montreal plus

RESTAURANTS

BARS

MOVIES

MUSIC

ENTERTAINMENT

CULTURE

TOURISM

NEWS

NEW CONTENT

Your **WEB** *Site*

www.montrealplus.ca

A **plus**

FOR YOU !

Focus Québec — 10,95 $

Enhanced by a hundred breathtaking photos, this magnificent book presents a spectacular overview of the historic and contemporary reality of the Québec City region.

Français
English
Español
Italiano
日本語
Deutch

Discover the way of life, the culture and the ancestral lands of the Québec's First peoples through more than 100 photos and illustrations.

Also available in French in a publication entitled *Le Québec amérindien et inuit.*

The Native Peoples of Québec — 14,95 $

The Mural of Quebecers — 9,95 $

Discover all the secrets of this Mural located at Place-Royal in Old Québec City !

Also available in French in a publication entitled *La Fresque des Québécois.*

Also available :

- A series of four superb, giant posters about Québec *9,95 $ each*

- The book *La Minganie vue par vingt grands reporters* *29,95 $*

All of our products are available in bookstore.
To place an order call toll-free
Canada and USA : **1 800 476-2068**
Québec area : **(418) 692-1336**

ÉDITIONS
SYLVAIN HARVEY

BED & BREAKFASTS
IN QUÉBEC 2000

AGRICOTOURS

Travel better, enjoy more
ULYSSES
Travel Guides

Project coordinators
Odette Chaput
(Féd. Agricotours)
Pascale Couture
André Duchesne
(Ulysses)

Collaboration
Odile Bélanger
Diane Drapeau
Isabelle Larocque
Andrée Lyne Allaire
Louis Hébert

Illustrations of houses
Marie-Annick Viatour
Lorette Pierson
Sandrine Delbaen
Myriam Gagné
Sylvie Darèche
Louca
Stéphanie Thellen

Translation
Danielle Gauthier
Tara Salman
Myles McKelvey

Cartography
André Duchesne
Patrick Thivierge
Yanik Landreville

Photo cover page
La Maison Lebreux
Petite Vallée, Gaspésie

Correction
Tara Salman

Graphic desing
Stéphanie Routhier

Cover page print
Typo Express

Page layout
Julie Brodeur

Distributors

AUSTRALIA: Little Hills Press, 11/37-43 Alexander St., Crows Nest NSW 2065, ☎ (612) 437-6995, Fax: (612) 438-5762

CANADA: Ulysses Books & Maps, 4176 Saint-Denis, Montréal, Québec, H2W 2M5,
☎ (514) 843-9882, ext.2232, 800-748-9171, Fax: 514-843-9448, info@ulysses.ca, www.ulyssesguides.com

GERMANY and **AUSTRIA**: Brettschneider, Femreisebedarf, Feldfirchner Strasse 2, D-85551 Heimstetten, München,
☎ 89-99 02 03 30, Fax: 89-99 02 03 31, cf@brettschneider.de

GREAT BRITAIN and **IRELAND**: World Leisure Marketing, Unit 11, Newmarket Court, Newmartket Drive, Derby DE24 8NW,
☎ 1 332 57 37 37, Fax: 1 332 57 33 99, office@wlmsales.co.uk

ITALY: Centro Cartografico del Riccio, Via di Soffiano 164/A, 50143 Firenze, ☎ (055) 71 33 33, Fax: (055) 71 63 50

PORTUGAL: Dinapress, Lg. Dr. Antonio de Sousa de Macedo, 2, Lisboa 1200, ☎ (1) 395 52 70, Fax: (1) 395 03 90

SCANDINAVIA: Scanvik, Esplanaden 8B, 1263 Copenhagen K, DK, ☎ (45) 33.12.77.66, Fax: (45) 33.91.28.82

SPAIN: Altaïr, Balmes 69, E-08007 Barcelona, ☎ 454 29 66, Fax: 451 25 59, altair@globalcom.es

SWITZERLAND: OLF, P.O. Box 1061, CH-1701 Fribourg, ☎ (026) 467.51.11, Fax: (026) 467.54.66

U.S.A.: The Globe Pequot Press, 246 Goose Lane, Guilford, CT 06437-0480, ☎ 1-800-243-0495, Fax: 800-820-2329, sales@globe-pequot.com

OTHER COUNTRIES: Ulysses Books & Maps, 4176 Saint-Denis, Montréal, Québec, H2W 2M5,
☎ (514) 843-9882, ext.2232, 800-748-9171, Fax: 514-843-9448, info@ulysses.ca, www.ulyssesguides.com

For information on the Fédération des Agricotours network:

Fédération des Agricotours du Québec
4545, av. Pierre de Coubertin
C.P. 1000, Succursale M.
Montréal, Québec
H1V 3R2
(514) 252-3138
fax (514) 252-3173
internet http://www.agricotours.qc.ca
E-mail agricotours-q@sympatico.ca

Issued also in French under the title: Gîtes du passant au Québec 2000

TABLE OF CONTENTS

INTRODUCTION

"Bed & Breakfasts in Québec 2000" is the largest edition ever: 680 properties categorized under six "authentic" and "quality" vacation and leisure formulas.

453 **Bed & Breakfasts** Gites du Passant[MD]*
89 **Country Inns** Auberges du Passant[MC]*
89 **Country and City Homes**
23 **Farm Stays**
19 **Country-style Dining** Tables Champêtres[MC]*
7 **Farm Excursions**

---

* **Mark of certification and trademarks registered to the Fédération des Agricotours du Québec. Only members may use this designation.**

Formulas where the warmth and hospitality of host-members, a family atmosphere and pleasant surroundings await you. "Bed & Breakfasts in Québec 2000" is perfect to discover the best of Québec. This guide is a judicious choice for its wealth of information, reservation advice, tourist maps, colour photos and descriptions of each property: illustration, price, itinerary, details about rooms, bathrooms and menus, etc. For explanations about each of the six formulas, see **page 10**.

FARM ACTIVITIES ♠

Take a "nature" break... At the end of each region in the "B&B and Country-Style Inns" section of the guide, you will find a list of farm activities that include accommodation, dining and entertainment possibilities.

TAXES

As per federal and provincial laws, customers may have to pay federal Goods and Services tax (7%) and the provincial tax (7.5%). Establishments that charged taxes are marked "Taxes extra". Foreign visitors can be refunded upon presentation of their receipts.
According to provincial law, some tourist regions (i.e. Montréal, Laval) must charge an additional tax of $2 per night for each unit rented. This tax goes toward a partnership fund which is used to promote the region's tourist offerings.

ANNUAL REVISION OF THE GUIDE

Though the guide is revised each year, all information contained herein is subject to change without notice (i.e. increase in taxes). However, the prices listed for each establishment are valid until the publication of the next edition, expected in Febuary 2001.

QUALITY CONTROL

All the establishments in this guide have submitted a request for accreditation review to the Fédération des Agricotours and must agree to respect a code of ethics as well as certain hospitality, room arrangement, security, hygiene, comfort and food quality standards. To ensure that our norms are being respected, each establishment in the nerwork is inspected regularly by the federation, and must conform to precise standards of security, cleanliness, comfort and quality of service. On site, a sign indicating Agricotours membership is your assurance that the owners belong to the Fédération des Agricotours du Québec. To further assure guests a quality stay, each establishment offering accommodation must display a certificate in each room stating that it has been verified by Agricotours and is in compliance with their quality standards.

EVALUATION FORMS

Do not hesitate to complete the "Evaluation Forms" sheets at the end of the book, as well as those available in the rooms (or dining rooms in Country-style Dining), to let us know how you enjoyed your Agricotours experience. We need your feedback, suggestions and criticism to continue to improve the quality of the network and the services provided.

EXCELLENCE PRIZE

Each year, the Fédération honours its members with two awards in two different categories:
- The "People's Favourite" category: awards the hosts who stood out for their hospitality at all times. Candidates in this category are selected from customers' opinion cards.
- The "Merit" category: awarded to the hosts who stood out for their efforts to develop, promote and offer a quality service.
You will find a list of the 1999 nominees in both categories on the next page.

WIN A STAY

By filling out and sending your Evaluation Form, you get the chance of winning a two-night stay for two people in one of our member-establishments.

25 years of hospitality
1975 - 2000

For 25 years, the host members of the
Fédération des Agricotours du Québec
have been committed to offering you
genuine, high-quality choices
for accommodation and agricultural tourism.

This has made Agricotours the largest
high-quality network in Quebec, and
your confidence has helped in its success.

For this reason, our network host members hope
that they may, with their traditional warm
welcome, continue to help you discover the
best of Quebec for many more years to come.

You'll always feel welcome
in the Agricotours network.

The Fédération des Agricotours du Québec

AGRICOTOURS

"*People's Special Favourite*"
Category

"Congratulations to these hosts ans hostesses for the remarkable welcome and service they have consistently offered their guests."

Accommodation Sector
The Provincial Grand Prize-winner is

Gîte l'Écume de Mer
Andréa Neu
La Martre, GASPÉSIE

Country-Style Dining Sector
The Provincial Prize-winner is

Domaine de la Templerie
Chantale Legault et Roland Guillon
Huntingdon, MONTÉRÉGIE

Accommodation Sector
The Regional Prize-winners are

BAS-ST-LAURENT
Chez Marie-Roses
Jacqueline et Jean-Guy Caron
Bic

CANTONS-DE-L'EST
Domaine sur la Colline B&B
Nicole et Gilles Deslauriers
Cowansville

CHARLEVOIX
Chez Gertrude
Gertrude et Raymonde Tremblay
St-Urbain

CHAUDIÈRE-APPALACHES
Auberge des Glacis
Micheline Sibuet et Pierre Watters
St-Eugène-de-l'Islet

CÔTE-NORD
La Maison Harvey-Lessard
Sabine Lessard et Luc Harvey
Tadoussac

GASPÉSIE
Gîte l'Écume de Mer
Andréa Neu
La Martre

LANAUDIÈRE
Chez Marie-Christine
Micheline Adam
Ste-Élisabeth

LAURENTIDES
Les Jardins de la Gare B&B
Françoise et Alain Guénette
Val-Morin

MAURICIE
Maison Emery Jacob
Lucie Verret et Réal Trépanier
St-Tite

MONTÉRÉGIE
Au Jardin d'Alexandre
Diane et Jean-Marie Caissie
Brossard

OUTAOUAIS
Maison la Crémaillère
Andrée et André Dompierre
Messines

RÉGION DE MONTRÉAL
Au Gîte Olympique
Denis Boulianne
Montréal

RÉGION DE QUÉBEC
Chez Monsieur Gilles[2]
Gilles Clavet
Québec

SAGUENAY-LAC-ST-JEAN
Les Gîtes Makadan
Micheline Villeneuve et Daniel Bergeron
Normandin

... *Excellence*
1999

"*Success*"
Category

Congratulations to these hosts ans hostesses for the remarkable way they have developed, promoted and offered high-quality services.

Agricultural Tourism Sector
The Regional Prize-winner is

Les Douces Heures d'Antan
Francine Gareau et Claude Barabé
Tingwick, CENTRE-DU-QUÉBEC
(Farm Stay)

Accommodation Sector
The Regional Prize-winner is

L'Air du Temps
Lucie Chrétien et Daniel Desgagné
Chambly, MONTÉRÉGIE
(Bed & Breakfast)

Special Mention by the Jury
A group of 4 establishments in the LAURENTIDES :

L'Auberge de la Tour du Lac
Jean-Léo Legault
Ste-Agathe-des-Monts

Les Jardins de la Gare B&B
Françoise et Alain Guénette
Val-Morin

La Bonne Adresse
Odette Bélanger et Jean-Marie Noël
St-Faustin

Le Provincialat
Pierre Seers et Guillaume Petit
Lac-Nominingue

The Fédération des Agricotours du Québec
25 years of hospitality
1975 – 2000

SIX ACTIVITY AND HOLIDAY PACKAGES

BED AND BREAKFASTS

This option, known as the **Gîte du Passant** ^{MC}*, offers bed and breakfast in a private residence in the country, on a farm, in a village, in the suburbs or in the city. There are as many different kinds of lodgings and friendly hosts as there are warm welcomes and varieties of facilities and comforts... and flexible prices. The Gîte du Passant offers up to five rooms per residence. For a long or short stay, choose one of the 453 Gîte du Passant throughout the regions of Québec. **Section p 44**.

COUNTRY INNS

Bed and breakfast in a small country inn with a relaxed atmosphere. These 89 establishments offer up to 12 rooms in the main residence or adjoining buildings, some also provide additional meals in a dining room. Known as **Auberge du Passant** ^{MC}*, these inns distinguish themselves from traditional hotels by their uniqueness and personalized attention to detail. Though inns accommodate more guests that B&Bs, you'll find the same friendly welcome. **See complete list p 45**.

COUNTRY AND CITY HOMES

This may take the form of a fully equipped house, cottage, apartment or studio, and is ideal for an independent holiday in the city or country. Wheter you want to enjoy the beauty of nature or lose yourself in the city, you'll be warmly welcomed into one of the 89 country or city homes to ensure a perfect stay. Monthly, weekly, weekend and even daily rates are available. **See complete list p 47**.

FARM STAYS

This fun-filled holiday package consists of bed and full board or half board in a farm house, where hosts invite you to discover life on a farm. The activities on each farm differ according to the type of animals and farming. Certain farms will allow children without adults. 21 Farm Stays in the province ensure a fun and unique holiday in natural settings for the whole family. **Section p 36**.

COUNRTY-STYLE DINING ^{MC}*

For getting together with family and friends, celebrating an anniversary, reunion or another special occasion, the hosts of Country-Style Dining will warmly welcome you either to the dining room of their house or a lovely, authentically decorated adjoining room. Throughout the year, they offer high-quality, home-made meals using regional products or produce from their farm. The 19 Country-Style Dining establishments also distinguish themselves in that they have a relaxing atmosphere that encourages cultural exchange. The hosts invite their guests to partake in their way of life by offering a guided tour of their farm, and some offer other recreational activities. **Section p 14**.

FARM EXCURSIONS

Farmers invite you to spend several hours outdoors or a day at the farm. Different recreational and educational activities are offered to promote farm life. Whether it's a family get-together, a picnic with friends, a country hike or a school outing, farm excursions offer children as much as families, friends and people of all ages, a whole range of activities to enjoy. **Section p 28**.

---

*Mark of certification and trademarks registered to the Fédération des Agricotours du Québec. Only members of the federation may use this designation.

TABLE OF SYMBOLS

F	French spoken fluently		Swimming on premises
f	Some French spoken		Pick-up from public transportation with or without additional charge
E	English spoken fluently (50% of establishments)		Pets on the premises
e	Some English spoken		Restaurant on site
	Guests are requested to refrain from smoking	R4	Distance (km) to nearest restaurant
	Wheelchair access	M4	Distance (km) to nearest grocery store
P	Private parking	TA	Establishment that accepts travel agency reservations
★	Country Inns Classification (p 12)		Bed and Breakfast Classification (p 12)
	Classification in progress		

ACTIVITIES

	Art gallery, museum		Cycling path
	Summer theatre		Horseback riding
	Boat cruise		Snowmobile
	Swimming		Downhill skiing
	Golf		Cross-country skiing
	Hiking		Dog-sledding

METHOD OF PAYMENT

VS	Visa	ER	En Route
MC	MasterCard	IT	Interact payment
AM	American Express		

PRACTICAL INFORMATION

In this guide, the hosts briefly describe the unique characteristics of their home, its decor and surroundings. Information is also given on the activities available in the region. You will also find a detailed itinerary to help you make your choice.

COUNTRY-STYLE DINING

– Menus:

The menus given in this guide are examples of the type of meals served. In addition to the menu presented, the hosts may offer you a variety of other menus at various prices. These menus are always made with fresh farm or local products.

At the request of the hosts, the menus have been left in their original French to preserve their authenticity. Bring your own wine because it is not available on site.

– Number of people:

The number of people welcomed during the week and on weekends is given for each establishment. The minimum may vary depending on the season. Note that some hosts can accomodate more than one group at a time. In these cases, depending on the minimum number of people anticipated by the owners, it is possible to reserve the whole establishment for your group.

– Rates:

Certain places offer reduced rates for children 12 years an under. Hosts may reserve the right to charge for the number of places reserved even if the actual number of guests is less. Service charge are not included in the prices, this is left to the discretion of the patrons.

– Reservations, deposit and cancellation:

You must reserve with the hosts directly. It is always advisable to book several weeks in advance. A maximum deposit of 50% of the total price may be required to confirm the reservation.

If you cannot honour your reservation, flexible cancellation rules may apply. It is a good idea to get these specifications in wtrittig. However, if no written agreement is produced, the cancellation policy is as follow: 30 days or less before the reservation date, the entire deposit is retained.

When cancelling, it is advisable to postpone the reservation to avoid losing the deposit.

FARM EXCURSIONS

– Reservations, deposit and cancellation:

Reservation should be made directly to the selected farm. A 40% deposit (minimum $20) may be required to confirm your reservation.

If you cannot honour your reservation, flexible cancellation rules may apply. It is a good idea to get these specifications in writing. However, if no written agreement is produced, the money foreseen and received as a deposit will be kept by the host for damage according to the following rules:

• 8 to 15 days' notice, 50% of the deposit will be retained (minimum $20);

• 7 days or less before the reservation date, the entire deposit will be retained.

When cancelling, it is advisable to postpone the reservation to avoid losing your deposit. More flexible rules may apply.

BED AND BREAKFAST
COUNTRY INNS
COUNTRY AND CITY HOMES

– **Reservations and method of payment:**

It is always advisable to reserve in advance to be sure of getting the size and type of accommodation you want, especially in high season (July and August). For reservations, contact the establishment directly, either by mail, by telephone or by e-mail. Since each place is different, it is usually a good idea to confirm details with your host: the type of room, the number of beds per room, whether the places has single or double beds, what restaurant facilities are nearby, what time you plan on arriving, up until what time your reservation should be held in case of delay, what forms of payment are accepted, etc. Generally, expect to pay with traveller's cheques or cash. The establishments that accept credit cards have VS, MC, AM, ER, IT written under their rate charts. Also, if you have any conditions which might prove pertinent (example is you are allergic to pets), you are strongly encouraged to check with your hosts before making reservations.

– **Deposit and cancellation:**

For B&Bs and Inns, a deposit of 40% or a minimum of $20 may be required to confirm a reservation. The balance of the fee will be paid during your stay. If you cannot honour your reservation, flexible cancellation rules may apply. It is a good idea to get these specifications in writting. However, if no written agreement is produced, the money foreseen and received as a deposit will be kept by the host for damages according to the following rules:
- 8 to 15 day's notice: 50% of deposit (minimum $20) is retained;
- 7 or fewer days' notice: entire deposit is retained.
If your stay must be cut short before the end, 40% of the unused portion of the stay may be retained. When cancelling, it is advisable to postpone the reservation to avoid losing your deposit.

For country and city homes, check with owners of country houses for their individual deposit and cancellation policies.

– **For European customers:**

There are several ways to reserve your stay in advance: either contact the establishment directly, use a travel agent or contact Tourisme Chez l'Habitant in France or Hospitality Canada.

Tourisme chez l'habitant: Reservations can be made by mail or by telephone with a credit card. All arrangements and payment are made in advance, so you head for Québec with address in hand! An additional charge is added to the price for all reservation services. Information is sent free of charge.

Tourisme chez l'habitant
15 rue des Pas Perdus, B.P. 8338
95 804 - Cergy St-Christophe cedex
Tel: (1) 34.25.44.44
Fax (1) 34.25.44.45

Hospitality Canada: For a stay of 2 nights of more, you can reserve through the Hospitality Canada network. There is no charge for these reservations from France, Belgium or Switzerland by calling 0-800-90-3355. Or from North America by calling 1-800-665-1528

You can also make your reservations by telephone after you arrive or by visiting their offices located in the tourist offices in Montréal and Québec City:

By telephone: **(514) 287-9049**
By fax: **(514) 287-1220**
internet: www.hospitality-canada.com
e-mail: hosp.cam@iq.ca

In person:
Centre Infotouriste
1001 Square Dorchester
Montréal
(corner Ste-Catherine & Peel)

Maison du tourisme
12, rue Sainte-Anne
Vieux-Québec
Opposite the Château Frontenac

CLASSIFICATION «HÉBERGEMENT QUÉBEC»

To better serve tourists, Hébergement Québec started a hotel-classification program in 1998 followed by a bed and breakfast classification-program in 1999.

*NOTE: Since not every establishment adheres to «Hébergement Québec» by choice, there are two reasons why a classification may not be written:
• **The establishment decided not to publish its classification**
• **The establishment decided not to be evaluated by «Hébergement Québec»**
The ✎ means the establishment is in the process of being classified.

In accordance with international standards and Québec norms for tourist accomodations, the establishments in this guide have been classified as follow: 0 to 5 **stars** for hotels and 0 to 5 **suns** for bed and breakfast.

BED AND BREAKFAST RATINGS

The bed and breakfast rating system was establish recently in Québec in order to assist tourists choosing among the widely varied number of bed and breakfasts in the province.

A bed and breakfast is defined as a tourist lodging in a private residence that does not exceed 5 bedrooms, offers a shared or private bathroom, and includes breakfast service in the price. However, the rating of a bed and breakfast cannot be compared to a similar one for a hotel, since the evaluation criteria are not the same. This is why we have used different symbols for both types of establishments.

The new symbol used exclusively for bed and breakfast rating is the **sun**. The **sun** reflects the personal hospitality and the particular ambiance related to receiving people «at home», whether the home is modest or luxurious.

In order to determine the different levels of comfort and quality of bed and breakfast, the number of suns (from 0 to 5) is based on the following qualitative and quantitative criteria:

- **The exterior of the house and its environment** (condition of the building, its architecture, landscaping and parking amenities, etc.);
- **The interior of the house** (decor and layout of common rooms, breakfast, etc.);
- **Bedrooms** (size, furniture, bed linen, elements of comfort, etc.);
- **Bathrooms** (shared or private, size, plumbing, appliances, linen, supply, etc.).

BED & BREAKFAST CLASSIFICATION	
NO SUN	BED AND BREAKFAST CONFORMING TO MINIMUM STANDARDS OF THE REGULATIONS RESPECTING TOURIST ESTABLISHEMENTS (***None of the establishments in this guide correspond to the «no sun» classification. See note, left side of this page**)
☀	BASIC COMFORT BED AND BREAKFAST
☀☀	GOOD COMFORT AND QUALITY BED AND BREAKFAST
☀☀☀	VERY COMFORTABLE AND GOOD QUALITY BED AND BREAKFAST
☀☀☀☀	SUPERIOR COMFORT AND QUALITY BED AND BREAKFAST
☀☀☀☀☀	EXEPTIONAL QUALITY AND COMFORT, REFINED AND LUXURIOUS BED AND BREAKFAST

COUNTRY INNS CLASSIFICATION	
NO STAR	ESTABLISHEMENT MEETS THE MINIMUM STANDARDS OF THE REGULATION ON TOURIST ESTABLISHEMENTS (***None of the establishment in this guide correspond to the no star definition. See note, left side of this page**)
★	ESTABLISHEMENT WITH BASIC FACILITIES AND SERVICES THAT MEET QUALITY STANDARDS
★★	COMFORTABLE ESTABLISHMENT WITH GOOD QUALITY FACILITIES, PROVIDING SOME SERVICES AND AMENITIES
★★★	VERY COMFORTABLE ESTABLISHMENT, WITH EXCELLENT FACILITIES, OFFERING MANY SERVICES AND AMENITIES
★★★★	ESTABLISHMENT OFFERING SUPERIOR COMFORT, AMONG THE BEST, WITH SUPERB FACILITIES AND A WIDE RANGE OF SERVICES AND AMENITIES
★★★★★	EXEPTIONAL ESTABLISHMENT, IN TERMS OF COMFORT AND FACILITIES AND THE MANY AMENITIES AND IMPECCABLE SERVICES OFFERED

Contact CSETQ at : www.hebergementquebec.com

Bed and Breakfasts and Country-style Inns are presented in the following format:

Country-style Homes and City Homes are presented in the following format:

Legend

A. Number corresponding to the one on the regional map

B. Localization of house

C. Type of service offered

D. Classification of Country Inns

E. Classification of Bed and Breakfasts

F. See table of symbols p. 9

G. Rate table (see the box on right)

H. Information about additional taxes and accepted methods of payment

I. Dates open and reduced rate period

J. Room and bathroom information

K. Nearby activities, see p 9

L. House information and table rates

G.
Shared room rates

B&B
Bed and Breakfast

MAP
Modified American Plan: breakfast and supper

*Child
12 years and younger staying in parents' room

When two prices are given, they refer to the comfort level of the room and not to high and low seasons.

Country-Style Dining

COUNTRY-STYLE DINING

1. Dunham
2. Magog
3. Saint-Léon-de-Standon
4. Saint-Ambroise-de-Kildare
5. Saint-Jacques-de-Montcalm
6. L'Annonciation
7. Lachute, Argenteuil
8. Mirabel
9. Mirabel, Sainte-Scholastique
10. Saint-André-Est
11. Saint-Eustache
12. Sainte-Anne-des-Plaines
13. Louiseville
14. Huntingdon
15. Saint-Rémi-de-Napierville
16. Saint-Urbain-Premier
17. Saint-Valérien
18. Sainte-Justine-de-Newton
19. Saint-Sixte

1. DUNHAM

LA CHÈVRERIE DES ACACIAS
Renée Ducharme and Gérard Landry
356, chemin Bruce (route 202)
Dunham J0E 1M0
(450) 295-2548

On the road to the vineyards, our homestead is a major goat-breeding, fodder-crop and poultry farm. The originality of the food served in the ambiance of a 19th-century house will charm you. Our menu constitutes a gastronomic adventure orchestrated around our farm products combined with those of our neighbours. Our home is just the place to end an unforgettable day in the region.

Located 1hr from the Champlain bridge. From Montreal or Sherbrooke: Hwy 10, Exit 68 for Cowansville Rte 139. Then take Rte 202 to Dunham. In the village, turn on Chemin Bruce (Rte 202) at the corner of "Estrie Gaz". The goat farm is 1.2km from the village.

Open year round

Activities: 🚶 🚲 🐎 ⛷ 🏃

Jus de légumes et fruits frais
Fromage au pesto et pâté de foie
sur bruschetta
Mosaïque de légumes
au fromage frais de chèvre
Potage croustillant aux amandes
Chabrot, surprise à découvrir
Gigot de chevreau au cari ou
Magret de canard, sauce aux cerises de terre
Granité aux trois melons
Salade de betteraves à l'aïoli
Meringue aux trois fruits
Other menus upon request

Meal: $35 taxes extra	
week:12 to 30 people	w/e: 12 to 30 people
Only one group at a time	

Includes: visit of the farm

2. MAGOG

AUX JARDINS CHAMPÊTRES
Monique Dubuc and Yvon Plourde
1575, chemin des Pères, R.R.4
Magog J1X 5R9
(819) 868-0665
toll free 1-877-868-0665
fax (819) 868-6744
www.auxjardinschampetres.com
auxjardinschampetres@qc.aira.com

Just steps from Magog and Orford in the magnificent Eastern Townships region, you'll give in to the charming countryside, the warmth of our hundred-year-old house, as well as the "pure delights" that we will serve you. Our dishes are concocted from our various farm animals, organic vegetables and edible flowers. Do not resist, rather enjoy it with your friends and while staying at our B&B. One and two-day packages starting at $74 per person, double occupancy. Bring your own wine. **B&B p 76. See colour photos.**

From Montréal, Hwy 10 East, Exit 115 South-Magog/ St-Benoît-du-Lac, drive 1.8km. Turn right on Chemin des Pères twd St-Benoît-du-Lac/Austin. Drive 6.1km, look for sign on your right. We are waiting for you!

Open year round

Activities: 🛶 🎿 🚶 🚲 🏃

Salade au confit de canard et vinaigrette tiède
balsamique ou Rillettes de lapin aux pistaches
Potage aux poires et cresson
Aumônière de poireaux sauce cheddar
et coulis de poivrons rouges ou
Foie de lapereau sauté aux champignons
sauce porto
Granité au calvados
Canard de barbarie sauce genièvre et caribou
ou Râble de lapin aux pruneaux et armagnac ou
Scalopini de volaille aux cerises de terre
Fromages de St-Benoît-du-Lac
Crêpes glacées aux pommes et figues ou
Gâteau à la pâte d'amande ou
Soufflé aux marrons et
Sabayon au Grand Marnier

Meal: $39 taxes extra / VS MC IT	
week: 1 to 50 people	w/e: 1 to 50 people
Min. number of guests vary with the season	
Able to accommodate more than 1 gr./ 4 dining rooms	
(exclusive use depends on number of people)	

Includes: visit of the farm (in season)

3. ST-LÉON-DE-STANDON

FERME LA COLOMBE
Rita Grégoire and Jean-Yves Marleau
104, rang Sainte-Anne
St-Léon-de-Standon GOR 4L0
(418) 642-5152
fax (418) 642-2991
www.fermelacolombe.qc.ca

Fromage frais aux fleurs d'onagre
Poitrine de dindon sauvage fumée en papillon
Velouté de citrouille et fromage de chèvre
Aumônière de pintade ou Râble de lapin au
cidre de pomme ou
Poitrine de poulet de grain à l'abbaye
Pomme de terre noisette
Tonnelle de courgette
Salade fleurie
Mousse aux pétales de rose
Fondant au chocolat et coulis de gadelles
noires
Thé, café, tisane
Other menus upon request

Tourism Grand Prize 1997. One hour from Québec City in the heart of the Appalachians, come and experience the gourmet adventure of the Ferme La Colombe. You'll relish every moment in our cosy hewn-timber dining room, made all the more charming by the crackling fireplace and the beautiful panoramic view from the window. You will be won over by our exotic cuisine, made of wild turkey, guinea fowl, rabbit and trout, while enjoying the lovely view and garden of edible flowers. B&B and Cuntry-style dining packages available. **Farm excursion p 29, Farm stay p 38 and B&B p 114.**

From Québec City, Hwy 20 E., Exit 325 twd Lac-Etchemin, Rtes 173 S. and 277 S. to Saint-Léon-de-Standon, Rue Principale. Go 0.9 km beyond the church, cross the 277 at the stop sign, left on the Village road and drive 4 km. Turn right on rang Ste-Anne and drive 2 km.

Meal: $30-34 taxes extra	
week: 8 to 25 people	w/e: 8 to 25 people
Only one group at a time	

Includes: visit of the farm

Open year round

Activities: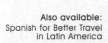

4. ST-AMBROISE-DE-KILDARE

BERGERIE DES NEIGES
Desneiges Pepin and Pierre Juillet
1401, Rang 5
St-Ambroise-de-Kildare J0K 1C0
tel/fax (450) 756-8395
bergeriedesneiges@moncourrier.com

A life's dream... Goodbye law practice, so long teacher's summer holidays... Desneiges Pepin and Pierre Juillet (two "dyed in the wool" city dwellers) took over this farm and settled with 11 ewes in 1985. What do they do for fun? They share their experience and show guests the daily renewed life of the farm. How? Over a good meal. More than 11 years and 400 ewes later, they have retained that "city kid" enthusiasm for the country. They offer you a gastronomic adventure at La Bergerie des Neiges. **B&B p 160.**

From Montréal, Hwy 40 E., Exit 122, Hwy 31 N. Rte 158, 1km, left on Rte 343 N., drive for 15km to St-Ambroise. At the flashing yellow light, go left on Rang 5 for 2km. The farm is white and pink, on the left!

Open year round

Activities:

Merguez maison et mayonnaise harissa
Potage de carottes du rang 5
Rillettes d'agneau et compote d'oignons
Duo d'agneau, sauce ricaneuse
Légumes de Lanaudière
Salade de fromage feta de brebis
Tulipe et glace maison sur coulis de fruits
Thé, café, tisanes
Other menus upon request

Meal: $37 taxes extra / VS
week:12to 36 people   w/e: 12 to 36 people
Min. number of guests vary with the seasons
Only one group at a time

Includes: visit of the farm

5. ST-JACQUES-DE-MONTCALM

BERGERIE VOYNE
Lise Savard and Mario Gagnon
2795, rang St-Jacques, route 341
St-Jacques-de-Montcalm J0K 2R0
(450) 839-6583

In the beautiful Lanaudière region, we raise lambs and produce our own maple syrup. The ancestral home of the Venne family, also known as "Voyne", in green and white cedar, is ready for your visit. Lamb is featured in our cuisine, and the shepherd knows all the secrets of its preparation. You can see the herd on a tour of the farm.

From Montréal, Hwy 25 North to St-Esprit (40km). Rte 158 East to St-Jacques, left on Rte 341 North. It's 4.8km from the intersection with Rte 158.

Open year round

Activities:

Terrine de campagne
Tourte aux poireaux ou Feuilleté de canard, gelée de thym sauvage
Potage saisonnier
Gigot d'agneau sauce au porto blanc ou Rôti de veau forestière
Salade du potager
Plateau de fromages fermiers de la région
Fondue à l'érable ou Gâteau aux noisettes et sucre d'érable ou Parfait aux bleuets et chocolat blanc
Café, thé, infusion
Other menus upon request

Meal: $35-36
week: 8 to 20 people   w/e: 10 to 20 people
Only one group at a time

Includes: visit of the farm

6. L'ANNONCIATION

LA CLAIRIÈRE DE LA CÔTE
Monique Lanthier and Yves Bégin
16, chemin Laliberté
L'Annonciation J0T 1T0
(819) 275-2877

In the Hautes Laurentiennes, you are invited to our table to spend some peaceful hours in the clearing of a forest of varied species. We live in harmony with nature amongst a variety of small animals (lambs, rabbits, grain-fed chickens, calves and deer), which become succulent dishes accompanied by fresh vegetables from our organic gardens. **Farm stay p 39 and B&B p 169.**

From Montréal, Hwy 15 North and Rte 117 to L'Annonciation. Drive 4.3km beyond the hospital. Turn left on Chemin Laliberté. First house on right (almond Canadian-style house).

Open: Dec. 1 to Mar. 31, May 1 to Oct. 31

Activities:

Rougette crémière
Foie gras poulette
Pesto en pâte
Velouté de saison
Tournedos dindonneau au fouillis jardinier
Verdoyant potager, crémerie de fines herbes
Fromagerie raisinet
Fruiterie sauvagine en velours
Pouding paysan sirop d'érable
Thé, café, tisane
Other menus upon request

Meal: $30	
week: 6 to 20 people	w/e: 6 to 20 people
Only one group at a time	

Includes: visit of the farm

7. LACHUTE, ARGENTEUIL

AU PIED DE LA CHUTE
Deschênes family
273, Route 329 Nord
Lachute J8H 3W9
(450) 562-3147
fax (450) 562-1056

In the calm of the country, our wood house offers charm, comfort and the delicacies of reputed country-style dining, where poultry and lamb are the specialties. Family-style welcome is both warm and personalized. Pastoral walks near our pond and at the foot of the falls will add to the magic of the countryside and the pleasures of dining. Welcome to our place!

From Montréal, Hwy 15 N., Exit 35. Hwy 50 to Côte St-Louis, go right to Rte 158 W., left to Rte 329 N. At the flashing yellow light, go right for exactly 1.5km. It's on your left.

Open year round

Activities:

Bouchées miniatures de bienvenue
Feuilleté d'agneau au curry
ou Rillettes de lapin, marmelade de pommes
ou Ballotine de volaille à l'échalote
ou Confit de pintade aux champignons
ou Croustillant de légumes marinés
Potage deux saveurs
Gigot d'agneau et sa ratatouillle au basilic
ou Chapon braisé à la moutarde et coriandre
ou Civet de lapereau aux pruneaux
ou Saisie de pintade au miel et gingembre
ou Daim braisé aux pommes et groseilles
Salade campagnarde à l'érable
Raclette d'Argenteuil à la gelée de Sauternes
Duo de desserts «surprise» sur coulis
Also: Menu de méchoui
Other menus upon request

Meal: $35-40 taxes extra/VS MC IT	
Reduced rates: Mar. 1 to Apr. 15	
week: 6 to 30 people	w/e: 14 to 30 people
Only one group at a time	

Includes: visit of the farm

8. MIRABEL, LACHUTE

LES RONDINS
Lorraine Douesnard and François Bernard
3015, Sir Wilfrid Laurier, route 158
Mirabel J7N 3B3
(450) 562-7215
(450) 258-2467
fax (450) 258-2347

45 minutes from Montréal, come share the intimacy of our house built in 1860. The Victorian decor, the fireplaces, the piano and the furnishings will take you slowly back in time. Dishes are made from our own veal, grain-fed chickens and Muscovy ducks. The old stove cooks country-style bread and products from our own maple grove.

From Montréal, Hwy 15 North, Exit 35. Follow Hwy 50 West, take Chemin Louis Exit 272. Turn right, continue to traffic light. Turn left onto Rte 158 West, drive 1km, 3rd farmhouse on the right. Or, Hwy 15 North, Exit 39, Lachute-bound Rte 158 West, drive 20.7km.

Open year round

Activities:

Bouchées d'avant
Roulade de chapon farcie
Potage «Mirabel»
Salade tiède au confit de canard
Canard de barbarie à la framboise ou
Mijoton de veau au basilic ou
Suprême de volaille aux mûres
Fromage fermier «La Longeraie »
Gâteau rhubarbe et mousse au sirop d'érable
Parfait maison
Other menus upon request

Meal: $35-37
week:10 to 26 people   w/e: 14 to 26 people
Min. number of guests vary with the season
Only one group at a time

Includes: visit of the farm (in season)

9. MIRABEL, STE-SCHOLASTIQUE

AUX DOUCEURS DE LA RUCHE
Danielle Rochon and Mario Morrissette
10351, St-Vincent
Mirabel, Ste-Scholastique J7N 2V7
tel/fax (514) 990-2450
(450) 258-3122
www3.sympatico.ca/douceurs.ruche/
douceurs.ruche@sympatico.ca

Excellence Prize 1997-98. In the lovely Basses-Laurentides region, only 40 min from Montréal, come rediscover the calm of the countryside. A majestic drive lined by spruce trees leads to a home that has witnessed Québec's history. It is here that we await you. In the kitchen, our fowl is slowly being roasted and the sweet scent of warm honey house fills the room. A visit of the honey-house will reveal the secret world of bees; you'll also taste "beehive sweets". A wood fire is already warming the dining room; the only thing missing is you.

From Montréal, Hwy 15 North, Exit 20 West, Hwy 640 West, Exit 11 Boul Arthur-Sauvé, towards Lachute. Drive 17.5km. After Belle-Rivière Restaurant turn right on St-Vincent. 5km to 10351. We await your arrival at the end of the spruce drive.

Open year round

Activities:

Mousse de foies de volaille au cognac
Jus de légumes frais
Oeufs de caille dans leur nid et
Terrine de volaille
Velouté de navet aux pommes
Perdrix rôtie, sauce moutarde au miel
Riz sauvage aux fines herbes ou
pommes de terre
Petits légumes de saison
Salade «Miramiel»
Fromages de chèvre frais
La ruche et ses ouvrières
Thé, tisanes, café
Pain maison, douceur «chocomiel»
Other menus upon request

Meal: $37 taxes extra
week: 4 to 32 people   w/e: 4 to 32 people
Min. number of guests vary with the season
Able to accommodate more than 1 group
(exclusive use depends on season, nb. of people)

Includes: visit of the farm

10. ST-ANDRÉ EST

LA FERME DE CATHERINE
Marie Marchand and Robert Dorais
2045, Route 344
St-André Est J0V 1X0
(450) 537-3704
fax (450) 537-1362
fermecatherine@videotron.ca

Marie, Catherine and Robert invite you to come enjoy family ambience and country cooking close to the old wood stove whose warmth mixes with the warmth of the hosts. Robert will take you around the farm where you can admire a superb view of Lake of Two Mountains and its surroundings. If you love good food, have a seat and let the feast begin!

From Montréal, Hwy 13 or 15 to Hwy 640 twd of Oka. From Oka, take Hwy 344 for 19km. On the 344 it's 6km after St-Placide. The road gets narrower and winding as you arrive at La Ferme de Catherine.

Open year round

Activities:

Crémant de pomme
Saucisse deux viandes sur
tombée de tomates ou
Tourte aux marinades fruitées
Terrine de bison au confit d'oignons
Potage fermière
Rôti de bison ou
de bœuf braisé aux fines herbes
Salade trois feuilles
Assiette de fromages assortis et fruits
Délices de la saison
Thé, café ou infusion
Other menus upon request

Meal: $36-42
week:12 to 36 people   w/e: 12 to 36 people
Only one group at a time

Includes: visit of the farm

11. ST-EUSTACHE

LE RÉGALIN
Réjean Brouillard
991, boul. Arthur-Sauvé,
route 148 ouest
St-Eustache J7R 4K3
tel/fax (450) 623-9668
toll free 1-877-523-9668
www.web-solut.com/leregalin
regalin@total.net

Less than 30 minutes from Montréal, in the maple area of St-Eustache, a beautiful, typical old house with dormer windows overlooking a large orchard extending as far as the eye can see. Farm animals (rabbits, pheasants, guinea fowl, geese, ducks and ostriches) inspire the planning of our menus. We offer dinner concerts for one and all, and we are able to accomodate 2 groups in separate and exlusive dining rooms.

From Montréal, Hwy 15 North, Exit 20 West, Hwy 640 West, Exit 11. Boul. Arthur-Sauvé twd Lachute. 5 km from the exit, 8 houses after the Pépinière Eco-Verdure (tree nursery) on the right side.

Open year round

Activities:

Mousse de foies de lapereau et pain maison
Feuilleté de faisan au poivre vert ou
Aumonières de pintade à l'érable
Potage de saison
Lapin aux abricots, au cidre ou à l'érable ou
Rotisson d'autruche à l'hydromel ou
Suprême de faisan au poivre rose
Salade verdurette
Plateau de fromages fins
Profiteroles au chocolat ou
Gâteau mousse aux abricots
Café, thé, infusions
Other menus upon request

Meal: $35-40
week:15 to 50 people   w/e: 15 to 50 people
Min. number of guests vary with the season
Able to accomodate more than one group

Includes: visit of the farm

12. STE-ANNE-DES-PLAINES

LA CONCLUSION
Chantal and Gilles Fournier
172, rang La Plaine (rte 335)
Ste-Anne-des-Plaines JON 1H0
(514) 990-7085 ou (450) 478-2598
fax (450) 478-0209
www.web-solut.com/laconclusion
laconclusion@web-solut.com

Adventure after adventure... There is much to discover and share at our house: the warm welcome and all the small considerations for which we are famous; warm bread and refined cuisine; farm-bred rabbits, quail and pheasants; fresh garden vegetables, flowers and herbs; a cozy Victorian-style house and a friendly, romantic ambiance. And in Conclusion, our history... In short, a memorable culinary experience you'll want to repeat.

From Montréal, Hwy 15, Exit 31, eastbound Rue Victor for 10.7km, which then turns into Rang Lepage. At the flashing light, left on Rte 335 for 7.7km, follow directions for Rte 335 North. Or Hwy 640, Exit 28, Rte 335 North for about 17km, follow directions for Rte 335 North.

> *Potage ou crème du jardin*
> *Pain maison aux cinq grains*
> *Caille glacée au vinaigre de framboises ou*
> *Gâteau de lapin au vin blanc ou*
> *aumônière de foies de lapin à la crème*
> *Assortiment de pâtés*
> *Lapin aux pommes et raisins ou*
> *Lapin farci aux abricots ou*
> *Lapin chasseur aux olives ou*
> *Cailles rôties, sauce porto et raisins verts*
> *Salade de saison*
> *Tarte aux framboises glacée au sirop d'érable*
> *ou Gâteau mousse aux fraises et à la rhubarbe*
> *ou Crêpes de blé au Cointreau et bleuets ou*
> *Gâteau moka et mousse d'amandes*
> *Crème glacée maison et gourmandises*
> *Goat cheese available upon request*
> **Other menus upon request**

Open year round

Activities:

Meal: $27-42	
week: 2 to 30 people	w/e: 2 to 30 people
Min. number of guests vary with the season	
Able to accommodate more than one group (exclusive use depends on season,nb.of people)	

Includes: visit of the farm (in season)

13. LOUISEVILLE

60 min from Montréal, La Seigneurie looks forward to spoiling you in its cosy home! You'll delight in our 9-course meal composed of produce from our small traditional farm. The vegetable garden, flower beds and herb garden make our food healthy, while the colours make for an attractive presentation. After a feast complemented by wine, what could be better than joining Morpheus in one of our B&B's 5 cosy rooms! **Farm Excursion (tour of the gardens) p 32, Farm Stay p 40, B&B p 194 and Country Home (La Maison du Jardinier) p 200. Ad end of the guide.**

From Montréal or Québec City, Hwy 40 Exit 166, Rte 138 E., 2.4km to Rte 348 W. At the lights, left twd Ste-Ursule, 1.5km, 1st road on the right, 1st house tucked away behind the trees.

Open year round

Activities: 🏛 👥 🚶 🚲 🐕

LA TABLE DE LA SEIGNEURIE
Michel Gilbert
480, chemin du Golf
Louiseville J5V 2L4
tel/fax (819) 228-8224

Bouchées cordiales à l'apéritif
Feuilleté de filet de perchaude
du Lac Saint-Pierre
Soupière de Bortsch québécois
Granité Bienfaisant
Le porc, le veau, le lapin ou
l'agneau de la Seigneurie sont à l'honneur
Légumes potagers
Laitue, vinaigrette «Fin Palais»
Éphémère triangle de fromages
Bagatelle «Seigneuriale» au sherry
Douceurs inoubliables
Other menus upon request
Exceptional menus inspired from Monet and Colette's cuisine

Meal: $39 taxes extra
week: 8 to 26 people   w/e: 10 to 26 people
Min. number of guests vary with the season
Able to accommodate more than one group
(exclusive use depends on season, nb. of people)
Includes: visit of the farm (in season)

14. HUNTINGDON

Provincial 1999 Excellence Prize. Nestled in fields and woods, our ancestral home awaits you. Walking in the forest, visiting the sugar shack, outdoor activities. At your discretion: soccer field, volleyball court, bowling green and horseshoe space. Our farm-bred geese, guinea fowl, pheasants and ducks will treat you to an unforgettable concert. You will enjoy succulent dishes prepared by your host, who has some 30 years' cooking experience, in a relaxed ambiance. **See colour photos.**

From Montréal, Rte 138 West twd Huntingdon. 9km after the stop in Ormstown, turn right at the Chemin Seigneurial, drive 4.7km, turn left chemin de la Templerie, 350m at stop. New Erin 1km.

Open year round

Activities: 🦢 🐿 🚶 🚴

DOMAINE DE LA TEMPLERIE
Chantale Legault and Roland Guillon
312, chemin New Erin
Godmanchester (Huntingdon) JOS 1HO
tel/fax (450) 264-9405

Petits fours apéritif, Velouté en cachette
Plateau de trois charcuteries fines, au choix :
Truite farcie en croûte, Foie de veau au raisin,
Ris de veau aux poires, Mousse de saumon.
Selon votre goût : Filet d'oie sauce Bordelaise,
Suprême de faisan au cognac, confit de canard
sauce béarnaise, Sauté d'agneau paysanne,
Tournedos de canard au roquefort, Médaillon
d'autruche à l'hydromel et bleuets
Également nous vous offrons :
Chapon, lapin, pintadeau, porc et caille
Pommes château, jardinière de légumes
Salade de cœurs et de gésiers confits
Plateau de fromages, Crêpes soufflée au
Grand-Marnier, Clafoutis aux fruits de saison,
Coupe de la Templerie
Café, thé, infusion
Other menus upon request

Meal: $35-45
week:10 to 38 people   w/e: 12 to 38 people
Min. number of guests vary with the season

Only one group at a time

Includes: visit of the farm (in season)

15. ST-RÉMI-DE-NAPIERVILLE

On the wide expanses of the Rive-Sud, only 15 minutes from Montréal, come experience true gastronomy. A charming entrance, lined with apple trees and forest, and a dining room redolent with the wonderful smell of well-browned chicken at the edge of a property near a pond provide a warm and soothing ambiance. While we prepare a feast for you, what could be better than an early evening drink on the terrace whose charm is only enhanced by your presence.

From the Champlain bridge, Hwy 15 twd the U.S.A., Exit 42 (Rte 132). Rte 209 South, to St-Rémi. From the church, drive 2.2km, 1st road on the right is Rang St-Antoine. Or from the Mercier bridge, Rte 207 South and 221 South until Rte 209 South, to St-Rémi.

Open year round

Activities: 🚶 🚴 🐎

FERME KOSA
Ada and Lajos Kosa
1845, rang St-Antoine
St-Rémi-de-Napierville J0L 2L0
(450) 454-4490

Cocktail de bienvenue
Amuse-gueule
Crème de légumes de saison
Tomate à l'antiboise
Tagliatelle aux asperges ou aux poivrons
Magrets de canard au vinaigre balsamique
et aux navets confits
Légumes du potager
Salade de saison
Quelques fromages fermiers (chèvre)
Couronne de pommes
caramélisée au jus de cidre
Café, thé, infusion
Other menus upon request

Meal: $35
week:10 to 40 people   w/e: 14 to 40 people
Min. number of guests vary with the season

Only one group at a time

Includes: visit of the farm (in season)

16. ST-URBAIN-PREMIER

LA BERGERIE DU SUROÎT
Nathalie Laberge and Stéphane Couture
440, rang Double
St-Urbain-Premier J0S 1Y0
(450) 427-1235

A country house set back from the road, nestled in the midst of a perennial-flower garden and hilly fields. In season, outdoor games let you appreciate the setting. Inside, the fire crackles in the woodstove, the table sports its Sunday tablecloth with place settings from the pine cupboard. We'll share with you little details on lamb breeding, growing mixed herbs and edible flowers. Welcoming you to our home is both a pleasure and a passion.

From the Champlain bridge, Hwy 15 S., Exit 42 (Rte 132). At 5th light, take Rte 209 S. twd St-Rémi. Drive 26.6km. Then take Rte 205 for 2.4km. From the Mercier bridge, toward Rte 138 W., 1st exit right on Rte 221 to St-Rémi for 7km. Rte 207 S. Drive twd St-Isidore for 16km. Rte 205 S. for 3.4km.

Open year round

Activities:

Pâté de foie et son confit d'oignons *Potage de cresson et champignons ou du jardin* *Feuilles de vignes farcies sur coulis* *d'abricots ou papillottes d'agneau* *sauce au yogourt* *Carré d'agneau aux herbes de Provence ou* *Gigot d'agneau aux trois parfums* *Brunoise de légumes croquants ou* *Brochette de légumes marinés* *Verdure aux herbes fraîches ou* *Salade de mer et d'agrumes* *Aumônière de pommes et fromage* *Douceur glacée aux fruits de la saison* *ou Surprise chocolatée*

Meal: $36
week:10 to 24 people   w/e: 10 to 24 people
Only one group at a time

Includes: visit of the farm

17. ST-VALÉRIEN

LA RABOUILLÈRE
Pierre Pilon
1073, rang de l'Égypte
St-Valérien J0H 2B0
(450) 793-4998
fax (450) 793-2529

Depending on the season, you will be welcomed either by our gardens or a fire in the hearth. Rabbit is on the menu, as well as lamb and farm birds including delicious young pigeon, our new dish. Edible flowers cheer up and flavour our dishes. Arrive early, as there is a lot to see. **Farm Excursion p 33, Farm stay p 41, B&B p 210.**

20 minutes from St-Hyacinthe or from Granby. From Montréal, Hwy 20 East, Exit 141 to St-Valérien. In the village, take Chemin Milton and the 1st road on the right (2nd flashing light). Or Hwy 10, Exit 68, Rte 139 towards Granby. Rte 112 and Rte 137 North to Ste-Cécile. After Ste-Cécile, right on Chemin St-Valérien to the first flashing light, turn left.

Open year round

Cocktail de fruits *et assiette de canapés* *Terrine de pintadeau aux avelines ou* *foies de lapin au porto* *Potage provençal (tomates, ail,* *pesto, chèvre frais)* *Cuisseau de lapin farci à l'estragon ou* *Pigeonneau à la niçoise ou Suprême de pintade* *aux pommes et au cidre ou Magret* *de canard au vinaigre de frambroises* *ou gigot d'agneau au miel et au romarin* *Salade mille fleurs (in season)* *Fromages de chèvre* *Gâteau au fromage, amande et* *fruits sur crème anglaise* *Also menus brunch, méchoui* **Other menus upon request**

Meal: $35-42 *Taxes extra*
week:12 to 100 p.   w/e: 15 to 100 people
Min. nb. of guests may vary with the season
Able to accommodate more than one group/ 3 dining rooms available (exclusive use depends on seasons, nb. of people)

Includes: visit of the farm

18. STE-JUSTINE-DE-NEWTON

LA SEIGNEURIE DE NEWTON
Lucille F. Lavallée
750, 3ᵉ Rang
Ste-Justine-de-Newton J0P 1T0
(450) 764-3420

At the heart of a farming region, share the intimacy of our hundred-year-old house with Victorian decor. Enjoy meals with fresh bread baked daily in our authentic bread oven. The piano is always at your disposal. Full range of products from our maple grove. Visit the pheasants, horses, chickens and other animals at our farm. Percheron horses can take you for a carriage or sleigh ride (reservation). Our windmill pumps water for the garden. Welcome!

From Montréal, Hwy 40 W., twd Ottawa, Exit 17 (Montée Lavigne). Left on Rte 201 S. for 9.6km to Rang Ste-Marie-de-Ste-Marthe. Take this for 4.6km, at the first stop, go left for 5.1km

Open year round

Activities:

Spécialité faisan :
Terrine de foies de faisan et
Rillettes au poivre vert
Potage saisonnier
Feuilleté aux épinards
Faisan au cognac
Carottes persillées ou Légumes saisonniers
Riz aux fines herbes
Salade de la maison centennaire
Fins fromages régionaux
Crêpes divines à l'érable et
Tartelettes paysannes au sirop d'érable
Café, thé, infusions
2nd menu: Festin d'agneau
Other menus upon request

Meal: $35-40	
week:10 to 24 people	w/e: 10 to 24 people
Only one group at a time	

Includes: visit of the farm

19. ST-SIXTE

FERME CAVALIER
Gertie and Marc Cavalier
39, montée St-André
St-Sixte J0X 3B0
(819) 985-2490
fax (819) 985-1411
marc.cavalier@sympatico.ca

In our beautiful valley, beside the Rivière St-Sixte, lamb and poultry from our farm are served in two traditions: the richness of French gastronomy and the exotism of Moroccan cuisine. Give in to temptation with our changing menu, depending on the seasons, available products and the vision of your hosts. And don't forget our package including accommodation in a cosy and comfortable B&B.

One hour from Hull, 2 from Montréal. From Hull, Hwy 50 to Masson, then Rte 148 to Thurso. Route 317 North for 18km to Montée Paquette. Turn and continue to Montée St-André. Turn left, the farm is 800m away.

Open year round

Activities: ● ⚸ 🎿 ⛷ 🛷 🐎

Velouté de saison
Filet de truite et sa crème de persil
Noisettes d'agneau marinées aux herbes
Raviole aux champignons des bois
Flan de courgettes et tomates
Bouquet de fraîcheur du jardin
Fromages de la Petite Nation avec pain
aux noix et au miel
Mille-feuille à la mousse d'érable
Café, thé, tisanes, pain maison
**Ask about our Moroccan menus
and other specialties.
We can assist you in
planning your special occasions.**

Meal: $23-35 *Taxes extra*
week:10 to 25 people   w/e: 14 to 25 people
Min. nb. of guests may vary with the season
Able to accommodate more than one group/ 2 dining rooms available
(exclusive use depends on season, nb. of people)

Includes: visit of the farm (in season)

Farm Excursions

1. ST-LÉON-DE-STANDON

JARDINS DES TOURTEREAUX
DE LA FERME LA COLOMBE
Jean-Yves Marleau
104, rang Ste-Anne
St-Léon-de-Standon
GOR 4L0
(418) 883-5833
(418) 642-5152
fax (418) 642-2991
www.fermelacolombe.qc.ca

*90km from
St-Georges de Beauce
100km from Québec
70km from Lévis*

A booklet enables you to discover the great number of plants laid out in 10 thematic gardens. Trails, a pergola, swings, little bridges spanning ponds are graced with aviaries and an animal park. Come enjoy a relaxing picnic by the gently babbling brook. These unique gardens, situated in the heart of the mountains, will fill your everyday life with romanticism and reverie. A stay or country-style dining at La Colombe farm B&B will allow you to further enjoy our gardens. **Country-style dining p 17, farm stay p 38 and B&B p 114.**

From Québec City, Hwy 20 East, Exit 325 twd Lac-Etchemin, rtes 173 and 277 South twd St-Leon-de-Standon. From the church, drive 0.9km. At the stop sing, cross Rte 277 and turn left on Rte du Village, 4km. Right on Rg Ste-Anne, 2km.

FOR FAMILIES AND SMALL GROUPS : mid-June to beginning of September
(Tuesday to Sunday 9am to 4pm)
For groups of 20 to 80 personnes : May to November (with reservation)

- Horticultural farm: tending and reproducing plants
- Visiting the various theme gardens:
- edible flowers (75 varieties)
- fragrant flowers (rose gardens, lilacs, etc.)
- gardens of colours or garden of Eden
- garden of birds and hummingbirds
- secret garden
- garden of indigenous plants
- berry garden
- lovers' garden
- water garden (6 ponds and a lake)
- nature-interpretation relay

- Dinner on the farm and feeding the animals*
  - For school groups: "Tour of Noah's ark"*
- guided visit of the animals (20 species)
- treasure hunt
- flower sampling gardens
- cutting and vegetal multiplication activities
- tour of gardens

Rates:
$3.50 per person
$3.00 senior citizens
$2.50 students
$1.00 children from 2 to 6
Taxes extra
*additional charge

2. RAWDON

ARCHE DE NOÉ
Bernard Boucher
4117, ch. Greene
Rawdon
JOK 1SO
(450) 834-7874
(450) 834-3934
fax (450) 834-5090

55km from Montréal
80km from Longueuil
30km from Joliette

You can begin your stroll immediately upon your arrival by visiting the different animals. This guided tour through the property introduces you to more than 15 animal species, some of which run free. The flower gardens and the different landscapes are sure to make your visit most enchanting. You may make reservations to take part in the daily tasks of farm life. Moreover, pleasant footpaths lead you through our valleys to peaceful picnic and rest stops. We can organize a party*, a spit-roasted-lamb barbecue* or an other event* for you: just contact us!

From Montréal, Hwy 25 North to Rawdon. Rte 337 North, left on Rue Queen (at the IGA). Cross the village to 16e Avenue, then turn left at the Chemin Morgan intersection. We are 6km farther.

For families, small groups and groups of 15 people and more : May 1 to October 31

- The Arche de Noé is 1 hour from Montréal!
- Ostriches, boars, Vietnamese pot-bellied pigs, miniature goats, horses, (Limousin) cattle, birds, cats and dog.
- Footpaths and picnic areas able to accommodate up to 200 people.

- Landscaped volleyball court and horseshoe space.
- Unforgettable scenery and family ambiance that will brighten up your day!
  Rates:
  $6 per person
  $20 for groups of 4 people or more
  groups on reservation

3. MIRABEL, ST-BENOIT

INTERMIEL
Viviane and Christian Macle
10291, La Fresnière
Mirabel, St-Benoît J7N 3M3
(450) 258-2713
fax (450) 258-2708
www.intermiel.com
intermiel@sympatico.ca

15km from St-Eustache
45km from Montréal
25km from Mirabel airport

In St-Benoît, come to the largest beekeeping area in Québec. The guided tour includes a visit to the mead cellar, a video, demonstrations, educational games room, opening of the hives in season. The "honey boutique"carries our various products made of honey and maple...wich you can taste!

From Montréal, Hwy 15 North, Exit 8. Follow the blue tourist information signs (18km).

Open year round, 7 days a week
Groups: with reservations
adults $3.00 children $1.00 *Taxes included*
Guided tours (1h30 long) including honey/mead sampling.
School package: 2-hour educational visit in 4 workshops
Price: $5.50 (includes snack and a pot of honey)
other packages available (mini barn)

- Movie on the beekeeping activities
- Learn about farm's bee
- Observation of living hives
- Handling of an active hive by the beekeeper (in summer)
- Demonstration of prodution techniques
- Visit to the mead cellar

- Tasting the beehive products (ganache au miel, caramel)
- Educational games room
- Marionette theatre
- Hydromel sampling (honey wine)
- Exhibition shop (candles, wrapping, gifts, cosmetics, maple product...)
- Picnic area (interior space in case of rain)
- Mini-barn

4. LOUISEVILLE

LES JARDINS
DE LA SEIGNEURIE
Michel Gilbert
480, chemin du Golf
Louiseville J5V 2L4
tel/fax (819) 228-8224

26km from Trois-Rivières
160km from Québec
120km from Montréal

All around a traditional little farm, these gardens have been restored and enlarged, taking inspiration from 19th-century bourgeois farm life. You'll get an inside look at Québec's natural farming heritage, raising animals, ecological farming, and the art of country living. Your five senses will be charmed. "One of 20 gardens to visit in Quebec" (*l'Essentiel*, July 98; *La Semaine Verte*, August 98). **The B&B de La Seigneurie p 194, Farm Stay p 40, Maison du Jardinier p 200, Country-style dining p 23,** are the best places to stay to take advantage of these romantic gardens. **Ad end of the guide.**

From Montréal or Québec City, Hwy 40 Exit 166, Rte 138 E., 2.4km to Rte 348 W. At the lights, left twd Ste-Ursule, 1.5 km, 1st road on the right, 1st house tucked away behind the trees.

FOR FAMILIES AND SMALL GROUPS: June 15 to September15 (with reservations)
For groups of 10 to 40 people: June 15 to September 15 (with reservations)

- Identification of old flower varieties, fruits and vegetables in flower beds, a rose garden, groves and vegetable gardens
- Enclosed herb garden and an exhibition on their medicinal properties
- Buckwheat fields
- Composting and complementary gardening
- The advantages of a greenhouse
- Visit sheep, goat and horse pastures
- Demonstration on how to use some old gardening tools
- Identification of 60 tree varieties
- Visit the farmyard (turkeys, geese, chickens, ducks, guinea-fowl)

- Iroquois vegetable garden
- Cut-flower garden (900 gladiola)
- Visit heritage buildings and their "residents": pigs, calves, rabbits, cats, goats and sheeps.

Rates:
$6 per person including tasting of farm products in the garden.
Schedule: guided tour (90 min) every day at 3 pm or otherwise with reservations.
Supper on the farm (5 courses, $20) is available after the tour, with reservations. The tour is free for those staying at the Seigneurie.

5. ST-VALÉRIEN

LA RABOUILLÈRE
Pierre Pilon
1073, rang de l'Égypte
St-Valérien JOH 2B0
(450) 793-4998
fax (450) 793-2529

80km from Montréal
20km from St-Hyacinthe
20 from de Granby

La Rabouillère, a unique farm. Your host, a veterinarian, has an infectious enthusiasm for animals and flowers... A unique collection of many animal species and breeds in magnificent countryside. (Ideal site for family parties, anniversaries, weddings, etc.). **Country-Style Dining also available see p. 25, Farm stay p 41, B&B p 210.**

From Montréal, Hwy 20 East, Exit 141, twd St-Valérien. In the village, take Chemin Milton, and the first road on the right (2nd flashing light). Or from Hwy 10, Exit 68, Rte 139 twd Granby, then Rte 112 and 137 North twd St-Hyacinthe. After Ste-Cécile, Chemin St-Valérien to the right, to the next flashing light turn left.

Our farm is now open from May to October, weather permitting,
for families and small or large groups.
RESERVATIONS ALWAYS REQUIRED
Snacks available upon request*

- The garden: large variety of perennials and herbs (flowers in the kitchen, composting, water garden, flora and fauna)
- The rabbit hutch: different breeds of rabbits (giant, dwarf, Angora...)
- Goats: care of the different breeds (milk, Angora, dwarf)
- Horse breeding: visit the stables, care and training of foals
- The farmyard: more than 50 types of birds
- The sheepfold (rare breeds): four-horned Jacob Sheep, Barbarian sheep and Katahdin (wool-less)

- Curiosities: llamas, donkeys, miniature horses...
- Other activities: pony rides, pool, volleyball, musical shows (folksinger or classical)*, campfire*, spit-roasted lamb (méchoui)*, corn on the cob*, brunch*, snack of terrines, pâtés and brochettes*
Rates:
$5 per person
* additional charge

6. ST-PIE

FERME JEAN DUCHESNE
Diane Authier and
Jean Duchesne
1981-84,
Haut-de-la-Rivière Sud
St-Pie J0H 1W0
(450) 772-6512
fax (450) 772-2491

60km from Montréal
20km from St-Hyacinthe
15km from Granby

Set between the mountains and river, our unique farm is one where horses, sheep, rabbits, emus and many other animals live in perfect harmony. Treat your family to an exceptional experience and relive childhood memories... Our farm turns your children into little farmers, with everything designed for them through a guided tour (see various options). The adventure is crowned with a "Farmer For A Day" certificate of merit awarded by the "Big Farmer".

Hwy 20, St-Hyacinthe Exit 123. At stop sign, left on Rte 235 South to St-Pie. At the flashing light, after St-Pie bridge, left on Rang Emille Ville and left twice more. Hwy 10, Exit 55, Rte 235 North twd Rang Emille Ville (right at the flashing light), then left and left again.

FOR FAMILIES AND SMALL GROUPS: 1 to 30 people April to October (with reservations)
For groups of 2 to 150 people: April 9 to October 11 (with reservations)

- Guided tours: educational, recreational, experimental (close contact with animals) programs adapted for different age groups.
- Introduction to various farm-bred animals: the rabbit and its hutch, the cow and its dairy, the goat and its milking facilities, interpreting animal languages, etc.
- Feeding animals, milking goats, etc. Visit to our sheepfold. Hay ride from the sheep pen. Wow, what an adventure!
- Awarding of a "Farmer For A Day" certificate of merit with the farmer's official handshake.

- Farm games (hay, kittens...) and several surprises!
- Facilities: designed in case of rain, adapted for children and wheelchairs, ind./out. picnic and play areas, local- and farm-products shop.
- Options: Day farmer 10am to 3pm, night farmer 6pm to 9pm, kid farmer 10am to 3pm (Sun. only, Jun to Aug). Orchard farmer for the new school year 10am to 3pm*.
- Farm parties: Children's birthday parties, catered* or uncatered private receptions, cornhusking party*.

Rates :
$6 per person
$5 For groups of 25 to 150 people
* additional charge

7. PIERREFONDS ⬧

FERME ÉCOLOGIQUE DU
PARC-NATURE DU
CAP-SAINT-JACQUES
D-TROIS-PIERRES
183, ch. du Cap-Saint-Jacques
Pierrefonds H9K 1C6
(514) 280-6743
fax (514) 624-0725
www.d3pierres.qc.ca
info@d3pierres.qc.ca

30km from Montréal
100km from Joliette
180km from Hull

On the western part of the island of Montreal, immerse yourself in a universe of organic agriculture. We are the only farm in Canada associated with an international organization of educational farms. More than 15 species, greenhouse displaying cultivation, organic garden, cultivation fields. Everything to introduce the young and old alike to the agricultural world. We also offer a whole range of complementary services. The country ambiance will charm you!

Hwy 40, Exit 49. Follow the blue singposts. The park entry is at 20099 Boul. Gouin Ouest. Inside the park, follow «La Ferme Écologique» indications.

Free visit for families each year, animation service: Feb. 15 to Oct. 31, weekends.
Guided visit for groups of 10 to 120 ppl.: Feb. 15 to Oct. 31, by reservation. Price $5/pers.
Sugar Shack*: Feb. 15 to April 15, visit and traditional meal, by reservation.

- Free, animated visits on weekends (mid-Feb/late October).
- Guided visits: educational/recreational program adapted to age groups.
- "Farm Visit": May/late October.
- Special programs*: sugar shack, farm/beach, Halloween.
- More than 15 species in their indoor and outdo- or habitats.
- Organic greenhouse cultivation.
- Organic garden: identifying crops, composting...
- Sleigh ride*
- Interpretation centre (February/late October).

- General store, local farm and craft products.
- Dining,
- Hiking trails and picnic site,
- Cross-country ski trails,
- playground, thematic festivals, harvest festival* (2nd Sunday in August)
- Complementary services*: country-style dinners, children's birthday parties, conference and reception rooms, off-site reception rooms
  * Additional charge
  Rate:
  Parking $4

Farm Stays

		RATES		ANIMALS	ACTIVITIES
		2 meals	3 meals		
BAS-ST-LAURENT					
St-Jean-de-Dieu Ferme Paysagée ☎ (418) 963-3315 (page 60)	single double child child alone	--- --- --- ---	40 35 de-pends on age	Deer, lamas, golden pheasant, hens, ponies, sheeps, goats, rabbits, quails, ducks, cows, peacocks.	Milking a cow, bringing the cows in from pasture, gathering eggs from chickens and quails. Feeding the small animals. Trout fishing. Walking along our trails and through our fields. **See advertisement end of Bas-St-Laurent region (accommodation section).**
CANTONS-DE-L'EST					
Courcelles Ferme Auberge d'Andromède ☎ (418) 483-5442 (418) 486-7135 (page 68)	single double child child alone	50-60 50-60 30 ---	--- --- --- ---	Pinto pony, French Percheron and Appaloosa horses, Labrador and Irish setter dogs, cat, hens, rabbits, quails, pigs, ducks, chickens, geese.	Come enjoy yourselves at our Townships farm, running, strolling, frolicking in the fields and the forest on our 76-acre property. Cuddle the kittens, pet "Tite-toune" the Dalmatian and "Ducky" the brown Labrador. Feed the animals, rabbits and our four horses. Savour fresh eggs, maple waffles with raspberries and pancakes from our saphouse for breakfast. A great getaway for couples. Period decor and comfort await you in exceptional surroundings. **Ad end of the Cantons-de-l'Est region.**
Danville Le Clos des Pins ☎ (819) 839-3521 (page 69)	single double child child alone	55-70 45-53 20-25 ---	--- --- --- ---	Cows, calves, goats, horses, pigs, cats, sheeps, rabbits, hens, quail, guinea-fowl, Bernese bouvier dogs.	Walks (135 acres), horse-drawn carriage rides, animal care, swimming, campfires, outdoor games, fruit picking, maintaining the organic vegetable garden, swing, children's playground. Daycare available for a small fee.

		RATES		ANIMALS	ACTIVITIES
		2 meals	3 meals		
CENTRE-DU-QUÉBEC					
Tingwick Les Douces Heures d'Antan ☎ (819) 359-2813 (page 88)	single double child child alone	--- 65 47.⁵⁰ 25 ---	--- --- --- ---	Sheep pen, rabbits, ponies, cow and calf, variety of poultry, quails, ducks, pheasant, goat, pigs, trout-fishing ponds, dog and cat.	**1999 Provincial Agrotourism Award.** We invite you to relive the pleasures of yesteryear on our peaceful 27-acre farm. Help take care of animals and participate in farm work. Enjoy trout fishing, picking berries, gardening in our large organic vegetable gardens and smelling our thousands of perennials. Give in to the pleasures of our table garnished with fresh farm products, and finally, warm up by the campfire. **See colour photos.**
CHAUDIÈRES-APPALACHES					
St-Cyprien, Barré Le Jardins des Mésanges ☎ (418) 383-5777 (page 110)	single double child child alone	--- 50 37.⁵⁰ 15-25 ---	--- --- --- ---	Ponies, laying hens, corn-fed chickens, quails, geese, rabbits, dog, cat, cow and calf.	As the seasons drift by, discover different activities. In spring, participate in maple-syrup making in our sugar shack. In summer, discover the organic garden and its original produce, as well as the flowers and the birds. Visit the region on the bike paths. Enjoy the beautiful colours of autumn while hiking, wood cutting or picking mushrooms. In winter, skate on the lake or do some snowshoeing. B&B accessible by skidoo. In summer, you can garden for a small additional charge.
St-Léon-de-Standon Ferme la Colombe ☎ (418) 642-5152 (page 114)	single double child child alone	--- 50 42-45 15-30 ---	--- --- --- ---	Goat, partridge, sheeps, rabbits, various fowl, guinea-fowl, wild turkeys, quails, ducks, cats and dog.	Visit of thematic gardens, nature interpretation, feeding the animals. Our family-style cuisine will win you over! Trout fishing, swimming, canoeing, play-ground, bicycling, camp fires, fruit-picking, rest, birdwatching, winter sports, ski packages, skating rink on site. **Country-style dining p 15 and Farm excursion p 29**

		RATES		ANIMALS	ACTIVITIES
		2 meals	3 meals		
CÔTE-NORD					
Sacré-Coeur Ferme -5- Étoiles ☎ (418) 236-4551 (418) 236-4833 (page 123)	single double child child alone	69 49 29 ---	--- --- --- ---	Buffalo, stags, deers, boars, wolves, cows, horses, more than 32 species of farm birds...	Guided tour of the farm and its animals, the daily care of the animals, tractor and horse rides, excursions: hiking, all-terrain vehicles, kayaking, sailing or boat trips on the Saguenay Fjord, whale-watching cruises, backcountry camping. **Country Home p 128. For activities: see advertisement in Côte-Nord and Saguenay-Lac-St-Jean regions.**
GASPÉSIE					
St-René-de-Matane Gîte des Sommets ☎ (418) 224-3497 (page 141)	single double child child alone	40 32.50 12.50 15 with res.	50 42.50 17.50 20 with res.	Cattle breeding, goat farm, hens, rabbits and Ti-Lou, our friendly dog.	Guided tours of the farm and hiking. Fishing in the brook, mountain biking, picnics, campfires, mushroom picking, wildberry picking, photo safari. Mountain climbing, visit to beaver pond. In winter season: snowshoeing, cross-country skiing, sliding, skidooing (equipment not provided).
LAURENTIDES					
L'Annonciation La Clairière de la Côte ☎ (819) 275-2877 (page 169)	single double child child alone	60 40 20-25 ---	65 45 30 ---	Cows, calves, goats, sheeps, rabbits, hens, turkeys, geese, grain-fed chickens, dog and cats.	Visit of the farm. Forest walks (300 acres). Organic gardens, fine herbs, flowers, greenhouse. See chicks hatch. Transformation of farm products. Smoking of meat and fish. Rest areas. Campfires. Games. Life on the farm is busy. **Country-Style Dining p 19.**
St-Faustin Ferme de la Butte Magique ☎ (819) 425-5688 (page 174)	single double child child alone	67-77 53.50 28 ---	--- --- --- ---	Ewes, lambs and other breeds; East Friesian dairy, Merino, Jacob, and Icelandic (for wool), chickens, roosters and chicks, pigs in the forest, lama, colley dogs and 3 differently coloured cats.	Come discover the magic....From the daily care of the animals, through the cycle of seasons, experience: lambing, ewe milking, cheesemaking, wool shearing and hand spinning, maple sugaring, organic gardenning...Plus swimming, hiking to the 3 big birches, playing in the sheperd's hut, evening campfire and more! We also invite young «artist» girls from 10-12 years old to a very special one-week «wool camp». Contact us!

		RATES		ANIMALS	ACTIVITIES
		2 meals	3 meals		

MAURICIE

		RATES		ANIMALS	ACTIVITIES
		2 meals	3 meals		
Hérouxville Accueil les Semailles ☎ (418) 365-5190 (page 193)	single double child child alone	43 33 15 ---	51 41 18 ---	Cattle for slaughter, horses, goats, sheep, pig, rabbits, kittens, ducks, pheasants, turkeys, hens, grain-fed chickens.	Children enjoy feeding the animals and gathering eggs. Guests have the use of outdoor facilities: pool, swing set, volleyball court, sandbox, horseshoes, campfire and kitchen garden. Witness farm work with the changing seasons.
Louiseville Ferme de la Seigneurie ☎ (819) 228-8224 (page 194)	single double child child alone	45-70 52-65 30 ---	--- --- --- ---	Goats, calves, sheep, horses, rabbits, ducks, turkeys, hens, geese, guinea-fowl, dogs, cats.	Get close to nature at this small traditional farm: observe and feed fowl and other animals, identify birds. 60 varieties of trees, 86 varieties of flowers and medicinal herbs. Learn about the organic farming of the large vegetable garden and go all the way to the river through the fields. The guided tour of the farm and its gardens, at 3pm, is free. Winter: dogsledding excursions. Ask for farm pic-nic package. **Country Home p 200, Country-Style Dining p 23, Farm Excursion p 32. Ad end of the guide.**

MONTÉRÉGIE

		RATES		ANIMALS	ACTIVITIES
		2 meals	3 meals		
Howick (Riverfield) Auberge La Chaumière ☎ (450) 825-0702 (page 206)	single double child child alone	47 37 18 37	53 43 23 43	Horses, sheep, donkey, dogs and cats.	Walks, cycling, swimming, canoeing, fishing, cross-country skiing, skating, snowshoeing, horseback riding, golfing, dogsledding, ornithology. **Country home p 212.**

MONTÉRÉGIE

		RATES		ANIMALS	ACTIVITIES
		2 meals	3 meals		
Howick Hazelbrae Farm ☎ (450) 825-2390 (page 206)	single double child child alone	--- --- --- ---	45 45 12-30 ---	Cows and variety of small animals.	Campfire, carriage ride, pool, bikes, farm activities. Observe the milking of the cows, haymaking.
St-Valérien La Rabouillère ☎ (450) 793-2329 (page 210)	single double child child alone	60-75 50-60 25 ---	--- --- --- ---	Exotic animals (llama, donkeys, miniature horses, bearded sheep, Katahdin, Jacob, Boer and pygmy goats, pot-bellied pigs, rabbit hutch, 50 varieties of birds, peacocks, pheasants, geese, ducks, hens, pigeons and more.	Observation and care of animals, identification, feeding, gathering eggs, incubator, births. Tour of gardens and organic kitchen gardens (perennials, herbs, edible flowers). Forest walks (marked trails, plantings, mushroom and berry picking, peat bog, ornithology). Fishing, swimming and canoeing in ponds. Pool, playground, summer theatre, zoo, downhill skiing, bike paths. **Country-style dining p 25, Farm walks p 33, B&B p 210.**
Ste-Agnès-de-Dundee Chez Mimi ☎ (450) 264-4115 1-877-264-4115 (page 210)	single double child child alone	55 45 25 ---	70 60 35 ---	Bullock, cows, cats, dogs, hens, rabbits.	Taking care of the garden and flowers. Feed the rabbits, collect eggs, make hay, pick vegetables. Bird-watching, river fishing, golf courses, snowmobile stopovers, horseback riding, country walks, bike paths, archeology.

		RATES		ANIMALS	ACTIVITIES
		2 meals	3 meals		
OUTAOUAIS					
Vinoy, Chénéville Les Jardins de Vinoy ☎ (819) 428-3774 (page 234)	single double child child alone	69-84 51-59 24.⁵⁰ ---	84-99 59-74 28.⁵⁰ ---	Goats, pigs, rabbits, sheep, wild boar, geese, guinea-fowl, ducks, chickens, hens, dog, cats.	Yesteryear's charm, modern comforts. Animal husbandry, old-time sugaring off, sleigh rides (dogs, horses), soap-making, jams, preserves, bread making, spinning, medicinal plants, forest trekking, cross-country skiing, snowshoeing, playground, campfire, organic garden, regional table d'hôte. **See colour photos.**
QUÉBEC CITY REGION					
St-Gabriel-de-Valcartier Le Gîte des Equerres ☎ (418) 844-2424 toll free : 1-877-844-2424 (page 258)	single double child child alone	80 60-70 40 ---	--- --- --- ---	A unique forestry farm in Quebec. Vast plantation of noble trees, broad-leaved trees and conifers. Also, market and horticultural gardening. To the delight of children, 2 dogs, hens and rabbits.	Unique outdoor setting. 200 acres between fields, river, lake and forest. Boundless valley! A paradise of activities for young and old alike. Kilometres of walking, mountain-biking, cross-country-skiing and snowshoeing trails. Fishing, campfire, indoor pool, private tennis court. Bird-watching station, small and big game. Near water park, rafting, horseback riding, golf courses, ski resorts. The back country 30min from the city. **Country Home p 262.**
SAGUENAY - LAC-SAINT-JEAN					
Hébertville Carole et Jacques Martel ☎ (418) 344-1323 (page 267)	single double child child alone	--- --- --- ---	35 35 15 ---	Cows, heifers, calves, dogs, cats.	Tour of the farm and observation of farm activities (milking, maintenance, etc.) Grain farming with square and round hay chaff. Capacity: 10 people.

		RATES		ANIMALS	ACTIVITIES
		2 meals	3 meals		
SAGUENAY - LAC-SAINT-JEAN					
La Baie Chez Grand-Maman ☎ (418) 544-7396 (page 270)	single double child child alone	60 50 15-20 ---	--- --- --- ---	Cows, calves, chickens, hens, turkeys, cats, dog.	Try milking a cow. Feed the animals and see to their care. Walk along the shores of the Baie des HA! HA!. Outdoor fireplace, pool, and ice-fishing during winter.
Lac-à-la-Croix Céline et Georges Martin ☎ (418) 349-2583 (page 272)	single double child child alone	40 34 16 ---	--- --- --- ---	Cows, heifers, calves, dog.	Visit of the farm.
Normandin Ferme Nordan ☎ (418) 274-2867 (page 275)	single double child child alone	60 45 25 ---	--- --- --- ---	Dairy cows, rabbits, hens, calves, goat and other varieties of small animals.	Cute little farm where everyone can feed the animals, help care for them, collect eggs and pet these adorable creatures. Visit to the dairy farm and observation of activities (milking, maintenance, etc.). Camp fire, swimming pool and swing.
St-Félix-d'Otis Gîte de la Basse-Cour ☎ (418) 544-8766 (page 278)	single double child child alone	60 50 15-20 ---	--- --- --- ---	Sheep, hens, ducks, rabbits, partridges, pigeons, quails, cats and dog.	Observing and feeding the animals, collecting eggs, feeding trout, bird watching and identification, tending of organic vegetable garden, vegetable and berry picking, preparing and baking bread in the outdoor bread oven, hiking, campfires, regional table d'hôte. Winter: cross-country skiing, snowshoeing, walking, skidooing (local trail 383 only 3 kilometres away). Available with reservation: kayaking on the fjord, dogsledding, ice fishing and skidoo rental.

Bed and Breakfasts

Country Inns

Country Homes

City Homes

WHERE TO FIND THE...

46.

COUNTRY HOMES

CITY HOMES (APPARTMENTS & STUDIOS)

ABITIBI-TÉMISCAMINGUE

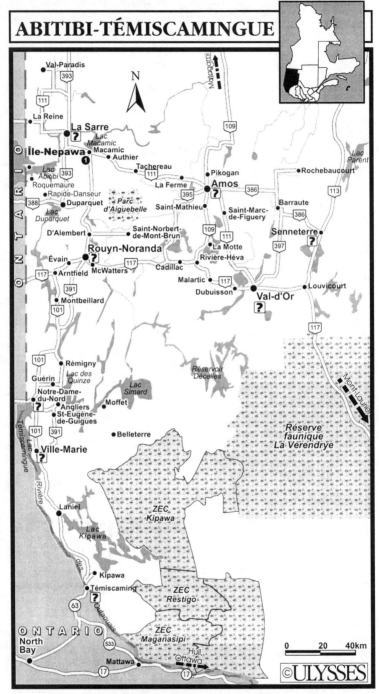

* The numbers on the map refer to the numbering of the establishments of this region

1. ÎLE-NEPAWA

F E 🐕 🚗 P 🏊 R30 M10

Three comfortable chalets in the wilderness on the shores of Lac Abitibi, including a Swiss-style with fireplace, as well as two bungalows. We raise cattle, goats and horses. Water sports, hunting and fishing. Near the Aiguebelle conservation park. Come and enjoy a visit with Quebecers of German descent.

From Rouyn, Rte 101 to La Sarre. 3 km past La Sarre, follow the signs for Ste-Hélène and Île Nepawa, half-paved gravel road. 1st house on the right after the bridge to the island.

COUNTRY HOME
FERME VACANCES

Hélène and Hermann Wille
695 Île-Nepawa, R.R. # 1
Ste-Hélène-de-Mancebourg
JOZ 2T0
(819) 333-6103

No. houses	3
No. rooms	2-3
No. people	6-8
WEEK-SUMMER	$250
W/E-SUMMER	$125
DAY-SUMMER	$50

Open: May 1 to Oct. 31

Activities: 🛶 🚶 🐎

BAS-SAINT-LAURENT

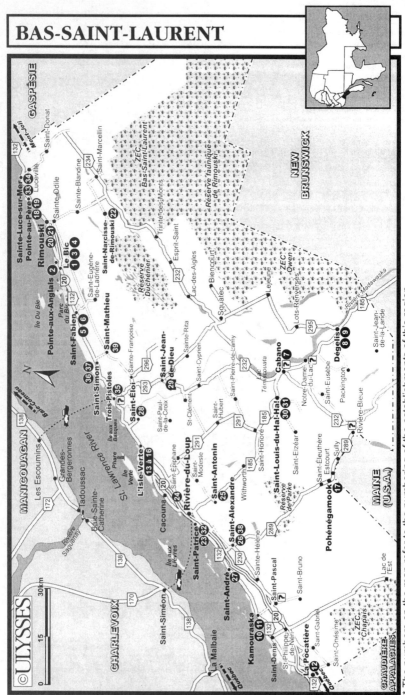

* The numbers on the map refer to the numbering of the establishments of this region

1. BIC, LE

★★★ F e ⊘ ✗ 🚗 P R.2 TA

Bas-St-Laurent Excellence Prize 1999. Hundred-year-old house deep in the country. Great sunsets on Rivière-Hâtée cove. Ambiance where flowers meet the magic of Christmas. King-sized beds, private bathrooms. Old-fashioned or healthy breakfast, tea time, outdoor barbecues. Hiking in the mountain, or on the sea shore. Patio, balcony, family garden. Enjoy seaside solitude.

From Québec City, Hwy 20 E., Rte 132 E. At East Bic exit, left at flashing light on Rte 132, about 2km. From Ste-Flavie or Mont-Joli, Rte 132 W. twd Bic.

INN
AUBERGE CHEZ MARIE-ROSES

Jacqueline Caron
2322, Route 132 Est
Bic G0L 1B0
(418) 736-5311
(418) 736-4954
fax (418) 736-5955
www.marie-roses.qc.ca
marieroses@globetrotter.net

B&B	
single	$55-60
double	$65-75
triple	$80-90
child	$10

Taxes extra VS MC IT

Reduced rates: Oct. 15 to May 31
Open: Feb. 15 to Jan. 5

Number of rooms	7
rooms with private bath	5
rooms in basement	1
shared wc	1
shared bathrooms	1

Activities: 🏛 🍂 🛶 🚶 🚴

2. BIC, LE

☀☀☀ F E ⊘ P 🚗 🐕 R2 TA

On the shore of the St. Lawrence, in Bic Harbour, our century-old house awaits you in its calm setting with its old-fashioned decor and ambiance. Idyllically situated hugging the seashore. From the porch, a spectacle of sea birds follows the eternal movement of the tides.

From Québec City, Hwy 20 East, Rte 132 to Bic. Take the Aux Cormorans and Club de Golf exit. Drive 2km. On the point, «Aux Cormorans» is the last house on the left, on the seashore.

B&B
AUX CORMORANS

Judy Parceaud
213, chemin du Golf
Pointe-aux-Anglais
Bic G0L 1B0
(418) 736-8113
fax (418) 736-4216
www.bbcanada.
com/2982.html
cormoran@globetrotter.qc.ca

B&B	
single	$40-75
double	$50-75
triple	$60-65
child	$10

VS MC

Open year round

Number of rooms	5
rooms with private bath	1
shared bathrooms	2

Activities: 🏛 🍂 🛶 🚶

3. BIC, LE

☀☀☀ F e 🐕 ✗ 🚗 P R3 TA

Quintessential Québec house dating from 1830. Aux 5 Lucarnes offers you 4 large rooms with sink, a «table d'hôte» prepared with local products, sea-kayak packages and access to the sea... Lunchbox service for your hikes. And so much more...

From Québec City, Hwy 20 East and Rte 132 East. At Bic exit, left at flashing light, about 3km along Rte 132.

B&B
AUX 5 LUCARNES

Johanne Desjardins
2175, Route 132 Rivière-Hâtée
Bic G0L 1B0
tel/fax (418) 736-5435
www.cam.org/~bsl/lucarnes/
polyfilm@globetrotter.net

	B&B	MAP
single	$45	$70
double	$55	$105
triple	$70	$145
quad.	$85	$185
child	$10	$20

Taxes extra VS MC ER

Reduced rates: Oct. 16 to May 15
Open year round

Number of rooms	4
rooms with sink	4
shared bathrooms	2

Activities: 🍂 🚶 🚴

4. BIC, LE

☀☀☀ F e 🐕 P R3 TA

A charming Norman-style house with antique furniture, this B&B overlooks the river and offers you a magnificent view of islands and mountains. Two rooms have their own bathroom and private entrance with view over the river. In a secluded setting, discover the wide expanses...

3 hours from Québec City, Hwy 20 East, Rte 132 East to Bic. First exit turn right on Rue Ste-Cécile. Turn right on the first small cross street, Rue Voyer. Voyer becomes 2e Rang Ouest. Drive 4km.

B&B
LA PETITE NORMANDE

Claire Beaudoin
456, Rang 2 Ouest
C. P. 2009
Bic G0L 1B0
(418) 736-5897

B&B	
single	$50-60
double	$55-70
child	$15

Reduced rates: Oct. 20 to May 1
Open year round

Number of rooms	4
rooms with private bath	2
shared bathrooms	1
rooms in semi-basement	2

Activities: 🍁 ⛵ 🚶 🎿 🚴

---

5. BIC, ST-FABIEN

☀☀☀ F E 🚫 🚗 P R3 TA

At the gates of Parc du Bic, I invite you to share with me the charm of yesteryear, modern comfort, tranquillity (away from Rte 132) and a hearty breakfast of home-made bread and jam. Warm welcome. I love company! Dinner on request.

Rte 132 from Gaspé or Montréal. In St-Simon, 11km from Petro Canada. Left on Rang 1 for 2km (white house, red roof). In St-Fabien, 3km from art mill. Right on Rang 1.

B&B
CLAIREVALLÉE

Marguerite Voyer
178, Rte 132 ouest
St-Fabien G0L 2Z0
tel/fax (418) 869-3582
(450) 922-9054
www.cam.org/
~bsl/clairevallee/

B&B	
single	$40-50
double	$55-65
triple	$70-80
quad.	$85-95

VS

Open: May 1 to Oct. 31

Number of rooms	5
rooms with private bath	1
shared bathrooms	3

Activities: 🍁 ⛵ 🎿 🚶 🚴

---

6. BIC, ST-FABIEN

☀☀ F e ✕ P R1 TA

Right next to Parc Bic, a former shoemaker's home warmly welcomes you, with the smell of fresh bread and «joie de vivre» amidst its turn-of-the-century decor. Next to the home, a pretty café and a terrace are ideal for meeting villagers. Little flea market at the back of the house.

From Québec City, Hwy 20 East, Rte 132 East to St-Fabien. At the heart of the village near the caisse populaire. Yellow wood house.

B&B
LA MAISON DU
CORDONNIER

Réal Houle
26, 7ᵉ Avenue C.P. 488
St-Fabien G0L 2Z0
(418) 869-2002
fax (418) 869-2022

	B&B	MAP
single	$38	$56
double	$50	$86
triple	$62	$116
quad	$74	$146
child	$10	$22

Taxes extra VS

Open year round

Number of rooms	4
shared wc	1
shared bathrooms	1

Activities: 🍁 ⛵ 🚶 🚴 🛷

7. CABANO

★★ F E ✖ 🚗 P R.3 TA

Located near Lac Témiscouata and the bike path, guests at the Auberge du Chemin Faisant enjoy our fine Magdalen Island-style cuisine, as well as our delectable breakfasts. Your host will entertain you on the piano, and the fireplace completes the cosy atmosphere. A great place for rest and relaxation.

From Québec City, Hwy 20 E., at Rivière-du-Loup, Rte 185 S. At Cabano, first exit, Rue Commercial for 1km, then turn right at Vieux Chemin.

INN
AUBERGE DU CHEMIN FAISANT

Liette Fortin and Hugues Massey
12, Vieux Chemin
Cabano G0L 1E0
(418) 854-9342
toll free 1-877-954-9342
www.cheminfaisant.qc.ca
info@cheminfaisant.qc.ca

	B&B	MAP
single	$45-85	$65-105
double	$50-90	$90-130
triple	$60-100	$120-160
quad.	$70-110	$150-190
child	$10	$10

Taxes extra VS MC

Reduced rates: 3 nights or more, 5$/night
Open year round

Number of rooms	7
rooms with private bath	3
rooms with sink	2
rooms in basement	1
shared bathrooms	1
shared wc	1

Activities: 🚣 ⛷ 🚴 🛶 ⛷

---

8. DÉGELIS

☀☀☀ F E 🚫 🐕 🚗 P 🏊 R1.5

Located in a forest by Lac Témiscouata. Great comfort, clear panoramic view of the lake, famous à-la-carte breakfast. Come nightfall, around a fire on the beach, the song of the loon and golden sparks meeting the stars make up nature's sound and light show. Reserve from Oct. 15 to May 15.

Hwy 20, Exit 499, Rte 185 South. In Dégelis, Rte 295 North twd Auclair, for 6km. By bike, cross the Dégelis dam and follow the 295 North, turn left and ride 2.5km.

B&B
GÎTE AU TOIT ROUGE

Dominique Lagarde and
André Demers
441, Route 295
Dégelis G5T 1R2
(418) 853-3036
(418) 853-2294

B&B	
single	$40-50
double	$55-65
triple	$70-80
quad.	$80-95
child	$5-12

Reduced rates: Oct. 15 to Apr. 15
Open: Jan. 6 to Dec. 20

Number of rooms	4
rooms with private bath	1
rooms with sink	3
shared bathrooms	1

Activities: 🚣 ⛷ 🚴 🐎 🚶

---

9. DÉGELIS

☀☀☀ F e P 🚗 R.13

Welcome to our welcoming B&B: water garden and falls, fragrant with flowers. Private entrance, big parking lot. Direct access to "Le Petit Témis" bike path; bike storage. Balcony, lounge, TV, fridge. Lavish breakfast in sunroom. Family picnics in gazebo. Restaurant nearby. Children welcome. See you soon!

From Québec City, Hwy 20 E. to Riv.-du-Loup, Rte 185 S. In Dégelis, 1st exit on left on Ave Principale. From New Brunswick Rte 185 N. In Dégelis, 1st exit on right, Ave Principale.

B&B
LA BELLE MAISON BLANCHE

Monique and André Lavoie
513, av. Principale
Dégelis G5T 1L8
(418) 853-3324
fax (418) 853-5507
www.destinationquébec.com

B&B	
single	$40
double	$55-60
triple	$70-80
quad.	$80-90
child	$15

Reduced rates: Nov. 1 to April 30
Open year round

Number of rooms	5
shared wc	1
shared showers	1
shared bathrooms	1

Activities: ⛷ 🚶 🚴 🐎 🛶

10. KAMOURASKA

☀☀☀ F e ☒ �car P TA

Situated on a hilltop, the Auberge Des Îles has a magnificent view of the Kamouraskan Islands and the sunsets. In the evening, whether you're in the dining room, solarium or in your room, the twinkling lights on the north coast will captivate you. A cordial welcome with a touch of class, as well as some little extras, will make your stay a memorable one.

Hwy 20, Exit 465. Drive to Kamouraska. Once in the village, turn left on Av. Morel (Rte 132). Drive 1.5km.

INN
AUBERGE DES ÎLES

Liette and Rita Lévesque
198, avenue Morel
Kamouraska G0L 1M0
(418) 492-7561
fax (418) 492-7695

B&B	
single	$40-49
double	$49-58
child	$10

Taxes extra VS MC IT

Reduced rates: Nov 1 to Dec. 31
Open: May 1 to Oct. 31,
Nov 1 to Dec. 31, on reservation

Number of rooms	5
rooms with private bath	2
rooms with sink	1
shared bathrooms	1
shared wc	1

Activities: 🏛 ⛵ ⚲ 🚶 🐎

11. KAMOURASKA

☀☀☀ F e ⊘ P 🚗 R.5 TA

This beautiful century-old house will leave you with unforgettable memories, marked by the rhythm of the wind and the tide. Comfort, cleanliness, and *joie de vivre* await. Close to the sea, with a 2km-long promenade: what memories are made of. The sea air will whet your appetite for the gourmet breakfast to come. Bas-St-Laurent Excellence Prize 1995-96. Access to the St. Lawrence River.

From Québec City, Hwy 20 East, Exit 465. Drive 5km to Kamouraska. Once in the village, left on Ave. Morel (Rte 132). The second house after the church.

B&B
CHEZ JEAN ET NICOLE

Nicole and Jean Bossé
81, av. Morel, route 132
Kamouraska G0L 1M0
(418) 492-2921
www.total.net/
~stefnat/gite.html

B&B	
single	$45
double	$55-65
triple	$80
child	$10

VS

Open year round

Number of rooms	4
rooms with private bath	1
shared wc	1
shared bathrooms	1

Activities: 🛥 ⚲ 🚶 🚲 🐎

12. LA POCATIÈRE

☀☀☀☀ F e ♿ 🚗 P 🏊 TA

More than an inn, this is a place where we get to know our guests. A place whose charm and landscape inspires peace and love, where the aromas of regional dishes mingle with the fragrances of the ancient woods. Discounts for longer stays. Children welcome; 3 kilometres from various attractions...

One hour from Québec City, Hwy 20 East, Exit 436, turn right (west) at the stop, continue for 500 metres and you're here. From Gaspé, Exit 436...

B&B
AUBERGE AU DIABLO-VERT

Manon Brochu and Luc Gagnon
72, route 132 Ouest B.P.9
La Pocatière G0R 1Z0
(418) 856-4117
fax (418) 856-5161
www.québecweb.
com/diablovert
diablove@globetrotter.net

B&B	
single	$55
double	$65
triple	$75

VS MC AM IT

Reduced rates: Sept 1 to May 31
or 20% more than 3 nights
Open year round

Number of rooms	5
shared bathrooms	3

Activities: 🏛 ⛵ 🛥 ⚲

13. L'ISLE-VERTE

☀☀☀ | F | e | 🚫 | P | R1 | TA

Would you like to relive a page of our history, while admiring the accomplishments of our ancestors? We would like to share our large 150-year-old seigneurial house with you. Interior decor inspired by the highlights of the Victorian era: flowers, lace... You'll find charm, warm, old-fashioned hospitality and copious breakfasts.

From Québec City, Hwy 20, Rte 132 East. Turn right before the bridge at the flashing light. Or from Rimouski, Rte 132 West, turn left after the bridge at the flashing light. 1st house on the right on a hill.

B&B
AUX BERGES DE LA RIVIÈRE

Eve and Noëlla Caron
24, rue Villeray
L'Isle-Verte G0L 1L0
(418) 898-2501
(418) 862-8547
noella@icrdl.net

B&B	
single	$45
double	$50
triple	$65
quad.	$80
child	$10

Reduced rates: 10% 2 or 3 nights, 15% 4 nights and more
Open: June 15 to Sep. 15

Number of rooms	5
shared bathrooms	2

Activities: 🐚 ⛴ 🚣 🏃 🚲

14. L'ISLE -VERTE

☀☀☀ | F | E | 🐕 | 🚗 | P | R1 | TA

La Grande Ourse is a 19th-century Anglo-Norman house. The babbling Rivière Verte is just a stone's throw away from our flower garden, where birds congregate. In winter, warm up by the hearth before going off to your cosy bed. In the morning, a hearty breakfast awaits. Welcome to La Grande Ourse!

From Québec City, Hwy 20 East, Rte 132 East. After the Rivière Verte bridge, turn right and then right again. From Rimouski, Rte 132 West, L'Isle Verte exit, straight until end of the village, then left.

B&B
LA GRANDE OURSE

Martine Girard and
Paul-André Laberge
6, rue du Verger
L'Isle-Verte G0L 1K0
(418) 898-2763
fax (418) 898-3717

B&B	
single	$45-80
double	$55-80
triple	$70-80
quad.	$80
child	$0-10

Open year round

Number of rooms	5
shared wc	1
shared bathrooms	2

Activities: 🏛 🐚 ⛴ 🏃 🚲

15. L'ISLE-VERTE

☀☀ | F | e | 🐕 | P | R.5

A Victorian-style house with centenary charm that extends a warm and genuine welcome. Large tree-lined property. In the early morning wake up to the crowing of the cock and birdsong mingled with the aroma of a hearty breakfast. View of the river and access to nearby leisure activities. Make yourselves at home.

From Québec City, Hwy 20 East, Rte 132 East. In the village, turn right at the caisse populaire. House on the left, on the hill. From Rimouski: Rte 132 West, turn left at the caisse populaire...

B&B
LA MAISON ANCESTRALE

Diane Lévesque and
Joseph-Marie Fraser
5, rue Béland C.P. 245
L'Isle-Verte G0L 1K0
(418) 898-2633
(418) 898-2053

B&B	
single	$40
double	$50
triple	$65
child	$10

Open: June to Sep. 15

Number of rooms	4
shared wc	1
shared bathrooms	2

Activities: 🏛 🐚 ⛴ 🏃 🏃

16. L'ISLE-VERTE

☀☀ F 🚗 P R.5 TA

A B&B to discover on the road to Gaspésie. Warm, friendly welcome. Our goal: to make your stay a pleasant one. Clean, comfortable rooms; lounge; large living room with TV; wood-burning stove. After a good night's rest, enjoy a hearty breakfast of muffins and homemade jams. Near many services; bike shed. The only thing missing is you! See you soon!

From Québec City, Hwy 20 East, Rte 132 East. After the flashing light, Rte 132 for 0.5km, left on Rue Louis-Bertrand. From Gaspé, Rte 132 to L'Isle-Verte, right on 2nd street. 1km from the island ferry.

B&B
LES CAPUCINES

Marie-Anna and Yvon Lafrance
31, Louis-Bertrand, C.P. 105
L'Isle-Verte G0L 1K0
(418) 898-3276

B&B	
single	$40
double	$55
triple	$70
quad.	$80
child	$10

Reduced rates: 5% 3 nights or more from Nov. 1 to Apr. 30
Open year round

Number of rooms	3
rooms in basement	1
shared bathrooms	2

Activities: 🏛 🍴 ⛵ 🎣 🏃

17. POHÉNÉGAMOOK

☀☀ F e 🚗 P R.02 TA

Located near three borders (Québec, New Brunswick and Maine), La Bohème has an enchanting setting where legends combine with the history of the region. It offers a beautiful view of the lake and easy access to leisure activities: swimming, golfing, skiing, biking, hiking and snowmobiling. Breakfast is served up in a warm, cosy atmosphere.

From Québec City, Hwy 20 East, Exit 488 to Pohénégamook, Rte 289 South. After the second church, turn on Rédemptoristes, then left on Rue Beaupré, 2nd-to-last house.

B&B
LA BOHÈME

Jacqueline Gagné
1268, rue Beaupré
Pohénégamook G0L 1J0
(418) 859-3476

B&B	
single	$30
double	$40
child	$10

Reduced rates: Oct.1 to Mar. 31
Open year round

Number of rooms	3
shared batrooms	2

Activities: ⛷ 🎣 🚲 ⛵ 🏃

18. POINTE-AU-PÈRE

★★★ F e 🍽 P

Come to our Victorian home, built around 1860, and dream of travelling. Former property of Sieur Louis-Marie Lavoie, known as "Louis XVI", who was master-pilot on the St. Lawrence and upriver for the city of Québec. This charming home has since become an inn where you'll be spoiled by serenity and a warm welcome. **See colour photos.**

From Québec City, Hwy 20 East, Rte 132 to Rimouski, Rte 132 to Pointe-au-Père, drive 1km past the church.

INN
AUBERGE LA MARÉE DOUCE

Marguerite Lévesque
1329, boul. Ste-Anne
Pointe-au-Père, Rimouski
G5M 1W2
(418) 722-0822
(418) 723-4512
fax (418) 736-5167

B&B	
single	$70-80
double	$75-85
triple	$100
quad.	$110
child	$15

Taxes extra VS MC

Reduced rates: May, Oct. 1 to Dec 23
Open: May 1 to Dec 23

Number of rooms	9
rooms with private bath	9

Activities: 🏛 🍴 🎣 🏃 🚲

19. POINTE-AU-PÈRE

☀☀ F E 🚫 P 🚗 R.5 TA

Magnificent location, panoramic view, warm welcome, comfortable bed, affable host, nearby restaurant, quiet walks, beach campfires, starry nights, northern lights, lapping waves, deep sleep. Quiet mornings, fragrant coffee, talks... Activities: kayaking, museum, cycling, hiking... Enjoy your stay, *Sonia & André*.

Drop anchor at the end of the 20! Past Rimouski, Rte 132 East, between Bic and Métis, below the Pointe-au-Père lighthouse (Rue du Phare).

B&B
GÎTE DE LA POINTE

Sonia Soucy and
André Gamache
1046, rue du Phare
Pointe-au-Père G5M 1L8
(418) 724-6614
(418) 750-3332

B&B	
single	$40
double	$50
triple	$60

Taxes extra VS

Reduced rates: Sep. 15 to June 15
Open: Jan. 15 to Dec. 15

Number of rooms	5
rooms in semi-basement	4
shared wc	3
shared bathrooms	1

Activities: 🏛 ⛴ 🚶 🚴 🎿

20. RIMOUSKI

🖊 F E 🚫 🚗 P R2

At Chez Charles et Marguerite, visitors are greeted with a sincere and friendly welcome and the hosts respect your privacy. Breakfast is served in the dining room and solarium, with soft music playing in the background. Located close to the centre of town, this large, beautifully landscaped property has bike and walking paths that lead through the woods near the seashore. A wonderful opportunity to discover the lively, artistic character of the region!

From Québec City, hwy 20 East, Rte 132 East. At the eastern Bic exit, turn left at the flashing light, Rte 132. Drive 1.3km past the church.

B&B
CHEZ CHARLES ET MARGUERITE

Carmen Parent
686, boul. St-Germain ouest
Rimouski G5L 3S4
(418) 723-3938

B&B	
single	$45
double	$60
triple	$70
quad.	$85
child	$15

VS

Open: June 1 to Sept 10

Number of rooms	3
shared wc	1
shared batrooms	1

Activities: 🏛 🏊 🚶 🎿 🚴

21. RIMOUSKI, BIC

☀☀☀ F e 🐕 🚗 P R6 TA

An ancestral home
A family farm
A friendly ambiance
Amazing breakfasts
Enticing eggs, crepes
That young and old alike will enjoy
The house, the rooms, the stay
Are lovingly decorated
So that you will always remember
That at La Maison Bérubé
You are like family
Who visit us yearly

3 hours from Québec City, Hwy 20 East, Rte 132 East. At the Eastern Bic exit, at the flashing light turn left Rte 132. Drive for 6.4km to the left. 11.5km from Rimouski.

B&B
LA MAISON BÉRUBÉ

Louise Brunet and
Marcel Bérubé
1216, boul. St-Germain Ouest,
route 132
Rimouski G5L 8Y9
tel/fax (418) 723-1578

B&B	
single	$45
double	$55
triple	$75
quad.	$90
child	$5-15

Reduced rates: Oct. 1 to Apr. 30
Open year round

Number of rooms	5
rooms with sink	1
shared wc	1
shared bathrooms	2

Activities: 🏛 🏊 ⛴ 🚶 🐎

22. RIMOUSKI, ST-NARCISSE

F e ♿ P ⌂ R4

Quebecers find this B&B a comfortable chalet, while people from France consider it a trapper house. Log-house interior, quiet and very comfortable. Bears, deer, moose and beavers nearby. Breakfast in the solarium with view of the private lake teeming with trout. Free canoeing and swimming. 10min from «Canyon des Portes de l'Enfer». A real vacation only 15min from Rimouski.

From Québec City, Hwy 20 East, Exit 610, Rte 232 West for 16km. Stay on Rte 232; 1km past St-Narcisse intersection, left on Rang 1.

B&B
DOMAINE DU BON
VIEUX TEMPS

Hélène Rioux and
Régis Gauthier
89-1, chemin de l'Écluse
Rimouski-St-Narcisse G0K 1S0
(418) 735-5646
www.chez.com/
bonvieuxtemps
lacabane@globetrotter.qc.ca

B&B	
single	$45
double	$50-65
child	$10-15

Open year round

Number of rooms	3
rooms with private wc	2
shared bathrooms	1

Activities: ⚓ 🚣 ⛷ 🏃 🐕

---

23. RIVIÈRE-DU-LOUP

☀☀☀ F E 🚭 P R1

A superb 1895 Victorian house. Admire the sunsets from the solarium while breathing in the salty air. Rest in the shade of hundred-year-old trees. Two lounges suitable for relaxation. Prime Ministers John A. MacDonald and Louis St-Laurent once stayed in the neighbourhood. Magnificent surroundings!

Via Hwy 20, Exit 503, turn left at the stop, 11th house on the left. Located on Rte 132 between Notre-Dame-du-Portage and Rivière-du-Loup.

B&B
AUBERGE LA SABLINE

Monique Gaudet and
Jean Cousineau
343, Fraser ouest
Rivière-du-Loup G5R 5S9
(418) 867-4890

B&B	
single	$60-75
double	$65-80
triple	$80-95
child	$10

Taxes extra VS MC IT

Reduced rates: Sep. 5 to June 21
Open year round

Number of rooms	3
rooms with private bath	1
shared wc	1
shared bathrooms	1

Activities: 🛥 ⚓ 🚶 🚴

---

24. RIVIÈRE-DU-LOUP

☀☀☀ F E P 🚗 🍽 TA

"Who sleeps, eats" at Au Bonheur du Jour, a rural B&B between the road and the sea in L'Anse-au-Persil. As night falls the dining room offers 5-course meals to guests with reservations. The next morning there will be fresh bread toasted on the wood stove. Bring your own wine and binoculars. Io parlo più che meno l'italiano.

L'Anse-au-Persil is between Rivière-du-Loup and Cacouna. From Riv.-du-Loup, Rte 132 East to #284. A short, private marked road leads to the B&B hidden from the road.

B&B
AU BONHEUR DU JOUR

Marie Anne Rainville
284, Anse-au-Persil, rte 132
Rivière-du-Loup G5R 5Z6
tel/fax (418) 862-3670
www.destinationquebec.
com/ftpdocs/occas/occasa.htm

	B&B	MAP
single	$45	$65
double	$55	$100
triple	$70	$140
child	$10	$35

Open: June 20 to Aug. 30

Number of rooms	3
shared bathrooms	1

Activities: 🦆 ⚓ 🚶 🚴

25. RIVIÈRE-DU-LOUP, ST-ANTONIN

F e P R.5 TA

Located less than 5 kilometres from Rivière-du-Loup, on the road to Edmunston, "La Maison de Mon Enfance" awaits you. For your relaxation: books, photos and old artifacts. For your leisure: cruise packages, museums, theatre, Petit Témis cycling path 1 kilometre away. See you soon, *Roseline*.

Rte 185, in St-Antonin, at the flashing light turn toward the Trans Canadien restaurant, it's at the stop. From Riv.-du-Loup, twd Edmunston, Jct. 185 for 4km.

B&B

LA MAISON DE MON ENFANCE

Roseline Desrosiers
718, ch. Rivière-Verte
St-Antonin G0L 2J0
(418) 862-3624
fax (418) 862-8969

B&B	
single	$40-50
double	$50-60
triple	$60-70
quad.	$80

VS IT

Open: June 15 to Sep. 15

Number of rooms	5
shared wc	1
shared bathrooms	2

Activities:

26. ST-ALEXANDRE, KAMOURASKA

F e P R.3 TA

Spend your holidays in the beautiful ancestral home of Marie-Alice Dumont, first professional photographer in Eastern Québec. Mouthwatering breakfasts served by the stained-glass window of the former photography studio. The warmest of welcomes awaits. Bas St-Laurent Excellence Prize 1994-95.

From Québec City, Hwy 20 East, Exit 488 to St-Alexandre. The "Maison au Toit Bleu" is in the village, at the intersection of Rtes 230 and 289, near the large cross.

B&B

LA MAISON AU TOIT BLEU

Madame Daria Dumont
490, av. St-Clovis
St-Alexandre G0L 2G0
(418) 495-2701
tel/fax (418) 495-2368

B&B	
single	$45
double	$60
child	$10

Open year round

Number of rooms	3
shared wc	1
shared bathrooms	1

Activities:

27. ST-ANDRÉ, KAMOURASKA

F e P TA

A charming inn, La Solaillerie welcomes you with open arms. Rustic rooms with period decor, in the ancestral house that invites you to dream of the past or luxury room with romantic decor in which to lounge with your loved one under the goosedown duvet. We also offer the best food in the region: creative, refined, lavish regional cuisine. Tourism 1999 Grand Prize: "Hospitality and Customer Service". **See colour photos.**

Hwy 20, Exit 480 to St-André. In the village, turn right on Rue Principale. We are located next to the post office. Or via Rte 132.

INN

AUBERGE LA SOLAILLERIE

Isabelle Poyau and Yvon Robert
112, rue Principale
St-André-de-Kamouraska
G0L 2H0
(418) 493-2914
fax (418) 493-2243

B&B	
single	$45-82
double	$55-89
triple	$114
child	$16

Taxes extra VS MC IT

Reduced rates: May, June, Sep. and Oct. 10% the room if dinning at the Inn.

Open: May 1 to Oct. 31

Number of rooms	11
rooms with private bath	6
rooms with bath and sink	3
rooms with sink	2
shared wc	2
shared bathrooms	1

Activities:

28. ST-ÉLOI

Come and share the comfort and tranquillity of a more-than-hundred-year-old presbytery near l'Isle-Verte. Breathe in the fresh air in this peaceful village, explore the building and admire the view of the St. Lawrence. Copious breakfasts. Children welcome. Visits to the family farm also possible. **Advertisement end of this region. See colour photos.**

From Québec City, Hwy 20 East, Rte 132 East for 19km to the Rte St-Éloi Exit. Drive 5km twd the town of St-Éloi. Turn left on Rue Principale.

INN
AU VIEUX PRESBYTÈRE

Raymonde and Yvon Pettigrew
350, rue Principale Est
St-Éloi G0L 2V0
(418) 898-6147
toll free 1-888-833-6147
aubergeauvieux@qc.aira.com

	B&B	MAP
single	$38-40	$53
double	$53-55	$83
triple	$68-70	$113
quad.	$85	$145
child	$10	$20

Taxes extra VS, IT

Reduced rates: Nov. 1 to May 1
Open year round

Number of rooms	4
rooms with sink	4
shared bathrooms	2

Activities: 🏛 ❀ ⛴ 🚶 🚲

29. ST-JEAN-DE-DIEU

Family with children, all happy to have you as guests. Dairy farm. Fishing and small animals: peacocks, ducks, rabbits, sheep, goats, deer, llamas... Crepes with maple syrup for breakfast. A warm atmosphere and healthy food. 20 min from the river. Families welcome. **Farm Stay p 37. Advertisement end of this region.**

From Québec City, Hwy 20 East, Rte 132 East to Trois-Pístoles. Rte 293 South to St-Jean-de-Dieu. Drive 4km past the church.

B&B
LA FERME PAYSAGÉE

Gabrielle and Régis Rouleau
121, Route 293 Sud
St-Jean-de-Dieu G0L 3M0
(418) 963-3315
www.lafermepaysagee.
freeservers.com
rouls@globetrotter.net

B&B	
single	$30
double	$40
child	$10

Open year round

Number of rooms	3
shared bathrooms	2

Activities: ❀ 🎣 🚶 🚴 🐎

30. ST-LOUIS-DU-HA! HA!

Located right on the "Petit Témis" bicycle path, Au Doux Repaire is aptly named. Deep in the country, this former post office offers quiet, comfort and originality. A living room next to the rooms is reserved for guests. Enchanting terrace and outdoor pool with view of the mountains.

From Québec City, Hwy 20, Exit 499. Rte 185 South, 7km from St-Honoré entrance. Turn right on Rang Vauban, right on Rte Bossé. From the south, 5.2km from St-Louis-du-Ha! Ha!

B&B
AU DOUX REPAIRE

Elyse Cossette and
Gilles Gagné
26, route Bossé
St-Louis-du-Ha!Ha! G0L 3S0
(418) 854-9851
gite26@globetrotter.net

B&B	
single	$35
double	$50
triple	$60
child	$5

Reduced rates: Oct. 15 to Jan. 1 and March 15 to June 15
Open year round

Number of rooms	4
shared bathrooms	2

Activities: 🎣 🚶 🚴 ⛵ 🎿

31. ST-LOUIS-DU-HA! HA!

☀☀☀ F e 🚐 P R6 TA

Looking for a warm ambiance, cleanliness, quiet and comfort? Then drop by our home, a typical 1920s house offering a magnificent view of the Témis mountains and a delicious breakfast of homemade products. Family-size room. Bike shed and shuttle service. A good stop on the road to the Maritimes.

From Québec City, Hwy 20 to Rivière-du-Loup. Rte 185 South for 60km. Turn right at the flashing light, continue for 1.6km. Turn left on Rang Beauséjour, continue for 5km.

B&B
GÎTE BEAU-SÉJOUR

Louiselle Ouellet and
Paul Gauvin
145, rang Beauséjour
St-Louis-du-Ha! Ha! G0L 3S0
(418) 854-0559
fax (418) 854-2691
lgauvin@sympatico.ca

B&B	
single	$40
double	$50
triple	$60
quad.	$70
child	$5

Reduced rates: Oct. 15 to May 15 or 10% 4 nights and more
Open year round

Number of rooms	3
shared bathrooms	2

Activities: 🕊 🎣 🚶 🚴 🐎

---

32. ST-PATRICE-DE-RIVIÈRE-DU-LOUP

☀☀☀ F E 🚫 ⛵ P R3

Summer residence of Canada's first Prime Minister, Sir John A. Macdonald from 1872 to 1890. Magnificient heritage house which gives visitors a splendid view across the St. Lawrence River to the mountainous north shore. Enjoy your stay in a quiet and peaceful environment, as well as our delicious home-made breakfast. Many activities and day trips nearby. **Country Home in Percé, Gaspésie region, p 152, no 58.**

Hwy 20 to Rivière-du-Loup then west on Hwy 132 twd St-Patrice.

B&B
LES ROCHERS

L'Héritage Canadien du Québec
336, rue Fraser
St-Patrice, Rivière-du-Loup
G5R 5S8
(514) 393-1417
(418) 868-1435
fax (514) 393-9444
www.total.net/~chq
chq@total.net

B&B	
single	$65-75
double	$70-85
triple	$80-95
child	$10

VS MC

Open: June 1 to Sep. 1

Number of rooms	5
rooms with private bath	2
rooms with sink	3
shared bathrooms	3

Activities: 🛥 🚤 🕊 🎣 🚶

---

33. STE-LUCE-SUR-MER

F E ♿ 🍽 P ⛵ TA

Right on the beach and just a few kilometres from the Jardins de Métis, we offer an oasis of peace in harmony with the rhythm of the seas. In concert with the setting sun and our fine regional cuisine (included in the menu), you will experience a magical sound and light show. **See colour photos.**

From Québec City, Hwy 20 East, Rte 132 twd Ste-Flavie. After Pte-au-Père, watch for "Camping La Luciole", drive 500 ft. and turn left, then right on Route du Fleuve.

INN
AUBERGE DE L'EIDER

Johanne Cloutier
and Maurice Gendron
90, route du Fleuve Est
Ste-Luce-sur-Mer G0K 1P0
tel/fax (450) 448-5110
(418) 739-3535
auberge.eider@sympatico.ca

B&B	
single	$55-65
double	$60-85
triple	$75-95
quad.	$105
child	$10

Taxes extra VS MC ER

Open: June 15 to Sep. 15

Number of rooms	14
rooms with private bath	14

Activities: 🛥 🚤 🕊 🎣 🚴

34. STE-LUCE-SUR-MER

F E P ◈ ◈ ◈ R.1 TA

On the banks of the St. Lawrence, charming 1920 house with country colours, landscaped grounds and private beach. Creative "eye-catching" breakfast will whet your appetite. Relaxing gazebo. Unforgettable evening show as the fiery sun kisses the sea. Cocktail hour. 15 minutes from Jardins de Métis, Parc du Bic, Côte-Nord ferry.

Mid-way between Rimouski and Mont-Joli via Rte 132. Enter the picturesque village of Ste-Luce along the river; we are 0.2km west of the church, near the river.

B&B
MAISON DES GALLANT

Nicole Dumont and
Jean Gallant
40, du Fleuve Ouest, C.P. 52
Ste-Luce-sur-Mer G0K 1P0
(418) 739-3512
toll free 1-888-739-3512
www.bbcanada.
com/1992.html
jean.gallant@cgocable.ca

B&B	
single	$45
double	$55
triple	$75
child	$10

Open year round

Number of rooms	3
shared wc	1
shared bathrooms	1

Activities: 🏛 ◈ 🏃 🚴 ⛷

35. TROIS-PISTOLES

☀☀☀ F ◈ P R4

Bas-St-Laurent Excellence Prize 1997-98. It's so good to be home! Enjoy a stay on our farm in the quiet countryside, in a 100-year-old house furnished with antiques. Hearty breakfast of homemade jams and bread. Near ferry to the north shore. Grand Prize Winner of 1999 Bas-St-Laurent Tourism Award "small tourism-related business". **Ad end of this region.**

From Québec City, Hwy 20 East, Rte 132 East to Trois-Pistoles. Rte 293 South, 1km, right on Rang 2 Ouest, 2.7km. From ferry, 1st street on the left, Jean-Rioux, at 2nd light, 1km along Rte 293 South, turn right, 2.7km.

B&B
FERME LE TERROIR
DES BASQUES

Marguerite and
Pierre-Paul Belzile
65, Rang 2 Ouest
Trois-Pistoles G0L 4K0
tel/fax (418) 851-2001

B&B	
single	$45
double	$55
triple	$75
quad.	$95
child	$10

Open: May 1to Oct. 31

Number of rooms	4
rooms with sink	2
shared bathrooms	2

Activities: 🏛 🛶 ⛴ 🏃 🚴

36. TROIS-PISTOLES, ST-SIMON

☀☀☀ F E ◈ P ◈ R4 TA

Ancestral (1820) house. Bucolic setting. Farmhouse. Rooms with old baths. Private beach. Packages: excursions (Îles aux Basques, whale-watching), theatre. Footpaths: Trois-Pistoles river, Parc du Bic... Skiing, snowmobiling. Hearty breakfasts, homemade bread. Cooking opportunities. Reduced rates off-season, group packages. **Ad end of this region.**

Direct access via eastbound Rte 132, 7km east of Trois-Pistoles. Heading west, 4km west of St-Simon. 10min from the ferry.

B&B
CHEZ CHOINIÈRE

Alain Choinière
71, rue Principale Ouest
St-Simon G0L 4C0
(418) 738-2245
www.bbcanada.
com/chezchoiniere
chezchoiniere@hotmail.com

B&B	
single	$40
double	$60
triple	$75
quad.	$90
child	$10

Reduced rates: 20% for 3 nights and more, Oct. 15 to June 15
Open year round

Number of rooms	5
rooms with sink and bath	2
rooms with private bath	3
shared bathrooms	1

Activities: 🏛 🛶 ⛴ 🏃 🏃

37. TROIS-PISTOLES, ST-SIMON

✻✻✻ | F | E | 🚫 | 🚗 | P | R.5 | TA |

Located 15km west of Parc du Bic, our large century-old house has preserved its original character and charm. Guests enjoy our peaceful setting and cordial welcome. Breakfast includes home-made *reine-claude* (greengage) plum jams, as well as pancakes, maple syrup, muffins and excellent coffee. See you soon! **Ad end of this region.**

From Québec City, Hwy 20 East, then Rte 132 East to Saint-Simon, 15km east of Trois-Pistoles. Turn right on Rue de l'Église and drive to 39.

B&B
GÎTE DE LA REINE-CLAUDE

Jane O'Brien and Claude Daoust
39, rue de l'Église
Saint-Simon-de-Rimouski
G0L 4C0
tel/fax (418) 738-2609
www.bbcanada.com/3325.html
jcdaoust@quebectel.com

B&B	
single	$38-48
double	$50-60
triple	$70
quad.	$80
child	$10

Open year round

Number of rooms	4
shared wc	2
shared bathrooms	1

Activities: 🦪 🛥 🛶 🧍 🚲

---

25 years of hospitality
1975 - 2000

For 25 years, the host members of the Fédération des Agricotours du Québec have been committed to offering you genuine, high-quality choices for accommodation and agricultural tourism.

This has made Agricotours the largest high-quality network in Quebec, and your confidence has helped in its success.

For this reason, our network host members hope that they may, with their traditional warm welcome, continue to help you discover the best of Quebec for many more years to come.

You'll always feel welcome in the Agricotours network.

38. ST-ALEXANDRE, KAMOURASKA

 F e [symbols] M19 TA

Unique outdoor experiences on our forested farm: 3 lakes, 2 rivers, fauna, flora, 11.4km of trails, lookouts, cycling, snowshoeing, X-country skiing, snowmobiling, winter camping, rides on horse sleighs and carriages... Meals upon request. Free farm tour. You'll feel at home in the beautiful Québec country side. **See colour photos.**

From Montréal, Hwy 20 East, Exit 488. Rte 289 turn right, drive 20km (15 minutes from Hwy 20). Or, from Gaspésie, Hwy 20, Exit 488, Rte 289 turn left, drive 20km.

COUNTRY HOME
LE REFUGE FORESTIER

Réal Sorel
Havre du Parke,
Route 289, C.P. 220
St-Alexandre G0L 2G0
(418) 495-2333
toll free 1-888-495-2333
fax (418) 495-2509

No. houses	2
No. rooms	3-34
No. people	12-60
WEEK-SUMMER	$495-1995
WEEK-WINTER	$495-1995
W/E-SUMMER	$295-1195
W/E-WINTER	$295-1195
DAY-SUMMER	$125-495
DAY-WINTER	$125-495

Taxes extra VS IT

Open year round

Activities: [symbols]

---

39. ST-MATHIEU-DE-RIOUX

F E [symbols] P [symbols] R6 M6 TA

Magnificent spot, large plot of land, tranquillity, panoramic view, mountains, St. Lawrence River; 2-kilometre-long wild private lake, with clear unpolluted water, surrounded by a forest. Large, renovated 2-storey house with cachet, 4-sided porch, veranda, cathedral roof, equipped kitchen, fireplace, 2 bathrooms. **City Home, Québec region p 262, no 76.**

From St-Simon (on Rte 132 East of Rivière-du-Loup) take 1st road on right, east of the village towards St-Mathieu. From St-Mathieu, 1st road on right, east of the village, to rang 4 then Rang 5 East.

COUNTRY HOME
MAISON BRISSON

Chantal Brisson and
Serge Thibaudeau
307, rang 5 Est
St-Mathieu-de-Rioux G0L 3T0
(418) 640-9255
fax (418) 640-0795
www.craph.org/mti
sthibau@globetrotter.net

No. houses	1
No. rooms	4
No. people	8
WEEK-SUMMER	$800
WEEK-WINTER	$800
W/E-SUMMER	$400
W/E-WINTER	$400

Open year round

Activities: [symbols]

FARM ACTIVITIES

Farm Stay:

CANTONS-DE-L'EST

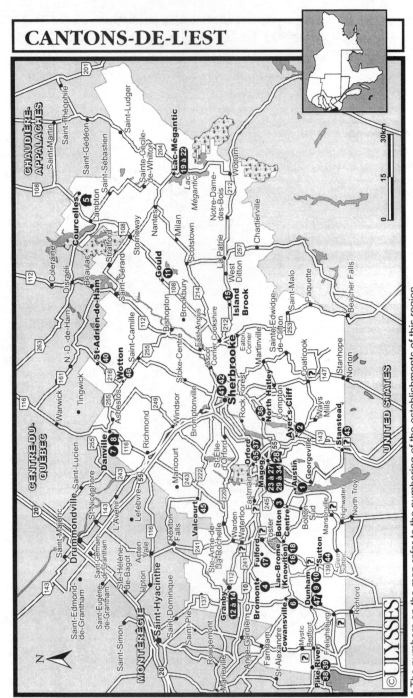

* The numbers on the map refer to the numbering of the establishments of this region

© ULYSSES

1. AUSTIN

☀☀☀☀☀ F e ✕ 🚗 P TA

This Georgian manor is located in an impressive setting with a breathtaking view of Abbaye Saint-Benoît-du-Lac, Lac Memphrémagog and Mont Owl's Head. Depending on the season: ski, golf or summer theatre packages can be booked. Lovely scenery. Enjoy the fine local cuisine, which offers a choice of four different *table d'hôte* with five or six-course dinners. Bring your own wine. **See colour photos.**

From Montréal, Hwy 10, Exit 115, drive to Austin and St-Benoît-du-Lac, about 12km.

INN
AUBERGE LES PIGNONS VERTS

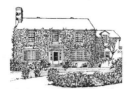

Raymonde and
Florian Landry
2158, chemin Nicolas-Austin
Austin J0B 1B0
tel/fax (819) 847-1272

	B&B	MAP
single	$70-80	$95-105
double	$90-100	$140-150
triple	$120	$205
quad.	$150	$250

Taxes extra VS MC IT

Open year round

Number of rooms	5
rooms with private bath	5

Activities: 🏊 🚣 🚶 🚴 🏊

2. AYER'S CLIFF

F P R5

Hundred-year-old house in the country, panoramic view, quiet place. Home cooking. Swimming in Lake Massawippi 3km away, summer theatre, Coaticook Gorge, cross-country skiing, downhill skiing 15 min. away, 8 min. from golf, 200 ft. from skidooing. Near North Hatley, Mont Orford and Magog. Horseback riding 15 min. away. Ideal for hiking and cycling.

From Montréal, Hwy 10 East, Exit 121. Hwy 55 South, Exit 21, Rte 141 South. About 2.5km. after intersection of Rte 143, left on Chemin Audet. Big white house on the hill.

B&B
CÉCILE LAUZIER

Cécile Lauzier
3119 ch. Audet, Kingscroft
Ayer's Cliff J0B 1C0
(819) 838-4433

	B&B
single	$45-50
double	$55-65
triple	$75

Open year round

Number of rooms	3
shared bathrooms	2

Activities: 🏊 🚣 🚶 🚴 🛷

3. BOLTON CENTRE

☀☀☀☀ F E ♿ 🚗 P R12

The "Mère Poule" takes you under her wing in her 19th-century home. It's a charming and magical little nest with eclectic cuisine, vegetarian dishes (by special request), a tea room, a reading room, hammocks, a cosy fireplace, a slide, home-made soup at 4pm in winter, and a terrace with flowers and chirping birds in the summer. You can even have the pleasure of being an innkeeper the time of a wonderful retreat! **See colour photos.**

From Montréal, Hwy 10, Exit 106, Rte 245 South. From Québec, Hwy 20, 55 South, 10 West, etc.

B&B
CHEZ LA MÈRE POULE

Lise and Réal Savaria
900, route 245, ch. Missisquoi
Bolton Centre J0E 1G0
(450) 292-4548
(450) 292-0226
www.abacom.com/merepoule
merepoule@abacom.com

	B&B	MAP
single	$65	$87.50
double	$85-95	$130-140
triple	$115	$182.50
quad.	$135	$205
child	---	$10

Taxes extra IT

Reduced rates: 10% to 20%, 3 nights and more
Open year round

Number of rooms	5
rooms with private bath	5

Activities: 🏊 🚶 🎿 ⛷ 🏃

4. BROMONT

 F E P R4 TA

This completely renovated B&B in Bromont combines quality, tranquillity and hospitality. Located in an idyllic setting in the middle of a vast, wooded 19-acre area dotted with lakes and rivers, La Clairière has large, tastefully decorated rooms with an added personal touch. Our breakfasts are a gourmet delight. Less than 10min from all the region's attractions.

From Montréal, Hwy 10 Exit 78. At the light, right on Rue Shefford. At the stop sign, left on Rue Gaspé, 6km. Left on Rue Frontenac, 2km. Right on Rue des Perdrix, then first street on your left.

B&B
LA CLAIRIÈRE

Lyne and François Girardin
3, des Mésanges
Bromont J2L 1Y8
(450) 260-1954
fax (450) 260-1955
pages.infinit.net/girardin
la.clairiere@videotron.ca

B&B	
single	$65-85
double	$75-95
triple	$90-110
child	$15

Reduced rates: Nov. and Apr., 10% 2 nights and more
Open year round

Number of rooms	3
rooms with private bath	1
rooms with sink	3
shared wc	1
shared bathrooms	1

Activities:

---

5. COURCELLES

F E P TA

Our farm-inn offers you fine regional cuisine. Savour our dishes in a magnificent sunroom looking over flowers, horses and fawns. Enjoy the period decor with your hosts Gina and Gilles, who will introduce you to fine food and attractions. Delicious and rejuvenating holiday. **Farm Stay p 37. Ad end of this region.**

Hwy 10 E. Exit Boul Université to Lennoxville, Rte 108 twd Beauceville. In Beauceville, 108 W. twd Courcelles.

B&B
L'AUBERGE D'ANDROMÈDE

Gina Hallé and Gilles Leclerc
495, Rang 6
Courcelles G0M 1C0
tel/fax (418) 483-5442
(418) 486-7135
www3.sympatico.ca
/andromedetour
andromedetour@sympatico.ca

	B&B	MAP
single	$45	$80
double	$70	$145

VS

Reduced rates: Jan. 1 to Apr. 1
Open year round

Number of rooms	3
rooms with private bath	3

Activities: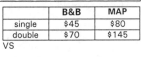

---

6. COWANSVILLE

 F E P R.5 TA

Cantons-de-l'Est Excellence Prize 1999. Enchanting site near Bromont and Lac Brome. Discover our paradise on a 10-acre hill, overlooking Lac d'Avignon with view over the mountains. Flowery expanses, pond, footpaths, in-ground pool, VIP suites, hearty and varied breakfasts. Near cultural and sports activities. Gift certificates and "golf" packages available. "Sheer bliss."

From Montréal or Sherbrooke, Hwy 10, Exit 74, Boul Pierre Laporte twd Cowansville. At BMP hospital, left on Rue Principale drive 0.5km.

B&B
DOMAINE SUR LA COLLINE B&B

Nicole and Gilles Deslauriers
1221, rue Principale
Cowansville J2K 1K7
(450) 266-1910
toll free 1-888-222-1692
fax (450) 266-4320
www.surlacolline.qc.ca
info@surlacolline.qc.ca

B&B	
single	$70-100
double	$75-115
triple	$135
quad.	$150
child	$10-20

VS MC

Reduced rates: Oct. 16 to Dec. 10 and Jan. 15 to May 13
Open year round

Number of rooms	4
rooms with private bath	2
shared wc	1
shared bathrooms	1

Activities:

7. DANVILLE

★★★ F E P R.2 TA

In the heart of a town born with the "grand tronc," Auberge Jeffery is a completely restored Victorian-style house built in 1875. We are located just a few steps from the famous "Le Temps des Cerises" restaurant, which offers tasty local cuisine in a beautiful Presbyterian chapel. A great place to drop anchor between Montréal and Québec City.

From Montréal, Hwy 20, Exit 147, Rte 116 East. At Danville, turn right Rte 255 North at the light. From Québec City, Hwy 20, Exit 253, Rte 116 West. At Danville, turn left at the light onto Rte 255 North.

INN
AUBERGE JEFFERY

Martine and Patrick Satre
91, rue Water, C.P. 496
Danville J0A 1A0
(819) 839-2711
toll free 1-888-302-2711
fax (819) 839-2186
www.cerises.com
jeffery@cerises.com

	B&B	MAP
single	$70	$92
double	$75	$121
triple	$90	$160

Taxes extra VS MC AM ER IT

Open year round

Number of rooms	6
rooms with private bath	6

Activities: 🦆 🍴 🚶 🚴 🏃

8. DANVILLE

☀☀☀ F e 🚫 🚗 P 🏖 ✕ R3

Nature lovers: spacious estate with forest, trails and animals, where only the beauty of the landscapes rivals the peace and quiet. Table d'hôte served by the fire or on the terrace in summer. Hiking, cycling (path), swimming, X-country skiing. Packages: theatre, golf, cycling, riding. **Farm Stay p 37.**

From Montréal, Hwy 20, Exit 147, Rte 116 East. In Richmond, at lights, drive 13.9km, left on Demers drive 2.5km. From Québec City, Hwy 20, Exit 253, Rte 116 W. In Danville at lights 3km, Demers to the right 2.5km.

B&B
LE CLOS DES PINS

Josée Brouillette and
Daniel Godbout
60, chemin Boisvert
Danville J0A 1A0
tel/fax (819) 839-3521
www.closdespins.qc.ca
closdespins@sympatico.ca

	B&B	MAP
single	$45-60	$60-75
double	$60-75	$90-105
triple	$90	$135
quad.	$105	$165
child	$10	$20-25

Taxes extra

Reduced rates: Nov. 15 to Dec. 15 and Jan. 15 to May 15
Open year round

Number of rooms	4
shared bathrooms	2

Activities: 🦆 🍴 🚴 🐎 🛷

9. DUNHAM

☀☀☀ F E 🚗 P 🏖 R5

Pierre Foglia of La Presse newspaper called it a "a great find, with a lovely name... A superb house run by a young couple. The stately trees along the path here form a leafy tunnel... just like being in Vermont... lavish breakfast..." Hiking path, spa, heated swimming pool. 10$ off/additional night or the equivalence in our maple grove product.

Hwy 10, Exit 68, Rte 139 South (20km). At the 2nd traffic lights in Cowansville, turn right, Rte 202 South to Dunham (2km). Left Ch. Fitchett, (2km) left Rang Vail (2km).

B&B
AU TEMPS DES MÛRES

Marie-Josée Potvin and
Pierre Cormier
2024, chemin Vail
Dunham J0E 1M0
(450) 266-1319
fax (450) 266-1303
toll free 1-888-708-8050

	B&B
single	$45-60
double	$65-75
child	$0-25

VS MC

Reduced rates: 10$, see the text
Open year round

Number of rooms	5
rooms with private bath	3
shared bathrooms	2

Activities: 🚣 🍴 🚶 🚴 🏃

10. DUNHAM

✹✹✹✹✹ F e 🚳 P R.25

After touring the vineyards, unwind at our magnificent Victorian manor. Terrace, living room with fireplace, air-conditioned suites and private bathrooms. House with a dream-like environnement and many possibilities. We look forward to seeing you soon.

Hwy 10, Exit 68, Rte 139 to Cowansville (18km). At traffic light, take Rte 202 to Dunham (8km). 200 metres past the corner store, Rue du Collège (left).

B&B
AUX DOUCES HEURES

Lyette Leroux Dumoulin and
André Dumoulin
110, rue du Collège C.P. 40
Dunham J0E 1M0
(450) 295-2476
toll free 1-877-295-2476

B&B	
single	$50
double	$75
child	$15

Taxes extra

Open: Mar. 1to Nov. 30

Number of rooms	5
rooms with private bath	5
shared wc	1

Activities: 🏊 🚶 🚲 ⛷ 🎿

---

11. GOULD

✏ F E P 🐕 🏔 ✗ R.15 TA

Scottish village founded around 1837, 12 rooms throughout 3 historic buildings with period furnishings. Original woodwork. Traditional ambiance and Scottish- and Québec-inspired cuisine. Access to the river; magnificent, pristine nature all year round. Breakfast in the general store's atmosphere of yore.

From Montréal, Hwy 10, Exit 143, Rte 112 E. In East Angus, Rtes 214 and 108 E. From the U.S., Rtes 3 and 257 N. From Québec City, Hwy 73 twd Ste-Marie, Rte 173 twd Vallée-Jct, Rte 112 twd Thetford and Weedon, Rte 257 S.

INN
LA RUÉE VERS GOULD

Daniel Audet and
Jacques Cloutier
19, Route 108
Gould, Lingwick J0B 2Z0
tel/fax (819) 877-3446
toll free 1-888-305-3526
www.gitestrie.com

	B&B	MAP
single	$40-55	$65-80
double	$55-70	$105-120
child	$15	

Taxes extra VS MC IT

Open: Feb. 1 to Jan. 10

Number of rooms	12
rooms with private bath	1
rooms with sink	2
shared bathrooms	4

Activities: 🏛 🍷 🏊 🚶 🚲

---

12. GRANBY

✹✹✹ F E 🚳 ♿ 🚗 P 🛥 R.5

Right near the zoo, a unique concept ideal for families & groups (16 people): four 2-room units (suites) with private bathroom. Air condition. Children's game room, private entrance, modern kitchen for your stay. Special family and group packages for the Granby Zoo.

From Hwy 10, follow directions to Zoo. On Boul. David Bouchard at traffic light, south St-Hubert. 2 stops. Turn left on Bourget Ouest.

B&B
AUBERGE DU ZOO

Ginette Marcoux and
Claude Gladu
347, Bourget Ouest
Granby J2G 1E8
(450) 378-6161
toll free 1-888-882-5252
fax (450) 378-0470
www.aubergeduzoo.com

B&B	
single	$55-65
double	$75-85
triple	$95-105
quad.	$115-125
child	$10

Taxes extra VS MC IT

Reduced rates: 20% 3 nights or more, special 3 days: zoo, amazoo
Open: June 1 to Oct 1

Number of rooms	4
rooms with private bath	4

Activities: 🍷 🏊 🚶 🚲

13. GRANBY

✹✹✹✹✹ F E 🚗 P 🚫 R1 TA

Located on the shores of Lac Boivin, a short bike ride away from l'Estriade, we offer guests stunning sunsets in an enchanting setting. Private lounge with fireplace, terrace and barbecue in season, skiing, skating, hiking, horseback riding: everything for your comfort and relaxation.

Hwy 10, Exit 74 twd Granby. At end of Pierre Laporte, left on Rte 112, right from L'Iris, left from the Potentille and left from Nénuphar.

B&B
LA MAISON DUCLAS

Ginette Canuel and
Camil Duchesne
213, du Nénuphar
Granby J2H 2J9
(450) 360-0641
www.maisonduclas.com
info@maisonduclas.com

B&B	
single	$50
double	$65
triple	$85
child	$10

Reduced rates: Nov. 15 to May 1
Open year round

Number of rooms	2
rooms with private bath	2
rooms in basement	2

Activities: 🍂 🎣 🚴 ⛷ 🏃

14. GRANBY

☀☀☀ F E 🏊 🚫 P R.2 TA

Carole and Michel welcome you to their charming raspberry-coloured house. Let us mapper you in this relaxing setting on Lac Boivin located near a park. Enjoy coffee on the waterfront among flowers and facing the Estriade cycling path. Close to the downtown shops and restaurants. Rooms with air conditionning. **See colour photos.**

From Montréal, Hwy 10 East. Exit 74, Rte 112 West to Granby. Right at the 1st traffic lights on Rue Church, right on Drummond.

B&B
A FLOWER ON THE
RIVER FRONT

Carole Bélanger and
Michel Iannantuono
90, Drummond
Granby J2G 2S6
tel/fax (450) 776-1141
1-888-375-1747
busines hours only - toll free
www.clubtrs.ca/fleurvtg
fleurvtg@login.net

B&B	
single	$50-65
double	$55-70
child	$10

Taxes extra VS MC AM

Reduced rates: Jan. 8 to Apr. 15,
Oct. 31 to Dec. 15
Open year round

Number of rooms	4
rooms with private bath	2
shared bathrooms	1

Activities: 🍂 🏊 🎣 🚴 ⛷

15. ISLAND BROOK

★★★ F E ✗ P

From the windows of our inn built in 1865 with victorian charm, you can see the mountains of Maine and the lush countryside, one of the clearest skies in Québec. Suites, king-size bed, whirlpool for two and fireplace. Superb local cuisine, quality, intimacy, comfort and luxurious accommodations. Close to tourist and cultural attractions. Rest and tender moments are to be had here. **Ad at end of guide.**

From Montréal, Hwy 10 E. From Québec City, Hwy 55 to Sherbrooke, Exit 143, 112 E. to East-Angus, 253 South to Cookshire and 212 East to La Patrie. From U.S., via Hwy 161.

INN
BOUGIES BOUFFE & BISOUS
LA CHARMILLE

Lise Martel
1409 Rte 212
C.P. 965
Island Brook, Qc.
J0B 1M0
tel/fax (819) 875-3141

	B&B	MAP
single	$85-105	$110-130
double	$138-158	$198-218
triple	$163-183	$248-268
quad.	$188-208	$298-318
child	$25	$45

Taxes extra VS MC

Reduced rates: 20% 2 nights and more
Open year round

Number of rooms	4
rooms with private bath	4

Activities: 🎣 🏃 🚴 🐎 🛷

16. KNOWLTON, LAC BROME

☀☀☀☀☀ F E ⊗ 🐾 ➤ P R4 TA

Our B&B offers a breathtaking panoramic view. All three rooms have a balcony, a homey décor and a window with a beautiful view of the stars. Comfort, tranquillity and relaxation guaranteed, not to mention a hearty breakfast!

Hwy 10, Exit 90, Rte 243 South to Knowlton. After two stops, exit Rte 243 in the centre of town. Straight down Chemin Mt. Écho for 4km, 2nd street on your left is Rue Benjamin.

B&B
RÊVERIE AUX QUATRE-VENTS

Jacqueline and Guy LeRoyer
46, rue Benjamin, C.P. 82
Knowlton Lac Brome
JOE 1V0
(450) 243-0867

B&B	
single	$65
double	$75
triple	$90

Open year round

Number of rooms	3
shared bathrooms	2

Activities: 🚣 🐎 🚶 🚴 🎿

---

17. LAC-BROME, FULFORD

F E P 🐾 🏊 R5 TA

A warm welcome to our English "Tudor" house, located between Bromont and Knowlton. Come and stroke our pure-bred norwegian horses (Fjord). Enjoy a walk on our property of 26 acres. You'll find a brook, a wooded countryside, a pool and patios. Golf club 5 min. away. Snowshoeing on the site and snowmobile trail access 35-45.

Exit 78 on Hwy 10 to Bromont. Straight ahead for 7km, turn right at red flashing light (Brome road). We are 1km further on your left.

B&B
LE TU-DOR

Ghislaine Lemay and
Jean-Guy Laforce
394, chemin Brome
Fulford, Lac-Brome
JOE 1SO
(450) 534-3947
fax (450) 534-5543

B&B	
single	$50-55
double	$70-75
triple	$90-95
quad.	$110-115
child	$15

VS MC

Reduced rates: Nov 1 to Apr. 30 except for hollidays, and 3 nights or more
Open year round

Number of rooms	4
rooms with private bath	4

Activities: 🚶 🚴 🐎 🏊 🏃

---

18. LAC-BROME, KNOWLTON

☀☀☀ F E ⊗ 🐾 ➤ P R.5 TA

Take a break and enjoy of our peaceful ancestral home, the only B&B located within walking distance of the village. We offer you a warm welcome - just like a member of the family! Our specialty: fruit-filled crepes, a recipe passed down by our great-grandmother.

From Montréal, Hwy 10, Exit 90, Rte 243 to Knowlton, turn right at 2nd stop sign, Rte 104, 0.8km. From Québec City, Hwy 20, Hwy 55 South, Hwy 10, Exit 90, Rte 243...

B&B
LA DORMANCE

Jocelyne Rollin and
Normand Faubert
402, ch. Knowlton, C.P. 795
Lac-Brome, Knowlton JOE 1V0
(450) 242-1217
www3.sympatico.ca/
ladormance
ladormance@sympatico.ca

B&B	
single	$70-80
double	$80-90
triple	$95-105
quad.	$110-120
child	$10

VS

Reduced rates: Nov 1 to May 1, 20% 3 nights or more
Open year round

Number of rooms	4
rooms with private bath	4

Activities: 🎿 🚣 🚶 🚴 🎿

19. LAC-MÉGANTIC

☀☀☀☀☀ F E 🚭 P 🛶 R1

Provincial Excellence Prize 1997-98. Modern, cedar house in an enchanting setting. Fish for trout off the pier, swim off our beach, boat ramp. Near 18-hole golf course and 2 provincial parks including the Astrolab (astronomy study centre). Breakfast in the solarium or in the gazebo, watching the loons.

Hwy 10, Exit 143, then Rtes 108 East and 161 South In Mégantic, 10km after the bridge or Exit 143, take Rtes 112 and 212 twd Mont Mégantic then 14km along 161 North.

B&B
AU CHANT DU HUARD

Françoise and Gérald Périnet
850, Route 161
Lac-Mégantic G6B 2S1
tel/fax (819) 583-4795
www.destinationquebec.
com/ftpdocs/huard/huard.htm
cduhuard@megantic.net

B&B	
single	$50-85
double	$60-95

Open: May 1 to Oct 15

Number of rooms	4
rooms with private bath	1
rooms with sink	3
shared bathrooms	2

Activities: 🏛 ⛴ 🚣 🎣 🚴

20. LAC-MÉGANTIC

☀☀☀☀ F E P 🚭 R1

Visit our B&B perched on a hill overlooking the lake, located 1km. from the golf course. Near the Observatoire & Astrolab. Peaceful setting. 34 hectares of woodlands. Ponds and trails leading to the beaver dam. Panoramic view, ideal for fall colours. Private beach nearby. 2 large rooms with queen-size beds. Breakfast on solarium overlooking the lake.

From Montréal or Sherbrooke, Hwy 10, Rtes 143 S., 108 E., 161 S. From Mégantic, 8km twd golf club. From N.D. des Bois, Rtes 212 E., 161 N., 1km after golf course.

B&B
AU SOLEIL COUCHANT

Nicole and Gérard Théberge
1137, Route 161
Lac-Mégantic G6B 2S1
tel/fax (819) 583-4900
www.destinationquebec.com

B&B	
single	$50-60
double	$60-75

Open: May 1 to Oct. 31

Number of rooms	4
rooms in basement	2
rooms with private bath	2
shared bathrooms	1

Activities: 🏛 🚣 🎣 🚶 🚴

21. LAC-MÉGANTIC

☀☀☀ F E P 🚭 🐕 R4

Tastefully decorated warm and cosy house, located in the town centre in a quiet residential neighbourhood near the lake, marina and restaurants. Our breakfasts are also very generous; guests benefit from air conditioning in summer.

From Sherbrooke Rte 161. Left at 2nd light, Rue Maisonneuve, right on Rue Dollard. From Québec City or Woburn, cross downtown after railway, right on Rue Villeneuve, left on Dollard.

B&B
LA MAISON BLANCHE

Noreen Kavanagh Legendre
4850, rue Dollard
Lac-Mégantic G6B 1G8
(819) 583-2665

B&B	
single	$55
double	$55

Reduced rates: after Thanksgiving
Open year round

Number of rooms	2
rooms with private bath	2

Activities: ⛴ 🚣 🎣 🚴 ⛷

22. LAC-MÉGANTIC ★★★ F E P ✕

Built in 1891 on the lakeshore, the Manoir D'Orsennens was completely restored and expanded. It offers the comfort of a large hotel with the charm of a small inn, well-equiped rooms, excellent cuisine and a unique décor. Near numerous tourist attractions, guests are greeted with a warm welcome and personalized service. You will definitely want to come back! Packages available. 75km from St-George-de-Beauce, 100km from Sherbrooke.

From Montréal or Sherbrooke, Hwy 10, Rtes 143 South, 108 East and 161 South. Cross the town. After the bridge, keep right.

INN
MANOIR D'ORSENNENS

Nathalie Michaud
3502, rue Agnès
Lac-Mégantic G6B 1L3
(819) 583-3515
toll free 1-877-583-3515
fax (819) 583-0308

	B&B	MAP
single	$77-82	$102-107
double	$95-100	$145-150
triple	$123	$198
quad.	$146	$246
child	$15-20	$23-28

Taxes extra VS MC AM ER IT

Reduced rates: corporatives rates
Open year round

Number of rooms	12
rooms with private bath	12
shared wc	2

Activities: 🦆 ⛷ 🚶 🚴 🏃

---

23. MAGOG ☀☀☀☀ F E ✕ 🚭 🛏 P R.01 TA

Let us greet you with a touch of conviviality in our ancestral home. Our neo-gothical style B&B, part of the historical circuit, is situated in beautiful downtown Magog on a small and quiet street. We will guide you towards the best restaurants and suggest interesting surroundings activities. Woodburning stove, piano, heartwarming atmosphere all year. We enjoy conversational exchanges on history, music and mostly travel. Hoping to see you soon! Welcome!

From Montréal, Hwy 10 Exit 118. Twd Magog, 4km. Left at 2nd stop, right at the first street.

B&B
À L'ANCESTRALE

Monique Poirier
200 Abbott
Magog J1X 2H5
tel/fax (819) 847-5555
toll free 1-888-847-5507
www.bbcanada.com/ancestrale

	B&B
	B&B
single	$50-60
double	$60-80

VS MC IT

Reduced rates: 20% 3 nights, Oct 1 to May 31
Open year round

Number of rooms	4
rooms with private bath	2
rooms with sink	2
shared wc	1
shared bathrooms	1

Activities: 🐕 ⛷ 🚶 🚴 🏃

---

24. MAGOG ☀☀☀ F e P R.2 TA

Welcome to our 100-year-old (1875) house, with cozy country-style rooms with queen-size beds and whirlpool baths. Explore Magog and its sights. 2 min from the town centre and Lake Memphrémagog, with its park, beaches and bicycle path; Mont Orford and the art centre. Enjoy activities available year round.

Hwy 10, Magog-bound Exit 118, Rte 141 South. At the McDonald's, turn left onto Chemin Hatley. Keep left; 1st house on the cape.

B&B
AMOUR ET AMITIÉ

Nathalie and
Pascal Coulaudoux
600, ch. Hatley Ouest
Magog J1X 3G4
(819) 868-1945
amouretamitie@sympatico.ca

	B&B
	B&B
single	$60-95
double	$70-105
triple	$75-125
quad.	$135-150
child	$0-15

Taxes extra

Reduced rates: Oct. 15 to Dec. 15 and Jan. 15 to May 15
Open year round

Number of rooms	5
rooms with private bath	5

Activities: 🏛 🏊 🦆 🚴 🎣

25. MAGOG

☀☀☀☀ F E 🚗 P 🐕 R.1 TA

Awaiting you is our elegant Victorian home, its luxuriant yard, a warm atmosphere and gourmet breakfasts with international fine cuisine menus. Lounges, fireplace, sunroom, kitchenette. Within steps: majestic lake, dining, shops, cultural activities, bike path. 8km to Mt Orford park. Well-located to discover Township charms. Package-deals. Bikes to lend. A home away from home! **Ad on back cover.**

From Montréal or Sherbrooke, Hwy 10, Exit 118 twd Magog. After the Magog River, turn left at the flashing light. 3rd house on the right.

B&B
À TOUT VENANT

Margaret McCulloch and Marc Grenier
624, Bellevue Ouest
Magog J1X 3H4
(819) 868-0419
toll free 1-888-611-5577
fax (819) 868-5115
www3.sympatico.ca/atoutvenant
atoutvenant@sympatico.ca

B&B	
single	$59-64
double	$65-74
triple	$89-94
quad.	$109-114
child	$0-15

Taxes extra

Reduced rates: Sep.15 to June 15
Open year round

Number of rooms	5
rooms with private bath	5

Activities: 🏛 🍴 🛥 🚲 🎣

26. MAGOG

☀☀☀ F E 🚭 🚗 P 🐕 ♿ R.1 TA

Charming good spirits and the comfort of a hundred-year-old house (fireplace, terrace). Located near restaurants and the beach, on the wine route and the road to Mont Orford. Gourmet lunch made by a French pastrychef. Cultural and summer/winter outdoor activities (hiking, skiing, snowshoeing, skidoo, skating, fishing...) Packages. See you soon. **See colour photos.**

From Montréal or Sherbrooke, Hwy 10, Exit 118 for Magog. Rte 141, Rue Merry North. From Québec City, Hwy 20 West, Hwy 55 South, 10 West, Exit 118 for Magog.

B&B
AU SAUT DU LIT

Lydia Paraskéva and Patrick Bonnot
224, rue Merry Nord
Magog J1X 2E8
tel/fax (819) 847-3074
toll free 1-888-833-3074
www.bbcanada.com/1557.html
ausaudulit@qc.aira.com

B&B	
single	$65
double	$74
child	$0-20

Taxes extra VS MC

Reduced rates: Oct. 15 to May 15, 3 nights and more
Open year round

Number of rooms	5
rooms with private bath	5

Activities: 🍴 🎣 🚲 ⛷ 🐕

27. MAGOG

✒ F E 🚭 🚗 P R.05

A calm and friendly red-brick Loyalist home near all of the outdoor and cultural activities in Magog-Orford. The inviting, cosy rooms face the cardinal points, so you can go to sleep or wake up with the sun. Our scrumptious breakfasts will delight both athletes and connoisseurs. Guided sports excursions available. Non-smoking B&B.

Hwy 10, Exit 118 for Magog. Drive 3km, you will be on Merry North. Turn left before the church.

B&B
AU VIRAGE

Louise Vachon and Jean Barbès
172, Merry Nord
Magog J1X 2E8
tel/fax (819) 868-5828
barbesjean@sympatico.ca

B&B	
single	$55-90
double	$60-95

Taxes extra VS

Reduced rates: Oct 15 to May 15
Open year round

Number of rooms	5
rooms with private bath	3
rooms with sink	2
shared wc	1
shared bathrooms	1

Activities: 🍴 🛥 🎣 🚲 ⛷

28. MAGOG

✎ | F | E | 🛏 | P | ⛵ | ✕ | R6 | TA

Enjoy a change of scenery and breathe in the fresh country air. Savour an unforgettable 5-course breakfast by the fireside or a country dinner on our terrace near the pool. After a walk through our flowered gardens, to the small farm or stream, you will have but one desire: to come back! **Country-style Dining p 16. See colour photos.**

From Montréal, Hwy 10, Exit 115 South-Magog/St-Benoît-de-Lac, drive 1.8km. Right on Chemin des Pères, twd St-Benoît-du-Lac/Austin. Drive 6.1km. Watch for the sign on your right. We're waiting for you.

INN
AUX JARDINS CHAMPÊTRES

Monique Dubuc and
Yvon Plourde
1575, ch. des Pères, R.R. 4
Magog J1X 5R9
(819) 868-0665
toll free 1-877-868-0665
fax (819) 868-6744
www.auxjardins
champetres.com
auxjardinschampetres@
qc.aira.com

	B&B	MAP
single	$65-89	$104-128
double	$74-94	$152-172
triple	$94-114	$211-231
child	$20	$40

Taxes extra VS MC IT

Open year round

Number of rooms	5
rooms with private bath	1
shared wc	1
shared bathrooms	2

Activities: 🚣 🚤 🚲 🏊 🏃

29. MAGOG

🌼🌼🌼🌼🌼 | F | E | 🚭 | 🚗 | P | R.5 | TA

A place for rest and relaxation par *excellence!* Surrounded by hundred-year-old maple trees, our warm and inviting Victorian house will delight you. Unique decor, 5 rooms with fireplace and air-conditioning. Homestyle cuisine served in the solarium or on the terrace. Vast landscaped garden with spa. Limousine service in an antique car and boating excursions. Café Crème B&B is located two steps away from all the activities: Mt-Orford, the lake, shows, restaurants, etc.

From Montréal, Hwy 10 East, Exit 118, twd Magog. 2nd stop sign, MacDonalds, left. 2nd street, turn right onto Des Pins.

B&B
CAFÉ CRÈME B&B

Annick and Christophe Balayer
235 des Pins
Magog J1X 2H8
(819) 868-7222
toll free 1-877-631-7222
fax (819) 868-0050
www.bbcafecreme.com
info@bbcafecreme.com

	B&B
single	$90-105
double	$90-105
child	$40

Taxes extra VS MC

Reduced rates: Nov. 1 to Jan. 31, 15% off, 2 nights and more
Open year round

Number of rooms	5
rooms with private bath	5

Activities: 🚣 🚶 🚲 🏊 🐎

30. MAGOG

🌼🌼🌼 | F | E | 🚭 | P | R.1 | TA

Escape to the Eastern Townships! This warm 1880 house will delight you with its creature comforts, guaranteed peace and quiet and sublime breakfasts. Take a nap beneath the apple trees or discover the peacefulness of Lake Memphrémagog or, again, the bustle of the Main Street. **See colour photos.**

From Montréal or Sherbrooke, Hwy 10 Exit 118, toward Magog Rte 141, for 3km. At traffic light, turn left on St-Patrice West, then 1st left on Abbott.

B&B
LA BELLE ÉCHAPPÉE

Louise Fournier
145, rue Abbott
Magog J1X 2H4
tel/fax (819) 843-8061
toll free 1-877-843-8061

	B&B
single	$45-75
double	$60-90
child	$15

VS MC

Reduced rates: Nov. 1 to June 1
Open year round

Number of rooms	5
rooms with private bath	1
rooms with sink	2
shared bathrooms	2

Activities: 🏊 🚤 🚶 🚲 🎿

31. MAGOG

☀☀☀☀ | F | E | 🚫 | 🚗 | P | R.1 | TA

Steps from downtown and Memphrémagog Lake, Victorian residence from 19th century surrounded by splendid gardens. Exquisite interior decorated with unique hand-painted objects. Painting workshop session packages. Ski, water sports, vineyards, horse-back riding.

From Montréal, Hwy 10 East, Exit 118, twd Magog, 3km on Rte 141/Rue Merry Nord. From Québec City, Hwys 20 West, 55 South, 10 West, exit 118, twd Magog, 3km on Rte 141/Rue Merry Nord.

B&B
LA BELLE VICTORIENNE

Louise De Roy and
Jean-Philippe Camboursier
142, rue Merry Nord
Magog J1X 2E8
tel/fax (819) 847-0476
http://pages.infinit.net/bellevic
labelvic@videotron.ca

B&B	
single	$65-85
double	$70-90
triple	$105
child	$10

Taxes extra MC

Reduced rates: mid-Oct. to mid-May
Open year round

Number of rooms	5
rooms with private bath	3
shared bathrooms	2

Activities: 🏛 🍂 ⚓ 🎿 🚲

32. MAGOG

☀☀☀☀ | F | E | P | 🚗 | R.1 | TA

Hike, cycle, bird watch or let us take you on our sailboat to discover one of our best kept secrets, Lake Mempremagog. In winter enjoy the Mt. Orford region in a sleigh, a dog sled or on skis. A warm welcome and all the comforts of home await you at La Maison Campbell. We hope our attractive rooms, our cozy fireplace, our café au lait and lovely home cooked breakfasts will make your stay here a memorable one. **Ad on back cover.**

From Mtl or Sherbrooke, Hwy 10, Exit 118 twd Magog. Pass over the Magog river turn left at the flashing yellow light, dir. Ayer's Cliff, keep to the right (becomes Bellevue Street).

B&B
LA MAISON CAMPBELL

Francine Guérin and
Louise Hodder
584, rue Bellevue Ouest
Magog J1X 3H2
(819) 843-9000
fax (819) 843-3352
www3.sympatico.ca/
maisoncampbell
maisoncampbell@sympatico.ca

B&B	
single	$65-75
double	$70-80
child	$0-20

Taxes extra

Reduced rates: Oct. 15 to June 15
Open year round

Number of rooms	5
rooms with private bath	3
shared bathrooms	1

Activities: ⛴ 🚶 🚲 🏃 🐕

33. MAGOG

☀☀☀☀ | F | e | 🚫 | P | 🏖 | R.1 | TA

An oasis of peace in the heart of Magog. Between the pool's clear refreshing water and the cosy fireplace, you will be pleasantly surprised by your attentive hosts' warm welcome. We will turn your dreams of such moments into reality. Package deals available (sports and culture). Near Lake Magog, bike path, downtown and mountain. **Ad on back cover.**

Hwy 10, Exit 118 twd Magog. Rue Merry Nord. After crossing the main street, you are on Rue Merry Sud. We are steps from McDonald's.

B&B
LE MANOIR DE
LA RUE MERRY

Jocelyne Gobeil and
Alain Tremblay
92, rue Merry Sud
Magog J1X 3L3
toll free 1-800-450-1860
(819) 868-1860

B&B	
single	$80
double	$80-90
triple	$100-110
quad.	$120-130
child	$20

Taxes extra VS MC IT

Reduced rates: mid-Sep. to mid-May
Open year round

Number of rooms	5
rooms with private bath	5

Activities: 🍂 ⚓ 🎿 🚲 🏊

34. MAGOG

☀☀☀☀ F E ⊘ 🚗 P 🏠 R.2 TA

A haven of tranquillity in downtown Magog. Your hosts, Pauline and Roger, invite you to share the comforts of their centennial home, to relax on the veranda or in the shade of majestic trees, to cool off in the in-ground pool or to cuddle up in front of the fireplace. You'll be enticed to a breakfast you will not soon forget by the aroma of freshly brewed coffee.

Hwy 10, Exit 118. Rte 141 S., 3km. The B&B parking is at 190 Merry Nord.

B&B
Ô BOIS DORMANT

Pauline and Roger St-Aubin
205 Abbott
Magog J1X 2H4
tel/fax (819) 843-0450
www.oboisdormant.qc.ca
dormant@oboisdormant.qc.ca

B&B	
single	$50-75
double	$55-80
triple	$80-95
quad.	$105
child	$0-15

Taxes extra VS MC AM

Reduced rates: 15% Sep. 15 to May 31
Open year round

Number of rooms	4
roooms with private bath	2
rooms with sink	2
shared wc	1
shared bathrooms	1

Activities: 🍁 🕴 🚴 🎿 🏃

---

35. MAGOG, ORFORD

☀☀☀ F e ⊘ ♿ 🍴 P 🏊 R1.5 TA

In the peaceful forest and 5min from Magog (with all of its attractions, not to mention the lake), Gîte Domaine de la Forêt is the perfect B&B for R&R (rest and relaxation). It has a pool, skating rink and gourmet dinners prepared by a French chef. Great variety of activities nearby: skiing, hiking, cycling and snowmobiling path, dogsledding, golfing and horse-drawn sleigh rides. One room equipped for the handicapped.

From Montréal, Hwy 10 or from Québec City, Hwy 20 and 55, Exit 123 Omerville. At the first light, turn right on St-Jacques Ouest, second stop, right on St-Michel to the end on your left.

B&B
GÎTE DOMAINE DE LA FORÊT

Marie-Evelyne Malatchoumy
935, rue St-Michel
Orford J1X 7H4
tel/fax (819) 847-2153
www.bbcanada.
com/domainedelaforet
domaine.de.la.foret
@sympatico.ca

	B&B	MAP
single	$65-80	$90-105
double	$70-90	$119-139
triple	$90-110	$165-185
quad.	$110-130	$210-230
child	$20	on request

Taxes extra VS

Open year round

Number of rooms	4
rooms with private bath	4

Activities: 🍁 🛷 🕴 🚴 🎿

---

36. NORTH HATLEY

★★★ F E 🐕 P R.5

Built around 1860, this prestigious property faces the golf course at the exit from North Hatley, and it's the choice establishment for discriminating vacationers. This elegant Bourgeois character home exudes discreet luxury. The large peaceful garden is an extension of the patio, which is decked with flowers and surrounded by majestic evergreens. Refined, cosy ambiance, classy décor, spacious and lots of grandeur. "La Raveaudière is an exceptionally high-quality B&B lodge." *The Gazette*, 1999.

From Montréal, Hwy 10, Exit 121, Hwy 55 South Exit 29. Rte 108 East 0.5km from town.

INN
LA RAVEAUDIÈRE

Michel Lefebvre and
André Person
11, chemin Hatley C.P. 8
North Hatley J0B 2C0
(819) 842-2554
fax (819) 842-1304
www.bbcanada.com/2925.html
aperson@accglobal.net

B&B	
single	$90-120
double	$115-145

Taxes extra VS MC IT

Open year round

Number of rooms	7
rooms with private bath	7

Activities: 🏛 🛶 🕴 🚴 🏃

37. ORFORD

✹✹✹✹✹ F E ⛰ 🐴 P R.5

Magnificient country home with rural charm, grange, wooden silo, and large property connected to a golf course. Cosy interior decor with fireplaces, pine accents, parquet floors and solariums. Well-kept rooms of superior comfort with private bathrooms, air conditionning, tv and VCR. Terrace, gardens, heated swimming pool. All this at Orford, between lakes and mountains, for a vacation with class. Gastronomical breakfast. **See coulor photos.**

From Montréal or Sherbrooke, Hwy 10 Exit 118 twd Orford. At the village exit, drive along the golf course. Right on Alfred-Desrochers, 500 m.

B&B
AUBERGE DE LA TOUR

Francine Gouin and
André Taillefer
1837, chemin
Alfred-Desrochers
Orford J1X 6J4
(819) 868-0763
fax (819) 868-4091
www.auberge-de-la-tour.com
franny@
auberge-de-la-tour.com

B&B	
single	$75
double	$85-95
triple	$110-120
child	$15

Taxes extra VS MC AM ER

Open year round

Number of rooms	4
rooms with private bath	4
shared wc	1

Activities: 🚣 👤 🚴 ⛷ 🎿

38. PIKE-RIVER

✹✹✹ F E 🚭 P ⊠ TA

Located in the heart of farming country. We are a Swiss family that has lived here for 30 years. In our small restaurant we serve Swiss home-cooked meals and produce home-made breads, jams and sauces. Take long quiet walks on the 100 acres of land surrounding our inn. We look forward to meeting you.

From Montréal, Champlain bridge, Hwy 10 East, Exit 22 St-Jean-sur-Richelieu. Hwy 35 South to Rte 133 South (30 min), brown house on left. Or from US, Interstate 89 North to Philipsburg, then Rte 133 North, about 13km on the right.

INN
AUBERGE LA SUISSE

Dora and Roger Baertschi
119, Route 133
St-Pierre-de-Véronne-à-
Pike-River J0J 1P0
(450) 244-5870
fax (450) 244-5181
www.bbcanada.com/lasuisse
aubergelasuisse@hotmail.com

B&B	
single	$55-60
double	$65-75
child	$25

Taxes extra VS MC AM IT

Reduced rates: Feb. 1 to Apr. 30, Dec.
Open: Feb. 1to Dec. 31

Number of rooms	4
rooms with private bath	4

Activities: 🏛 🍷 👤 🚴 🐎

39. PIKE-RIVER

✹✹✹ F E 🚭 🚗 P 🏊 🐕 R2

One hour from Montréal and 10 min from Vermont: on the riverbank, an opulent, flowery B&B invites you for a restful break in a cosy atmosphere. Hearty Swiss breakfast with home-made bread and goods from our farm. Bicycling tours. Near the wildlife reserve, the Musée Missisquoi and the vineyards.

From Montréal, Champlain bridge. Hwy 10 East, Exit 22 twd St-Jean, Rte 35 South then Rte 133 twd St-Pierre-de-Vérone-à-Pike-River. In the curve, turn left on Chemin des Rivières. Drive 1.5km.

B&B
LA VILLA DES CHÊNES

Noëlle and Rolf Gasser
300, Desrivières
Pike-River J0J 1P0
(450) 296-8848
fax (450) 296-4990

B&B	
single	$40-45
double	$60-65
child	$10

Reduced rates: 10% 3 nights and more
Open: Feb. 1 to Nov. 30

Number of rooms	4
rooms with private bath	1
rooms in basement	1
shared bathrooms	2

Activities: 🏛 🚣 👤 🚴 🎿

40. ST-ADRIEN-DE-HAM

Overlooking the village, our French cottage-style house warmly welcomes you with its gardens and stretches of water over 119 acres of land. Located 8 kilometres from Mont-Ham. On site: footpaths, cross-country skiing, snowshoeing and massage. Nearby: cycling path, golf, summer theatre, downhill skiing, skidooing and fishing.

From Montréal: Hwy 20, Exit 147, Rte 116 to Danville, Rte 255 South, Rte 216 East, about 8km from St-Adrien.

B&B
EAU SOLEIL LE VENT

Jacqueline Sauriol and
Yves Castonguay
1200, Route 216
St-Adrien-de-Ham J0A 1C0
(819) 828-0919
dodu@sympatico.ca

B&B	
single	$40-60
double	$50-70
triple	$85-95
child	$10

VS MC

Open year round

Number of rooms	4
shared wc	1
shared bathrooms	2
rooms in basement	1

Activities: 🍴 🍷 🧍 🚲 🎿

41. SHERBROOKE

In the heart of a 19th-c. residential district, this superb Second Empire-style house transports you to Provence. A setting of warm coulours with soothing lavender scents. Pastis and olives offered as cokctails on the sun terrace in summer, by the fire in winter. Discover "the charms of the country in the city, the attractions of the city in the country".

From Montréal, Hwy 10. From Québec City, Hwy 20 and 55 Exit 140, Hwy 410 to Boul. Portland, then follow it for 4km. After the Domaine Howard park, turn left on Rue Québec.

B&B
CHARMES DE PROVENCE

Céline Desrosiers and
Alexis Rampin
350, rue du Québec
Sherbrooke J1H 3L8
(819) 348-1147
www.tourisme-cantons.qc.ca/
charmes-de-provence

B&B	
single	$50
double	$65
triple	$80
quad.	$95
child	$10

Taxes extra

Reduced rates: 10% 3 nights and more
Open year round

Number of rooms	3
shared wc	1
shared bathrooms	1

Activities: 🏛 🧍 🧍 🚲 🎿

42. SHERBROOKE

Sample the charms of this vast, old presbytery in a warm and refined setting. Lounge about in the solarium or the private living room, luxuriate in the warmth of its fireplace, woodwork, antiques and friendly young hosts! Give in to the morning feast, a sinful delight! Ready for paradise, in the heart of the historic district.

From Montréal, Hwy 10; from Québec City, Hwy 20 and 55, Exit 140, Rte 410 to Boul. de Portland. Continue for 4km.

B&B
COUETTE ET CAFÉ
LE VIEUX PRESBYTÈRE

Flore Béland and Carl Thibeault
1162, boul. de Portland
Sherbrooke J1H 1H9
(819) 346-1665
www.levieuxpresbytere.qc.ca
carl.thibeault@sympatico.ca

B&B	
single	$50-60
double	$65-75
triple	$80-90
child	$10

Open: May 1 to Sep. 30

Number of rooms	5
rooms with private bath	1
shared bathrooms	2

Activities: 🏛 🍴 🧍 🧍 🚲

43. STANSTEAD
☀☀☀ F E 🚗 P R2.5

Dating from 1940, this residence is situated on one of the only border streets in North America. Everything is done to ensure you have a pleasant stay in our peaceful and relaxed environment. Delicious five-course breakfast are served. Located only 5min from Parc Weir (swimming and boat launch). Excursions on Lac Memphrémagog are possible and the property links up with a bike path. There's also a museum, opera house, antique shop and much more. See you soon!

From Montréal, Hwy 10 twd Sherbrooke, Exit 121. Hwy 55 twd Stantead. Vermont, Exit 1 Rte 247 twd Stantead (Beebe plain) 4.5km.

B&B
LA GRENOUILLÈRE DES
TROIS VILLAGES

Francyne and Serge Tougas
25, Canusa
Stanstead J0B 3E5
tel/fax (819) 876-5599
stougas@abacom.com

B&B	
single	$55-70
double	$60-75

Taxes extra VS MC AM

Open year round

Number of rooms	3
rooms with private bath	1
shared wc	1
shared bathrooms	1

Activities: 🏛 🚣 🎣 🚲 🎿

44. SUTTON
☀☀☀☀ F E P R1

With its slate roof and lavish pine woodwork, this gigantic Victorian home will charm even the most discriminating guest. Recommended by a *Journal de Montréal* editorial, Les Caprices de Victoria concocts refreshing strawberry *coulis* with *crème anglaise* and *café au lait*, an and delightful mixture of colours and flavours! The refined décor blends well with the original Victorian style. "A restful sleep and an enchanting awakening."

Hwy 10, Exit 74 for Cowansville. Follow the signs for Sutton, Rte 139 South.

B&B
LES CAPRICES DE VICTORIA

Hugo Sénécal and
Jean-Sylvain Murray
63, Principale Nord
Sutton J0E 2K0
(450) 538-1551
www.capricesdevictoria.qc.ca
b.b@capricesdevictoria.qc.ca

B&B	
single	$65-105
double	$75-115
child	$15

Taxes extra VS MC AM

Open year round

Number of rooms	4
rooms with private bath	2
rooms with sink	2
shared bathrooms	1

Activities: 🎣 🎿 🚲 🎿 🏃

45. VALCOURT
☀☀☀ F E 🚗 P 🏊 R10 TA

In the calm and tranquillity of the Township countryside, the Auberge Boscobel offers you 120 acres of nature in all its forms: forest, maple grove, stream, lake, fields... and spectacular wildlife. You'll savour home-made goods. 10km from the Musée Bombardier.

Hwy 10, Exit 78. Rte 241 North to Warden, then Rte 243 North. Or Hwy 20, Exit 147, Rtes 116 East, 139 South, 222 East. In Valcourt at the stop sign, Ch. de la Montagne twd Roxton Falls, 2.8km. Ch. Boscobel, 5.3km. At the fork, left on 10e Rang, 2km.

B&B
AUBERGE BOSCOBEL

Sandra and Jean-Pierre Simon
6387, 10e Rang Nord
Valcourt J0E 2L0
tel/fax (450) 548-2442
www.bbcanada.com/
2108.html
jpsimon@total.net

B&B	
single	$31
double	$53

Open year round

Number of rooms	3
rooms with private bath	1
shared bathrooms	2

Activities: 🦆 🚣 🚲 🎿 🏃

46. WOTTON

| F | P | R5 | M4 |

Cosy cottage with old-fashioned charm and magnificent view of the lakes. Activities include pedal-boats, canoeing, snowmobiling, hiking through forests and fields. Cross-country skiing, snowshoeing, golf and swimming close by. 4km from Asbestos.

From Montréal, Hwy 20 East, Exit 147. Rte 116 East to Danville, Rte 255 South to Wotton. 4km after crossing Rte 249, turn left on Route des Lacs, drive 2km.

COUNTRY HOME
LA MAISON DES LACS

Monique and Jean Mercier
28, chemin des Lacs
Wotton JOA 1N0
(819) 346-3575
pager (819) 573-9478

No.houses	1
No. rooms	5
No. people	10
WEEK-SUMMER	$500
W/E-SUMMER	$250
W/E-WINTER	$250
DAY-SUMMER	$150
DAY-WINTER	$150

Open: weekends only from Sep. 1 to June 30, anytime during July and Aug.

Activities: 🏛 🛶 ⛷ 🛷 🏃

FARM ACTIVITIES

Farm Stays:

Country-style Dining*:

* Registered trademark.

CENTRE-DU-QUÉBEC

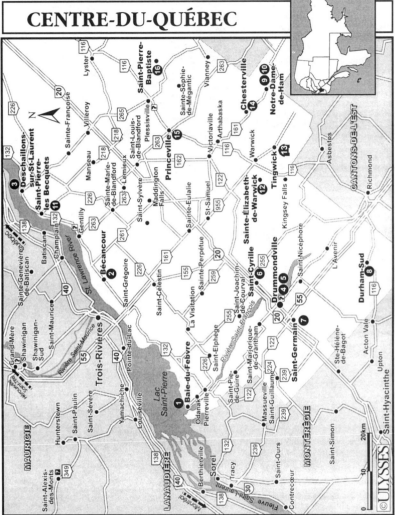

* The numbers on the map refer to the numbering of the establishments of this region

1. BAIE-DU-FEBVRE

☀☀☀☀ F e P ☒

If Morpheus (the Greek god of sleep) existed, he would live at Au Bout des D'Oies. An old wooden door welcomes you into an interior whose colours are inspired by various local birds: snow goose, shoveler duck brown, thrush blue and teal duck green. For a gourmet feast worthy of the greatest kings, come dine with us and taste our delicious goose. Reservations required. Member of the Québec regional cuisine organization.

Hwy 20, Exit 185, Rte 255 for Baie-du-Febvre.

INN
AU BOUT DES D'OIES

Manon Chapdelaine and Mario Laliberté
440 rue Principale
Baie-du-Febvre J0G 1A0
(450) 783-3333
fax (450) 783-3331

B&B	
single	$50
double	$65
triple	$80
quad.	$95

Taxes extra VS IT

Open year round

Number of rooms	4
shared bathrooms	2

Activities: 🚶 🏃 🚴 🛷 ⛷

2. BÉCANCOUR

☀☀☀☀ F E ☒ P TA

We are renowned for our welcome, our food and our B&B inside a sumptuous Victorian house. We serve: ostrich, buffalo, caribou, venison, duck, rabbit, beef, seafood and perch. Refined local cuisine. Right nearby: canoeing, tennis, horseback riding, snowmobiling, swimming, fishing, tourist attractions.

From Montréal or Québec City, Hwy 40. In Trois-Rivières, cross the Laviolette bridge, Rte 132 East. Bécancour Exit. Rue Nicolas Perrot. We are next to the church.

INN
MANOIR BÉCANCOURT

Yvon Beaulieu
3255, Nicolas Perrot
Bécancour G0X 1B0
(819) 294-9068
fax (819) 294-9060

	B&B	MAP
single	$35	$55
double	$50	$90
child	$15	$30

Taxes extra VS MC

Open year round

Number of rooms	5
shared wc	4
shared bathrooms	2

Activities: 🏛 ♣ 🛶 🚶 🚴

3. DESCHAILLONS-SUR-SAINT-LAURENT

☀☀☀ F E P R.5 TA

La Petite Diligence brings the beautiful romances of times past to life. Come explore the St. Lawrence River, its spectacular landscapes and singular promontories. Let yourselves be won over by its vivacity, and lulled by its fabulous sunsets. The river, our roots, our history. Come take a look!

Rte 132 runs along the St. Lawrence River's south shore, halfway between the Québec City and Trois-Rivières bridges. From Hwy 20, Exit 253, Rte 265 North to the river, left about 1km.

B&B
LA PETITE DILIGENCE

Claire Duhamel
1545, Marie-Victorin, C.P. 26
Deschaillons-sur-Saint-Laurent
G0S 1G0
(819) 292-3119
(819) 292-3106
fax (819) 292-2925

B&B	
single	$30
double	$40

Open year round

Number of rooms	2
shared bathrooms	1

Activities: 🏃 🚴 🐎 🛷 ⛷

4. DRUMMONDVILLE

✹✹✹ F E 🚫 🚗 P ⛵ R1 TA

"Experience the house from long ago, where both roses and children grow. "Our small" family (11) welcomes you to its table set with home-made bread and jams, fresh eggs, juice and aromatic coffee. Make yourself at home! Halfway between Montréal and Québec City, between Sherbrooke and Trois-Rivières.

Hwy 20, Exit 175 to Drummondville (Boul. Lemire Sud), 300 m from Hwy 20.

B&B
LE GÎTE DES ROSES

Diane and Denis Lampron
215, boul. Lemire, R.R. #6
Drummondville J2C 7X2
(819) 474-4587
fax (819) 474-1500
rose.qc.ca/gite
gite@rose.qc.ca

B&B	
single	$40
double	$55
triple	$65
quad.	$75
child	$10

Open year round
closed from Aug. 5 to Aug. 20

Number of rooms	3
shared bathrooms	3

Activities: 🏛 🍂 🗝 🚶 🚴

---

5. DRUMMONDVILLE

✹✹✹✹ F E ♿ ✂️ 🚗 🦮 P R5 TA

A continually well-kept B&B by the St-François River awaits you. Surrounded by woodlands, greenery and flowers, near a brook. Quiet nights. Complete, refined breakfast on the spot or in the house next door, on the same property. We are 12 minutes from the town centre. Meals upon request.

Hwy 20, Exit 55 twd Sherbrooke, then Rte 139 Exit twd St-Nicéphore. Go through the village and continue to the airport near the river. Turn right and drive 1.2km.

B&B
MAISON LA COULÉE

Beldora and Daniel Roy
4890, boul. Allard
Drummondville J2B 6V3
(819) 477-4359
fax (819) 477-0672
www.quebecweb.com/
lacoulee/
daniel.roy@dr.cgocable.ca

	B&B	MAP
single	$45-75	$60-90
double	$60-80	$90-110
triple	$110-130	$155-175
child	$10-15-20	on request

Open year round

Number of rooms	5
rooms with private bath	2
rooms with sink	2
shared bathrooms	2

Activities: 🏛 🍂 🗝 🚶 🚴

---

6. DRUMMONDVILLE, ST-CYRILLE

F e 🚫 P 🦮 R4 TA

Halfway between Montreal and Québec City, 5km from Drummondville. Amidst vast spaces, trees, flowers, water gardens and waterfall. Non-smoking B&B with fireplace and air conditioning. Healthy homemade breakfasts. 4km from Village d'Antan and Légendes Fantastiques, local festivals, health clinic, cross-country skiing and bike path.

Hwy 20, Exit 185, drive 2km to the church, turn right on Rte 122, continue for 1km.

B&B
L'OASIS

Johanna Beier Putzke
3500, Route 122
St-Cyrille-de-Wendover
J1Z 1C3
(819) 397-2917

B&B	
single	$35
double	$45-60
child	$0-10

Reduced rates: Oct. 1 to May 1
Open year round

Number of rooms	3
rooms with private bath	1
rooms with sink	1
shared bathrooms	1

Activities: 🍂 🚶 🚴 🐕 🏃

7. DRUMMONDVILLE, ST-GERMAIN

☀☀☀ F E ⊗ 🚗 P R6 TA

Old-world charm, good living. Large, secluded 1916 country house amidst vast, flowery expanses. Hearty gourmet breakfast of homemade goods in the solarium overlooking the garden. Québec «Village d'Antan», Légendes Fantastiques, "La Campagnarde" bike path. Welcome to the heart of Québec.

From Québec City, Hwy 20, Exit 166, left on 10e Rang to Rte 239 North. From Montréal, Hwy 20, Exit 166, right on 10e Rang to Rte 239 North, continue for 3km.

B&B
LE MADAWASKA

Juliette Levasseur
644, Route 239 Nord
St-Germain J0C 1K0
(819) 395-4318

B&B	
single	$40
double	$55
triple	$65
child	$10

Open: May 1 to Oct. 15

Number of rooms	3
shared bathrooms	2

Activities: 🏛 🥾 🎣 🚲

---

8. DURHAM-SUD

☀☀☀ F E ⊗ P 🚤 🐕 R5 TA

We welcome you to our sixth generation farm where you can wake up to the chimes following a peaceful night. A tantalizing breakfast of homemade goodies will awaken all your senses. A walk through the rolling fields, a snooze in the hammock, petting baby rabbits, or visiting the numerous activities around are all at your disposal.

From Hwy 20, Exit 147, Rte 116 East to Durham-Sud. From flashing light another 2km on Rte 116, left on Mooney Rd, 3km. From Hwy 55 Exit 88, Rte 116 West 12km, right on Mooney Rd, 3km.

B&B
LA SIXIÈME GÉNÉRATION

Heather Lunan and
Norman Carson
415, chemin Mooney
Durham-Sud J0H 2C0
(819) 858-2539
fax (819) 858-2001
www.sixiemegeneration.qc.ca
6genbb@dr.cgocable.ca

B&B	
single	$40-45
double	$55-60
triple	$75
quad.	$90
child	$0-10

Taxes extra

Open: June 1 to Oct. 31

Number of rooms	3
shared wc	1
shared bathrooms	1

Activities: 🏛 🎣 🚲 ⛷ 🏃

---

9. NOTRE-DAME-DE-HAM

F E 🐕 🚗 P R5 TA

Fairytale house in a little village in the heart of the Appalachians, where Morpheus, the god of sleep and dreams warmly welcomes you to his magical little wooden home. The river, the trout, the falls invite you as I await you in the privacy of my own home.

Hwy 20, Jean-Lesage twd Québec city, Exit 210. In Victoriaville, twd the Laurier museum or S.Q. Boul. Laurier South (Rte 161 South). Notre-Dame-De-Ham 26km.

B&B
LA MAISON DE MORPHÉE

Madeleine Codère
23, Principale
Notre-Dame-de-Ham, G0P 1C0
tel/fax (819) 344-5476

B&B	
single	$45-50
double	$55-65
triple	$85
child	$12

Taxes extra

Open year round

Number of rooms	3
rooms with private bath	1
shared bathrooms	1

Activities: 🏛 🥾 🎣 🚲

10. NOTRE-DAME-DE-HAM

F E 🚫 P 🐴 R5

In the heart of the majestic Appalachians, our Victorian house is similar in style to our New England neighbours: antique furniture, warm atmosphere, Swiss-like landscapes. Our knowledge of local history is much appreciated by guests. Our little anecdotes are amusing, and sometimes hard to believe, but we assure they are true!

Jean-Lesage Hwy 20 twd Québec City, Exit 210. At Victoriaville, twd Musée Laurier or S.Q., Boul. Laurier South (Rte 161 South). Notre-Dame-de-Ham, 26km.

B&B
LE GÎTE J.D. TROTTIER

Jeanne D. Trottier
37, rue Principale
Notre-Dame-de-Ham G0P 1C0
tel/fax (819) 344-5640
jdarc@boisfrancs.qc.ca

B&B	
single	$40
double	$55
triple	$70
child	$12

VS MC

Open year round

Number of rooms	3
shared bathrooms	2

Activities: 🏛 🦪 🍴 🚲 🏃

11. ST-PIERRE-LES-BECQUETS

☀☀☀ F E P 🏊 🐴 R1

Come live according to the rhythm of the tides, the life of the river, the country and a village that takes the time to welcome you. We offer you rest and comfort in a welcoming home with unique vistas. Heated pool in season. Unforgettable sunrises and sunsets.

From Montréal, Hwy 40 East. In Trois-Rivières, Laviolette Bridge, Hwy 30 East, which becomes Rte 132 East, to St-Pierre. Or from Québec City, bridge twd Nicolet, Rte 132 West to St-Pierre.

B&B
LA MAISON SUR LE FLEUVE

Suzanne Chartrand
and Jacques Lefebvre
136, Marie-Victorin
St-Pierre-les-Becquets
G0X 2Z0
(819) 263-2761
fax (819) 375-2512

B&B	
single	$35
double	$50
child	$5-15

Open: Apr. 1 to Nov. 1

Number of rooms	3
shared wc	1
shared bathrooms	1

Activities: 🍴 🚲 🐎 🛶 🏃

closed.

12. STE-ÉLIZABETH-DE-WARWICK

☀☀☀ F e 🏊 🚗 P ✕ R6 TA

Enjoy the relaxing wide expanses and the quiet countryside. Kitchen garden, orchard and flower gardens surround our home. For more action less than 6 kilometres away, bike along the country road (110km) or enjoy yourselves at the Grands-Chênes theatre in Kingsey Falls. Tempted? Pack your bags, we await you! Packages: cycling, canoeing, theatre.

Hwy 20, Exit 210. Rte 955 to St-Albert, follow signs for Warwick, turn right on 4e Rang (6km). After the village of Ste-Élizabeth, left on Rte Mondoux, drive 1.5km.

B&B
LE PETIT BALUCHON

Marie-France, Maude and
Jean-René Dumas
305, route Mondoux
Ste-Élizabeth-de-Warwick
J0A 1M0
(819) 358-2406

	B&B	MAP
single	$40	$55
double	$58	$88
child	$5-10	$10-20

Taxes extra

Open year round

Number of rooms	5
shared bathrooms	2

Activities: 🏛 🦪 🍴 🚲 🐎

13. TINGWICK

☀☀☀ F e ☒ 🚗 P 🏊 R7 TA

Provincial Excellence Prize Success 1999 and Tourisme Québec Régional Prize, Hospitality and Customer Service 1999. Come enjoy the hospitality and pleasures of yesteryear in our little paradise. Meet our animals, tour our large gardens and relax in the spa, near the brook. **Farm Stay, p 38. See colour photos.**

Hwy 20, Exit 210, Rte 955 South twd St-Albert. At the end, turn right, 1km, turn left twd Warwick, straight ahead to Tingwick. At the stop sign, straight ahead for 4km. At Rang 7, turn left and continue for 3.4km.

B&B
LES DOUCES HEURES D'ANTAN

Francine Gareau
and Claude Barabé
703, Rang 7
Tingwick JOA 1L0
(819) 359-2813
fax (819) 359-3229
www.login.net/dhdantan
dhdantan@login.net

	B&B	MAP
single	$50	$65
double	$65	$95
triple	$85	$130
quad.	$100	$160
child	$10	$25

Taxes extra VS

Reduced rates: 10% Nov. 1 to Apr. 1 or 3 nights and more (year round)
Open year round

Number of rooms	4
rooms with sink	3
shared bathrooms	2

Activities: 🦫 🛶 🚶 🚴 🎿

14. CHESTERVILLE

`F` `e` `♿` `🐕` `🚗` `P` `M15` `R7` `TA`

Nestled at the summit of a mountain in the middle of the forest, a rustic and comfortable cottage is waiting for you. By bike, on foot or on skis, discover the tranquillity and *joie de vivre* of the Appalachian Mountains. Theatre and music complete the perfect picture. Our home is your home!

Between Montréal and Québec City, Hwy 20, Exit 210, Rte 955 South to Warwick, then Tingwick. Turn left at the stop sign and head to Warwick. Once in Warwick, turn right at the stop sign onto St-Philippe and then drive to Fréchette.

COUNTRY HOME
LE RELAIS DE LA
PETITE MONTAGNE

Hélène Rollan
771, rang Fréchette
Chesterville GOP 1J0
(819) 382-9979
fax (819) 382-2197
relaismontagne@citenet.net

No. houses	1
No. rooms	4
No. people	2-22
WEEK-SUMMER	$805-1565
WEEK-WINTER	$890-1 700
W/E-SUMMER	$340-635
W/E-WINTER	$385-680
DAY-SUMMER	$215-340
DAY-WINTER	$235-385

Taxes extra

Reduced rates: Oct. 15 to Dec. 15 and Jan. 15 to Apr. 15
Open year round

Activities: 🍷 👣 🧍 🚲 ⛷

15. PRINCEVILLE

`F` `e` `🐕` `🚗` `P` `R3` `M3`

Heidi and her grandfather knew about the richness of wide expanses, the beauty of nature. The peace and comfort of "Paradis d'Émy" also makes us embrace nature again. A stone's throw from the farm are the pleasures of skiing, golfing, cycling, snowmobiling. This cozy paradise is a dream come true!

Between Québec City and Montréal. Hwy 20, Exit 235, for Princeville. Rte 263 South. Drive 15km, turn left on Rang 7 Est. From Rte 116 in Princeville, take the 263 North, 3km, first right onto Rang 7 Est.

COUNTRY HOME
AU PARADIS D'ÉMY

Joceline Desfossés and
Normand Jutras
7, Rang 7 Est
Princeville G6L 4C2
(819) 364-2840
fax (819) 364-5426
www.pearle.net/
~pcboss/emy.htm
pcboss@pearle.net

No. houses	1
No. rooms	4
No. people	2-14
WEEK-SUMMER	$350-1022
WEEK-WINTER	$350-1022
W/E-SUMMER	$130-370
W/E-WINTER	$130-370
DAY-SUMMER	$65-185
DAY-WINTER	$65-185

Taxes extra

Open year round

Activities: 🍷 🛶 🧍 🏇 🐎

16. ST-PIERRE-BAPTISTE

`F` `e` `♿` `🐕` `P` `〰` `R6` `M6`

Lovely house in the Appalachian foothills: natural wood and brick interior. During the cold season, a crackling fire awaits you. Handwoven bedding and rugs. All necessary cooking equipment, 2 bathrooms. On the farm: trails, cross-country skiing, small animals. Nearby: snowmobile trails, swimming at the falls.

From Montréal Hwy 20, Exit 228, from Québec City, Exit 253 to Thetford Mines. Drive 11km past Plessisville, turn left on St-Pierre-Baptiste for 4km. Left at the church 100 m, right on Route Roy; drive 5km. Right Gîte Domaine des Pins.

COUNTRY HOME
DOMAINE DES PINS

Danielle Pelletier and
Yvon Gingras
2108, rang Scott
St-Pierre-Baptiste GOP 1K0
(418) 453-2088
fax (418) 453-2760
www.domaine.qc.ca

No. houses	1
No rooms	5
No. people	2-16
WEEK-SUMMER	$300-450
WEEK-WINTER	$350-500
W/E-SUMMER	$200-300
W/E-WINTER	$300-350
DAY-SUMMER	$125
DAY-WINTER	$150

Taxes extra

Open year round

Activities: 🏛 🍷 🛶 🧍 🛷

FARM ACTIVITIES

Farm Stay:

13 LES DOUCES HEURES D'ANTAN, Tingwick 38

* Registered trademark.

To Ensure Your Satisfation

Bed & Breakfast, Country Inn,
Country and City Homes, Farm Stay,
Country-Style Dining, Farm Excursion :

680 establishments fall into these
6 categories, and all are accredited and regularly
inspected according to a code of ethics and standards
of quality for hospitality, layout and decor, safety,
cleanliness, comfort and meals served.

The Fédération des Agricotours du Québec
25 years of hospitality
1975-2000

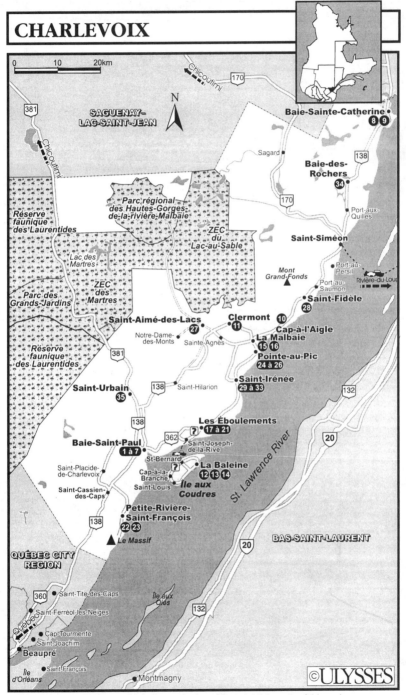

CHARLEVOIX

SAGUENAY–
LAC-SAINT-JEAN

Baie-Sainte-Catherine
8 9

Sagard

Baie-des-
Rochers
34

Réserve
faunique
des Laurentides

Parc régional
des Hautes-Gorges-
de-la-rivière-Malbaie

ZEC
du
Lac-au-Sable

Port-aux-
Quilles

Saint-Siméon

Lac des
Martres

Port-au-
Persil
Rivière-du-Loup

Mont
Grand-Fonds

Port-au-
Saumon

Parc des
Grands-Jardins

ZEC
des
Martres

Saint-Fidèle
28

Réserve
faunique
des Laurentides

Saint-Aimé-des-Lacs
27

Clermont
11

Cap-à-l'Aigle
10

Notre-Dame-
des-Monts

Sainte-Agnès

La Malbaie
15 16

Pointe-au-Pic
24 à 26

Saint-Urbain
35

Saint-Hilarion

Saint-Irénée
29 à 33

Les Éboulements
17 à 21

Baie-Saint-Paul
1 à 7

Saint-Joseph-
de-la-Rive

Saint-Placide-
de-Charlevoix

St-Bernard

Cap-à-la-
Branche

La Baleine
12 13 14

St. Lawrence River

Saint-Cassien-
des-Caps

Saint-Louis

Île aux
Coudres

Petite-Rivière-
Saint-François
22 23

Le Massif

BAS-SAINT-LAURENT

QUÉBEC CITY
REGION

Saint-Tite-des-Caps

Île aux
Oies

Saint-Ferréol-les-Neiges

Cap-Tourmente

Saint-Joachim

Beaupré

Saint-François

Île
d'Orléans

Montmagny

©ULYSSES

* The numbers on the map refer to the numbering of the establishments of this region

1. BAIE-ST-PAUL

☀☀☀☀☀ F E 🚭 P 🚗 ⛵ R.2 TA

An old, colourful house in the heart of artistic Baie-St-Paul. Woodwork, lace, duvet. Wood-burning stove for chilly mornings. Piano, reading room. Terraces and flowery gardens looking out onto the countryside, mountains and the magical seasons. Local and homemade goods at breakfast. Access to kitchen. Packages: skiing, whale-watching, music. **See colour photos.**

From Québec City, Rte 138 East, 100km. In Baie-St-Paul, Rte 362 East. At the church, turn right on Rue Ste-Anne. At the fork, blue house on the right.

B&B
À LA CHOUETTE

Ginette Guérette and
François Rivard
2, rue Leblanc
Baie-St-Paul G3Z 1W9
(418) 435-3217

B&B	
single	$70
double	$80
triple	$95
child	$5-10

Reduced rates: Apr. 5 to May 15, Oct. 11 to Dec. 23
Open year round

Number of rooms	4
rooms with private bath	4

Activities: 🏛 🚤 🧍 🎿 🏃

2. BAIE-ST-PAUL

★★ F e 🚭 🐕 P 🚗 ✕ TA

Peace, serenity, soft music, hospitality and fine food. A Victorian house with centenary charm nestled beneath the maples in the heart of the village. Fireplace, terrace and garden. Near shops, the Massif and a host of activities, parks, golf, casino, cruise... In summer, MAP plan only. **See colour photos.**

100km from Québec City twd Ste-Anne-de-Beaupré, Rte 138 E. At Baie-St-Paul, Rte 362 E. At church, left on Rue St-Jean-Baptiste. Or from La Malbaie, Rtes 138 or 362 West.

INN
AUBERGE LA MUSE

Evelyne Tremblay and
Robert Arsenault
39, rue St-Jean-Baptiste
Baie-St-Paul, G3Z 1M3
(418) 435-6839
fax (418) 435-6289
toll free 1-800-841-6839
www.lamuse.com
lamuse@charlevoix.net

	B&B	MAP
single	$80	$102
double	$90-110	$135-155
triple	$120-130	$180-190
quad.	$140-150	$215-225
child	$10-20	$15-30

Taxes extra VS MC ER IT

Reduced rates: Apr. 24 to June 15 and Oct. 22 to Dec. 22
Open year round

Number of rooms	10
rooms with private bath	10

Activities: 🏛 🚶 🧍 🎿 🏃

3. BAIE-ST-PAUL

☀☀☀ F e 🚭 🐕 P R.5 TA

Located on one of the most picturesque streets in town, our 100-year-old house, whose garden extends to the St. Lawrence River, is yours to appreciate. Steps away from good restaurants, art galleries, shops and the exhibition centre. 15 min from "Au Massif de Petite Rivière St-François" ski resort. Hearty breakfasts await.

From Québec City, twd Ste-Anne-de-Beaupré, Rte 138 East, 100km. In Baie-St-Paul, Rte 362 East. At the church, cross the bridge, 1st street on the right.

B&B
AU CLOCHETON

Johanne and Laurette Robin
50, rue St-Joseph,
Baie-St-Paul G3Z 1H7
(418) 435-3393
toll free 1-877-435-3393
fax (418) 435-6432

B&B	
single	$45-65
double	$60-80
triple	$80-95
quad.	$110
child	$5-10

MC

Reduced rates: Apr. 3 to May 15, Oct.15 to Dec. 20
Open year round

Number of rooms	4
rooms with sink	4
rooms with private bath	1
shared bathrooms	1

Activities: 🏛 🧍 🎿 🏃

4. BAIE-ST-PAUL

F E P R3.5

Come discover one of the loveliest places in Charlevoix! Exceptional view of the St. Lawrence River. Peaceful environment. Picturesque house built on the mountainside. Rooms with panoramic view, private entrance and terrace. Lounge. Therapeutic massage on the premises. Massif ski package. 5 minutes from downtown.

From Québec, Rte 138 E. twd Ste-Anne-de-Beaupré for 100km. At the Baie-St-Paul church, Rte 362 E. for 2km. At the sign for "Les Encadrements du Cap" turn right on Chemin Cap-aux-Rets. 2nd house on the left, after the cross.

B&B

AU PERCHOIR

Jacinthe Tremblay
and Réjean Thériault
443, Cap-aux-Rets
Baie-St-Paul G3Z 1C1
tel/fax (418) 435-6955
www.quebecweb.com/perchoir

B&B	
single	$80-105
double	$85-110
triple	$100-125
quad.	$115-140
child	$10-15

Taxes extra VS

Reduced rates: Apr. 9 to June 16, Oct. 9 to 23 Dec. and during the week, except in the summer

Open year round

Number of rooms	3
rooms with private bath	3

Activities:

5. BAIE-ST-PAUL

F e P R.1 TA

Amidst tourist activities, away from the bustle but near galleries and restaurants, 15 min from the Massif. A house with the charm of yesteryear, with its high ceilings and large balcony. Rooms decorated in art-related themes. Queen-size beds. Gourmet breakfast. Back bungalow with 3 self-catering, soundproofed, fully equipped suites for 2 to 4 people. **See colour photos.**

From Québec City, Rte 138 East. In Baie-St-Paul, on Rte 362, opposite the hospital.

INN

AUX PETITS OISEAUX

Danielle Trussart and
Jacques Roussel
30, boul. Fafard, Rte 362
Baie-St-Paul G3Z 2J4
(418) 435-3888
toll free 1-877-435-3888
fax (418) 435-0465
www.quebecweb.com/oiseaux
trussel@charlevoix.net

B&B	
single	$60
double	$65-85
triple	$85-100
quad.	$115
child	$10-15

Taxes extra

Reduced rates: Oct. 15 to Dec. 15 Apr. 15 to June 15

Open year round

Number of rooms	10
rooms with sink	2
rooms with private bath	8
shared bathrooms	1

Activities:

6. BAIE-ST-PAUL

F E P R2 TA

This 200-year-old house was renowned for its hospitality towards homeless people, and it has kept its shelter charm and vocation. Wake up to the smell of a crackling fire and enjoy a copious home-made breakfast with regional accents. Our home has a lavishly decorated interior. In the rooms, queen-size beds, view of the St. Lawrence River and L'Île aux Coudres. Packages and group rates. Near the Massif ski resort. Come visit us!

From Québec City, Rte 138 East. At the tourist info. bureau before Baie-St-Paul, turn right, follow St-Antoine S. at left. Drive 500m, 1st street on right.

B&B

GÎTE LE NOBLE QUÊTEUX

Marie Lou Jacques and
Claude Marin
8, côte du Quêteux
rang St-Antoine Sud
Baie-St-Paul G3Z 2C7
(418) 240-2352
fax (418) 240-2377
queteux@charlevoix.net

B&B	
single	$50-60
double	$55-65
triple	$70-80
quad.	$85-95

Reduced rates: Oct. 11 to Dec. 20, Apr. 25 to May 18

Open year round

Number of rooms	5
rooms with private bath	2
rooms in basement	2
shared bathrooms	1

Activities:

7. BAIE-ST-PAUL

☀☀☀ F E P 🐕 R.1 TA

This turn-of-the-century former rooming house has found its calling again with the arrival of your host Jean, who will help make your stay here an unforgettable one. Savour the greatest variety of jams, jellies and marmalades made in «home of Charlevoix». Make the most of the nearby and animated downtown Baie-St-Paul.

Located a stone's throw from the Baie-St-Paul church on Rue Ste-Anne (street where the pier is).

B&B
L'ARTOÎT

Jean Perron
50, rue Ste-Anne
Baie-St-Paul G3Z 1P2
tel/fax (418) 435-4091
www.quebecweb.
com/gpc/artoit/

B&B	
single	$50
double	$60
triple	$80
quad.	$120
child	$15

Reduced rates: Oct.15 to May 15
Open year round

Number of rooms	3
shared wc	1
shared bathrooms	1

Activities: 🏛 🧍 ⛷ 🎿 🐎

8. BAIE-STE-CATHERINE

☀☀☀ F e 🚭 🚗 P 🐕 🗡 R1 TA

Now swept away by the fury of the waves, now enchanted by the tranquillity of the woods, N.-D. de l'Espace watches over the secret world of whales and our village. Anne-Marie's table d'hôte, regional home cooking. Dogsled, cruise tickets. Charlevoix Excellence Prize 1994-95.

From Québec City, Rte 138 East twd La Malbaie. At bridge, twd Tadoussac. At Baie-Ste-Catherine watch for blue tourist sign, drive 1km. From Tadoussac, 4km.

B&B
ENTRE MER ET MONTS

Anne-Marie and Réal Savard
476, Route 138
Baie-Ste-Catherine G0T 1A0
(418) 237-4391
fax (418) 237-4252
www.fjord-best.com/
entre-mer-et-monts
entre-mer-et-monts@
fjord-best.com

	B&B	MAP
single	$35-40	$50-55
double	$45-50	$75-80
triple	$65-70	$110-115
child	$15-20	$27.⁵⁰-30

VS MC

Reduced rates: Nov. 1 to May 31
Open year round

Number of rooms	5
rooms with sink	3
rooms in basement	3
shared wc	1
shared bathrooms	2

Activities: 🛶 🧍 🧍 🛷 🐎

9. BAIE-STE-CATHERINE

F 🚗 P 🏊 R.5 TA

Beautifully located in a magnificent bay, near a little church at the heart of a peaceful village, come and immerse yourself in the beautiful countryside. Discover the beauty of the sea. Far from the noise of Rte 138 for peaceful and restful nights. Rooms on the main floor or in the basement. Boat cruise tickets for sale.

From Québec City, Rte 138 E. twd Tadoussac. From the Baie-Ste-Catherine "Bienvenue" (welcome) sign, drive 4km. First road on the left. Watch for the provincial sign on Rte 138.

B&B
GÎTE DU CAPITAINE

Etiennette and Benoit Imbeault
343, rue Leclerc
Baie-Ste-Catherine G0T 1A0
(418) 237-4320
(418) 237-4359

B&B	
single	$40
double	$50
triple	$70
quad.	$90
child	$15-20

VS

Open: May 1 to Oct. 31

Number of rooms	5
rooms in basement	2
shared bathrooms	2

Activities: 🏛 🧍 🛶 🧍 🐎

10. CAP-À-L'AIGLE

★★★ F E ♿ 🚗 P 🐾 R.8 TA

Auberge Fleurs de Lune is a charming inn located in the heart of Cap-à-l'Aigle, near the casino and all the attractions in Charlevoix. Our rooms have all the modern conveniences, a sophisticated decor, balcony and a breathtaking view of the St. Lawrence River. Some rooms have a fireplace and whirlpool. The lodge has two rooms with living room and fully equipped kitchen. Choice of breakfasts served at your table. "Like a flower in Charlevoix" (Gilles Toupin, *La Presse*).

From Québec City, Rte 138 East for Cap-à-l'Aigle.

INN
AUBERGE FLEURS DE LUNE

Monique and André Vaillancourt
301, St-Raphaël
Cap-à-l'Aigle G0T 1B0
(418) 665-1090
toll free 1-888-665-1020
fax (418) 665-4458
www.quebecweb.
com/fleursdelune

B&B	
single	$85-125
double	$105-175
triple	$150
quad.	$180

Taxes extra VS MC AM IT

Reduced rates: Oct. 15 to June 15, except on holidays
Open year round

Number of rooms	11
shared wc	1
rooms with private bath	11

Activities: 🛷 🛷 ⚜ 🚶 🎿

11. CLERMONT

☀☀☀ F e P R1

In the heart of Charlevoix, you will experience a personal warmth and hospitality, as well as our fondness for the country. In the comfort of our large home, your history will fascinate us while ours will enchant you. Come and relax in the gentle warmth of our company.

From Québec City, Rte 138 E. drive 130km to Clermont. From La Malbaie, Rte 138 W., drive 7km to Clermont.

B&B
LA MAISON GAUDREAULT

Jeannine and Antonio
230, boul. Notre-Dame
Route 138
Clermont G4A 1E9
(418) 439-4149
antonio.gaudreault
@sympatico.ca

B&B	
single	$40
double	$50
child	$0-15

Open year round

Number of rooms	5
shared bathrooms	2

Activities: 🏛 🎿 ⚜ 🛷 🐎

12. ISLE-AUX-COUDRES

☀☀☀☀ F e 🚗 P R2

Large, peaceful, beautiful and welcoming house where your hosts Rita and Vincent offer you warm hearts and good food. Steps from the river and near cultural and tourist activities. Let yourself be soothed and pampered by the rhythm of the tides in a unique setting.

From Québec City, Rte 138 E. twd Baie-St-Paul. Rte 362 to St-Joseph-de-la-Rive ferry. On the island, left at stop sign, drive 3km.

B&B
GÎTE LA MAISON BLANCHE

Rita and Vincent Laurin
232, Royale Est, C.P. 238
Isle-aux-Coudres G0A 3J0
(418) 438-2883

B&B	
single	$50
double	$70

Reduced rates: Oct. 15 to June 15
Open year round

Number of rooms	5
rooms with private bath	1
rooms with sink	4
shared wc	2
shared bathrooms	2

Activities: 🛷 🚤 🚶 🚴 🎿

13. ISLE-AUX-COUDRES ☀☀☀ F 🚗 P R2 TA

Excellence Prize Charlevoix 1997-98. Let yourselves be pampered and charmed by Uncle Wilfrid's house, where we can chitchat in a setting redolent of yesteryear. Cycling, walks, browsing handicraft shops and other activities... will help you digest Isle-aux-Coudriers' typical dish «le p'tit pâté croche».

From Québec City, Rte 138 E. twd Baie-St-Paul. Rte 362 to the ferry. On the island, straight ahead after the stop for 3km, turn right at the 2nd stop, drive 2km.

B&B
GÎTE LA RIVERAINE

Lise Dufour
6, rue Principale
La Baleine, Isle-aux-Coudres
G0A 2A0
(418) 438-2831

B&B	
single	$40-55
double	$55-65
child	$10

Open: May 1 to Oct. 31

Number of rooms	5
rooms with private bath	1
rooms with sink	4
shared bathrooms	2

Activities: 🍴 🛶 🚲 🛷 🤸

---

14. ISLE-AUX-COUDRES ☀☀☀ F e P 🚗 🐕 R1 TA

Away from the bustle of the city, on an enchanting island. As if time had stopped. Wake up to birds chirping and breakfast on the terrace. Relaxing, large, sunny and flowered living-room. For a unique holiday: bring your hat, I'll supply the brushes, and together we'll do a painting.

From Québec City, Rte 138 E. twd Baie-St-Paul. Rte 362 to St-Joseph-de-la-Rive ferry. On the island, right at flashing light, drive 10km. 500 ft after St-Louis church.

B&B
VILLA DU MOULIN

Louise F. Belley
252, chemin des Moulins
Isle-aux-Coudres G0A 1X0
(418) 438-2649
(418) 665-6126
toll free 1-888-824-6263
patriot@cam.org

B&B	
single	$40
double	$60
triple	$75
quad.	$90
child	$10

Open: Apr. 1 to Oct. 31

Number of rooms	5
shared bathrooms	2

Activities: 🏛 🍴 🛶 🐟 🚲

---

15. LA MALBAIE ☀☀☀ F E 🚗 P 🏊 R4.5 TA

In the mood to hit the casino? It's only 130 seconds away! How about mountains, lakes and attractions? They are all near our residence, where guests are always warmly greeted in a quiet, enchanting setting. Welcome.

Whether you're coming from Rtes 138 or 362, by the river, the exit before or after traffic light at the shopping centre, turn and it's the 3rd house on the right.

B&B
GÎTE E.T. HARVEY

Etudienne Tremblay and
Jacques Harvey
19, rue Laure-Conan
La Malbaie Pointe-au-Pic
G5A 1H8
tel/fax (418) 665-2779
www.bbcanada.
com/2779.html

B&B	
single	$40
double	$45-50
triple	$60-65
child	$15

Reduced rates: Oct. 30 to
Apr. 30, 3 nights or more
Open year round

Number of rooms	4
rooms in basement	1
shared wc	1
shared bathrooms	1

Activities: 🏛 🚲 🎿 🐎

16. LA MALBAIE

☀☀☀ F e 🛶 P 🏊 R.7 TA

Our B&B offers rest and relaxation, with its flowery garden, indoor and outdoor fireplaces, outdoor spa, 2-person therapeutic bath, sound-proof rooms, TV, small lounge, front and back balconies with view of the river. Not to mention the delicious breakfasts, from orange crepes to Yvonne's brioches.

2km from the casino. Rte 138 E. twd La Malbaie 1st street on your right after the tourist office then left on Rue Laure-Conan. Or Rte 362 to La Malbaie, 2nd street after shopping centre. Left side.

B&B
LA MAISON
DUFOUR-BOUCHARD

Micheline Dufour
18, rue Laure-Conan
La Malbaie G5A 1H8
(418) 665-4982

B&B	
single	$35-45
double	$45-55
triple	$60-70
quad.	$80-85
child	$5-15

Open: May 15 to Oct. 15

Number of rooms	4
shared bathrooms	2

Activities: 🍷 🚤 🏇 🐎

---

17. LES ÉBOULEMENTS

★★ F E ♿ 🛶 P 🐕 R.5

Up in the heights of Les Éboulements, overlooking the St. Lawrence and Isle-aux-Coudres and centred among the marvels of Charlevoix, Auberge La Bouclée is a haven of peace for your vacation. Fall in love... An old-fashioned charm that thrills many a heart. For groups, families or sweethearts, young and old, our family welcomes you into its home.

From Baie St-Paul, Rte 362 E. twd La Malbaie/Isle-aux-Coudres, drive about 16km. Right at the flashing light. Left after 500m. Welcome.

INN
AUBERGE LA BOUCLÉE

Ginette and Mario Ouellet
6, route du Port
Les Éboulements G0A 2M0
(418) 635-2531
toll free 1-888-635-2531
www.quebecweb.com/
labouclee

B&B	
single	$52
double	$69-89
triple	$104
quad.	$119
child	$0-15

Taxes extra VS MC ER IT

Reduced rates: Oct. 20 to June 20
Open year round

Number of rooms	9
rooms with sink	9
shared wc	1
shared bathrooms	4

Activities: 🏛 🏇 🛷 🎿 🏃

---

18. LES ÉBOULEMENTS

★★★ F e P 🛶 ✕ TA

Amidst cultural and sports activities, inn Le Surouêt (southwest wind) offers an unobstructed view of Île-aux-Coudres, a grand decor, luxury rooms with balcony and fireplace, dining room, terrace, tea room, fine cuisine, art gallery and gift shop. All under the same roof for an unforgettable stay.

From Baie-St-Paul. Rte 362 E. for 16km. 700m from flashing light. We are on the right. Welcome.

INN
AUBERGE LE SUROUÊT

Micheline and Rhéaume Gélinas
195, rue Principale
Les Éboulements G0A 2M0
(418) 635-1401
toll free 1-888- 935-1401
fax (418) 635-1404

	B&B	MAP
single	$82-$102	$110-130
double	$105-125	$160-180
triple	$140	$215
child	$17.⁵⁰	$27.⁵⁰

Taxes extra VS MC AM ER IT

Reduced rates: 10 % from Sep. 15 to June 15
Open year round

Number of rooms	5
rooms with private bath	5

Activities: 🏛 🍷 🏃 🎿 🐎

19. LES ÉBOULEMENTS

☀☀☀ F e ♿ P 🐕 R2

Experience an extraordinary holiday with me in my ancestral home, located in the middle of Charlevoix. In the mountains with a view of the St. Lawrence, in the great outdoors yet close to all the great tourist attractions: whales, casino, Île-aux-Coudres, Baie-St-Paul, etc.

From Québec City, via Rte 138, enter Baie-St-Paul, twd the church, straight to Les Éboulements, Rte 362 E., for about 14km.

B&B
GÎTE DU VACANCIER

Jacqueline Audet
104, Route 362
Rang St-Joseph
Les Éboulements G0A 2M0
(418) 635-2736
(418) 653-5861
www.quebecweb.com/gpc

B&B	
single	$35-45
double	$45-60
triple	$60-75
quad.	$65-80
child	$10-15

Open: June 15 to Oct. 15

Number of rooms	5
rooms with private bath	1
rooms with sink	4
shared bathrooms	2

Activities: 🏛 🛶 ⛴ 🚶 🚴

20. LES ÉBOULEMENTS

☀☀☀ F e 🚗 P R2

Ancestral house facing Île-aux-Coudres. The village's first hotel in 1930. Decor in the style of yesteryear. Relax on the big porch and admire the mountains and the river that runs between the houses. A paradise to discover, amidst the region's tourist attractions. Varied all-you-can-eat breakfast complemented by little treats lovingly prepared by your hosts.

From Québec City, Rte 138 East to Baie-St-Paul. From Baie-St-Paul, Rte 362 East to Les Éboulements.

B&B
GÎTE VILLA DES ROSES

Pierrette Simard and
Leonce Tremblay
290, rue Principale, C.P. 28
Les Éboulements G0A 2M0
(418) 635-2733

B&B	
single	$40
double	$50
triple	$70
child	$0-15

Reduced rates: Oct. 15 to June 15
Open year round

Number of rooms	5
rooms with sink	4
shared wc	3
shared bathrooms	2

Activities: 🏛 🛶 🚴 🎿 🐎

21. LES ÉBOULEMENTS

☀☀☀ F e P R1.5 TA

Nestled between the mountains and the river, this 200-year-old house offers, calm, reverie and peace of mind. Comfortable familly-size rooms with private bathrooms, antique furniture, a smiling welcome and the delight of home-made pastries and jams make for a veritable Nid-Chouette, or cute little nest!

From Québec City, twd Ste-Anne-de-Beaupré, Rte 138 E. to Baie-St-Paul (about 100km). From Baie-St-Paul, Rte 362 E. to Les Éboulements, drive 20km. Or from La Malbaie, Rte 362 W. for 25km.

B&B
LE NICHOUETTE

Gilberte Tremblay
216, rue Principale
Les Éboulements G0A 2M0
(418) 635-2458
www.chouette.freeservers.
com/nichouette.html
chouette@cite.net

B&B	
single	$40
double	$50
triple	$70
quad.	$90
child	$0-12

VS MC

Open: May 1 to Oct. 31

Number of rooms	3
rooms with private bath	3

Activities: 🏛 🍷 ⛴ 🚶 🚶

22. PETITE-RIVIÈRE-ST-FRANÇOIS ★★★ F e 🚗 P 🛥 ✕ R1.5 TA

Located by the majestic St. Lawrence River and near the "Le Massif" ski resort, our house is a haven of peace. Enjoy an exhilarating holiday, a good chat, a delicious meal and the luxury of a cosy *courtepointe* or quilt. Come and get to know us. "Bonnes Tables du Québec" directory, 3-star hotel. Panoramic view.
Your hosts,
Alice and Maurice.

From Québec City twd Baie-St-Paul, 90km. Right at Petite-Rivière-St-François sign, for 8km, left on Rue Racine.

INN
AUBERGE LA COURTEPOINTE

Alice and Maurice Bouchard
8, rue Racine
Petite-Rivière-St-François
GOA 2LO
(418) 632-5858
fax (418) 632-5786
www.aubergelacourtepointe.
qbc.net

	B&B	MAP
single	$50	$70
double	$90	$130

Taxes extra VS MC AM ER IT

Open year round

Number of rooms	8
rooms with private bath	8

Activities: 🏛 ⛏ 🏃 🎿 🏃

23. PETITE-RIVIÈRE-ST-FRANÇOIS ☀☀☀☀ F E 🚭 P R4 TA

Charlevoix Excellence Prize 1996-97. Mountain B&B in the Rivière-du-Sot valley near the Massif ski resort and Baie-St-Paul. Balcony overlooking the river with a view of Charlevoix's "extravagant" landscape. And of course... the VIP treatment... **See colour photos.**

From Québec City, drive 90km twd Baie-St-Paul. At the Petite-Rivière-St-François sign turn right. Drive 3km, our house is 200m back on the left-hand side of the road.

B&B
TOURLOGNON

Lise Archambault and
Irénée Marier
279, rue Principale
Petite-Rivière-St-François
GOA 2LO
tel/fax (418) 632-5708
toll free 1-888-868-7564
www.quebecweb.
com/tourlognon
irenee@charlevoix.net

B&B	
single	$65-70
double	$80-90
triple	$100-105
child	$15

Taxes extra MC

Open year round

Number of rooms	5
rooms with private bath	5

Activities: 🏛 🛷 🏃 🎿 🏃

24. POINTE-AU-PIC ☀☀☀ F e ♿ 🐕 P R1 TA

My ready smile and Charlevoix's down-to-earth people bid you a warm welcome. Clean, spacious rooms with antique decor and copious breakfasts. We have been told: "your warm welcome makes us feel right at home". Near major tourist attractions: casino, museum, golf, etc. Let yourselves be pampered!

From Québec City, Rte 138 E. twd La Malbaie. At Manoir Richelieu, straight for about 1km, left from the hill. Or Rte 362 twd Pointe-au-Pic, 2km from Golf du Manoir, right from the hill.

B&B
GÎTE BELLEVUE

Louise Forgues
107, côte Bellevue
Pointe-au-Pic GOT 1MO
(418) 665-6126
(418) 438-2649
toll free 1-888-824-6263
patriot@cam.org

B&B	
single	$45-55
double	$55-90
triple	$75-100
quad.	$100-120
child	$10

Reduced rates: 10% Feb. to Apr.
Open year round

Number of rooms	5
rooms with private bath	1
shared bathrooms	2

Activities: 🏛 🚣 ⛏ 🛷 🎿

25. POINTE-AU-PIC

☀☀☀☀ F E 🐕 P 🚗 R.5 TA

Charlevoix Excellence Prize 1995-96. Come enjoy peace and comfort in a warm and cozy Austrian house overlooking the winding St. Lawrence River and away from the main road, designed with you in mind. Private entrance, fireplace, balcony, terraces, flowery gardens and varied breakfasts! In the midst of activities, 5 min from the casino.

Québec City, Rte 138 E to La Malbaie. Leclerc bridge: Rte 362 W, 4.4km, left on Côteau-sur-Mer. From Baie-St-Paul, Rte 362 E to La Malbaie, Pointe-au-Pic. 2km from Manoir Richelieu golf club, right on Côteau-sur-Mer.

B&B
LA MAISON FRIZZI

Raymonde Vermette
8, Côteau-sur-Mer, C.P. 526
La Malbaie, Pointe-au-Pic
G0T 1M0
(418) 665-4668
fax (418) 665-1143
www.quebecweb.
com/gpc/maisonfrizzi/
introfranc.htm

B&B	
single	$50-60
double	$65-75
triple	$85-95
child	$0-15

VS MC

Reduced rates: Oct. 15 to Dec. 20, Apr. 1 to June 1
Open year round

Number of rooms	4
rooms with sink	4
shared bathrooms	2

Activities: 🏛 🛷 🐕 🛶 🎿

---

26. POINTE-AU-PIC

★★ F E 🚗 P R1 TA

The ancestral Eau Berge house faces the river and welcomes you with its unique decor. The rooms are particulary comfortable and inviting. Choice of healthy breakfast, or otherwise! Come and be refreshed. Close to the casino and other activities. See you soon.

From Québec City, twd Ste-Anne-de-Beaupré. Rte 138 E. twd La Malbaie. At the traffic lights of the bridge, continue straight. 500m from the shopping centre. On the right across from the "Irving". Or Rte 362 to Pointe-au-Pic, staight beside the river, on the boulevard. At the "Irving" on the left.

INN
L'EAU BERGE

Claudette Dessureault
1220, boul. De Comporte, C.P. 152
Pointe-au-Pic G0T 1M0
(418) 665-3003
fax (418) 665-2480
www.quebecweb.
com/leauberge

B&B	
single	$60-100
double	$65-105
triple	$90-125
quad.	$145
child	$15-20

Taxes extra VS MC

Open: Jan. 20 to Oct. 31

Number of rooms	7
rooms with sink	1
rooms with private bath	2
shared wc	1
shared bathrooms	2

Activities: 🏛 🛶 🛷 🐕 🎿

---

27. ST-AIMÉ-DES-LACS

★★ F E ♿ P 🐴 ✕ TA

Large property in the mountains with spacious rooms, relaxation at the field-stone fireplace, cozy bar, dinning room with panoramic view of the surrounding heights, and a menu featuring refined cuisine made with regional products. Gather around the outdoor fireplace, or the gazebo, in the terraced flower gardens. Hiking trails, outdoor activities, park, and a lookout onto the great hinterland of the Menaud country.

Rte 138 between St-Hilarion and Clermont, St-Aimé Exit, follow blue tourist signs. We are 13km from the start, passed a little white bridge, on your right, at 23km from the Parc des Hautes-Gorges.

INN
AUBERGE LE RELAIS DES
HAUTES GORGES

Lucille Dazé and Rhéal Séguin
317, rue Principale
St-Aimé-des-Lacs G0T 1S0
tel/fax (418) 439-5110
toll free 1-800-889-7655
www.quebecweb.com/relais

	B&B	MAP
single	$55-70	$85-120
double	$68-80	$110-130
triple	$95-100	$155-175
quad.	$120-130	$195-210
child	$0-15	$0-30

Taxes extra VS MC

Reduced rates: Nov. and Apr.
Open year round

Number of rooms	8
rooms with private bath	8
shared wc	2

Activities: 🛶 🐴 🛶 🚴 🐎

28. ST-FIDÈLE

☀☀☀ F e 🐾 🛏 P R.5

Situated in St-Fidèle, about 10km from La Malbaie/Pointe-au-Pic, Gîte Le Savayard has a charming decor furnished with genuine antiques. Nestled in a small corner of paradise surrounded by flowers in the summertime. You will be welcomed like one of the family here in our typically Québécois home. Enjoy a healthy breakfast facing the garden. Open year round. We look forward to seeing you soon!

From Québec City, Rte 138 East for Tadousac.

B&B
LE SAVAYARD

Lisette Savard
142 rue Principale
St-Fidèle G0T 1T0
(418) 434-2837

B&B	
single	$30
double	$45
child	$10

Open year round

Number of rooms	4
shared bathrooms	2

Activities: 🏛 🛷 🎿 ⛷ 🏃

29. ST-IRÉNÉE

F E 🛏 P R1 TA

Our cosy B&B offers a peaceful haven with a beautiful view of the St. Lawrence River. Your host Danielle welcomes you with open arms. She will make you feel at home, and will ensure that you are pampered with fine cuisine and interesting excursions, such as the "Domaine Forget concerts" or whale cruises. Welcome home!

From Québec City, Rte 138 East for Baie-St-Paul, Rte 362 East for St-Irénée, 25km. From La Malbaie, Rte 362 West about 15km.

B&B
AUX 5 PIGNONS

Danielle Papineau
1021 rang Terrebonne
St-Irénée
G0T 1V0
(418) 452-8151

B&B	
single	$45-55
double	$55-65
triple	$70-80
quad.	$15

Taxes extra VS MC

Open year round

Number of rooms	5
rooms with private bath	2
shared wc	1
shared bathrooms	1

Activities: 🛶 🎿 🏃 🐎 ⛷

30. ST-IRÉNÉE

F e ♿ 🛏 P TA

After 35 years of living in Saint-Irénée, I had the chance to purchase a classic Charlevoix house set on the edge of a one-of-a-kind beach on the St. Lawrence. Come get away from it all in this extremely relaxing setting.
Lucie Tremblay.

From Québec City, Route 138, about 120km. Route 362 across from the Baie-St-Paul church. Scenic highway to Saint-Irénée, 25km. From La Malbaie, Route 362 West for about 15km.

INN
LA LUCIOLE

Lucie Tremblay
178, chemin les Bains
St-Irénée G0T 1V0
(418) 452-8283
www.quebecweb.com/luciole
lucie.tremblay2@sympatico.ca

B&B	
single	$50
double	$55-65-85
triple	$75
child	$10

VS

Open year round

Number of rooms	6
rooms with private bath	1
rooms with sink	1
shared bathrooms	2
shared wc	1

Activities: 🏛 🛷 🛶 🎿 🏃

31. ST-IRÉNÉE

F E ☒ P TA

Nestled in the heart of the St-Irénée hills overlooking the sea, Le Rustique stands out among other B&Bs in Charlevoix. Because his owner is well travelled, this beautiful residence has a colourful ambiance and is renowned for its cuisine. Our B&B attracts city dwellers looking for a getaway, as well as music lovers (Domaine Forget concert packages).

From Québec, Rte 138 to Baie-St-Paul, 90km, Rte 362 to St-Irénée 25km, 500m right at the church. From La Malbaie, Rte 362 West, 15km.

INN
LE RUSTIQUE

Diane Lapointe
102, rue Principale
St-Irénée G0T 1V0
(418) 452-8250

B&B	
single	$45-55
double	$55-70
triple	$75-80
quad.	$85-90

Taxes extra VS MC IT

Reduced rates: May 1 to June 25, Sep. 3 to Oct. 26
Open: May 1 to Oct. 26

Number of rooms	6
shared wc	3
shared bathrooms	2

Activities: 🏛 ⛴ 🚤 🚶 🐎

32. ST-IRÉNÉE

✎ F E ♿ P 🚭 R3

Perched on the high cliffs of St-Irénée and next to the Domaine Forget concert hall, the Manoir offers spacious rooms and a breathtaking view of the St. Lawrence and Charlevoix mountains. 2-km-long seaside promenade in La Malbaie. Superb terrace for breakfast. Packages change with the seasons.

From Québec City, Rte 138 to Baie-St-Paul, then Rte 362 (La Panoramique) to St-Irénée, 25km. From La Malbaie, Rte 362 W., 15km.

B&B
MANOIR HORTENSIA

Alida Landry
320, chemin les Bains
St-Irénée G0T 1V0
(418) 452-8180
tel/fax (418) 452-3357
www.quebecweb.
com/hortensia
alidal@sympatico.ca

B&B	
single	$60-110
double	$75-125
child	$20

Taxes extra VS MC IT

Open year round

Number of rooms	5
rooms with private bath	4
shared wc	1
shared bathrooms	1

Activities: 🏛 ⛴ 🎿 🏃

33. ST-IRÉNÉE

☀☀☀ F E P R2

Come stay in our beautiful family home or in our lodge, which has kitchenettes. The rooms have panoramic views, some with balconies, verandas or fireplaces. From our 225 m altitude, you have a 100km-view of the shores of the St. Lawrence River. Located 2km from the St. Lawrence River and Domaine Forget. Come joke around with retired folks and history lovers.

From Québec City, Rte 138 East to Baie-St-Paul. Rte 362 to St- Irénée. 100m east of the pier, Chemin St-Antoine, drive 2km. From La Malbaie, Rte 362 West.

B&B
VILLA GRANDE VUE

Irène Desroches and
Gilles-M. Girard
325, St-Antoine
St-Irénée G0T 1V0
(418) 452-3209

B&B	
single	$40-65
double	$50-70
triple	$60-85

Reduced rates: 7 nights or more
Open year round

Number of rooms	5
rooms with private bath	2
rooms with sink	3
shared bathrooms	1

Activities: 🏊 ⛴ 🚤 🚶 🏃

34. ST-SIMÉON, BAIE-DES-ROCHERS

☀☀☀ F e P 🏊 🐕 R1 TA

You are invited to stop over in the hamlet of Baie-des-Rochers where warmth, peace and comfort come together. Nature awaits with the river flowing behind the house. The bay is 3km away, as is the network of hiking trails offering staggering panoramic views of the surroundings.

From Québec City, Rte 138 E. twd Tadoussac. 15km from St-Siméon at the corner store, sign indicating "Gîte de la Baie", turn right.

B&B
GÎTE DE LA BAIE

Judith and Maurice Morneau
68, rue de la Chapelle
Baie-des-Rochers
St-Siméon GOT 1X0
(418) 638-2821
www.quebecweb.
com/gpc/gitedelabaie
/introfranc.htm

B&B	
single	$30
double	$55
triple	$70
quad.	$80
child	$10

Open: June 1 to Oct. 13

Number of rooms	5
rooms with private bath	2
shared bathrooms	2

Activities: 🍷 ⛴ 🚤 🏃 🐎

35. ST-URBAIN

☀☀☀ F e 🚗 P R1.3 TA

Charlevoix 1999 Excellence Prize, Tourisme Québec, Regional Prize Hospitality and Customer Service 1999. 20-year-old B&B in the heart of Charlevoix. 10 min from Parc des Grands-Jardins, Mont du Lac des Cygnes, Baie-St-Paul; 30 min from Parc des Hautes-Gorges. Various activities, reservations possible. On site: salmon river, picnic (BBQ) area and emu farm. Ancestral house. Large lounge with TV. Varied breakfasts. See you soon! **See colour photos.**

From Québec City, Rte 138 East. 10km past Baie-St-Paul, Rte 381 North, continue for 3km.

B&B
CHEZ GERTRUDE

Gertrude and
RaymondeTremblay
706, St-Édouard, rte 381
C.P 293, St-Urbain GOA 4K0
(418) 639-2205
fax (418) 639-1130
www.quebecweb.com/gertrude
raymondetremblay
@videotron.ca

B&B	
single	$38-40
double	$50-55
triple	$65-70
quad.	$80-85
child	$10-15

Open year round

Number of rooms	5
rooms with sink	5
shared wc	4
shared bathrooms	2

Activities: 🏃 🚲 🎿 🏃 🐎

CHAUDIÈRE-APPALACHES

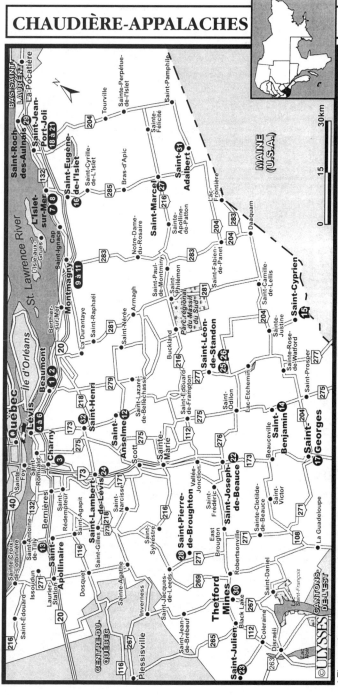

* The numbers on the map refer to the numbering of the establishments of this region

1. BEAUMONT

☀☀☀☀ F E 🚫 P 🐾 R5 TA

Chaudière Appalaches Excellence Prize 1997-1998. Warm and friendly hospitality in bicentenary Québec-style home with country decor and period furnishing. Snuggle up by the old fireplace or wood burning stove. Just 15 min from ferry boat to the heart of old Québec City and Irish Mem. Nat. Hist. Site. Ideal stop between Ontario and the Maritimes.

From Montréal, Québec City or Riv.-du-Loup, Rte 132 to Beaumont, turn on Rte 279 S. twd St-Charles. Pass the highway, 1st road right, Ch. St-Roch for 1.8 km.

B&B
AU GRÉ DU VENT

Michèle Fournier and Jean L'Heureux
220, chemin St-Roch
Beaumont G0R 1C0
(418) 838-9020
fax (418) 838-9074
www.bbcanada.
com/2487.html
augreduvent@msn.com

B&B	
single	$50-60
double	$55-65
triple	$70-80
quad.	$90
child	$0-15

VS

Open: May 1 to Sep. 30,
Oct. 1 to Apr. 30
(with reservation)

Number of rooms	3
rooms with sink	2
shared bathrooms	1

Activities: 🐚 🏛 🎿 🚶 🚴

2. BEAUMONT

☀☀☀☀☀ F E P 🛶 R1 TA

110-acre property overlooking the St. Lawrence River. 15min from the bridges and the Lévis/Québec ferry. Charming, restored 30-room mansion. Sumptuous and comfortable rooms. Antique decor, peaceful and romantic ambiance, breakfast with fine silver, view of more than 20 church steeples, heated pool, snowmobile. Chateau living! 20% low-season discounts.

From Québec City, Hwy 20 E., Exit 330 N., Rte 132 E. for 4km. From Riv.-du-Loup, Hwy 20 W., Exit 337 N., Rte 132 West for 1km.

B&B
MANOIR DE BEAUMONT

Denis Vézina
485, du Fleuve, route 132
Beaumont G0R 1C0
(418) 833-5635
fax (418) 833-7891
www.manoir
debeaumont.qbc.net
manoirbeaumont
@sympatico.ca

B&B	
single	$85-125
double	$100-150
triple	$150

Taxes extra VS MC AM IT

Reduced rates: 20% Jan. 1 to May 31 and Sep. 17 to Dec. 31
Open year round

Number of rooms	5
rooms with private bath	3
shared bathrooms	2

Activities: 🐚 🛶 🎿 🚴 🏃

3. CHARNY

☀☀☀ F E P 🚗 🚫 R.2

A place where one feels in the country while right by the bridges to Québec City, access to Boul. Champlain, which leads straight to old Québec City in 15min. Easy access to bike paths. Quiet area near many services. Relax and enjoy breakfast on the flowery terrace. Refined, varied breakfasts. Good value for the price.

From Montréal, Hwy 20; or from Québec City, Pierre-Laporte bridge twd Rivière-du-Loup, Charny Exit 175 South. At 1st lights, right on Ave. Sous le Vent, left on du Mistral, about 400m.

B&B
LE GÎTE DE LA
CHUTE CHAUDIÈRE

Yvette McIntyre
and Normand Beaudin
8069, du Mistral
Charny G6X 1G1
(418) 832-0728
www.bbcanada.com
/4090.html
normandbeaudin@videotron.ca

B&B	
single	$40
double	$50
child	$10

Open year round

Number of rooms	3
rooms with sink	3
rooms in basement	3
shared bathrooms	2

Activities: 🛶 🚴 🏇 🛷 ⛷

4. LÉVIS

\ F e 🚫 P R.5

Located in the heart of Vieux-Lévis, Auberge de la Visitation is a haven of peace in a wooded area next to a monastery. Learn about the history from the builders of Lévis who inhabited this area. Courteous service, cordial atmosphere and numerous activities within walking distance.

Hwy 20, Exit 325 North, straight on Président-Kennedy, drive 2.5km to St-Georges, turn right, 1km. From the ferryboat, Côte du Passage to St-Georges, turn left, drive 0.3km.

B&B
AUBERGE DE LA VISITATION

Ginette L'Heureux and
Martin Bergeron
6104, rue St-Georges
Lévis G6V 4J8
(418) 837-9619

B&B	
single	$45
double	$55
child	$10

VS MC

Open: May 1 to Sep.30, Oct. 1 to Apr. 30, with reservation except Dec. 24 to Jan. 2

Number of rooms	3
rooms with sink	3
shared wc	1
shared bathrooms	1

Activities: 🏛 🍴 🚣 🚶 🚴

---

5. LÉVIS

☀☀☀ F E 🚗 P R.5

Overlooking the St. Lawrence River, facing Old Québec. Near the ferry. Scenic tours. Enchanting light show, from the residence or terrace. Comfort. Relax by the fire. Central air conditioning. Welcome.

From Québec City or Riv.-du-Loup Hwy 20 Exit 327 right on Mgr-Bourget. After 2nd light, drive 1km, left on Champagnat. At 2nd stop right on Des Bosquets. From ferry, in Lévis, right on Côte du Passage, after 1st light left on Champagnat, after 6 stops, left on Des Bosquets.

B&B
GÎTE AUX BOSQUETS

Véronique and Émile Pelletier
162, rue des Bosquets
Lévis G6V 6V7
(418) 835-3494
fax (418) 835-0563
toll free for reservation only
1-888-335-3959

B&B	
single	$35-40
double	$50-60
triple	$70-75
quad.	$85

VS MC

Open year round

Number of rooms	3
rooms with private bath	2
shared bathrooms	1

Activities: 🏛 🚣 🚶 🚴

---

6. LÉVIS

☀☀☀☀ F e 🐕 🚗 P R.5 TA

La Maison sous L'Orme is an old renovated home in Vieux-Lévis that has a warm character and a large veranda overlooking Québec City. Located in a peaceful area of town, it has a private living room, food service, generous breakfast and queen beds. A 5min walk from the ferryboat takes you to the heart of Vieux-Québec.

Hwy 20, Exit 325 North or Rte 132 or the ferryboat. Follow the signs for the hospital. Before the hospital, Rue Wolfe. 150m, turn right on St-Félix.

B&B
LA MAISON SOUS L'ORME

Anne and André Carrier
1, rue St-Félix
Lévis G6V 5J1
(418) 833-0247
toll free 1-888-747-0247
sous.orme@qc.aira.com

B&B	
single	$65
double	$75
triple	$90
quad.	$105
child	$10

MC

Open year round

Number of rooms	3
rooms with private bath	3

Activities: 🍴 🚣 🚶 🚴 🛷

7. L'ISLET-SUR-MER

★★★ F E ⊘ ✕ 🛥 P R1 TA

We invite you to experience the history of the Côte-du-Sud in a large 5-dormer manor from the French regime (1754). Fully renovated. Quiet central air conditioning, queen-size beds, cable TV. Rooms: economy, standard, premium. Hearty breakfast, warm welcome. Packages: Grosse-Île, golf, cycling, theatre, ornithology, etc. In-house meals. 3-diamonds AAA (CAA).

100km from Québec City, south shore Hwy 20, Exit 400, Rte 285 North, 2.5km. Turn right on Rte 132 East, 1km, 150m east of the Maritime museum.

INN
AUBERGE LA MARGUERITE

Claire Leblanc
88, Des Pionniers Est, rte 132
L'Islet-sur-Mer G0R 2B0
(418) 247-5454
Canada toll free
1-877-788-5454
www.quebecweb.
com/lamarguerite

B&B	
single	$69-134
double	$84-148
child	$10-18

Taxes extra VS MC IT

Reduced rates: Nov. 1 to May 15, except for holidays and long week-ends
Open year round

Number of rooms	8
rooms with private bath	8
shared wc	1

Activities: 🏛 🦆 ⛴ 🚶 🚲

8. L'ISLET-SUR-MER

☀☀☀ F e ⊘ P 🛥 🐕 R.5 TA

A privileged place for relaxing to the sound of the waves. Charming, very comfortable hundred-year-old house specially decorated for you. Dreamy rooms and dining room on the river. Fancy health/delicacy breakfast. Snow geese in the fall, relaxation, photo-graphy, fresh air, music and hospitality. **Ad end of this region.**

One hour from Québec City or Riv.-du-Loup, 100km, Hwy 20, Exit L'Islet North, Rte 132 East Chemin des Pionniers East for 5km, or Exit St-Jean-Port-Joli North, Rte 132 West, 10km.

B&B
LES PIEDS DANS L'EAU

Solange Tremblay
549, des Pionniers Est
L'Islet-sur-Mer G0R 2B0
(418) 247-5575
fax (418) 247-7772
members.xoom.
com/presweb/lespiedsdansleau
seul@globetrotter.net

B&B	
single	$40-50
double	$55-75
triple	$80-100
quad.	$110-130
child	$20

Reduced rates: Dec. 1 to Feb. 1
Open year round

Number of rooms	4
rooms in basement	1
rooms with private bath	2
rooms with sink	1
shared wc	2
shared bathrooms	1

Activities: 🏛 ⛴ 🐎 🛷 🎿

9. MONTMAGNY

F E ✕ 🛥 P R.5 TA

This small corner of Europe in the middle of old Montmagny will delight you! Enjoy our warm welcome in this cosy, turn-of-the-century home with Victorian-style rooms. Sample the tasty, authentic cuisine in the quiet ambience of our dining room or stretch out on our sunny terrace. A variety of packages are offered: visiting Grosse-Île, golfing, flying, biking, skiing on a «lunar ground», snowmobiling, relax-ation—and much more.

Hwy 20 East, Exits 376 or 378 for the town centre or the scenic Rte 132. Snowmobilers: path 75 and 55.

INN
AUBERGE LA BELLE ÉPOQUE

Carole Gagné
100, St-Jean-Baptiste est
Montmagny G5V 1K3
(418) 248-3373
toll free 1-800-490-3373
fax (418) 248-7957
www.epoque.qc.ca
info@epoque.qc.ca

	B&B	MAP
single	$77-97	$99-119
double	$85-105	$130-150

Taxes extra VS MC

Open year round

Number of rooms	5
rooms with private bath	5

Activities: 🏛 ⛴ 🚶 🛷 🎿

10. MONTMAGNY

F | e | 🚭 | 🚗 | P | R1 | TA

Only 40 min from Québec City, discover the Snow Goose capital, nature, a superb woodland, a calm and inviting home. Comfortable rooms with fans. Wake up to the birds singing and enjoy a generous breakfast "à la Cécilienne". Golf, cruises to the national historic site of Grosse-Île and to Île-aux-Grues. World Accordion Jamboree festival and goose hunting. Welcome: make yourselves at home.

From Québec city, Hwy 20, Exit 376, ch. des Poiriers, rte 132 East, cross the bridge of Rivière-du-Sud, continue for 0.5km. The B&B is on the right.

B&B
LA CÉCILIENNE

Doris and Cécile Boudreau
340, boul. Taché Est
Montmagny G5V 1E1
(418) 248-0165
www.bbcanada.com/
2853.html

B&B	
single	$40-45
double	$55
child	$15-20

VS

Open year round

Number of rooms	4
shared bathrooms	2

Activities: 🏛 ♣ 🚤 🏃 🚲

11. MONTMAGNY

☀☀☀ | F | E | 🚭 | 🐕 | 🚗 | P | R.2

We would like to share the charm of our beautiful 200-years-old home with you. Furnished with pieces of period furniture, you will enjoy its peaceful, cheery atmosphere. You can either relax on our large land-scaped property or visit the activity centre 4min away. Generous break-fasts served up in a friendly home. A hearty welcome to all.

From Québec City, Hwy 20 East, Exit 376, Chemin des Poiriers, Rte 132 East, 1.1km. At the college, drive twd the centre of town, Rue Fabrique, 0.2km.

B&B
LES DEUX MARQUISES

Danielle Proulx
153 St-Joseph
Montmagny G5V 1H9
(418) 248-2178
les2.marquises@globetrotter.net

B&B	
single	$50
double	$60-65
child	$15

Open: Mar. 1 to Jan. 31

Number of rooms	4
rooms with private bath	1
rooms with sink	1
shared bathrooms	2

Activities: 🏛 🚤 🏃 🚲 🎿

12. ST-ANSELME ✕

☀☀☀☀ | F | e | 🚭 | P | 🏊 | R.5

In the heart of Chaudière-Appalaches, on the doorstep of the Beauce, a dreamy spot decorated to ensure comfort, escape relaxation. Soundproofed rooms, boudoirs, livingroom, fireplace, hot tub, etc. Outdoor fireplace, 40' heated pool, patio, terrace, flowery wooded property. Golf, cycling, skiing. Staying at Douces Évasions is energizing, enriching. Welcome! Room with kitchenette and living room in the basement.

20 min from Québec City. Hwy20, Exit 325 S. twd Lac Etchemin, right at the entrance of St-Anselme.

B&B
DOUCES ÉVASIONS

Gabrielle Corriveau and
Gérard Bilodeau
1043, boul. Bégin, rte 277
St-Anselme G0R 2N0
tel/fax (418) 885-9033
418-885-4533
www.quebecweb.
com/evasions
gabycor@globetrotter.net

B&B	
single	$50-55
double	$65
child	$15

Reduced rates: 10% for 5 nights and more
Open year round

Number of rooms	3
rooms with private bath	1
rooms in basement	1
shared bathrooms	2

Activities: ♣ 🚙 🚲 🏃 🎿

13. ST-APOLLINAIRE

❄❄❄ F e ⊘ ✕ P 🚗 R3 TA

Enjoy a stay at our bicentenary house, located just 20min from Québec City. A haven of peace and gourmet food await you here, as do horseback riding, carriage and sleigh rides, snowmobiling, farm activities... Packages available by reservation. Near bike path and skidoo trail, saphouse, Domaine Joly, St. Lawrence River.

Hwy 20, Exit 291, Rte 273 North twd St-Antoine-de-Tilly, continue for 2.5km. Turn right, 1.7km.

B&B
NOTRE CAMPAGNE D'ANTAN

Marie-Claude Roux and
Donald Foster
412, rang Bois-Franc Est
St-Apollinaire G0S 2E0
(418) 881-3418

B&B	
single	$45
double	$55
child	$20

Open year round

Number of rooms	2
shared bathrooms	1

Activities: 🎿 🚲 🐎 ⛷ 🏃

---

14. ST-BENJAMIN, BEAUCE

❄❄❄ F e P R.5 TA

In the heart of this lovely back-country village stands L'Antiquaille, filled with an atmosphere of yesteryear. Come admire our collection of antiques: wood-burning stoves, clawfoot baths, old curios, lace... Breakfast is the hostess' secret! Room with 1925 furniture.

Hwy 20, Exit Hwy 73 South twd St-Georges, Exit 173 South. In St-Odilon, turn right on Rte 275 South twd St-Benjamin.

B&B
L'ANTIQUAILLE

Jacqueline and Catherine
218, rue Principale
St-Benjamin G0M 1N0
(418) 594-8693

B&B	
single	$30
double	$45-50

Open: Apr. 1 to Oct. 30

Number of rooms	4
rooms in basement	1
shared wc	1
shared bathrooms	1

Activities: 🏛 🍷 🛶 🎿 🚲

---

15. ST-CYPRIEN

❄❄❄ F e ⊘ P R6

Our B&B is located in the heart of a luxuriant landscape in maple country. Discover: mini farm, organic garden, birds, etc. Healthy breakfast and treats: home-made jams and maple products. Cycling path and skidoo trail right nearby. Packages: health, exploring the maple grove and our saphouse. Hélène (the owner) is a nurse. We are pleased to welcome you. **Farm Stay p 38.**

From Québec City, Hwy 20 East, twd Lac-Etchemin Exit 325, Rte 277 South to Rte 204. Twd Ste-Justine for 7.8km, then right twd St-Cyprien.

B&B
LE JARDIN DES MÉSANGES

Hélène Couture and
Roger Provost
482, route Fortier
St-Cyprien, Barré G0R1B0
tel/fax (418) 383-5777

	B&B	MAP
single	$40	$50
double	$55	$75
triple	$70	$100
quad.	$85	$125
child	$5-15	$15-25

Taxes extra

Open year round

Number of rooms	4
shared bathrooms	3

Activities: 🏛 🍷 🏃 ⛷

16. ST-EUGÈNE-DE-L'ISLET

★★★ F e P ⊠ ☒ TA

Chaudière-Applalaches Excellence Prize 1999. Delightful former seigneurial mill will seduce you with its warm ambiance, country decor, gastronomic cuisine. In the heart of a vast estate, the inn boasts remarkable surroundings: river, swimming lake, bird-watching trails. Various packages (golf, cycling, cruise, massage, skiing) also offered. Very romantic! **See colour photos.**

On the south shore, 1 hour from Québec City. At Exit 400 off Hwy 20 E., turn left twd St-Eugène-de-L'Islet, left on Rang Lamartine and left on Route Tortue.

INN
AUBERGE DES GLACIS

Micheline Sibuet and
Pierre Walters
46, route de la Tortue
St-Eugène-de-l'Islet G0R 1X0
(418) 247-7486
toll free 1-877-245-2247
fax (418) 247-7182
www.aubergedesglacis.com
aubergedesglacis@hotmail.com

	B&B	MAP
single	$94-109	$124-139
double	$104-119	$164-179
suites-dbl	$129-149	$189-209

Taxes extra VS MC AM IT

Reduced rates: 3 to 5 nights during the the week and the low season (rates on request)
Open year round

Number of rooms	10
rooms with private bath	10

Activities: 🚤 ⛵ 🎣 🏃

17. ST-GEORGES, BEAUCE

☀☀☀ F e P R3 TA

Dream decor you will fall in love with. Large house with antiques. Sleep on a 125-year-old canopy bed... Romantic decor of old lamps and lace... Period photos of ancestors... Flowery countryside in beautiful region. Hearty breakfast, china wear and table lace. Golf, museum, warm welcome.

From Québec City, Rte 73 S. In Vallée-Jonction, Rte 173 S. twd St-Georges. After McDonald's, left on 90e Rue, drive 3km, left on 35e Ave, 9th house on the right.

B&B
GÎTE LA SÉRÉNADE

Berthe and Bernard Bisson
8835, 35th Av.
St-Georges-de-Beauce Est
G5Y 5C2
(418) 228-1059

	B&B
single	$49
double	$59
triple	$74
child	$15

VS

Open year round

Number of rooms	4
shared wc	1
shared bathrooms	1

Activities: 🏛 🍷 🎣 ⛷ 🏃

18. ST-JEAN-PORT-JOLI

☀☀☀ F E P R.1 TA

Authentic 200-year-old Canadian home located in the heart of the sculpture capital of Québec and by the St. Lawrence River. In our house it is our pleasure to receive you as a friend. Year-round package for maple grove visits and tastings. **Ad end of this region.**

From Montréal or Québec, Hwy 20 East, Exit 414, turn right, to Rte 132. At Rte 132 turn right, drive 0.5km. Large white house with red roof, 100m past the church.

B&B
AU BOISÉ JOLI

Michelle Bélanger and
Hermann Jalbert
41, de Gaspé Est
St-Jean-Port-Joli G0R 3G0
tel/fax (418) 598-6774
auboise@globetrotter.qc.ca

	B&B
single	$45
double	$50-55
triple	$65
child	$10

Taxes extra VS MC

Reduced rates: Sep. 7 to June 15
Open year round

Number of rooms	5
shared bathrooms	3
shared wc	1

Activities: 🏛 🍷 🚤 🎣 🚲

19. ST-JEAN-PORT-JOLI

F e ☒ 🚗 P 🏊 R.2 TA

Off the main street, 500m from services, 30m from the dock and the site of summer and winter festivals. A welcoming B&B by the St. Lawrence River; charming, comfortable rooms, including a family-size one. For early-birds: juice, coffee, newspapers. Lavish breakfast of homemade goods. Dinner by reservation. Packages: golf, cycling, health treatment on site.

Hwy 20, Exit 414, Rte 204 North, left on Rte 132. Follow signs on the right to "Marina, Quai". On Rue du Quai, left at the Des Pionniers junction.

B&B
GÎTE AUX VENTS ET MARÉES

Francine Bernier and
Henri Bélanger
15, rue Des Pionniers Ouest,
C.P. 769
St-Jean-Port-Joli G0R 3G0
tel/fax (418) 598-3112

	B&B	MAP
single	$40-45	$55-60
double	$50-60	$80-90
triple	$80	$125
quad.	$110	$170
child	$0-15	$5-30

VS

Reduced rates: 10% 3 nights and more, all year round
Open year round

Number of rooms	5
rooms with sink	2
rooms in basement	1
shared bathrooms	2

Activities: 🏄 🎣 🚶 🛷 🏃

---

20. ST-JEAN-PORT-JOLI

☀☀☀ F E 🚭 🐕 🚗 P 🏊 R.1 TA

Ancestral bicentennial house in the heart of the sculpture capital. Today's comforts meet those of yesteryear in a friendly and cordial atmosphere. Garden, flowers, woods, fireplace, pool and striking view of the Appalachians and the St. Lawrence River. Located in quiet countryside near various sites of artistic interest. Packages available. **Ad end of this region.**

1 hr from Québec, or from Riv.-du-Loup Hwy 20 Exit 414 to 132. Then 132 West 2.7km.

B&B
LA MAISON AUX LILAS

Joan Dubreuil and
Normand Brisebois
315, De Gaspé Ouest
St-Jean-Port-Joli G0R 3G0
(418) 598-6844
www.cam.org/~bblilas
bblilas@globetrotter.net

B&B	
single	$45-50
double	$50-55
triple	$65
child	$10

VS MC

Reduced rates: Aug. 20 to June 15
Open year round (with reservations from Nov. 1 to May 1)

Number of rooms	3
shared wc	1
shared bathrooms	1

Activities: 🏛 🍴 🛷 🎣 🚲

---

21. ST-JEAN-PORT-JOLI

☀☀☀ F E 🚭 🐕 P 🚗 R.3

Located in the village, a lovely Victorian home of yesteryear set back from the main road. Large plot of land by the river, next to the marina. A peaceful place in an intimate setting. Charming rooms and a lavish breakfast will enhance your stay. Welcome to our home. **Ad end of this region.**

From Montréal or Québec City, Hwy. 20 E., right on Exit 414 to Rte 132. Left on Rte 132 W. for 0.4km, right on Rue de l'Ermitage.

B&B
LA MAISON DE L'ERMITAGE

Johanne Grenier and
Adrien Gagnon
56, de l'Ermitage
St-Jean-Port-Joli G0R 3G0
(418) 598-7553
fax (418) 598-7667
www.bbcanada.com/ermitage
ermitage@globetrotter.net

B&B	
single	$50-70
double	$65-85
child	$15

Taxes extra VS MC

Reduced rates: Sep. 8 to June 15
Open year round

Number of rooms	5
rooms with private bath	1
rooms with sink	3
shared bathrooms	2

Activities: 🏛 🍴 🎣 🚶 🛷

22. ST-JOSEPH-DE-BEAUCE

☀☀☀ F e P R.5 TA

Discover the changeable aspects of the valley and the architecture of hundred-year-old houses, overlooking the mad course of the capricious Chaudière river toward the St. Lawrence River. A stunning panorama for every season... Play area, bike shed, pool. Welcoming you would be a great pleasure.

From Québec City, Hwy 73 S. In St-Joseph, south on Ave. du Palais to shopping centre. Rue St-Luc, house facing the curve.

B&B
«LES RÊVERIES»

Louise and Roland Doyon
1003, rue St-Luc
St-Joseph-de-Beauce G0S 2V0
(418) 397-4814
fax (418) 397-6439
reverie@microtec.net

B&B	
single	$35
double	$50
triple	$65
quad.	$80
child	$10-15

VS

Open year round

Number of rooms	2
rooms in basement	2
shared wc	1
shared bathrooms	1

Activities: 🏛 🐦 🚣 🎿 🏃

23. ST-JULIEN

☀☀☀ F e 🚭 P 🚗 ❌ R15

Chaudière-Appalaches Excellence Prize 1996-97. Nature-lovers, hikers, skiers and bikers, our cedar-shingled home awaits you in the Appalachians. Enjoy calm, views, armchair bird-watching and walks. After a good meal (available upon request), dream in front of the fireplace or on the terrace. Treat yourself! O'P'tits Oignons, the B&B difference.

Hwy 20, from Montréal Exit 228 or from Québec City Exit 253 twd Thetford-Mines. After the detour to Bernierville (St-Ferdinand) turn right on Rte 216 West to St-Julien. Turn right, before the village, to reach O' P'tits Oignons.

B&B
O' P'TITS OIGNONS

Brigitte and Gérard Marti
917, chemin Gosford,
route 216
St-Julien G0N 1B0
tel/fax (418) 423-2512
www.minfo.net/ptits-oignons/
bgmarti@megantic.net

	B&B	MAP
single	$45-55	$60-70
double	$50-60	$80-90

Reduced rates: 10% 3 nights and more
Open year round

Number of rooms	3
rooms with private bath	1
shared wc	1
shared bathrooms	1

Activities: 🏛 🐦 🚶 🏃 🐎

24. ST-LAMBERT-DE-LÉVIS

☀☀☀ F E 🚭 P 🚗 R2.5 TA

20 min from Old Québec City, enjoy the warm, welcoming atmosphere of a country setting. Large landscaped grounds, outdoor pool and flowery patio overlooking the Rivière Chaudière. In winter, relax by a cosy fire. Nearby: cycling, golf, swimming, horseback riding, cross-country skiing, skidooing and skating. Dogsledding package available upon request.

From Montréal Hwy 20 E.; from Québec City P.-Laporte bridge; from Riv.-du-Loup Hwy 20 W., Hwy 73 S., Exit 115 St-Lambert. Right on Du Pont 1km. Left on des Érables at the church, 1.5km. Right on Dufour.

B&B
LA MAISON BLEUE

Francine and Yvon Arsenault
122, rue Dufour
St-Lambert-de-Lévis G0S 2W0
(418) 889-0545
fax (418) 889-5122
pages.infinit.net/bleue/

B&B	
single	$40
double	$50
child	$10

Open year round

Number of rooms	2
shared wc	1
shared bathrooms	1

Activities: 🐦 🚣 🎿 🛷 🐎

25. ST-LÉON-DE-STANDON

F E ♿ P ☲ ✕ R4 TA

Discover our inn, an ancestral house, that can accommodate up to 26 guests with 3 private and 2 family-sized rooms with bunk beds. 1.3km² of land offering hiking, swimming (lake/river), cycling and fishing in summer, snowshoeing and skating in winter, or just simple tranquillity.

Hwy 20, Exit 325 Pintendre-Lac Etchemin. Rtes 173 S. and 277 S. In St-Léon, from Rte de l'Église, right on Rang St-François, drive 3.6km.

INN
AUBERGE TERRE DE RÊVE

Jean Comeau
65, rang St-François
St-Léon-de-Standon G0R 4L0
(418) 642-5559
fax (418) 642-2764
www.terredereve.com

B&B	
single	$40
double	$50
triple	$70
quad.	$90
child	$0-15

VS

Open year round

Number of rooms	5
rooms with private bath	1
rooms with sink	2
shared wc	4
shared bathrooms	2

Activities: 🚣 🏃 🛷 🎿 🐕

---

26. ST-LÉON-DE-STANDON

☀☀☀ F e 🚫 P 🚗 ✕ ☲ R7

Tourism Grand Prize 1997. Familial paradise 1 hr from Québec City. 100 yr-old house nestled in the Appalachians. Spacious rooms in the B&B or the log pavilion. Patio near private lake, beach, cascading river, trails. Ski & winter sports packages. Private dining and sitting rooms. Chaudière-Appalaches Excellence Prize 1995-96. **Country-style Dining p17, Farm Excursion p 29, Farm Stay p 38.**

From Québec City, Hwy 20 E., Exit 325 twd Lac-Etchemin, Rtes 173 S. and 27.7 S. to St-Léon-de-Standon. From the church 0.9km, at stop, cross Rte 277, left Rte du Village, 4km. Right Rang Ste-Anne, 2km.

B&B
FERME LA COLOMBE

Rita Grégoire and
Jean-Yves Marleau
104, rang Ste-Anne, route 277
St-Léon-de-Standon G0R 4L0
(418) 642-5152
fax (418) 642-2991
www.fermelacolombe.qc.ca

	B&B	MAP
single	$40	$50
double	$55-60	$84-90
triple	$75	$120
quad.	$85	$145
child	$5-10	

Taxes extra

Open year round

Number of rooms	2
rooms with private bath	2

Activities: 🚣 🏃 🐎 🎿 🏃

---

27. ST-MARCEL

✎ F e 🚫 ✕ 🚗 P R10 TA

Located in a peaceful town, this 100-year-old presbytery has retained is original charm. There's a museum on the premises, and you can find out how linen and animal fibres are transformed at the various workshops. You can also visit the «Ferme Jouvence», which has some rare animals. Nature area and gourmet restaurant with a healthy menu option on premises. Non-smoking. **Country Home p 116, no 31.**

Hwy 20 East, Exit 40, Rte 285 South 33.5km. Left on Rue Taché, 1km. Next to the church.

B&B
L'ANCIEN PRESBYTÈRE

Nicole Bélanger and
Raymond Raby
58, Taché Est
St-Marcel G0R 3R0
tel/fax (418) 356-5060
(418) 356-5663
raby@globetrotter.qc.ca

B&B	
single	$30
double	$40
triple	$55
quad.	$70
child	$5

Taxes extra VS

Open year round

Number of rooms	5
shared bathrooms	2

Activities: 🏃 🏃 🐎 🛷 🏃

28. ST-PIERRE-DE-BROUGHTON

F e P 🐕 🚤 ✕ R5 TA

Chateau life in a little corner of paradise! Have tea in the gazebo, learn the history of this large Victorian-style house, discover the "soapstone", swim in the pond, visit the farmyard, feed the deer/goats/rabbits/ponies, walk the trails! Make yourselves at home.

From Mtl, Hwy 20 E., Exit 228 Princeville, Rte 165 twd Black-Lake, Rte 112 to Québec City, drive 24km. Left, drive 2km. From Québec City Rte 173 Vallée-Jct Exit, Rte 112 to St-Pierre-de-Broughton, right, drive 2km.

B&B
AUBERGE DE LA
PIERRE FLEURIE

Pierrette Gagné and Pierre Cyr
193, Rang 11
St-Pierre-de-Broughton
G0N 1T0
(418) 424-3024
fax (418) 424-0452

	B&B	MAP
single	$40	$55
double	$45	$75

Taxes extra

Open year round

Number of rooms	4
shared bathrooms	2

Activities: 🏛 🍷 🎿 🚣 🐎

29. ST-ROCH-DES-AULNAIES

☀☀☀ F P 🚗 ✕ R.5 TA

A perfect dream! Fall under the charm of a 200-year-old house on an immense property bordering the St. Lawrence River. Dining room, view of the river, exquisite and copious breakfast. Let time drift by slowly. Marvel at the return of the snow geese, the sunsets, the tides, the winter storms, while keeping warm inside by the fireplace. Meal with reservations. 1 hour from Québec City, 45 min from Riv.-du-Loup **Ad end of this region.**

Hwy 20 Exit 430, left twd Seigneurie des Aulnaies. From Québec City, Rte 132, 15.5km from the St-Jean-Port-Joli church.

B&B
AU SOIR QUI PENCHE

Guy Gilbert
800, ch. de la Seigneurie
St-Roch-des-Aulnaies G0R 4E0
tel/fax (418) 354-7744
www.quebecweb.com/
ausoirquipenche
guygilb@globetrotter.net

B&B	
single	$40-45
double	$45-50
triple	$65
quad.	$75

Reduced rates: 10% 2 nights and more
Open year round

Number of rooms	4
rooms with sink	2
shared wc	1
shared bathrooms	2

Activities: 🍷 🚣 🎿 🚶 🤸

30. THETFORD MINES

☀☀☀☀ F E P 🚗 R.5

For a royal stay, little manor dating from 1930. Its yesteryear bourgeois look and charm invite you to a "halt" in time. The surrounding wooded grounds bordering a river contribute to the peaceful atmosphere. Near services and attractions. Complete breakfasts. Little extras included.

From Montréal (240km), Hwy Jean-Lesage (20 East), Exit 228, Rte 165 in Black Lake, Rte 112 East to downtown Thetford Mines. Or from Québec City (105km), Hwy Robert-Cliche (73 S.), Exit 81, in Vallée-Jonction Rte 112 West to downtown Thetford Mines.

B&B
LE KINGSVILLE

Thérèse Donovan
Rock Vachon
609, Notre-Dame Nord
Thetford Mines G6G 2S6
(418) 338-0538

B&B	
single	$45-55
double	$60-70
triple	$75-85
child	$15

Taxes extra VS MC

Open year round

Number of rooms	3
rooms with private bath	1
shared bathrooms	1

Activities: 🏛 🎿 🚲 🚣 ⛷

31. ST-ADALBERT

F e 🐕 ✂ 🚗 P 🏊 M10 TA

Experience a vacation in harmony with nature in a house located near our rare-animal breeding farm. Various workshops on request. Forest walks. Visit to maple grove. 20km from St-Pamphile golf course. **B&B p 114, n° 27.**

From Québec City, Hwy 20, Exit 400 for St-Eugène. Rte 285 South twd St-Marcel. Drive 41.5km, turn right at the "Rang 3, Rang 4" sign and continue for 2km.

COUNTRY HOME
FERME JOUVENCE

Nicole Bélanger
36 rang 4
St-Adalbert G0R 2M0
(418) 356-5060
(418)356-5663
fax (418) 356-5265
raby@globetrotter.qc.ca

No. houses	1
No. rooms	5
No. people	10
WEEK-SUMMER	$350-550
WEEK-WINTER	$350-550
W/E-SUMMER	$120-200
W/E-WINTER	$120-200
DAY-SUMMER	$60-100
DAY-WINTER	$60-100

Taxes extra

Open year round

Activities: 🚣 🎿 🚶 🐎 🏃

32. ST-HENRI-DE-LÉVIS

F e P R6 M8 TA

This spacious and well-lit cottage with cathedral roof and stone fireplace welcomes you to a quiet place. Located at the end of a country road, between fields and forest, it offers you the peace of its woodlands. Ambiance inspired by the seasons. Local tours, agrotourism, maple groves...

30 minutes from Vieux-Québec. Hwy 20, Exit 325 S. for Rivière-du-Loup, toward Pintendre, Lac Etchemin, Rte 173 South drive 10km, turn left on Chemin de la Tourbière, 2.5km, turn right, 2km.

COUNTRY HOME
TEMPÉRAMENT SAUVAGE

Sylvie Bouthillette and
Pier Grenier
523, chemin St-Jean-Baptiste
St-Henri G0R 3E0
(418) 882-0558
fax (418) 882-0458
www.cowboys-quebec.
com/Temperament.html

No. houses	1
No. rooms	2
No. people	4
WEEK-SUMMER	$535-715
WEEK-WINTER	$535-715
W/E-SUMMER	on request
W/E-WINTER	$195-255

MC

Open year round

Activities: 🏛 🚴 🐎 🛶 🏃

FARM ACTIVITIES

Farm Stays:

15 LE JARDIN DES MÉSANGES, St-Cyprien 38

26 FERME LA COLOMBE, St-Léon-de-Standon 38

Country-style Dining*:

26 FERME LA COLOMBE, St-Léon-de-Standon 17

Farm Excursions:

26 JARDINS DES TOURTEREAUX DE LA FERME LA COLOMBE, St-Léon- de-Standon 29

* Registered trademark.

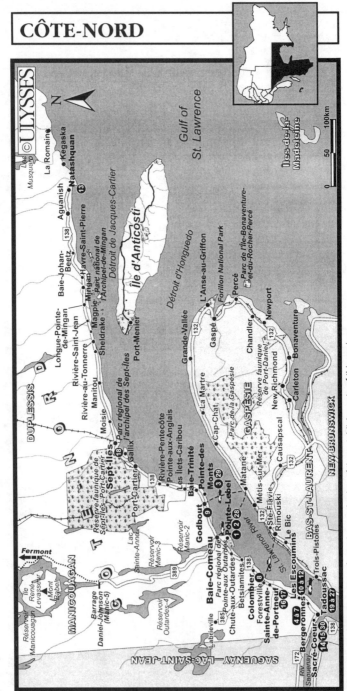

CÔTE-NORD

* The numbers on the map refer to the numbering of the establishments of this region

1. BAIE-COMEAU, POINTE-LEBEL

☀☀☀ F e P 🚗 🚤 R2

Calm, cosy and comfortable B&B to discover. Warm family welcome. Nature lovers will cherish the grandeur and beauty of our beach, where the St.Lawrence River meets the Manicouagan; swimming, walks and pool await you. Lavish home-made breakfast. Package deals upon reservation, from November to May. **Country Home p 128.**

From Québec City, Rte 138 E. to Baie-Comeau. 7.5km after Chute-aux-Outardes turn right at the traffic lights. Drive 14km to Pointe-Lebel.

B&B
AU PETIT BONHEUR

Carmen Poitras
and Mario Lévesque
1099, rue Granier
Pointe-Lebel G0H 1N0
(418) 589-6476
(418) 589-1294
fax (418) 295-3419

B&B	
single	$35-45
double	$45-55
triple	$65
quad.	$75
child	$10

Reduced rates: Nov. 1 to Apr 30, with reservation
Open year round

Number of rooms	4
rooms in basement	4
shared wc	1
shared bathrooms	2

Activities: 🍂 🎣 ⛷ 🚲 🛷

2. BAIE-COMEAU, POINTE-LEBEL

☀☀☀ F E 🚗 🐕 P 🚤 R1 TA

Côte-Nord Excellence Prize 1996-97. 14km from Baie-Comeau, 200m from an immense beach, between the St.Lawrence and the Rivière Manicouagan, discover a swimming, cycling, hiking and horseback-riding paradise. Big and cosy house with Victorian charm. Stylish rooms, quiet stay and hearty breakfast.

From Québec City, Rte 138 E. to Baie-Comeau. After Chute-aux-Outardes, drive 7.5km, right at the traffic lights and drive 11.5km. After the church, turn left on the 1st street.

B&B
LES TOURNE-PIERRES

Bernadette Vincent
and Jean-Yves Landry
18, rue Chouinard
Pointe-Lebel G0H 1N0
(418) 589-5432
fax (418) 589-1430
gite.tourne-pierres@
enter-net.com

B&B	
single	$40
double	$55
triple	$75
child	$15

MC

Reduced rates: Oct. 1 to May 31
Open year round

Number of rooms	5
shared wc	1
shared bathrooms	2

Activities: 🍂 🎣 ⛷ 🚶 🐎

3. BAIE-TRINITÉ

F E ✗ P TA

Old lighthouse: rooms upstairs. 2nd bathroom outside. Also, 7 cottages with bathrooms, by the sea, some of which are log houses. Breakfast service in the main house. Whale-, seal- and gannet-watching. Museum, excursion and fine-cuisine restaurant on site, from mid-June to late August. Outfitter classification: 4-star. **Country Home p 128. Ad end of this region.**

From Québec City or from the Matane-Godbout ferry, Rte 138 E., right at the entrance to Pointe-des-Monts, drive 11km. For reception cross footbridge.

INN
LE GÎTE DU PHARE DE
POINTE-DES-MONTS

Jean-Louis Frenette
Route du Vieux Phare
Baie-Trinité G0H 1A0
(418) 939-2332
(418) 589-8408
pointe-des-monts@
globetrotter.net

B&B	
single	$40
double	$49
triple	$58

Taxes extra VS MC IT

Open: June 15 to Sep. 15

Number of rooms	9
rooms with private bath	5
shared wc	2
shared bathrooms	1

Activities: 🚤 🎣 🚶 🚲

4. BERGERONNES

☀☀☀ F E 🚭 P 🚗 ⛴ R.2 TA

Quiet family house recommended by a French guide. Unlimited home-made jams. Lots of information about the region available. Whale-watching from shore. Numerous interpretation centres. Swimming. We look forward to meeting you.

3 hours from Québec City, Rte 138 E. 20 min from Tadoussac and 10 min from Escoumins from Trois-Pistoles by ferry. Kitty-corner from the church.

B&B
BIENVENUE
CHEZ LES PETIT

Janet Harvey
and Jean-Claude Petit
56, rue Principale
Bergeronnes G0T 1G0
(418) 232-6338
fax (418) 232-1117
www.ihcn.qc.ca/gitepetit
gitepetit@ihcn.qc.ca

B&B	
single	$40
double	$50
triple	$71
quad.	$92
child	$15

Reduced rates: Oct. 15 to May 15
Open year round

Number of rooms	5
rooms with sink	1
shared bathrooms	2

Activities: 🏛 🦆 ⛴ 🚶 🚲

5. BERGERONNES

F e 🍴 🚗 P

Auberge la Bergeronnette is a Victorian-style inn situated in the heart of the village, which lives in harmony with nature. Whale-wat-ching excursions, plane rides, sea kayak expeditions, interpretation centre, bike path and whale obser-vation points from the shore. *Table d'hôte*: game, seafood and fish. Packages available. Taxes and ser-vices extra.

24km from Tadoussac on Rte 138 East. 500m from the tourist office.

INN
LA BERGERONNETTE

Anne Roberge and
Daniel Brochu
65, Principale C.P. 134
Bergeronnes G0T 1G0
tel/fax **(418) 232-6642**
toll free 1-877-232-6605
www.bergeronnette.qc.ca
bergeronnette@ihcn.qc.ca

B&B	
single	$35-50
double	$50-65
child	$10

Taxes extra VS MC AM IT

Reduced rates: 20% Sep. 15 to Oct. 31, May 1 to June 15
Open: May 1 to Oct. 31

Number of rooms	8
rooms with private bath	1
rooms with sink	4
shared wc	1
shared bathrooms	3

Activities: 🦆 ⛴ 🚣 🚶 🚲

6. BERGERONNES

✎ F e 🚗 P R.1

Rock and chat on Petite Baleine's green veranda. The sloping hills unfold in front. Ducks and locals chat on Côte-à-Bouleau hill. One river flows by, then another and another. A smile invites you in. A spirit flows from room to room, breathing the perfumes of yester-day. A piano. A *catalogne* in bed inspires dreams. Sun beams dance across the crystal jam pots as if this were a ball, with Cinderella on the throne. Chicoutai charms our mor-ning table! **See colour photos.**

Near the church.

B&B
LA P'TITE BALEINE

Geneviève Ross
50, rue Principale
Bergeronnes G0T 1G0
(418) 232-6756
(418) 232-6653

B&B	
single	$40
double	$50
triple	$70

Reduced rates: 20% from Oct. 15 to May 15
Open year round

Number of rooms	5
rooms with sink	2
shared wc	2
shared bathrooms	2

Activities: 🏛 ⛴ 🚣 🚶 🚲

7. BERGERONNES

★ ★ ★ F E ♿ P 🚗 ✕

For a real holiday in whale country, come to the pink granite inn, in the heart of the village. Whale-watching cruises, skidoo, sea kayaking, scuba diving. 5km from Cap Bon-Désir, a whale-watching viewpoint, and only 2km to a prehistory interpretive centre. Bike rental on the premises. Regional menu between 6pm and 10pm. Whale watching packages $95 per person. Tx and service extra. TV.

24km from Tadoussac on Rte 138 E. Turn left after the tourist information booth. Follow the signs.

INN
LA ROSEPIERRE

Diane Gagnon
and Richard Bouchard
66, rue Principale, C.P. 116
Bergeronnes G0T 1G0
(418) 232-6543
toll free 1-888-264-6543
fax (418) 232-6215
rosepierre@mail.fjord-best.com

	B&B	MAP
single	$55-70	$95
double	$65-80	$135
triple	$80-95	$175
quad.	$95-110	$215
child	$15	

Taxes extra VS MC AM IT

Reduced rates: Oct. 1 to May 31
Open year round

Number of rooms	10
rooms with private bath	8
shared wc	1
shared bathrooms	1

Activities: 🏛 ⛴ 🚶 🎿 🚴

---

8. COLOMBIER

✹✹✹ F e 🚭 P 🏊 R25 TA

Private beach, showered in the salty waters of St.Lawrence River. A walk by the rocks on the shore will seduce nature lovers. Panoramic view. Comfortable new rooms of superior quality. Suite with front and back balconies. Rooms with private entrance. French, Spanish and some English spoken.

From Québec, Hwy 138 E., 300km. From Tadoussac, 100km. From Forestville, 27km. From the ferry Matane-Baie-Comeau, Hwy 138 W., 70km. From Papinachois Vacation Center, 25km.

B&B
GÎTE ANSE-AU-SABLE

Noëlla Thibault and
Jocelyn Gagnon
104 Anse-au-Sable
Colombier G0H 1P0
(418) 565-3047
(418) 587-3050
fax (418) 587-4808
ntibo@quebectel.com

B&B	
single	$65-100
double	$75-125
triple	$150
child	$10

VS IT

Open year round

Number of rooms	3
rooms with private bath	1
shared bathrooms	1

Activities: ⛴ 🏄 🚶 🎿

*130 km Tadoussac
70 km Baie-Comeau*

---

9. GODBOUT

✹✹ F E P 🚗 ✕

Stay by the sea, near the ferry. Breakfast served in our restaurant "Aux Berges". Dinner with reservations. Calm and beautiful landscape, beaches, fishing, excursions at sea. Check out waterfalls full of jumping salmon!

From Québec City, Rte 138 E. to Godbout. Located near the ferry.

INN
AUX BERGES

Lucie Cordeau and
Eric Deschênes
180, rue Pascal Comeau
Godbout G0H 1G0
(418) 568-7748
(418) 568-7816
fax (418) 568-7833

B&B	
single	$35
double	$45
triple	$55
child	$8-15

Taxes extra VS MC AM ER IT

Open: Apr. 1 to Oct. 31

Number of rooms	3
rooms with sink	3
shared bathrooms	1
shared wc	1

Activities: 🏛 ⛴ 🏄 🚶

10. LES ESCOUMINS

★ ★ F E 🚗 P ✕ R.5 TA

"A stop along the way to discovering the Côte-Nord..." Good beds, good cooking (meals with reservation). Personalized service whether you prefer to relax or explore: the sea, the river or the forest. Whales, salmon and trout are plentiful. Wonderful places for scuba-diving, snowmobiling. The inn is a cosy stop between the river and forest.

From Tadoussac, Rte 138 E., 40km. From Baie-Comeau, Rte 138 West 150km. 2km from the Les Escoumins-Trois-Pistoles ferry.

INN
AUBERGE DE LA BAIE

Esther Gagné
267, Route 138, C.P. 818
Les Escoumins G0T 1K0
(418) 233-2010
toll free 1-800-287-2010
fax (418) 233-3378

B&B	
single	$45-75
double	$55-75
triple	$65-85
quad.	$75-95
child	$10

Taxes extra VS MC AM ER

Reduced rates: Oct. 1to May 31
Open year round

Number of rooms	12
rooms with private bath	12

Activities: 🚤 ⛵ 🚶 🎿 🛷

11. LES ESCOUMINS

☀☀☀ F E P 🚗 🐕 R4

"Located right next to the ISSIPIT Indian reserve, come discover the sea, kayaking, sailing, scuba-diving, and in the winter, ice-fishing and snowmobile excursions. The shoreline follows the edge of Parc Saguenay-St-Laurent, the first marine park in Canada where you can see whales from the shore or from a boat. Quiet mornings and breakfasts."

30km east of Tadoussac, Rte 138, we are located on the edge of the ISSIPIT reserve. Follow the signs for the reserve, a flowery field on the left shows the way.

B&B
GÎTE DES GIROUETTES

Lucie Baillargeon
2, rue Roussel
Les Escoumins G0T 1K0
(418) 233-3297

B&B	
single	$45
double	$50

Open year round
(with reservation from Oct. 30)

Number of rooms	3
shared bathrooms	2

Activities: 🚤 ⛵ 🐎 🛷 🎿

12. LES ESCOUMINS

☀☀☀ F e 🚗 P R.5

Côte-Nord Excellence Prize 1997-98. 1998 Award of Excellence in Hospitality from the Assoc. Tour. Rég. Manicouagan. House located in the heart of the village, with view over the river. Charm, character and a warm ambiance. Rooms offering cosy comfort. All-you-can-eat breakfast in a laid-back, convivial atmosphere.

From Québec City, Rte 138 to Escoumins, go up to the church, turn left, 4th house.

B&B
LE GÎTE FLEURI

Marianne Roussel
21, de l'Église
Les Escoumins G0T 1K0
(418) 233-3155
fax (418) 233-3835

B&B	
single	$45
double	$55
triple	$70

Open year round

Number of rooms	4
shared bathrooms	2

Activities: 🚤 ⛵ 🚶 🚲 🛷

13. NATASHQUAN

★★ F e ♿ 🐕 🚗 P 🛥 R.5

Twenty feet from the sea, our inn offers relaxation, a warm welcome, personalized service. Fine-sand beaches, sea as warm as in New Brunswick. Footpaths along the river with sea eagles, ducks, birds. In winter: ice fishing, wide-open spaces, freedom. Nature lovers, snowmobilers, skiers, dogsledders, welcome to «plaquebière» (chicoutai) paradise.

Rte 138 East to Natashquan. From Rimouski, Nordik ferry (418) 723-8787. By snowmobile, Trans-Québec 3 trail.

INN
LE PORT D'ATTACHE

Nathalie Lapierre and Magella Landry
70, du Pré
Natashquan G0G 2E0
(418) 726-3569
(418) 726-3440
fax (418) 726-3767

B&B	
single	$50
double	$65

Taxes extra VS

Open year round

Number of rooms	8
shared bathrooms	3

Activities: 🚤 🧍 🚴 🛷 ⛷

---

14. SACRÉ-COEUR

★★ F E P 🚗 ✕ 🛥 R1 TA

Share in our family ambiance. "4-season" activities and packages. Québec cuisine also served to our customers staying in our country homes. No charge: visit or care of animals, sugar shack, tennis, pool, hiking trails, game park. Info and reservation service. **Farm Stay p 39, Country Home p 128. For activities, see ads in Côte-Nord and Saguenay-Lac-St-Jean.**

From Tadoussac, twd Chicoutimi, 17km from the intersection of Rtes 138 and 172, and 6km from the Sacré-Coeur church. From Chicoutimi North, Rte 172 S. to the right, 60m before the rest area.

B&B
FERME 5 ÉTOILES

Stéphanie and
Claude Deschênes
465, Route 172 Nord
Sacré-Cœur G0T 1Y0
(418) 236-4833
toll free 1- 877-236-4551
tel/fax (418) 236-4551
ferme5etoile@ihcn.qc.ca

	B&B	MAP
single	$40	$53
double	$45	$69
triple	$55	$90
child	$10	$16-18

Taxes extra VS MC AM IT

Open year round

Number of rooms	4
rooms with sink	2
shared bathrooms	2

Activities: 🛥 🚤 🧍 🛷 🐕

---

15. SACRÉ-COEUR

☀☀☀ F e P R2 TA

Modern house known for its large spaces, its cleanliness, the warmth and cheer of its residents. Breakfast served in the large solarium with a view of the lake, the geese, the ducks and other farm animals.

From Tadoussac, Rtes 138 E. and 172 N. Or from Chicoutimi North: Rte 172 S. Look for our sign: "Ferme Camil and Ghislaine".

B&B
GÎTE GHISLAINE

Ghislaine Gauthier
243, Route 172
Sacré-Coeur G0T 1Y0
(418) 236-4372

B&B	
single	$40
double	$45
triple	$60
quad.	$65
child	$10-15

Open: June 1 to Oct. 31

Number of rooms	3
rooms in basement	3
shared bathrooms	2

Activities: 🛥 🧍 🛷 ⛷ 🐕

16. STE-ANNE-DE-PORTNEUF

☀☀☀ F 🚫 P 🚗 R.1 TA

A warm welcome;
Dreamy rooms;
A well-earned sleep;
A generous breakfast;
Fresh fruit and vegetables;
Tides to behold;
A beach for strolling;
Birds to observe;
An enchanted forest;
Endless trails;
Friendship assured.
Tickets for boat cruises.
Provincial Excellence Prize 94-95.

From Québec City, Rte 138 E., 288km and 84km from Tadoussac. Or from Matane/Baie Comeau ferry, Rte 138 W., 135km. From Les Escoumins, 33km. From Forestville: 17km.

B&B
GÎTE LA NICHÉE

Camille and Joachim Tremblay
46, rue Principale, route 138
Ste-Anne-de-Portneuf
GOT 1P0
(418) 238-2825
fax (418) 238-5513

B&B	
single	$35
double	$45
triple	$60
child	$10

VS

Reduced rates: Nov 1 to Apr. 30
Open year round

Number of rooms	5
rooms with sink	5
shared wc	1
shared bathrooms	2

Activities: 🏛 🛥 🏊 🛶 🎿

17. STE-ANNE-DE-PORTNEUF

☀☀☀ F e P 🚗 R2 TA

Going to Germina's is like visiting your grandmother. Crepes, jams and giggling fits await you here. Stroll along the sandbank, see the birds, marina, blue whales and a centenary house with coloured past from the times of silent film and grocer's. Welcome to a region as big as the wind, sea and forest.

From Québec City, Rte 138 E., 288km. 3 houses from church. 84km from Tadoussac. Ferries: Escoumins: 33km, Forestville: 17km, Baie-Comeau: 135km, Godbout: 189km, Havre: 505km.

B&B
LA MAISON FLEURIE

Germina and Thérèse Fournier
193, Route 138, C.P. 40
Ste-Anne-de-Portneuf GOT 1P0
(418) 238-2153
fax (418) 238-2793
www.fjord-best.
com/portneuf/fournier.htm
maisonfleurie@moncourrier.com

B&B	
single	$35
double	$45-50
child	$10

Reduced rates: Nov. 1 to Apr. 30
Open year round

Number of rooms	3
shared bathrooms	2

Activities: 🏛 🛥 🏊 🛶 🎿

18. SEPT-ÎLES

☀☀☀ F e P R1 TA

Sept-Îles welcomes you. House located near the entrance of the town. Nearby: walking paths along the sea, bike paths and bikes available, horseback riding, snowmobiling trail, cross-country and downhill skiing. Large living room pool table. Simple and friendly hospitality. Breakfast served in a family atmosphere with home-made jam. Welcome!

In Sept-Îles head east, left on Rue Desmeules in front of the tourist information centre, turn right on Rue Fiset, 3 streets to Rue Thibault.

B&B
GÎTE DES ÎLES

Réjeanne and André Lemieux
50, rue Thibault
Sept-Îles G4S 1M7
(418) 962-6116

B&B	
single	$40
double	$50
triple	$65
child	$10

Open year round

Number of rooms	3
rooms in basement	1
shared bathrooms	2

Activities: 🏛 🛥 🚶 🏃 🚲

19. TADOUSSAC

★★ F E P 🚗 R.01 TA

Right next to the Saguenay fjord, the Maison Gagné inn welcomes you into an ambiance of warmth and friendship. Lovers of nature and the great outdoors, the seasons welcome you to our house. At the foot of one of the prettiest hiking trails in the province, you will spot whales, and will leave with precious memories of your stay.

From Québec City, Rte 138 E. Left once off the ferry, 400 m.

INN
AUBERGE «MAISON GAGNÉ»

Claire Gagné
139, rue Bateau-Passeur
Tadoussac G0T 2A0
(418) 235-4526
toll free 1-877-235-4526
fax (418) 235-4832
www.fjord-best.
com/maisongagné

B&B	
single	$59-69
double	$69-79
triple	$79-89
quad.	$89-99
child	$10

Taxes extra VS MC ER

Reduced rates: Sep. 15 to June 15
Open year round

Number of rooms	10
rooms in basement	2
rooms with private bath	10
shared wc	1

Activities: 🚤 🦭 🦌 🛷 🏃

20. TADOUSSAC

☀☀☀ F e 🚭 🚗 P R.3

Far from traffic, next to Parc du Saguenay, 3min from spectacular bay. Old-charm B&B with small, pretty, cozy rooms and friendly, family atmosphere. Delicious varied breakfasts. Everything within walking distance. Stays of 2 to 4 days, whale-watching cruises, bear and beaver watching. In-house info and ticket sales. Welcome to all.

Turn right at the village church, follow "Bord de l'eau", turn right at 1st street, left at "cul-de-sac" sign, 50m.

B&B
AUX SENTIERS DU FJORD

Elisabeth Mercier and
Xavier Abelé
148, Coupe de l'Islet
Tadoussac G0T 2A0
(418) 235-4934
fax (418) 235-4252
www.iquebec.com/fjord
elisabethmercier@hotmail.com

B&B	
single	$55
double	$60
triple	$90
child	$10-15

Taxes extra VS MC

Reduced rates: Sep.15 to June 15
Open year round

Number of rooms	5
rooms with sink	5
shared bathrooms	2

Activities: 🏛 🚤 🏃 🚲 🛷

21. TADOUSSAC

☀☀☀ F 🚗 P 🚭 R.1 TA

Comfortable and intimate rooms in our home. Enjoy magnificent views of the St.Lawrence River and the Saguenay Fjord from our solarium, where buffet breakfast awaits you in the morning. Rest in harmony with nature throughout the day. Tickets for cruises available.

From Québec City, Rte 138 E. Drive 0.5km from the Saguenay ferry. Right on Rue Des Pionniers, drive 0.3km, left on Rue de Forgerons, drive 0.3km. Right on de la Falaise, drive 0.1km.

B&B
GÎTE DE LA FALAISE

Émilienne and Fernand Simard
264, de la Falaise, C.P. 431
Tadoussac G0T 2A0
tel/fax (418) 235-4344
www.fjord-best.com/
gite-falaise
gite-falaise@mail.
fjord-best.com

B&B	
single	$45
double	$55
triple	$70
quad.	$85
child	$10

VS MC

Reduced rates: Apr. 1 to May 31 and Oct.
Open: Apr. 1 to Oct. 31

Number of rooms	5
rooms with sink	5
rooms in basement	1
shared bathrooms	2

Activities: 🏛 🚤 🏃 🦌 🚲

22. TADOUSSAC

☀☀☀ | F | e | 🚐 | P | R.25 | TA

A simple and warm welcome conducive to rest. A tranquil hideaway close to amenities. We will regale you with our generous home-made breakfasts. Whale-watching cruises. We have extensive knowledge of marine mammals. Tickets for sale here.

From Québec City, Rte 138 E. Drive 1.5km along road from Saguenay ferry. Right on Rue Bois-Franc, 300 ft, left on Rue des Bouleaux. We're waiting for you.

B&B
GÎTE DU BOULEAU

Claire-Hélène Boivin and
Jean-Yves Harvey
102, rue des Bouleaux,
C.P. 384
Tadoussac G0T 2A0
tel/fax (418) 235-4601

B&B	
single	$45
double	$50-60
triple	$65
quad.	$85

VS MC

Reduced rates: Apr. 1 to June 30 and Sep. 1 to Nov. 30
Open: Apr. 1 to Nov. 30

Number of rooms	5
shared bathrooms	3

Activities: 🏛 ⛵ 🚶 🚴

---

23. TADOUSSAC

☀☀☀ | F | E | 🚭 | P | �car | R1

A destination in itself. Welcome to our large, quiet restored house near the village. Soundproof rooms. As biologist and guide, we enjoy acquainting guests with our region. Trails, kayaking, whales, bears, beavers, birds, good advice and tickets on site. In winter: dogsledding, cross-country skiing, snowmobiling and fireplace...

After getting off the ferry, 1st street on the right, 1km from the church, 200m, turn left, past the golf course.

B&B
GÎTE DU MOULIN BAUDE

Virginie Chadenet and
Charles Breton
381, rue des Pionniers
C.P. 411
Tadoussac G0T 2A0
(418) 235-4765
www.ihcn.qc.ca
/moulinbaude/gite/
moulinbaude@ihcn.qc.ca

B&B	
single	$60
double	$65-75
triple	$90
quad.	$100
child	$10-15

VS MC
Reduced rates: Sep. 5 to July 6
Open year round

Number of rooms	4
rooms with private bath	4

Activities: ⛵ 🚶 🏃 🐕

---

24. TADOUSSAC

☀☀☀☀ | F | E | 🚭 | P | 🚐 | 🐕 | R.5

Côte-Nord Excellence Prize 1999. At the top of the village, tasteful, romantic, soundproof rooms with breathtaking view of the St.Lawrence River, fjord, lake, flower garden priv. balcony, queen-size beds. Lux. suite, therap. bath, king-size bed, a.c., TV. Ideal for couple. Hospitality. Copious, varied breakfasts. Bear-/whale-watching, fjord, seaplane tickets.

From the ferry, Rte 138, 1km. Halfway up the hill, at the roadsign, left on Rue des Forgerons, then Rue de la Montagne and Rue Bellevue. Watch for Maison Harvey-Lessard sign.

B&B
LA MAISON
HARVEY-LESSARD

Sabine Lessard and Luc Harvey
16, Rue Bellevue
Tadoussac G0T 2A0
in Tadoussac (418) 235-4802
in Québec (418) 827-5505
fax (418) 827-6926
www.dreamcite.
com/harveylessard/

B&B	
single	$80-85
double	$85-89
double suite	$145
child	$15-20

Reduced rates: May 1 to June 23, Oct. 1 to Oct. 31
Open: May 1 to Oct 31

Number of rooms	4
rooms with private bath	4
shared wc	1

Activities: ⛵ 🚤 🚶 🚴

25. TADOUSSAC

☀☀ F P R.1

We are happy to welcome you to our home. Seen from Tadoussac, the Saguenay is breathtaking. Cruises with whale watching. Bus service one kilometre away. Welcome to our home.

From Québec City, Rte 138 E. to the ferry across the Saguenay. Once off the ferry, take the first road on the right.

B&B
MAISON FORTIER

Madeleine B. Fortier
176, rue des Pionniers
Tadoussac G0T 2A0
(418) 235-4215
fax (418) 235-1029

B&B	
single	42 $
double	52 $
triple	67 $
child	10 $

Taxes extra VS

Open year round

Number of rooms	5
rooms with sink	5
shared wc	1
shared bathrooms	3

Activities: 🦪 ⛴ 🚤 🎿 🚶

26. TADOUSSAC

★★ F E ♿ P 🚗 R.4 TA

Cosy, comfortable hundred-year-old house with view of the Saguenay, on the shores of the lake, in the heart of the village of Tadoussac. 5 rooms with private bathrooms. Rooms with private baths also available in the annex the "Suites de l'Anse". Buffet breakfast served in the Maison Gauthier or in your room. Exceptional off-season rates.

From Québec City, Rte 138 East to the Saguenay ferry at Baie Ste-Catherine. Once off the ferry, 250 m on your left.

INN
MAISON GAUTHIER ET LES
SUITES DE L'ANSE

Lise and Paulin Hovington
159, du Bateau-Passeur
Tadoussac G0T 2A0
(418) 235-4525
(450) 671-4656
fax (418) 235-4897
fax (450) 671-7586

B&B	
single	$60
double	$60-80
triple	$85-95
quad.	$100-110
child	$10-15

Taxes extra VS MC IT

Reduced rates: May, June, Sep., Oct.
Open: May 1 to Oct. 31

Number of rooms	12
rooms with private bath	12

Activities: ⛴ 🚤 🎿 🚶 🚴

27. TADOUSSAC

☀☀☀ F E P 🚗 🐕 R.4

Century-old house with a view of the St.Lawrence River. Rooms with private bathroom. Buffet breakfast. Whale-watching. Near the bus station and restaurants. The Hovington family is proud to welcome you into their home. **See colour photos.**

From Québec City, Rte 138 East to Baie Ste-Catherine. Take the ferry. In Tadoussac take the first street on your right, Rue des Pionniers.

B&B
MAISON HOVINGTON

Lise and Paulin Hovington
285, rue des Pionniers
Tadoussac G0T 2A0
(418) 235-4466
(450) 671-4656
fax (418) 235-4897
fax (450) 671-7586

B&B	
single	$55-75
double	$60-75-80-100
triple	$100
quad.	$100-115
child	$15

Taxes extra VS MC IT

Reduced rates: May, June, Sep., Oct.
Open: May 1 to Oct.. 31

Number of rooms	5
rooms with private bath	5

Activities: ⛴ 🚤 🎿 🚶 🚴

28. BAIE-COMEAU, POINTE-LEBEL

F | e | P | M2 | R2 | TA

Peace, calm and rest await you here. Very relaxing site. On the premises: *jeu de fer*, petanque, pool and beach. You will fall in love with Villa Petit Bonheur! No one leaves 1097 Granier uncharmed! Carmen and Mario will give you a warm welcome, a custom of the house! **B&B p 119.**

From Québec, Rte 138 E. to Baie-Comeau. 7.5km after Chute-aux-Outardes turn right at the traffic light and head to Pointe Lebel, drive 14km.

COUNTRY HOME
VILLA PETIT BONHEUR

Carmen Poitras and
Mario Lévesque
1097, rue Granier
Pointe Lebel G0H 1N0
(418) 589-6476
(418) 589-1294
fax (418) 295-3419

No .houses	3
No. rooms	1-2
No. People	2-6
WEEK-SUMMER	350-500 $
WEEK-WINTER	300-450 $
W/E-SUMMER	150-180 $
W/E-WINTER	120-150 $
DAY-SUMMER	75-90 $
DAY-WINTER	60-75 $

Reduced rates: Oct. 1 to Nov. 30
Open: May 1 to Oct. 31, Dec. 1 to Jan. 31, with reservation

Activities:

---

29. BAIE-TRINITÉ

F | E | ♿ | 🐕 | P | ✕ | R1 | M14 | TA

7 comfortable chalets right by the sea, most of them loghouses, with kitchenette, bathroom and t.v. The Pointe-des-Monts headland juts out 11km into the Gulf of St.Lawrence. Right on the high seas! You'll see whales, seals and gannets from your kitchen window. Old lighthouse museum, excursions and gourmet restaurant all on site from mid-June to late August. Class. 4-stars oufitter. **Country Inn p 119. Ad end of this region.**

From Québec, Rte 138 E. Entrance to Pointe-des-Monts, 4km before Baie-Trinité (west), secondary road twd old lighthouse parking, 11km.

COUNTRY HOME
LE GÎTE DU PHARE DE
POINTE-DES-MONTS

Jean-Louis Frenette
Route du Vieux Phare
de Pointe-des-Monts
Baie-Trinité G0H 1A0
(418) 589-8408
(418) 939-2332

No. house	7
No. rooms	1-4
No. people	2-11
WEEK-SUMMER	$390-750
DAY-SUMMER	$62-150

Taxes extra VS MC IT

Reduced rates: ⅓ of the price from May 15 to June 5 and Sep. 6 to Oct. 15
Open: May 15 to Oct. 15

Activities:

---

30. SACRÉ-COEUR

F | E | ♿ | P | ✕ | R1 | M5 | TA

Share our family ambiance, our 700 acres of farm and forest, access to the fjord, our choice of activities and accommodations with bedding, kitchen and amenities, t.v. and services free of charge. Near Tadoussac and Sainte-Rose-du-Nord. **Farm Stay p 39, B&Bs p 123. For activities: see ads in Côte-Nord and Saguenay-Lac-St-Jean sections.**

From Tadoussac, twd Chicoutimi, 17km from the intersection of Rtes 138 and 172, and 6km from the Sacré-Coeur church. From Chicouti-mi-Nord, Rte 172 South to the right, 60m before the rest area.

COUNTRY HOME
FERME 5 ÉTOILES

Stéphanie and
Claude Deschênes
465, Route 172 Nord
Sacré-Cœur G0T 1Y0
(418) 236-4833
tel/fax (418) 236-4551
toll free 1-877-236-4551
ferme5etoile@ihcn.qc.ca

No. houses	9
No. rooms	1-3
No. people	2-8
WEEK-SUMMER	$410-1125
WEEK-WINTER	$285-910
W/E-SUMMER	$130-370
W/E-WINTER	$90-290
DAY-SUMMER	$40-55
DAY-WINTER	$40-50

Taxes extra VS MC AM IT

Reduced rates: Sep.10 to June 10
Open year round

Activities:

FARM ACTIVITIES

Farm Stay:

14 FERME 5 ÉTOILES, Sacré-Cœur 39

To Ensure Your Satisfaction

Bed & Breakfast, Country Inn,
Country and City Homes, Farm Stay,
Country-Style Dining, Farm Excursion :

680 establishments fall into these
6 categories, and all are accredited and regularly
inspected according to a code of ethics and standards
of quality for hospitality, layout and decor, safety,
cleanliness, comfort and meals served.

The Fédération des Agricotours du Québec
25 years of hospitality
1975-2000

Welcome to the Québec North Shore
10 minutes from Tadoussac

Ferme 5 étoiles

4 seasons
Rental activities
duration : between 2 and 3 hours

Spring-Summer-Fall
★ Beluga, seal and whale watching cruises
★ 4 wheel carts mountain excursions
★ Canoeing on lakes and rivers
★ Sea kayaking on the Saguenay fjord
★ Fishing (gear supplied)
★ Mountain bike and hiking trails
★ Bear and beaver watching
★ Hydroplane
★ Horseriding
★ The life of today's lumberjacks (4 saisons)
★ Museum

Winter
★ Ice fishing
★ Igloo lodging
★ Sliding on air tubes
★ Truckdriver journey (4 seasons)
★ Dogsleding and snowmobile : Initiation and excursion (possibility of many days packages)
★ Sugar shack, maple taffy tasting and traditions
★ Snowshoeing and cross country skiing trails along the Saguenay fjord

Packages

1. «Wild discoveries»
(2 days - 1 night)
One rental activity included (your choice)
according to the season :
★ «Goodies» of the farm
★ One night
★ One copious breakfast
★ One traditionnal supper

79 $ /pers./bed & breakfast

95 $ /pers./country home

2. «Wild exploration»
(3 days - 2 nights)
Two rental activities included (your choice)
according to the season :
★ «Goodies» of the farm
★ Two night
★ Two copious breakfast
★ Two traditionnal supper

154 $ /pers./bed & breakfast

185 $ /pers./country home

3. «A la carte» (3 days and up)
Ask us exactly what you want and we will make your «wilderness» dream come true!

Côte-Nord region
★ B&B's and Inns No. 14
★ Country homes No. 30

«Goodies» of the farm free for our clientele :
Guided tours of the farm and the sugar shack, animals daily care (for kids), hiking and cross country skiing trails, outdoor swiming pool, tennis, playground, outdoor fireplace, B.B.Q.

★ Children under 12 with adults : save 20% on adult rates
★ Lodging rates for 2 pers.
★ Taxes are not included with prices
★ Group rates (11 pers. and up)

Informations - reservations
Phone : (418) 236-4833 • Toll free : 1 877 236-4551 • Fax : (418) 236-4551
FERME 5 ÉTOILES, 465, route 172 Nord, Sacré-Coeur (Québec) G0T 1Y0 • E-mail : ferme5etoile@ihcn.qc.ca

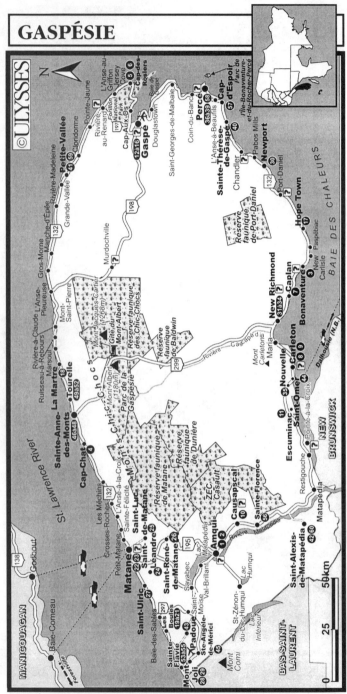

GASPÉSIE

© ULYSSES

* The numbers on the map refer to the numbering of the establishments of this region

1. AMQUI

☀☀☀ F e 🚭 P R4

House located on an old farm close to Lac Matapédia (5-min walk), private beach, a rest stop. Admire the differently coloured landscapes. Midway between Québec City and Percé or New-Brunswick. 4km away: summer theatre, fishing, canoeing, golf, park with bike paths and hiking. The generous homemade breakfast and friendly welcome will make you want to come again.

From Mont-Joli, Rte 132 E., watch for "Limites de la ville d'Amqui" sign, drive 2km. From Percé, Rte 132 W. through Amqui. 4km past the 2nd light. Right, after the camping site.

B&B
DOMAINE DU
LAC MATAPÉDIA

Carmelle and Roland Charest
780, Route 132 Ouest
Amqui G0J 1B0
(418) 629-5004
fax (418) 629-6606

B&B	
single	$45-55
double	$55-65
triple	$75-80
quad.	$80-95
child	$15

Reduced rates: Sep. 1 to Oct. 5
Open: June 15 to Oct. 5

Number of rooms	5
rooms with private bath	1
rooms with sink	4
shared wc	1
shared bathrooms	2

Activities: 🐚 ⛵ 🎿 🚶 🚴

2. AMQUI

☀☀☀ F 🚭 P 🚗 R.25 TA

Welcome to Amqui! House in the heart of downtown. Magnificent landscape with flower beds and vegetable garden. Walking distance from restaurants and activities (tennis, pool, etc.). Sincere, friendly hospitality. Home-made breakfast served in family ambiance. Welcome to our home.

From Mont-Joli, Rte 132 East. In Amqui, right at CN train station, across railway, straight ahead. From Gaspé, Rte 132 West. In Amqui, staight after the 2nd light, left at railway, then straight ahead.

B&B
GÎTE DE LA VIEILLE MAISON

Anita Guénette and
Roland Roy
21, rue Proulx, C.P. 179
Amqui G0J 1B0
tel/fax (418) 629-8184

B&B	
single	$45
double	$52
child	$10

Reduced rates: Oct. 1 to Apr. 30 with reservations
Open year round: with reservations

Number of rooms	3
shared wc	1
shared bathrooms	1

Activities: 🏛 🐚 ⛵ 🎿 🐎

3. BONAVENTURE

☀☀☀ F e 🐕 🚗 P 🏊 R5

For something a little out of the ordinary, we offer a youthful, colourful ambiance. Located near Rivière Bonaventure on the edge of the town, Gîte au Foin Fou was formerly a pioneer farm built in 1881. The facility has a terrace, hammock, artist workshop, swimming in the crystalline river, a campfire in the tipi, communal kitchen, laundromat, e-mail and bike shed. Enjoy a healthy breakfast, including an expresso. A great place to drop anchor for a few days.

At the traffic light, Rue Grand-Pré, drive straight for 5km.

B&B
GÎTE AU FOIN FOU

Manon Briand and
Hugues Arsenault
204 de la Rivière C.P. 592
Bonaventure G0C 1E0
(418) 534-4413
www.foinfou.qc.ca
foinfou@globetrotter.qc.ca

B&B	
single	$40
double	$55-60
triple	$70
quad.	$85
child	$10

Open: June 15 to Sep. 15

Number of rooms	5
rooms with sink	5
shared wc	1
shared bathrooms	2

Activities: 🏛 🐚 ⛵ 🎿 🐎

4. CAP-CHAT

☀☀☀☀ | F | E | 🚭 | 🏊 | P | 🚗 | ✕ | R2

Come join us to the sound of the waves and crying gulls. From our beach, see the whales disappear over the still horizon. At sunset, close your eyes and feel the very soul of Gaspé. Visit the 76-windmill park, the largest vertical-axis windmill and Parc de la Gaspésie. Our 10th year of welcoming guests. Dinner: seafood gratin, by reservation only.

From Québec City, Hwy 20 East, Rte 132 East to Cap-Chat. At west entrance, 3km from the windmill, and 2km from the Centre d'Interprétation du Vent et de la Mer.

B&B
AUBERGE «AU CRÉPUSCULE»

Monette Dion and Jean Ouellet
239, Notre-Dame Ouest,
Route 132
Cap-Chat GOJ 1EO
tel/fax (418) 786-5751
http://come.to/crepuscule
jeanou@globetrotter.net

B&B	
single	$40
double	$55-60
triple	$70
quad.	$85
child	$15

VS MC IT

Open year round

Number of rooms	5
rooms with sink	3
rooms with private bath	1
rooms in basement	2
shared bathrooms	4

Activities: 🚣 🧍 🚶 🐎 🎿

5. CAP-DES-ROSIERS, FORILLON

☀☀ | F | e | P | 🚗 | 🐕 | R.5

Friendly, welcoming B&B near Forillon Park, with its enchanting landscape and animal life. Visit the tallest lighthouse in the country and go on one of our cruises (whale, seal and bird watching). While savouring a copious breakfast, you'll be dazzled by a magnificent view of the sea. Welcome to our home.

From Québec City, Hwy 20 East and Rte 132 East to Cap-des-Rosiers. From Gaspé, Rte 132 to Cap-des-Rosiers; 3km from the entrance to the north part of Forillon Park.

B&B
AUX PÉTALES DE ROSE

Alvine Lebrun
1184, Cap-des-Rosiers
Gaspé GOE 1EO
(418) 892-5031

B&B	
single	$40
double	$55
triple	$70
quad.	$80
child	$10

Reduced rates: May 1 to June 1 and Sep. 15 to Oct. 25
Open: May 1 to Oct. 25

Number of rooms	5
rooms in basement	2
shared bathrooms	2

Activities: 🍷 🛶 🚣 🚲 🐎

6. CAP-DES-ROSIERS, FORILLON

✎ | F | e | 🚭 | 🚗 | P | R1 | TA

Located by the seashore and only 5min from Parc Forillon, our B&B awaits vacationers who are looking for calm and relaxation. You will love our delectable mega-breakfasts including jam, home-made bread and good black coffee. Numerous activities await: marine mammals, ferryboat, kayaking and much more. Less than 2km from the lighthouse. Welcome home!

From Québec, Hwy 20 East and Rte 132 East to Cap-des-Rosiers.

B&B
LA MAISON ROSE

Danielle Slonina
1182 route 132 est,
boul. Cap-de- Rosiers
Cap-des-Rosiers GOE 1EO
(418) 892-5602
(450) 666-0303
fax (450) 666-9749

B&B	
single	$40
double	$50
triple	$70
quad.	$85
child	$10

Reduced rates: 20% 3 nights and more
Open: July 1 to Sep. 4

Number of rooms	3
rooms with sink	1
shared wc	1
shared bathrooms	2

Activities: 🛥 🚣 🧍 🚲 🐎

7. CAPLAN

F E P R1 TA

Located between Bonaventure and Carleton, a memorable B&B overlooking Baie des Chaleurs – one you'll find hard to leave. Trails, beach, flowery gardens, farm animals. 10 minutes from Acadian Museum, Bioparc, adventure boats, golf, 2 salmon rivers, horseback riding. 20 minutes from St-Elzéar cave, British Heritage Centre. Lavish home-made breakfast. In the heart of Baie-des-Chaleurs. Health package: massage and sauna.

From Percé, Rte 132, after the bridge, 3km. In Caplan west side, 1.5km after the church.

B&B
À L'AUBERGE DE LA FERME

Jocelyn Brière
185, boul. Perron Est
Caplan G0C 1H0
tel/fax (418) 388-5603
(418) 392-9343
www.bbcanada.
com/2931.html
aubferme@globetrotter.net

B&B	
single	$30-35
double	$50
triple	$60-75
quad.	$80-90
child	$0-10

Taxes extra

Reduced rates: 15% Sep. 15 to May 31
Open year round

Number of rooms	5
shared wc	1
shared bathrooms	2

Activities:

8. CARLETON

★★ F e P R.1 TA

Located downtown, amidst all the activities. We can accommodate up to 16 guests. Tea time at 4 pm. It will be our pleasure to pick you up at the train or bus station. Free laundry service and bicycles. Packages available. Something for every season. Copious breakfast.

From Ste-Flavie, Rte 132 East. At entrance to Carleton, right at 1st light, Rte du Quai. From Percé, at entrance to Carleton, left at 2nd light, Rte du Quai. At corner of Rte 132 and Rte du Quai.

INN
AUBERGE LA VISITE SURPRISE

Isabelle Quinn and Lise Leblanc
527, boul. Perron
Carleton G0C 1J0
(418) 364-6553
fax (418) 364-6890
liselebl@globetrotter.net

B&B	
single	$35
double	$50
triple	$63
quad.	$76
child	$5-12

Taxes extra VS MC ER AM

Reduced rates: 10% Sep. 15 to June 15
Open year round

Number of rooms	7
rooms in semi-basement	4
rooms with sink	5
shared bathrooms	3

Activities:

9. CARLETON

F E P R1 TA

Two Acadians welcome you to their granite Canadian-style house. Spacious rooms, country decor. Large veranda with view of Mont St-Joseph, a few kilometres from the B&B. Children welcome. Near playground, beach, hiking trails, bird-watching tower. 25km from Parc de Miguasha.

From Québec City, Hwy 20 E., Rte 132 E. At the entrance to Carleton, next to "Optique Chaleurs". Entrance on Rue des Érables, 1st house on right. From Percé, drive 3km from the church, next to Motel l'Abri.

B&B
GÎTE LES LEBLANC

Jocelyne and Rosaire LeBlanc
346, boul. Perron C.P. 143
Carleton G0C 1J0
(418) 364-7601
(418) 364-3208
fax (418) 364-6333
indleb@globetrotter.net

B&B	
single	$40
double	$50
triple	$60
quad.	$70
child	$10

VS MC

Open: May 1 to Oct. 31

Number of rooms	4
rooms with sink	2
shared bathrooms	2

Activities:

10. CAUSAPSCAL ☀☀☀ F P R.2

B&B right in the heart of the village of Causapscal. Come relax in a setting typical of the Matapédia valley; it's just like being in a Swiss village. Enjoy a view of the Rivière Matapédia, where you'll see fishermen trying to catch salmon. Just the place for a pleasant stay!

Rte 132 West, Rue d'Anjou first street on the right after the traffic lights, left on Rue Belzile. Or Rte 132 East, Rue d'Anjou (by the «caisse populaire»), left on Rue Belzile.

B&B
LE GÎTE DE LA VALLÉE

Gilberte Barriault
71, rue Belzile
Causapscal G0J 1J0
(418) 756-5226
(418) 756-3072

B&B	
single	$35
double	$45
triple	$60
child	$10

Reduced rates: Nov. 1 to Apr. 30
Open: Jan. 16 to Dec. 14

Number of rooms	3
shared bathrooms	1

Activities: 🦪 🎣 🏃 🐕 🛷 🎿

---

11. ESCUMINAC, MIGUASHA F E 🚭 ♿ 🏊 P 🐕 R5 TA

Wanta-Qo-Ti, an experience worthy of its name: serenity. Located between the red cliffs of Miguasha and Baie des Chaleurs, facing the sea, this B&B was once a farm. Come discover this enchanting place. Right next to Parc de Miguasha, to the beaches of Carleton and Fort Listuguj.

From Carleton Rte 132 West to Nouvelle, twd Miguasha-Dalhousie ferry. At the ferry turn right on Rte Miguasha (becomes Pte-à-Fleurant) for 3.2km. From Matapédia Rte 132 East to Escuminac. Right at Parc Miguasha sign, 6.2km.

INN
AUBERGE WANTA-QO-TÍ

Bruce Wafer
77, chemin Pointe-Fleurant
Escuminac G0C 1N0
tel/fax (418) 788-5686
www.bbcanada.com/595.html
bwafer@globetrotter.net

B&B	
single	$40-43
double	$57-66
triple	$81
quad.	$96
child	$0-12

Taxes extra VS MC IT

Reduced rates: Sep. 15 to June 15
Open year round

Number of rooms	8
rooms with private bath	4
shared bathrooms	2

Activities: 🏛 🏄 🎣 🛷 🎿

---

12. GASPÉ ☀☀☀ F E 🚭 P 🚗 R.1 TA

Less than 30 minutes from Forillon Park, downtown, 3-storey house, close to one hundred years old, with great view of Baie de Gaspé. Walking distance from restaurants and museum, promenade, cathedral, marina. Cosy rooms and lounge, period decor and ambiance await you. Refined breakfasts to soft music.

From Percé, after the bridge, straight ahead to the first lights. From Forillon, turn right at the first lights. From Murdochville, turn left at the first lights. Everyone, turn left at the 2nd traffic lights and drive 100 m.

B&B
COUETTE-CAFÉ
LES PETITS MATINS

Noëlline Couture and
Guy Papillon
129, de la Reine,
Gaspé G4X 1T5
(418) 368-1370
gunoe@cablog.net

B&B	
single	$45-55
double	$55-65

VS MC

Open year round

Number of rooms	3
rooms with sink	1
shared wc	1
shared bathrooms	1

Activities: 🏛 🛷 🏃 🏃 🤸

13. GASPÉ

☀☀☀☀☀ F e ⊘ 🚗 P R.2

B&B
GÎTE DE GASPÉ

You will feel right at home upon entering the Gîte de Gaspé with Louisette and Gaétan's warm welcome. Enjoy a restful night and breakfast served with products from the family maple grove. Unforgettable! Panoramic view of Parc Forillon and the Gaspé bay from the terrace. Suggested activities.

From Québec City, Hwy 20 East, Rte 132 to Gaspé, toward town centre and Rue Jacques-Cartier up to Côte de la Légion turn right, continue for 75 m. Left on Rue Guignion.

Louisette Tapp and
Gaétan Poirier
201, rue Guignion
Gaspé G4X 1L3
(418) 368-5273
fax (418) 368-0119

B&B	
single	$45
double	$60
triple	$75
child	$10

Reduced rates: Avr. 1 to June 1, Oct. 1 to Nov. 30
Open: Apr. 1 to Nov. 30

Number of rooms	4
rooms with private bath	3
shared bathrooms	1
rooms in semi basement	1
rooms in basement	2

Activities: 🏛 ⛴ 🚣 🚶 🎿

14. GASPÉ

☀☀☀ F E ⊘ 🐕 🚗 P R1 TA

B&B
GÎTE HONEYS

Family house (3 generations). Built in 1922 with period furniture, Honeys' took in sailors during World War II. Enjoy a cocktail on the big porches facing the bay while admiring the superb sunsets. Next to the marina. Gaspesian breakfasts. Picnic on the grounds.

From Percé, right at flashing light after the tourist office. From Forillon, left at Gaspé bridge, left at flashing light. From Murdochville, right at the bridge, left at flashing light.

Françoise Lambert Kruse
and Harold Krusse
4, de la Marina
Gaspé G4X 3B1
tel/fax (418) 368-3294
www.gaspesie.qc.ca/honeys
honeys@cablog.net

B&B	
single	$50-55
double	$55-60
triple	$75
child	$10

VS

Open: May 1 to Oct. 31

Number of rooms	5
rooms with private wc	2
shared bathrooms	2

Activities: 🏛 ⛴ 🚣 🚲 🏇

15. GASPÉ

☀☀☀ F E ⊘ P 🐕 R.5 TA

B&B
GÎTE «LA CANADIENNE»

Close to Forillon National Park. A 5 min walk to all services. This Canadian house knows how to please with the welcome of its owners, its cleanliness, comfort and tranquillity. Documentation and information on our region's beautiful attractions available. Complete breakfast. See you soon!

Rte 132 or 198 to Gaspé. Rue Jacques-Cartier or Rue de la Reine to the cathedral where Rue Mgr Leblanc begins.

Hélène Pelletier and
Denis Bériault
201, Mgr. Leblanc
Gaspé G4X 1S3
tel/fax (418) 368-3806

B&B	
single	$45
double	$55
triple	$65
child	$10

Open: May 25 to Aug. 20

Number of rooms	5
rooms with private bath	5
rooms in semi-basement	5

Activities: 🏛 ⛴ 🚣 🚶 🎿

16. GASPÉ

☀☀☀☀☀ F E ✕ 🚗 P

Across from the town of Gaspé, discover a lovely, welcoming period house, with its carved staircase, panoramic view and rich history. Come sample delicious cuisine where seafood holds pride of place. Fresh lobster from the fish tank, terrace, fireplace.

Rte 132 to Gaspé. Located on Boul. York East or Rte 198, across from the town, on the bay, right near the tourist office.

INN
L'ANCÊTRE DE GASPÉ

Diane Lauzon and
Ronald Chevalier
55, boul. York Est
Gaspé G4X 2L1
(418) 368-4358
fax (418) 368-4054

B&B	
single	$55-75
double	$60-75
triple	$85
quad.	$95
child	$10

VS MC AM ER IT

Open: May 1 to Nov. 30

Number of rooms	3
rooms with private bath	1
shared wc	2
shared bathrooms	1

Activities: 🦞 🎿 🚶 🚴 🐎

---

17. HOPE TOWN, PASPÉBIAC

☀☀☀☀ F E 🚭 P 🚗 R4 TA

Provincial Excellence Grand Prize and the Regional Excellence Prize 1995-96. We invite you to join us in the comfort of our home for an unforgettable stay in our large, beautiful typical Gaspé house by the sea. The memory of our delightful 30ha estate and the visit to «Cabane au Canada», by a salmon river, will stay with you for a long time to come.

From Québec City, Hwy 20 East, Rte 132 East to Hopetown. 4km east of "Automobiles Roland Roussy". From Percé, Rte 132 West to Hopetown, 4km west of the village of St-Godefroi, on the right.

B&B
LA CLÉ DES CHAMPS

Jo-Anne Guimond and
Bernard Gauthier
254, Route 132
Hope Town, Paspébiac
G0C 2K0
tel/fax (418) 752-3113
toll free 1-800-693-3113
www.simarts.com/lacle.html
lacle@globetrotter.net

B&B	
single	$40-45
double	$50-55
child	$15

Open year round

Number of rooms	3
rooms with sink	1
shared wc	1
shared bathrooms	1

Activities: 🏛 🤿 🎿 🚶 🚴

---

18. LA MARTRE

☀☀☀ F E 🚭 P 🚗 R.5

Provincial Excellence Grand Prize 1999. Away from the noise of the 132, a cheerful ancestral house perched on a hill overlooking the sea and the picturesque village of La Martre. Spectacular panorama. Tour of the lighthouse, museum and archaeological digs, private forest chalet for meditation or picnic. Near Parc de la Gaspésie. We speak German. **See colour photos.**

From Québec City, Hwy 20 East and Rte 132 East. 25km east of Ste-Anne-des-Monts, 25km west of Mont-St-Pierre. At the lighthouse: Rue de l'Eglise, right on Rue des Ecoliers, 300 m.

B&B
GÎTE L'ÉCUME DE MER

Andréa Neu
21, rue des Écoliers
La Martre G0E 2H0
tel/fax (418) 288-5274
www.bbcanada.
com/3202.html
ecmer@globetrotter.qc.ca

B&B	
single	$45
double	$60
triple	$75
child	$0-15

Reduced rates: 10 %, for 3 nights and more
Open: June 1 to Sep. 30

Number of rooms	4
shared bathrooms	2

Activities: 🤿 🎿 🚶 🚴 ⛷

19. LES BOULES

★★ F e ♿ 🛏 P 🚗 ❌ TA

Jardins de Métis package in every season. Right on the beach, away from the 132, panoramic view, stunning sunsets, pleasures of the seashore. Seaside spa. Book-lovers' inn: haven of peace with reading room. Memories of Brittany. Delicious, healthy cuisine. Cheerful European ambiance. Family-size rooms in adjacent bungalow. Absolute peace and quiet.

On the way into Gaspésie, 35km before Matane, 10km past Jardins de Métis, left on Rte de Métis-sur-Mer, drive 6km, by the St. Lawrence River.

INN
AUBERGE DU GRAND FLEUVE

Marie-José Fradette and
Raynald Pay
47, Principale, C.P. 99
Les Boules G0J 1S0
tel/fax (418) 936-3332
aubergedugrandfleuve.qc.ca

	B&B	MAP
single	$45-80	$75-105
double	$52-80	$105-130
triple	$70-90	$145-165
quad.	$80-100	$180-200
child	$0-10	depend/age

Taxes extra VS MC IT

Open: Apr. 15 to Oct. 15

Number of rooms	12
rooms with sink	4
rooms with private bath	7
shared wc	2
shared bathrooms	2

Activities: 🦪 🚣 🎿 🚴 🐎

20. LES BOULES

☀️☀️☀️ F E 🚭 🐕 P R.3 TA

Near Jardins de Métis, we offer you a warm welcome in a spacious house located in a small, picturesque village by the sea. Golf course 2km away; 3km from a seafood restaurant. This part of the country is a must-see!

From Québec City, Hwy 20 E., Rte 132 E. 15 min past St-Flavie, after the Golf Boule Rock, go down twd the sea. At the church, turn left.

B&B
GÎTE AUX CAYOUX

Huguette, Gaétan,
Johanne Cayouette
80, rue Principale, C.P. 129
Les Boules G0J 1S0
(418) 936-3842

	B&B
single	$40
double	$45-55
triple	$65
child	$10-15

Open: May 15 to Oct. 1

Number of rooms	3
shared bathrooms	3

Activities: 🏛 🦪 🎿 🚣 🐎

21. LES BOULES

★★ F E P 🚗 ❌ TA

Open year round. Near the Jardins de Métis, our inn is licensed and offers refined cuisine. Choose the beauty of nature and the quietness of the countryside. Warm reception, copious breakfasts. Meet the innkeeper, who has lots of tales to tell and activities. Packages available.

Between Rimouski and Matane, following Rte 132, 10km from Jardins de Métis, after blue tourist sign, inland via Rte McNider, 4km, turn on 5e Rang.

INN
L'AUBERGE
«UNE FERME EN GASPÉSIE»

Pierre Dufort
1175, 5e Rang
Les Boules G0J 1S0
tel/fax (418) 936-3544

	B&B
single	$40
double	$60
triple	$70
quad.	$80
child	$10

Taxes extra VS MC

Reduced rates: Sep. 1 to July 1
Open year round

Number of rooms	6
shared bathrooms	3

Activities: 🎿 🚶 🐎 🛷 🐎

22. MATANE

★★ F e  P R1 TA

Former site of the Fraser seigneury, where the Rivière Matane joins the St. Lawrence River. Enjoy the calm and the fresh river air, near downtown Matane. Friendly, comfortable atmosphere. Sink in every room. Non-smoking B&B. Gaspésie Excellence Prize 1994-95.

From Québec City, Hwy 20 E., Rte 132 E. At Matane, Avenue du Phare, after the Tim Horton Donuts, right on Rue Druillette, at the 148, welcome and parking.

INN
AUBERGE LA SEIGNEURIE

Raymonde and Guy Fortin
621, rue St-Jérôme
Matane G4W 3M9
(418) 562-0021
toll free 1-877-783-4466
fax (418) 562-4455
www3.sympatico.ca/mercati/
seigneurie
mercanti@sympatico.ca

B&B	
single	$40-50
double	$60-70
triple	$75-85
quad.	$90-100
child	$10

Taxes extra VS MC IT

Reduced rates: Sep. 1 to May 31 20%3 nights and more year round
Open year round

Number of rooms	10
rooms with sink	5
rooms with private bath	5
shared wc	1
shared bathrooms	3

Activities: 🏛 🍴 👤 🚲 🏃

23. MATANE

☀☀☀ F E  P R.5 TA

Located right by the sea, our B&B offers an exceptional view! You will be treated to a warm welcome, a comfortable bed, a refined and lavish breakfast, as well as soft and relaxing music. Excellent restaurants in the vicinity. One kilometre from the town centre and the ferry.

On Route 132 in Matane, second house west of the lighthouse (Matane's Tourist Information Centre).

B&B
GÎTE DU PHARE

Josée Landry and
Gilles Blais
984, du Phare Ouest
Matane G4W 3M6
(418) 562-6606
fax (418) 562-8876
studpass@globetrotter.qc.ca

B&B	
single	$40-50
double	$50-60
triple	$70
quad.	$80
child	$10

VS

Open year round: with reservations from Oct. to May

Number of rooms	4
rooms with sink	2
shared bathrooms	2

Activities: 🛷 👤 🏊 🎿 🏃

24. MATANE, ST-LÉANDRE

☀☀☀☀ F E   P R14 TA

Lovely aeolian mountain hamlet near Matane (15 min). Fine home with ancestral old-manor decor of woodwork and antiques. In homage to Nelligan, poetry and song by the fire, singing around the piano. Refinement, merry mornings, gourmet food. 100-acre forest. Guided walk to the falls with golden retriever, natural spa. Total quiet. "Hospitality 97" award winner.

Rte 132, between Ste-Flavie and Matane, to St-Ulric south twd St-Léandre. On paved road, follow the 6 signposts.

B&B
LE JARDIN DE GIVRE

Ginette Couture and
Gérald Tremblay,
3263, route du Peintre
Matane, St-Léandre G0J 2V0
tel/fax (418) 737-4411
toll free 1-800-359-9133
www.bbcanada.com/866.html

B&B	
single	$40-50
double	$55-60-65
triple	$75
quad.	$90
child	$5-12

Taxes extra VS

Reduced rates: 15% 3 nights and more
Open year round

Number of rooms	5
rooms with private bath	2
shared wc	1
shared bathrooms	1

Activities: 🏛 🚶 👤 🚲 🐎

25. MATANE, ST-LUC

☀☀☀ F E P 🚗 🐕 R8 TA

Gaspésie Excellence Prize 1997-98. At 200 m. in altitude, away from Rte. 132, 5 min. from Matane. View over the St. Lawrence River and the region.Therapeutic bath, hearty breakfast, European coffee, near salmon pass, Matane/Baie-Comeau/Godbout ferry. Winter sports, visit the beaver pond, 8km, maple grove, 20km and «parc des origneaux», 28km.

In Matane, opposite Jean Coutu, Ave. Jacques-Cartier to lights, left on Ave. St-Rédempteur, continue for about 7km. Watch for blue "Gîte Le Panorama 1km" signpost, continue for 100m., left on Ch. Lebel, 700m.

B&B
LE PANORAMA

Marie-Jeanne and Hector Fortin
23, chemin Lebel
St-Luc-de-Matane G0J 2X0
tel/fax (418) 562-1100
toll free 1-800-473-3919

B&B	
single	$35-40
double	$50-55
triple	$75
quad.	$80
child	$10-15

VS

Open year round

Number of rooms	3
rooms in semi-basement	1
shared bathrooms	2

Activities: 🎿 🛶 🚶 🛷 🐎

26. MATANE, ST-RENÉ

☀☀ F e ♿ ❌ P R10 TA

Farmhouse fully renovated in the old-fashioned style, located by the road that once led to the village of Saint-Nil. Enjoy a wealth of outdoor activities while living in harmony with nature. Stay in the den of the settler who left his mark on these mountain tops... Your hosts await you. Dinner by reservation only. **Farm Stay p 39.**

From Matane, take southbound Rte 195. At the St-René church, drive 5.5km. Turn left on road to 10e and 11e Rang, then continue for 6.2km.

B&B
GÎTE DES SOMMETS

Marie-Hélène Mercier and
Louis-Philippe Bédard
161, Route 10ᵉ and 11ᵉ Rang
Saint-René-de-Matane G0J 3E0
(418) 224-3497

	B&B	MAP
single	$30	$40
double	$45	$65
triple	$65	$95
child	$10	$15

Open year round

Number of rooms	3
shared bathrooms	2

Activities: 🏛 👟 🚶 🎿 🤸

27. MATANE, ST-ULRIC

☀☀☀ F e P R5 TA

In Matane, see fishers at work, stock up on shrimp and visit the salmon run. In St-Ulric, take in the river's fresh air, watch superb sunsets and wind turbines, unique in Canada. Savour home-made jams, admire our magnificent vegetables and flower gardens, both different every year (winner of many prizes). Rooms with sinks. Welcome all.

From Montréal, Hwy 20 East, Rte 132 East. We are 45km east of Ste-Flavie and 18km west of Matane. From Gaspé, Rte 132 North. From Matane, drive 18km on Rte 132.

B&B
CHEZ NICOLE

Nicole and René Dubé
3371, Route 132,
St-Ulric-de-Matane
Matane G0J 3H0
tel/fax (418) 737-4896

B&B	
single	$35
double	$45-50
triple	$55
quad.	$65
child	$10

Open year round

Number of rooms	3
rooms with sink	3
shared wc	1
shared bathrooms	1

Activities: 🦪 👟 🚶 🛶 🎿

28. MONT-JOLI

☀☀☀ | F | e | P | 🚗 | 🐕 | R2 | TA

Our house, located on a plateau 2km from Mont-Joli and 7km from Ste-Flavie, offers a magnificent view of the river. Just minutes from the Jardins de Métis, the Atlantic Salmon Interpretation Centre and good restaurants. Lodging in winter with skiing right nearby. We'll be waiting with a hearty breakfast and traditional accordion music.

From Québec City, Hwy 20 East, Rte 132 East. Drive 2km from Mont-Joli. Or from the Vallée de la Matapédia, our home is located before Mont-Joli, 5 min from the shopping centre.

B&B
GÎTE BELLEVUE

Nicole and Émilien Cimon
2332, rue Principale,
route 132
Mont-Joli G5H 3N6
(418) 775-2402
toll free 1-888-551-2402

B&B	
single	$40
double	$50-55
triple	$65
quad.	$75
child	$10

Reduced rates: Sep. 1 to May 31
Open year round

Number of rooms	3
shared bathrooms	2

Activities: 🏛 🏊 🛶 🚶 🏃 🚴

29. MONT-JOLI

☀☀ | F | P | 🚗 | R.6

Come share in the calm of the countryside and the history surrounding the first schoolhouse of the region without going much out of your way. Warm welcome and splendid view of the St. Lawrence River from the hills. Enjoy the grandiose sunsets in a unique decor and atmosphere.

From Québec City, Hwy 20 East, Rte 132 East. In Ste-Flavie take 132 East to Mont-Joli for 7km until St-Joseph-de-Lepage. Right before the church, 2nd house on the right.

B&B
GÎTE DE LA VIEILLE ÉCOLE

Jeannine Migneault
90, du Lac
Mont-Joli, G5H 3P2
(418) 775-3504
fax (418) 739-3343

B&B	
single	$40
double	$50
triple	$65
quad.	$75
child	$10

Reduced rates: Sep. 1 to May 31
Open year round

Number of rooms	2
shared bathrooms	1
rooms with sink	1

Activities: 🏛 🦆 🛶 🚶 🏃

30. NEWPORT

☀☀☀ | F | e | 🚫 | 🏖 | P | 🚗 | R.4 | TA

A B&B to discover! A wealthy merchant's former estate spread over the loveliest beach in the township. Old-world charm, enchanting decor and cozy comfort. Delicious breakfasts. Evening restaurant package available. Nestled between Percé and Bonaventure, an ideal place for a long stay. Perfect for quiet nights and days of exploring. A fond memory.

From Ste-Flavie, Rte 132 East to Newport. 1.5km west of the church, house facing the islets.

B&B
AUBERGE LES DEUX ÎLOTS

Guylaine Michel and
André Lambert
207, Route 132, C.P. 223
Newport G0C 2A0
(418) 777-2801
toll free 1-888-404-2801
fax (418) 777-4719
www.bbcanada.
com/lesdeuxilots

B&B	
single	$45-55
double	$55-65
triple	$75-80
quad.	$90-95
child	$5-10

Taxes extra VS

Reduced rates: Sep. 15 to June 15
Open year round

Number of rooms	5
rooms with private bath	2
shared wc	1
shared bathrooms	2

Activities: 🏛 🚶 🏃 🐎 ⛷

31. NEW RICHMOND

☀☀☀ F E P 🚗 R.5 TA

Experience the atmosphere of a cosy Victorian and its exceptional view of Baie-des-Chaleurs. A large veranda looks out to the sea and the mountains. Spacious and comfortable rooms. The seashore is right nearby!

From Québec City, Hwy 20 East, Rte 132 East to New Richmond. At the intersection of Rte 299, turn right, drive 5km to Boul. Perron. Or from Percé, once in New Richmond, turn left on Boul. Perron.

B&B
AUBERGE L'ÉTOILE DE MER

Diane Bourdages and
Jacques Veillette
256, Perron ouest
New Richmond G0C 2B0
(418) 392-6246
www.bbcanada.com/3134.html
etoilebb@globetrotter.net

B&B	
single	$50
double	$55-65
triple	$70
quad.	$80
child	$10

Taxes extra VS

Open year round

Number of rooms	5
rooms with private bath	1
shared bathrooms	2

Activities: 🏛 🏖 🚶 🎿 🚴

---

32. NEW RICHMOND

☀☀☀ F e 🚭 🚗 P 🏊 R2 TA

Ancestral house surrounded by flowers, nestled in a peaceful spot in the heart Baie-des-Chaleurs. Your jovial and sociable hostess serves hearty breakfasts and brightens up your stay with suggestions of things to do in the maritime environment. Sailboat outings, hikes, everything possible to make your stay here an unforgettable one.

From Québec City, Hwy 20 East, Rte 132 East to New Richmond. Right at 3rd flashing light on Ch. St-Edgar, 1.7km, left on Ave. Leblanc, 150 m. From Percé: Rte 132, left at 1st flashing light on Ch. St-Edgar, 1.7km.

B&B
GÎTE DE LA MAISON LEVESQUE

Vyola A. Levesque
180, Avenue Leblanc
New-Richmond G0C 2B0
(418) 392-5267
toll free 1-888-405-5267
fax (418) 392-6948
blaster@globetrotter.qc.ca

B&B	
single	$30
double	$50
triple	$65
child	$10

Reduced rates: Sep. 1 to May 31
Open year round

Number of rooms	3
shared bathrooms	2

Activities: 🍷 🚶 🎿 🚴 🐎

---

33. NEW RICHMOND

☀☀☀ F E 🚭 🏊 P R2 TA

Amidst beautiful white birch on the Baie-des-Chaleurs, our cottage awaits you with a warm welcome. Wooded paths, access to the beach and peaceful surroundings are yours to enjoy.

From Québec City, Hwy 20 East, Rte 132 East to New Richmond. At the intersection of Rte 299, turn right, drive 3.5km to Rue de la Plage and turn right. From Percé, turn left at same intersection.

B&B
GÎTE «LES BOULEAUX»

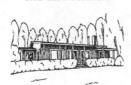

Patricia Fallu and
Charles Gauthier
142, de la Plage
New Richmond G0C 2B0
(418) 392-4111
fax (418) 392-6048

B&B	
single	$40
double	$45-60
triple	$60-75
quad.	$85
child	$5-10

VS

Open year round

Number of rooms	4
rooms with sink	3
rooms in basement	2
shared bathrooms	2

Activities: 🍷 🏖 🚶 🤸

34. NEW RICHMOND

We are located in an attractive little corner of New-Richmond. Relaxation, serenity, home-made breakfasts. The sea and the mountains are also on the menu. Fishing, hiking, cultural and outdoor activities. Our house is your house. I will be waiting for you.

From Québec City, Hwy 20 East, Rte 132 East to New Richmond. Take Chemin Cyr and Boul. Perron East, turn left, drive 2km. From Percé, Boul. Perron, drive 0.4km and turn right.

B&B
LA RELÂCHE

Émilienne Bourdages
108, Bellevue, C.P. 36
New Richmond, Cap-Noir
G0C 1C0
(418) 392-6749
fax (418) 392-6359
odini@globetrotter.net

B&B	
single	$35
double	$45-50
triple	$50-60
quad.	$80
child	$5-10

Open year round

Number of rooms	3
shared bathrooms	2

Activities: 🏛 ⛴ ⛵ ⛷

---

35. NOUVELLE-OUEST

In the middle of a sea of mountains, this B&B, which used to be a school and a general store, will greet you with a warm welcome. Only 10km away from Parc Miguasha, the ferryboat (which goes to New Brunswick) and the beach. Nearby: crystalline waters where you will find Salmo Salar, the king of our rivers, as well as sea trout—the envy of all fishermen.

From Québec City, Hwy 20 and 132 E. for Nouvelle. Drive 4km, turn left on Ch. Village Allard. From Gaspé, after the "Crevier" gas station in Nouvelle-Ouest, turn right onto Ch. Village Allard. Follow the signs.

B&B
GÎTE LA VIEILLE FORGE

Isabelle Caissy and
Urgel Vallières
605, chemin Village Allard
Nouvelle-Ouest G0C 2G0
(418) 794-2061
(418) 794-8139
urgel@globetrotter.net

B&B	
single	$35
double	$50
child	$10

VS MC

Open year round

Number of rooms	4
shared bathrooms	2

Activities: 🐚 ⛵ ⛷ 🚶 ⛸

---

36. PERCÉ

"La Rêvasse" is a dream come true. Why else visit Percé? Oh yes, the rock... The advantage of the B&B at the rock is that it is accessible at both low and high tides. Plus, it is inhabited by very friendly people... Thanks for the Percé welcome!' (*S. Bret, Lyon-France*) Excursion package: 2 nights, cruise to île Bonaventure, off-track guided tours on the mountains of Percé. 2 people/double $138.[25] with reservation only.

From Québec City, Hwy 20 East, Rte 132 East to Percé. Near the Palais de Justice, Rue St-Michel.

B&B
À LA RÊVASSE

Brenda Cain and
William Lambert
16, St-Michel, C.P. 281
Percé G0C 2L0
tel/fax (418) 782-2980
(418) 782-2102
http://membres.tripod.
fr/revasse/revasse.html
revasse@globetrotter.net

B&B	
single	$40-45
double	$50-60
triple	$70-75
quad.	$85-90
child	$15

Taxes extra

Open: May 1 to Oct. 15

Number of rooms	5
rooms with private bath	1
rooms in basement	1
rooms with sink	4
shared bathrooms	2

Activities: 🏛 ⛴ ⛵ 🚶

37. PERCÉ

☀☀ | F | E | 🐕 | 🚗 | P | R2 | TA

Lucille and Victor, 9 years old, invite you to their traditional family home situated just outside the affluent town centre of Percé. The setting exudes calm and tranquillity, and this vast landscaped property has a beautiful view of the sea. Generous breakfasts made from local products.

From Gaspé, Rte 132 W. for Percé. Only 3.1km from Percé Tourist information. From Carleton, Rte 132 E. for Percé. It's 12.6km from the Cap d'Espoir caisse populaire.

B&B
CHEZ DESPARD

Lucille Despard
468, route 132 ouest
Percé G0C 2L0
(418) 782-5446

B&B	
single	$35-40
double	$45-50
triple	$55-60
quad.	$65-70
child	$7

Reduced rates: Sep.1 to June 20
Open year round

Number of rooms	4
shared bathrooms	2

Activities: 🏛 🚤 ⚓ 🕴 🛷

38. PERCÉ

☀☀☀ | F | E | 🐕 | P | 🚗 | R.5 | TA

We are located in the centre of the village, behind the church. Everything is very quiet, especially at night. Spacious solarium, large rooms, home-made breakfasts. Here you will be able to park the car, relax and go for a walk. Everything is within reach: Île Bonaventure, Percé rock, mountains, restaurants, boutiques. We are from Percé, live hear year-round and can help you plan your activities.

Rte 132 East to the village of Percé. Take rue du Cap Barré to the last house.

B&B
GÎTE DU MONT STE-ANNE

Ginette Gagné and
Michel Méthot
44, Cap Barré
Percé G0C 2L0
tel/fax (418) 782-2739

B&B	
single	$45
double	$55
triple	$70
quad.	$85
child	$15

VS
Reduced rates: May 15 to
June 24, Sep. 15 to Oct. 15
Open: May 15 to Oct. 15

Number of rooms	5
rooms with sink	4
rooms in basement	2
shared bathrooms	2

Activities: 🏛 🚤 ⚓ 🕴 🕴

39. PERCÉ

F | E | 🚭 | P | R.1 | TA

We invite you to discover the charms of an ancestral house and of a rustic barn, right in the heart of Percé. We offer you: beautiful cozy rooms, nourishing breakfasts, lounge with fireplace, reading corner, solarium, terrace and balconies. Tennis court nearby. 5 min walk from the Percé Rock.

From Québec City, Hwy 20 East, Rte 132 East. In the village centre, facing court house, next to the sea.

INN
LA MAISON ROUGE

Stéphanie Grégoire and
Jean-Baptiste Silla
125, Route 132 Ouest
Percé G0C 2L0
(418) 782-2227

B&B	
single	$48
double	$60-67
triple	$75-82
quad.	$90-97
child	$15

Taxes extra VS

Open: June 1 to Sep. 30

Number of rooms	10
shared bathrooms	4

Activities: 🏛 🚤 ⚓ 🕴 🕴

40. PERCÉ, STE-THÉRÈSE

☀☀☀ | F | e | P | 🐕 | R1.5 | TA

Enjoy a stay in this picturesque fishing village. Upon entering our B&B, you will be greeted by an old fisherman carved into the door by a St-Jean-Port-Joli artist. Comfortable, well-decorated rooms. Lavish breakfasts in a spacious, Bahutier-style dining room next to the sunny-coloured kitchen. Warm-hearted hostess.

15 min from Percé, Rte 132 West. In Ste-Thérèse, halfway between the dock and the church. At the windmill, opposite the Bria restaurant.

B&B
GÎTE DU MOULIN À VENT

Jeannine Desbois
247, Route 132, C.P. 10
Ste-Thérèse-de-Gaspé
Percé-Ste-Thérèse
G0C 3B0
(418) 385-4922
tel/fax (418) 385-3103

B&B	
single	$35
double	$50-60
child	$10

Open: May 1 to Sep. 30

Number of rooms	4
shared bathrooms	2

Activities: 🏛 ⛵ 🚣 🧍 🚴

---

41. PETITE-VALLÉE

★ ★ | F | e | 🏊 | P | 🚗 | ✂ | R5 | TA

On a long headland, set back from Route 132 and one hour (70km) from Forillon Park, our centenary house opens its doors to offer you a family welcome and traditional cuisine, featuring fish and seafood. New glassed-in dining-room with superb sea view. **Country Home p 152. See colour photos.**

From Québec, Hwy 20 East, Rte 132 East to Petite-Vallée. At the entrance to the village, take the first street on the left, Longue-Pointe. At the fork, stay left.

INN
LA MAISON LEBREUX

Denise Lebreux
2, rue Longue Pointe,
Petite-Vallée G0E 1Y0
(418) 393-2662
tel/fax (418) 393-3105

	B&B	MAP
single	$40-45	$55-60
double	$50-60	$80-90
triple	$65	$110
quad.	$80	$140
child	$10	$20

Taxes extra VS IT MC

Open year round

Number of rooms	8
rooms with sink	4
shared bathrooms	3

Activities: 🐚 ⛵ 🧍 🚣 ⛷

---

42. ST-ALEXIS-DE-MATAPÉDIA

☀☀☀ | F | E | 🏊 | 🚭 | P | 🚗 | R1.5 | TA

Enjoy a unique stay on natural plateaus. Original house, extensive wooded grounds, trails, large heated in-ground pool under a dome. Activities, local history. In the area: panoramas, maple groves, guided wild-bear tour, canoeing, salmon fishing, Fort Listuguj (circa 1760), winter sports. Very warm welcome.

85km from Carleton. In Matapédia, cross the bridge, turn right twd St-Alexis, 10km. At the stop sign, straight ahead for 1.4km. 100km from Amqui, St-Alexis bridge, via St-Benoît, 10km.

B&B
AUX BOIS D'AVIGNON

Laura Chouinard
171, Rustico Nord
St-Alexis-de-Matapédia
G0J 2E0
(418) 299-2537
tel/fax (418) 299-2111
boisdavi@globetrotter.qc.ca

B&B	
single	$44
double	$52
triple	$60
quad.	$70
child	$9

Taxes extra

Reduced rates: Oct. 1 to June 1
Open year round

Number of rooms	3
shared bathrooms	2

Activities: 🧍 🚴 🚣 ⛸ ⛷

43. ST-ANTOINE-DE-PADOUE ☀☀☀ F e 🚗 P R11

Situated in the backcountry between the sea and the mountain near Matapédia River (15min from Rte 132), Gîte la Villa du Vieux Clocher used to be a presbytery (1910). It's now furnished with period furniture and filled with good humour and conviviality. A variety of activities await. Exquisite Gaspesian breakfasts and cosy room. A dream come true! The next chapter in this adventure story is waiting for you: a town to discover.

From Québec City, Hwy 20 E, Rte 132 E. In front of Jardins de Métis, take the 234 to St-Octave-de-Métis and Padoue.

B&B
GÎTE LA VILLA
DU VIEUX CLOCHER

Marjolaine Fournier
179, rue Beaulieu
Padoue G0J 1X0
(418) 775-9654
(418) 775-8208
marjolaine.fournier@ri.cgocable.ca

B&B	
single	$40-60
double	$55-75
child	$10

VS MC

Reduced rates: Oct.1 to May 31
Open year round

Number of rooms	5
rooms with private bath	1
shared bathrooms	3

Activities: 🏛 ¶ 🛷 ⛷ 🐎

44. ST-OMER ☀☀☀ F 🚫 P 🚗 R3 TA

Our home is your home. Small village between sea and mountains, with 1,300 residents, 10 min from Carleton. Quiet house ringed by trees, 91 m from Route 132; patio, porch, backyard, parking. 5 min from the beach, café, snackbars, 20 min from Parc Miguasha, salmon fishing. Restful rooms. Good breakfast. A true Gaspé welcome awaits you.

From Québec City, Hwy 20 East and Rte 132 East to St-Omer. 1.5km after Aux Flots Bleus campground. From Percé, 1 m from St-Omer church.

B&B
GÎTE LE ROITELET

Lucina Quinn and
Maurice Leblanc
108, route St-Louis
St-Omer G0C 2Z0
(418) 364-7436
fax (418) 364-2045

B&B	
single	$35-40
double	$50-55
triple	$65-70.⁵⁰
child	$10-15

VS

Reduced rates: Sep. 1 to June 30
Open year round

Number of rooms	5
shared bathrooms	2

Activities: 🏛 🐚 🚣 ¶ 🚶

45. STE-ANGÈLE-DE-MÉRICI ☀☀☀ F E 🚗 P 🏊 R.5 TA

14km from St-Flavie and the St. Lawrence River, in the heart of the village of Ste-Angèle, nature centre of the Métissienne region. Inground pool; cozy, comfortable rooms; hearty breakfast any time. 10 to 20km from Karting Lelièvre, Mont Comi, Jardins de Métis, salmon fishing on the Métis river 300 m, Ste-Luce beach, De La Pointe golf course, Mont-Joli airport.

Hwy 20 and Rte 132 East. In Ste-Flavie, twd Mont-Joli. 12km past Mont-Joli. In the village of Ste-Angèle, turn right onto Boul. de la Vallée.

B&B
LA GUIMONTIÈRE

Jeanne-Mance Guimont
515, av. Bernard Levesque
Ste-Angèle-de-Mérici G0J 2H0
(418) 775-5542

B&B	
single	$40
double	$55
triple	$75
quad.	$95
child	$10

Reduced rates: Sep.15 to June 15
Open year round

Number of rooms	3
shared bathrooms	1

Activities: 🚣 ¶ 🛷 ⛷ 🐎

46. STE-ANNE-DES-MONTS

Why Ste-Anne-des-Monts? Well, of course to discover the magnificent Parc de la Gaspésie, Mont Albert and Mont Jacques Cartier. Golf, Explorama, and a warm welcome from the locals. 10% reductions for stays of three days or more. Rooms in the basement have a separate entrance.

From Québec City, Hwy 20 East, Rte 132 East to Ste-Anne-des-Monts. Turn left before the bridge. At the stop sign turn left on 1st Avenue.

B&B
CHEZ MARTHE-ANGÈLE

Marthe-Angèle Lepage
268, 1ʳᵉ Avenue Ouest,
C.P. 3159
Ste-Anne-des-Monts G0E 2G0
tel/fax (418) 763-2692

B&B	
single	$38-40
double	$53-55
triple	$68-70
quad.	$80
child	$10-15

Reduced rates: 10% 3 nights and more
Open year round

Number of rooms	5
rooms with sink	3
rooms in basement	3
shared bathrooms	3

Activities:

47. STE-ANNE-DES-MONTS

Sept. 2, 1998
"Dear Julie,
Our experience with you has truly enriched our journey. You have shared your home with us in every sense, and your extreme warmth and generosity will always be remembered as the highlight of our visit to the Gaspé. The breakfast alone was worth the trip! We look forward to sharing your passions, goodness and kindness again!"
(Clients)

From Rimouski, Rte 132 East. 6.7km past the Cap-Chat church. Ste-Anne-des-Monts. White house with red roof.

B&B
GÎTE LES 2 COLOMBES

Julie Paquet
996, boul. Ste-Anne-Ouest,
C.P. 572
Ste-Anne-des-Monts G0E 2G0
(418) 763-3756

B&B	
single	$40-45
double	$50-60
triple	$75

Reduced rates: Nov. 1 to Apr. 30
Open year round

Number of rooms	4
rooms with sink	1
shared wc	1
shared bathrooms	2

Activities:

48. STE-ANNE-DES-MONTS

Our guests cherish our merry breakfasts of favourite treats like homemade bread, jams and pancakes; the quiet location near the park and the sea, far from Route 132; and the soothing sea breeze. Guests tell us our warm welcome makes them feel like family. Welcome!

From Quebec City, Hwy 20 East, Rte 132 East, at junction of Rte 299 (Rte du Parc) for 1km. Turn left on 2nd street after the bridge; or heading east from the church, 1km, on the right.

B&B
SOUS LA BONNE ÉTOILE

Denis Béchard
30, 5ᵉ Rue Est, C.P. 1132
Ste-Anne-des-Monts
G0E 2G0
(418) 763-3402
Fax (418) 763-3456

B&B	
single	$40
double	$55
triple	$70
quad.	$85
child	$10-15

VS

Reduced rates: Nov. 1 to May 31
Open year round

Number of rooms	4
rooms with sink	1
rooms in semi-basement	4
shared bathrooms	2

Activities:

49. STE-ANNE-DES-MONTS, TOURELLE

F E P R.5

At the heart of the Gaspé peninsula, outdoor terrace from which to admire marine mammals, superb sunsets and fishing village. Discover Parc de la Gaspésie, Mont Albert, Mont Jacques-Cartier, Explorama, walking by the river. Two rooms with private bathrooms. Copious breakfast. 10% reduction for 3 nights or more. Welcome.

From Québec City, Hwy 20 East, Rte 132 East to Tourelle. From the rest area, drive 0.2km, turn left, white house.

B&B
AU COURANT DE LA MER

Bibiane Miville and
Rino Cloutier
3, Belvédère, C.P. 191
Tourelle G0E 2J0
tel/fax (418) 763-5440
For reservation only:
1-800-230-6709
from 5 pm to 11 pm

B&B	
single	$35-50
double	$50-60
triple	$65
quad.	$75
child	$7-12

VS

Open: Mar. 1 to Nov. 30

Number of rooms	5
rooms with private bath	2
shared bathrooms	2
shared wc	1
rooms in basement	1

Activities: 🏛 🍵 🚣 ⛷ 🐎

50. STE-ANNE-DES-MONTS, TOURELLE

F e P R4 TA

Enjoy peace quiet and the rustic decor of our B&B. Lovely rooms with bathrooms for your comfort. Refuel on our delicious old-fashioned-style apple crepes. St. Lawrence River view. Relax on our flowery terrace. 10 min from Ste-Anne-des-Monts, don't miss the Parc de la Gaspésie! 215km or 2 hrs 30 min from Gaspé.

Hwy 20 East and Rte 132, 1 hr from Matane. In Tourelle, 4km from the church.

B&B
GÎTE DE LA NOUVELLE-FRANCE

Danielle Martin and
Jean-Guy Brisebois
203, boul. Perron Est
Ste-Anne-des-Monts, Tourelle
G0E 2J0
(418) 763-3338
fax (418) 763-2815

B&B	
single	$45
double	$55
triple	$70
quad.	$85
child	$10

VS

Reduced rates: 10% for group reservation, Mar. and Apr.
Open year round

Number of rooms	4
rooms with private bath	4

Activities: ⛷ 🐎 🎿 🐴

51. STE-ANNE-DES-MONTS, TOURELLE

F e P R3.5 TA

Welcome to our house at the foot of a lovely mountain by the "sea". You can walk along the shore to Tourelle and watch the fishermen in the harbour. Our breakfasts, complete with crepes and a selection of home-made preserves, go over big with guests – as does our Gaspé-style table talk. You'll feel right at home in our house.

From Québec City, Hwy 20 East, Rte 132 East to Tourelle. Drive 2km past the church (we are located 8 min from the intersection of the 299 - Parc de la Gaspésie Sainte-Anne-des-Monts).

B&B
GÎTE DE LA TOUR

Elise Dupuis and
Pierre Paul Labrie
151, boul. Perron Est C.P. 183
Tourelle G0E 2J0
tel/fax (418) 763-2802

B&B	
single	$35
double	$50
triple	$60
child	$5-10

VS

Open: June 1 to Oct. 15

Number of rooms	3
shared bathrooms	2

Activities: 🏛 ⛷ 🚶 🛷 🎿

52. STE-ANNE-DES-MONTS, TOURELLE

Ancestral house in Tourelle, a picturesque town sure to charm you. Warm welcome, making guests feel right at home. Clean, charming rooms; splendid antiques throughout the house; good food; very flexible schedule.

"A lovely B&B. I look forward to coming back." (a client)

From Montréal, Hwy 20 East, Rte 132 East to Tourelle. From Ste-Anne-des-Monts, at junction of Rte 299 (Rte du Parc), Rte 132 East twd Gaspé for 4km.

B&B
GÎTE DU PIONNIER
DE TOURELLE

Doris Therrien
87, boul. Perron Ouest,
Rte 132 C.P. 157
Tourelle G0E 2J0
(418) 763-7254

B&B	
single	$35-40
double	$50-55
triple	$70
quad.	$85
child	$10-15

Reduced rates: Nov. 1 to Avr. 30
Open year round

Number of rooms	3
shared wc	1
shared bathrooms	1

Activities: 🏛 ⚞ 🏃 ⚓ 🏃

53. STE-FLAVIE

Magnificent site, facing the majestic St. Lawrence River. Vast landscaped grounds. Small covered bridge across the river to the falls and the lake, where you can feed the trout. Welcome to snowmobilers; warm reception, memorable decor, lavish breakfasts. Jardins de Métis, 5km; art centre, 0.7km; snowmobiling, 1.5km. Family-size room available.

From Quebec City, Hwy 20 East, Rte 132 East to Ste-Flavie. Continue to 571 Route de la Mer.

B&B
AUX CHUTES

Nicole R. and Jocelyn Bélisle
571, route de la Mer
Ste-Flavie G0J 2L0
(418) 775-9432
fax (418) 775-5747
www.bbcanada.
com/1866.html

B&B	
single	$38-43
double	$45-65
triple	$55-75
quad.	$70-85
child	$10-15

VS MC

Reduced rates: 10% 3 nights and more from Otc. 15 to Apr. 15
Open year round

Number of rooms	5
rooms with sink	1
shared bathrooms	2

Activities: 🏛 🍴 ⚓ ⚞ 🏍

54. STE-FLAVIE

Come and experience traditional Gaspé hospitality in an ancestral home rich with the echoes of four generations of the same family. Magnificent sunsets over the St-Laurent will cast a spell. 6km from the famous Métis gardens and just a few steps from excellent restaurants.

Take Rte 132 East twd Gaspé, 24km beyond Rimouski, and 0.4km beyond the tourist information centre of Ste-Flavie.

B&B
LA MARÉE BLEUE

Jacqueline Paquet and
Peter Innis
411, route-de-la-Mer
Ste-Flavie G0J 2L0
(418) 775-7801
innisp@globetrotter.net

B&B	
single	$50
double	$55
child	$10

VS IT

Reduced rates: Sep.15 to June 15
Open year round

Number of rooms	4
shared bathrooms	2

Activities: 🏛 🍴 🐎 ⚞ 🚲

55. STE-FLAVIE

☀☀☀ F e P 🚗 🐾 R1 TA

I await you by the river at the gateway to the Gaspé region amongst the charm and comfort of a wooden house. Here, the day starts with the sound of waves lapping on the shore, warms up with the pleasant company and comes to a close with the colourful spectacle of the sunset.

From Québec City, Hwy 20 East, Rte 132 East to Ste-Flavie. 5km past the church, driving east along the shore. From Gaspé, Rte 132 West. 60km from Matane.

B&B
LA QUÉBÉCOISE

Cécile Wedge
705, de la Mer, route 132 Est
Ste-Flavie G0J 2L0
(418) 775-2898
(418) 775-3209
fax (418) 775-9793

B&B	
single	$40
double	$50-55

Reduced rates: Oct. 1 to May 31
Open year round

Number of rooms	3
shared wc	1
shared bathrooms	1

Activities: 🏛 🍂 🚣 🎿 🏃

---

56. STE-FLORENCE

☀☀ F e 🚭 🚗 P R1.5 TA

Situated away from the hustle and bustle, this ancient house used to be my grandparents' home. You will enjoy a refreshing sleep here. Behind the house, there's a stream, where you fish the trout or appreciate its natural surroundings. In front, there's a spectacular view of Rivière Matapédia, where fisherman catch large salmon. Delicious breakfasts served up with a smile.

From Québec City, Hwy 20, to Mont-Joli Rte 132 for Ste-Florence. In the town, at the railway crossing, turn right, 1km.

B&B
GÎTE DU VIEUX MOULIN

Réjeanne Doiron
314, Beaurivage nord C.P. 85
Sainte-Florence G0J 2M0
(418) 756-6208
www.multimania.com/
vieuxmoulin
vieux_moulin@hotmail.com

B&B	
single	$40
double	$50
child	$5

Reduced rates: Oct.15 to Apr. 30
Open year round

Number of rooms	4
shared bathrooms	2

Activities: 🏃 🎿 🚴 🛷 🏊

57. CAP-D'ESPOIR, PERCÉ

F | e | 🚗 | P | 🏊 | R5 | M.5 | TA

Come relax on the beach and be lulled to sleep by the sound of the waves. Share stories by the fire on the beach. Come and meet us. Three pleasantly fitted-out cottages (one on ground floor, one upstairs) with a view of Île Bonaventure are available. 10 minutes from a great attraction: Percé. Look up, you will see île Bonaventure. Welcome.

From Québec City, Hwy 20 E., Rte 132 E., located 12km west of Percé.

COUNTRY HOME
CHALETS DE LA PLAGE

Jason Pitre
mailing address:
1233, Principale, C.P. 26
Val-d'Espoir G0C 3G0
(418) 782-2181
fax (418) 782-5214

No. houses	3
No. rooms	2
No. people	4-8
WEEK-SUMMER	$650
DAY-SUMMER	$100

Reduced rates: May 1 to June 23, Sep. 1 to Oct. 31
Open: May 1 to Oct. 31

Activities: 🏛 ⛵ 🐎

58. PERCÉ

F | E | 🚫 | P | 🏊 | R1 | M1

La Maison Laberge is a typical Gaspé house located on Cap Mont-Joli. The house affords magnificent panoramas of the ledge known as the Trois Sœurs, which overlooks Cap Barré. To the east, the massive wall that is the Rocher Percé can be seen rising up behind Cap Mont-Joli. **B&B in Bas-St-Laurent section, p 61 no 32.**

From Québec City, Hwy 20 East, Rte 132 East. Located above the village on the cap Mont-Joli, on the ocean side.

COUNTRY HOME
LA MAISON LABERGE

Bertrand Daraiche and
Thérèse Ng Wai
232, Route 132 Est
Percé G0C 2L0
(418) 782-2816
(514) 393-1417
fax (514) 393-9444
www.total.net/~chq
chq@total.net

No. houses	1
No. rooms	2
No. people	6
WEEK-SUMMER	$700
DAY-SUMMER	$125

Open: June 1 to Sep.30

Activities: 🏛 ⛵ 🚲

59. PETITE-VALLÉE

F | e | ✖ | P | 🚗 | 🏊 | R5 | M1 | TA

On the coast, magnificent fully equipped chalets offer you the rest you want. You will go to sleep and wake up to the sound of the waves and watch the sun set or rise over the sea. This is what awaits you here! **Country Inn p 146. See colour photos.**

From Québec, Hwy 20 East, Rte 132 East to Petite-Vallée. At the entrance to the village, first street on the left, Longue Pointe. At the fork, stay left.

COUNTRY HOME
LA MAISON LEBREUX

Denise Lebreux
2, Longue Pointe
Petite-Vallée G0E 1Y0
(418) 393-2662
tel/fax (418) 393-3105

No. houses	4
No. rooms	1-2
No. people	2-4
WEEK-SUMMER	$525
WEEK-WINTER	$400
DAY-SUMMER	$80
DAY-WINTER	$60

Taxes extra MC VS IT

Reduced rates: Sep.16 to May 14
Open year round

Activities: 🦞 ⛵ 🎿

60. ST-ALEXIS-DE-MATAPÉDIA

F E ♿ 🚗 P R1 M4 TA

Holiday on a farm in Gaspésie? Why not! Bracing, edifying vacation: in dairy farm, woods, rivers, small, equipped house with wood-panelled interior. Fishing, canoeing, swimming, cycling, hunting, ice fishing, skidooing, maple grove, wilderness camping, sweat lodge, campfire, Acadian history. On way into Baie des Chaleurs and N.-B. Warm welcome. By reservation. RVs welcome.

From Mont-Joli to Matapédia, St-Alexis bridge, Rang St-Benoît, 6km. From Carleton to Matapédia, Matapédia bridge. 16km, right on Rang St-Benoît.

COUNTRY HOME
LA P'TITE MAISON
DES LEBLANC

René Leblanc
153 A, St-Benoit
St-Alexis-de-Matapédia
G0J 2E0
(418) 299-2106
tel/fax (418) 299-2443

No. houses	1
No. rooms	3
No. people	2-8
WEEK-SUMMER	$450-499
WEEK-WINTER	$350-400
DAY-SUMMER	$69-99
DAY-WINTER	$59-89

Reduced rates: Oct.15 to May 15
Open year round

Activities: 🏛 🚲 ⛷ 🎿

FARM ACTIVITIES

Farm Stay:

Maple Sugar Camp Adrien Marquis

1:30 hour guided tour of maple sugar production with free samples of maple sugar products.
$3 per adult, children under 12 free.

1580, rang des Bouffard G0J 1Y0
Tel.: (418) 562-1760

ÎLES-DE-LA-MADELEINE

Réserve écologique
de l'Île Brion

Gulf of
St. Lawrence

Grosse Île

Grosse-Île

Pointe-de-l'Est
National Wildlife
Area

Havre de la
Grande-Entrée

199

Grande-Entrée

Île de la
Grande Entrée

199

Île aux Loups

Pointe-aux-Loups

Lagune de la Grande-Entrée

Lagune du Havre aux Maisons

Dune-du-Sud

Île du Cap
aux Meules

Île du Havre
aux Maisons

Fatima

199

1

Havre-
aux-Maisons

Les Caps

? Meules

Cap-aux-

Gulf of
St. Lawrence

L'Étang-du-Nord

La Vernière

Anse aux
Étangs

L'Île-d'Entrée

Baie de
Plaisance

Île d'Entrée

Baie du
Havre aux
Basques

Dune de
Sandy Hook

Île du
Havre Aubert

La Grave

Havre-Aubert

L'Étang-
des-Caps

Solomon

L'Anse-à-
la-Cabane

Aurigny

Souris (P.E.I.)

Montréal

0   5   10 km

©ULYSSES

* The numbers on the map refer to the numbering of the establishments of this region

1. FATIMA

✹✹✹ F e 🚭 �car P R1.5

Enjoy the hospitality of a real "Madelinot" family. Quiet, wooded area, near services, in a residential district on the island of Cap-aux-Meules. Comfortable rooms, 1km from the beach. Hearty breakfasts for which we are now famous. Lounge with TV. Outdoor terrace at your disposal. Warm welcome, friendly atmosphere. Our home is your home; we await you.

From the ferry, Rte 199 East, Chemin Marconi to Chemin les Caps. In Fatima, near the church, take Chemin de l'Hôpital. Turn left on Chemin Thorne.

B&B
GÎTE BLANDINE ET THOMAS

Blandine and Thomas Thorne
56, chemin E. Thorne
Fatima GOB IGO
(418) 986-3006
fax (418) 986-6126
www.ilesdelamadeleine.
com/b+b/

B&B	
single	$45
double	$55
triple	$65
quad.	$75
child	$10

Open: May 1 to Oct. 31

Number of rooms	4
shared bathrooms	2
shared wc	1

Activities: 🥾 ⛵ ⚲ 🚲 🏇

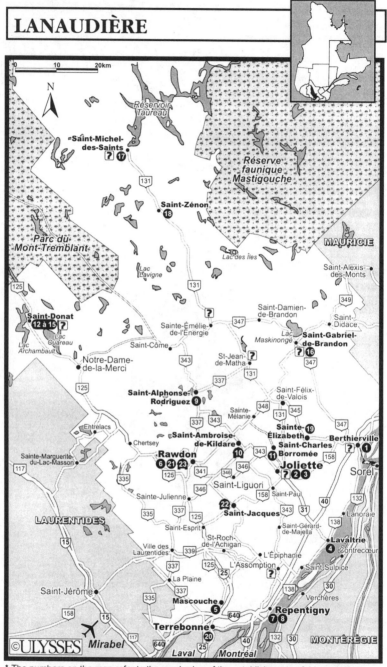

LANAUDIÈRE

1. BERTHIERVILLE

☀☀ F E 🐕 P R2 TA

This elegant Victorian house from 1888 offers you a warm welcome. Sylvie greets you with her little sweet treats that will introduce you to the region's culinary secrets. Make the most of this pied-à-terre and enhance your stay with many activities: music, nature, art and culture will convince you to stay more than a day. Impressive breakfast.

From Montréal, Hwy 40 East, toward Berthier, Exit 144. Rte 158 East to 138 East. Drive 1.5km, turn left just past the bridge, 3rd house on the right.

B&B
MANOIR LATOURELLE

Sylvie Couture, Roxane, Colette and Jules Rémillard
120, rivière Bayonne Nord
Berthierville J0K 1A0
(450) 836-1129
toll free 1-877-836-1129
fax (450) 836-2365
valremi@autray.net

B&B	
single	$45
double	$60
triple	$80
quad.	$100
child	$15

Taxes extra VS IT

Open year round

Number of rooms	4
shared bathrooms	2

Activities: 🏛 ⛴ 🚶 🏃 🚴

---

2. JOLIETTE

☀☀☀ F e 🚗 P 🐕 R.5 TA

Lanaudière Excellence Prize 1997-98. Enjoy comfort, human warmth, breakfast, the terrace, flowery garden and the soul of this hundred-year-old house. Located near the town centre, the amphitheatre, art museum, golf courses, bike paths, skating rink or boating on the river. Bikes available.

From Montréal or Québec city, Hwy 40, Exit 122 to Joliette. In Joliette, left on Rue Salaberry, facing the tourist office, to Boul Base-de-Roc, turn left.

B&B
GÎTE AUX P'TITS OISEAUX

Céline Coutu
722, boul. Base-de-Roc
Joliette J6E 5P7
(450) 752-1401
fax (450) 759-7836

B&B	
single	$45-50
double	$55-60-70
triple	$75
quad.	$100
child	$10

VS

Open year round

Number of rooms	4
rooms with private bath	1
rooms in basement	1
shared bathrooms	1

Activities: 🏛 🐚 🚶 🏃 🚴

---

3. JOLIETTE

F e 🚭 P 🏊 R2

Rest and relaxation await you at our friendly, down-to-earth B&B, where you will enjoy a scrumptious breakfast. Take a walk in our enchanting garden or huddle around a bonfire. Numerous activities nearby: music, golf (0.5km), bike path, amphitheatre (2km), Joliette (5km), art museum (6km). Indoor pool open May-Sep. Skating rink in winter. Visit to the greenhouses and guided tours of Joliette ($).

Hwy 40, Exit 122, Hwy 31 Exit 7 for St-Paul, first street on your right, 2.4km.

B&B
LA PETITE MONET

Francine and
Claude Coulombe
3306 Base-de-Roc
Joliette J6E 3Z1
tel/fax (450)759-5798

B&B	
single	$50
double	$60
child	$10

Open year round

Number of rooms	2
rooms in semi basement	2
shared wc	1
shared bathrooms	1

Activities: 🏛 🚶 🏃 🚴 ⛷

4. LAVALTRIE

☀☀☀ | F | E | 🚫 | 🐕 | 🚗 | P | 🏊 | R.5 | TA

At Au Gré du St-Laurent, all of your desires will be fulfilled. Situated 30min from Montréal, guests are dazzled by the panoramic view of the St. Lawrence River. Our B&B combines all of the modern conveniences with intimacy and charm. Guests enjoy generous home-made breakfasts and elegant rooms, whose colours are inspired by the seasons. Our smile and enthusiasm are catchy! Air conditioning, pool, antique shops and much more.

Hwy 40, Exit 122, Rte 131 South for Lavaltrie, about 5km. Turn right at the church, Rte 138 West, 1km. Left on Rue St-Thomas.

B&B
AU GRÉ DU ST-LAURENT

Diane Plasse St-Laurent
180, St-Thomas
Lavaltrie J0K 1H0
(450) 586-3257
(514) 386-1987
fax (450) 586-0981
http://users.mmic.net/cstl
cstl@mmic.net

B&B	
single	$45
double	$60
child	$15

Taxes extra

Open year round

Number of rooms	2
shared wc	1
shared bathrooms	1

Activities: 🏛 🏃 🚲 🐎 🏃

5. MASCOUCHE

☀☀ | F | e | ♿ | 🚫 | P | R3 | TA

30 min from downtown Montréal and Mirabel. Large sunny house in the country, surrounded by fields and greenery. Nearby: horseback riding, snowmobile trails. Parking. Warm and courteous welcome. Welcome to La Maison des Érables.

From Québec City, Hwy 40, Hwy 640 West and 25 North. From Montréal, Hwy 15 North, 440 East, 25 North. From Mirabel, Hwy 15 South, 640 East, 25 North. Exit 34, left on St-Henri, 1.5km.

B&B
LA MAISON DES ÉRABLES

Marie-Paule and Claude Potvin
2124, boul. St-Henri
Mascouche J7K 3C3
(450) 966-9508

B&B	
single	$40
double	$45
triple	$65
quad.	$85
child	$10

Open year round

Number of rooms	4
rooms with sink	3
shared wc	1
shared bathrooms	2

Activities: 🏛 🍎 🏃 🐎 🛷

6. RAWDON

☀☀☀ | F | E | 🚗 | P | R.1 | TA

A memorable stay in this Victorian house is offered to wilderness lovers, history buffs, skiers and golfers alike. Enjoy the mansard roofed bedrooms, the 5-course breakfast on the gallery or in the garden, and a guide for your cultural, gastronomic or sporting activities. My goal is your enjoyment! Mimi. Lanaudière Excellence Prize 1995-96.

From Montréal, Hwy 25 N. In St-Esprit take Rte 125 N. In Ste-Julienne take Rte 337 N. to Rawdon (Rue Queen is the main street). Or from Mirabel, Hwy 15 N., exit Rte 158 E. to Ville des Laurentides, then Rte 337 N... From Dorval, Hwy 40 E., 640 W., 25 N...

B&B
GÎTE DU CATALPA

Micheline Trudel
3730, rue Queen
Rawdon J0K 1S0
(450) 834-5253
www.did-dftg.com/
catalpa/index.htm

B&B	
single	$35-50
double	$50-65
triple	$75-90
quad.	$100-115
child	$15

Taxes extra VS

Open year round

Number of rooms	5
rooms with private bath	1
shared bathrooms	2

Activities: 🚴 🏃 🛷 🏃 🐎

7. REPENTIGNY

F E ⊘ 🐕 🚗 P 🛶 R.2

La Maison de Morphée is situated at the entrance of Repentigny on the outskirts of Montréal. You will find many different activities here: theatre, movies, cross-country skiing, walking, cycling, golfing, swimming... Whether you are out and about or snuggled up inside our home, you will enjoy unwinding in our spa, which has a whirpool bath, sauna and massage therapy. Our cosy rooms will deliver you into the arms of Morpheus, the god of sleep.

From Montréal or Québec city, Hwy 40, Exit 96 East twd Charlemagne. After the fourth light or Rte 138, twd Charlemagne.

B&B
LA MAISON DE MORPHÉE

Suzanne Le Brun and
Claude Mercier
221, Notre Dame des Champs
Repentigny J6A 3B4
(450) 582-2303

B&B	
single	$40
double	$70
triple	$95
quad.	$120
child	$0-15

VS MC IT

Open year round

Number of rooms	4
rooms with private bath	2
shared bathrooms	2

Activities: 🏊 ⛷ 🚶 🚴 🎿

---

8. REPENTIGNY

☀☀☀ F E 🚗 🐕 P 🛶 R.5 TA

Large, modern air-conditioned house near the St. Lawrence River. 30 min from Mirabel and Dorval airports; 15 min from the Biodome and the Olympic Stadium. Kitchen, parking, in-ground pool, fireplace. Accommodations for 12 people. Room with private entrance.

From Mirabel, Hwy 15 South, 640 East to Repentigny, left on l'Assomption, right on Perrault, left on Gaudreault. From Dorval, 520 East, 40 East, Charlemagne Exit 96 East...138, Claude David, Boul. l'Assomption, right on Perrault.

B&B
LA VILLA DES FLEURS

Denise Cloutier and
Claude Neveu
45, rue Gaudreault
Repentigny J6A 1M3
(450) 654-9209
fax (450) 654-1220
www3.sympatico.ca
/lavilladesfleurs
lavilladesfleurs@sympatico.ca

B&B	
single	$30-40-50
double	$40-50-60
triple	$60-70
quad.	$70-80-90
child	$10

VS AM

Open year round

Number of rooms	5
rooms with sink	3
rooms with private bath	1
shared bathrooms	2

Activities: 🏛 🏊 🚤 🚣 ⛷

---

9. ST-ALPHONSE-RODRIGUEZ

☀☀☀ F e ⊘ 🐕 P R2.5

Perched atop the Promontoire cross, in a relaxing setting, overlooking Lac Pierre, this "Swiss chalet" transports you to heaven. On site: fireplace, books, large plot of land. 500 metres away: beach, canoeing. Nearby: snowmobile trail, skiing, hiking, golf, horseback riding, music festival.

From Montréal, Hwy 40 East, Exit 122 twd Joliette, then Rte 343 North. In St-Alphonse, right at Lac Pierre, left on N.-Dame, past the church, Ch. Lac Pierre North. Drive along Rue Promontoire for 2km.

B&B
LA PETITE CHARTREUSE

Christiane Merle
771, rue Promontoire
St-Alphonse-Rodriguez
J0K 1W0
(450) 883-3961
www.megacom.net/~latitcha
latitcha@megacom.net

B&B	
single	$35-55
double	$50-70
triple	$65-85
quad.	$100

Open year round

Number of rooms	3
rooms with sink	1
shared bathrooms	2

Activities: 🚣 🚶 🎿 🛷 ⛷

10. ST-AMBROISE-DE-KILDARE

☀☀☀☀ | F | E | 🚗 | P | 🏊 | R2 | TA

A weekend at school? Why not if it is located on a farm with 400 sheep and offers: rooms with private bathrooms, communal kitchen, meeting room, heated in-ground pool and fine cuts of meat. Discover our breeding facilities, our region and wool fleece; we enthusiastically await you. **Country-style Dining p 18.**

From Montréal, Hwy 40 East, Exit 122, Hwy 31 North. Rte 158 West, 1km, right on Rte 343 North, drive 15km to St-Ambroise. Left at flashing yellow light on Rang 5, 2km. Pink-and-white farmhouse on the left!

B&B
BERGERIE DES NEIGES

Desneiges Pepin and
Pierre Juillet
1401, Rang 5
St-Ambroise-de-Kildare
J0K 1C0
tel/fax (450) 756-8395
bergeriedesneiges
@moncourrier.com

B&B	
single	$50
double	$65
child	$15

Taxes extra VS

Open year round

Number of rooms	4
rooms with private bath	4

Activities: 🚣 🚶 🚴 🎿

11. ST-CHARLES-BORROMÉE, JOLIETTE

☀☀☀☀ | F | e | 🚭 | P | R.5

Under hundred-year-old maple trees, our house opens its doors to relaxation. Located in a residential district near the Rivière Assomption, Gîte Sous Les Érables welcomes you to calm and comfort. Near golf courses, the biking trail, restaurants, the museum, the Festival International de Lanaudière and summer theatres.

Hwy 40, Exit 122, Rte 31 North twd downtown. After the cathedral, at the 5th light, turn right, 1km.

B&B
GÎTE SOUS LES ÉRABLES

Fernande Chamberland
and J.-Guy St-Arneault
90, Louis-Bazinet
St-Charles-Borromée, Joliette
J6E 6T6
(450) 755-2318
fax (450) 755-4429
mchamber@total.net

B&B	
single	$45
double	$55

VS MC

Open: May 1 to Dec. 15

Number of rooms	2
rooms with private bath	2

Activities: 🏛 🍴 🚶 🚴

12. ST-DONAT

☀☀☀ | F | E | ♿ | 🐟 | 🚗 | P | 🏊 | R1 | TA

Charm, warmth and comfort await you at this Canadian house right on Lac Archambault, across from the village and a 5 minute's walk via Parc des Pionniers. Private beach, fishing dock, pedal boat, canoe and bike supplied. Motor-boat rental. Mt-Tremblant Park: 12km away; Mt-Garceau: 3km away; snowmobile trail: 50 metres away; a few metres from cross-country ski trail; golf course: 4km away.

From Montréal, Hwy 25 North or 15 North, Exit 89 to St-Donat, left on Ave. du Lac, right on Chemin Bilodeau, right on Chemin La Marguerite.

B&B
AU PETIT CHÂTEAU DU LAC

Johanne Bertrand
59, chemin la Marguerite
St-Donat J0T 2C0
(819) 424-4768

B&B	
single	$55-65
double	$65-75
child	$15-20

Open: Dec. 1 to Mar. 31 and from May 15 to Oct. 15

Number of rooms	3
shared bathrooms	2

Activities: 🚣 🚶 🚤 🎿 🏃

AUBERGE LA MARÉE DOUCE, Pointe-au-Père, Bas-St-Laurent

LE REFUGE FORESTIER, Maison de campagne, St-Alexandre, Kamouraska, Bas-St-Laurent

AUBERGE LA SOLAILLERIE, St-André, Kamouraska, Bas-St-Laurent

AU VIEUX PRESBYTÈRE, St-Éloi, Bas-St-Laurent

AUBERGE DE L'EIDER, Ste-Luce-sur-Mer, Bas-St-Laurent

AUBERGE LES PIGNONS VERTS, Austin, Cantons-de-l'Est

CHEZ LA MÈRE POULE, Bolton Centre, Cantons-de-l'Est

UNE FLEUR AU BORD DE L'EAU, Granby, Cantons-de-l'Est

AUX JARDINS CHAMPÊTRES, Magog, Cantons-de-l'Est

AUBERGE DE LA TOUR, Orford, Cantons-de-l'Est

LA BELLE ÉCHAPPÉE, Magog, Cantons-de-l'Est

AU SAUT DU LIT, Magog, Cantons-de-l'Est

LES DOUCES HEURES D'ANTAN, Tingwick, Centre-du-Québec

AUBERGE LA MUSE, Baie-St-Paul, Charlevoix

À LA CHOUETTE, Baie-St-Paul, Charlevoix

AUX PETITS OISEAUX, Baie-St-Paul, Charlevoix

TOURLOGNON, Petite-Rivière-St-François, Charlevoix

Le Gîte Chez Gertrude

CHEZ GERTRUDE, St-Urbain, Charlevoix

AUBERGE DES GLACIS, St-Eugène-de-l'Islet, Chaudière-Appalaches

LA P'TITE BALEINE, Bergeronnes, Côte-Nord, Manicouagan-Duplessis

MAISON HOVINGTON, Tadoussac, Côte-Nord, Manicouagan-Duplessis

GÎTE L'ÉCUME DE MER, La Martre, Gaspésie

LA MAISON LEBREUX, Petite-Vallée, Gaspésie

CHALETS DES PINS, Maison de campagne, Rawdon, Lanaudière

LA VILLA DES FLEURS, Repentigny, Lanaudière

LE PROVINCIALAT, Lac-Nominingue, Laurentides

AUBERGE VILLA BELLERIVE, Lac-Nominingue, Laurentides

AUBERGE-RESTAURANT « CHEZ IGNACE », Lac-Nominingue, Laurentides

AUBERGE LA PETITE CACHÉE, Mont-Tremblant, Laurentides

AUBERGE LE LUPIN, Mont-Tremblant, Laurentides

L'AUBERGE À LA CROISÉE DES CHEMINS, Mont-Tremblant, La Conception, Laurentides

GÎTE ET COUVERT LA MARIE-CHAMPAGNE, Mont-Tremblant, Lac Supérieur, Laurentides

AUBERGE LAC DU PIN ROUGE, St-Hippolyte, Laurentides

Wilde's heath
B & B

LES JARDINS DU « LORD » WILDE (WILDE'S HEATH B&B), Mont-Tremblant, St-Jovite, Laurentides

LES JARDINS DE LA GARE, Val-Morin, Laurentides

AUBERGE DE LA GARE, Ste-Adèle, Laurentides

NID D'AMOUR, Val-Morin, Laurentides

La maison de l'Enclos

LA MAISON DE L'ENCLOS, Maison de campagne, Rosemère, Laurentides

MAISON EMERY JACOB, St-Tite, Mauricie

Gîte
Le St·Élias
BED & BREAKFAST

PRIX D'EXCELLENCE
RÉGIONAL
D'ACCUEIL
1995-96
AGRICOTOURS

LE ST-ÉLIAS, Batiscan, Mauricie

Auberge Le Château Crête

LE CHÂTEAU CRÊTE, Grandes-Piles, Mauricie

GÎTE DU PETIT COUVENT, Trois-Rivières, Mauricie

DOMAINE DE LA TEMPLERIE, Table champêtre, Huntingdon, Montérégie

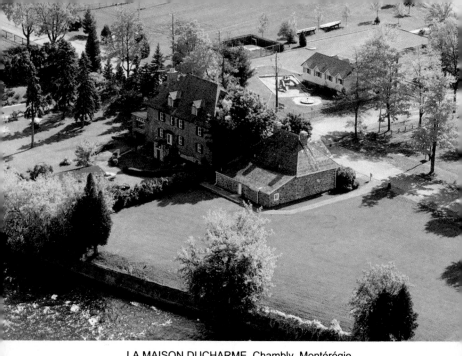

LA MAISON DUCHARME, Chambly, Montérégie

LA VICTORIENNE, rue Notre-Dame Est, Montréal, région de Montréal

L'air du Temps

AUBERGE L'AIR DU TEMPS, Chambly, Montérégie

PIERRE ET DOMINIQUE, Carré St-Louis, Montréal, région de Montréal

AUBERGE LA MAISON DES MERISIERS, Denholm, Outaouais

LES JARDINS DE VINOY, Vinoy, Chénéville, Outaouais

LA MAISON ANCESTRALE THOMASSIN, Québec, Beauport, région de Québec

AUBERGE CHEMIN DU ROY, Deschambault, région de Québec

AUX TROIS BALCONS, rue Saunders, Québec, région de Québec

HAYDEN'S WEXFORD HOUSE ET LES SUITES-APPARTEMENTS DU CAP-BLANC, rue Champlain, Québec, région de Québec

B&B MAISON LESAGE, chemin St-Louis, Québec, région de Québec

CHALETS-VILLAGE MONT-SAINTE-ANNE, Mont-Ste-Anne, St-Ferréol, région de Québec

AUBERGE PRESBYTÈRE MONT LAC VERT, Hébertville, Saguenay-Lac-St-Jean

AUBERGE LA MAISON LAMY, Métabetchouan, Saguenay-Lac-St-Jean

13. ST-DONAT

☀☀☀☀ F E P R1 TA

New, very sunny B&B with 5 spacious, soundproof rooms. Surrounded by lakes, 8 kilometres from Mont-Tremblant park. Lovely village with shops, bars and restaurants. Snowmobile paradise. Specials for groups and extended stays. "Meal" packages. Reduced rates for downhill skiing.
Your hosts, *Louise and Jean.*

From Montréal, Rte 125 North or Hwy 15 North, Exit 89, Rte 329 North to St-Donat. At the lights, in the centre of town, turn right on Allard street, 1km from church.

B&B
HALTE AUX PETITS OISEAUX

Sylvie Bouchard and
Jean L'Espérance
631, Allard
St-Donat J0T 2C0
(819) 424-3064
fax (819) 424-4367
www.st-donat.com/halte/

B&B	
single	$45
double	$65
triple	$90
quad.	$115
child	$10

Taxes extra VS MC AM

Reduced rates: Oct. 30 to Nov. 30 and Mar. 30 to May 30
Open year round

Number of rooms	5
rooms with private bath	5

Activities: 🛶 🎿 🚶 🛷 ⛷

14. ST-DONAT

☀☀ F e 🚗 P R.1 TA

Near many sports: winter and summer, I have 3 rooms for you, tv, sink, all the conveniences. Comfortable house with wrap-around veranda, close to a large clean lake, with clean beach and park for children. Warm welcome.

From Montréal, Hwy 25 and Rte 125 North to St-Donat. Or Hwy 15 North, Exit 89, Rte 329 North to St-Donat. At the flashing light, Rte 125 North. After the traffic light in the centre of town, at the second stop, left on Rue Bellevue.

B&B
LA MAISON ROBIDOUX

Annie Robidoux
284, rue Bellevue
St-Donat J0T 2C0
tel/fax (819) 424-2379

B&B	
single	$45
double	$60-65
triple	$80
quad.	$100
child	$10-15

VS MC

Reduced rates: Nov., Apr., May and more than 2 nights
Open year round

Number of rooms	4
rooms with sink	4
shared wc	1
shared bathrooms	2

Activities: 🚶 🏇 🛷 🎿 🐎

15. ST-DONAT

☀☀☀☀ F e 🚫 🚗 P 🏊 R2 TA

Ten kilometres from Mont-Tremblant park, at the foot of the ski hills, our modern, air-conditioned lakeside B&B boasts one room with queen-size bed and a family suite with private bathroom, fireplace and fridge. On site: fishing, motor-boat rental, pontoon with guide. Discount for 3 nights or more. Looking forward to welcoming you.

From Montréal, Hwy 25 and Rte 125 North to St-Donat or Hwy 15 North, Exit 89, Rte 329 North to St-Donat. At flashing light, Rte 125 North to traffic lights in the centre of the village, right on Rue Allard, drive 2km to end, left 1km.

B&B
LA MAISON SUR LE LAC

Line and Denis Boivin
103, chemin Lac Blanc
St-Donat J0T 2C0
(819) 424-5057
fax (819) 424-1795
www.st-donat.com/maison

B&B	
single	$50-55
double	$60-65
triple	$80
quad.	$95
child	$0-15

VS

Reduced rates: 15% 3 nights and more
Open year round

Number of rooms	2
rooms with private bath	1
shared bathrooms	1

Activities: 🛷 🛶 🎿 🚶 ⛷

16. ST-GABRIEL-DE-BRANDON

 F E 🚫 🐾 🚗 P 🏊 R1

Andante! Lento... Here everything is music! The gentle touch of the wind off the lake, the warmth of the hearth for peace and quiet, the spa's caresses for relaxation, Princesse's sweet purring, this B&B's special treats for pleasure! Need a little rest? We are waiting for you!

From Montréal, Hwy 40 East, Exit 144, right on Rte 158 for 2km, right on Rte 347 North, right twd St-Gabriel, drive about 30km.

B&B
L'ANDANTE

Lise Vézina and
Claude Perrault
480, rue Maskinongé
St-Gabriel-de-Brandon J0K 2N0
(450) 835-7658
www.bbcanada.com/andante
andante@pandore.qc.ca

B&B	
single	$40
double	$50

Open year round

Number of rooms	4
shared bathrooms	2

Activities: 🦆 🛶 🚲 🛷 🏃

17. ST-MICHEL-DES-SAINTS

 F e 🚗 P 🏊 R1 TA

Crowning the summit of Mont-Roberval, this big country house with chapel was once the home of the founder of Saint-Michel-des-Saints. Several lounges, fireplace, piano, sumptuous period decor, panorama over magnificent Lac Toro, forest trails, swimming pool, river and waterfall... A haven of peace near activities.

2 hours from Montréal: Hwy 40, Exit 122, Hwy 31 twd Joliette and Rte 131 North. In Saint-Michel-des-Saints: left at bowling alley onto Provost and right on Laforest to the end.

B&B
LE GÎTE SAINT-MICHEL

Robert Burelle
1090, rue Laforest
St-Michel-des-Saints J0K 3B0
(450) 833-6008
toll free 1-888-843-6008
bblegite@satelcom.qc.ca

B&B	
single	$43.^{50}-52
double	$61-78
triple	$87
child	$8.^{70}-13

Taxes extra VS

Open year round

Number of rooms	5
shared bathrooms	3

Activities: 🛶 🚶 🏃 🐕

18. ST-ZÉNON

 F e 🚗 P R.1 TA

Discover Matawinie and relax in a century-old house at the heart of the highest village in Québec. Warm welcome, comfortable rooms and generous breakfast. Nature, golf and history lovers will feel at home.

From Montréal, Hwy 40 East and Hwy 31 twd Joliette. Rte 131 twd St-Michel-des-Saints. Our place is located 300m from church. Bus service Saint-Zénon/Joliette/ Montréal.

B&B
AU VENT VERT

Denise and Marcel Plante
6300, rue Principale
St-Zénon J0K 3N0
(450) 884-0169

B&B	
single	$40
double	$50
child	$0-5

Open year round

Number of rooms	2
shared bathrooms	1

Activities: 🎿 🏃 🛷 🏃 🐕

19. STE-ÉLISABETH

✸✸✸ F E P R4

Lanaudière Excellence Prize 1999.
One hour from Montréal, a few minutes from Joliette, in a country setting. We welcome travelers from near and far. From here, a 30- to 60- minute drive takes you to the heart of a region of varied landscapes and flavours. A grand welcome and excellent breakfasts. Sampling of maple products.

One hour from Montréal, Hwy 40, exit 122, Hwy 31 and Rte 131 N. At Notre-Dame-de-Lourdes, twd Ste-Elisabeth, drive for 1.5km.

B&B
CHEZ MARIE-CHRISTINE

Micheline Adam
3120, Du Ruisseau
Ste-Élisabeth J0K 2J0
(450) 759-9336

B&B	
single	$45
double	$60
triple	$75

Open: May to Oct.

Number of rooms	3
shared wc	1
shared bathrooms	1

Activities: 🏛 🍁 🛶 🚶 🚴

20. TERREBONNE

F E 🚫 🚗 P R.25 TA

Set in vast woodlands, our large house awaits lovers of cultural activities, music, history, genealogy and ornithology, who enjoy the company of country folk. We are a few minutes' walking distance from old Terrebonne, Île des Moulins and public transportation. Quiet, restful place.

Hwy 440 or 640 to Hwy 25, Exit 22 Boul des Seigneurs, turn right at 1st street; on St-Michel, east of Chemin Gascon (Moody).

B&B
LE MARCHAND DE SABLE

Paule and Jacques Tremblay
658, St-Michel
Terrebonne J6W 3K2
(450) 964-6016
fax (450) 471-7127
pages.infinit.net/roussill
lemarchandde
sable@videotron.ca

B&B	
single	$45-54
double	$55-60

Open year round

Number of rooms	2
rooms with sink	2
shared wc	2
shared bathrooms	1

Activities: 🏛 🍁 👤 🚶 🚴

21. RAWDON

F E P  R7 M7

One hour north of Montréal. Nestled on the edge of pine lake in an enchanting setting, ideal for relaxation, mountainous. Cottage fully equipped, spotless, decorated in a country style, fireplace (wood furnished), whirlpool, natural lake, sandy beach, trails, hiking, biking and many 4-season activities close by. See you soon. **See colour photos.**

From Montréal, Hwy 25 North and 125 North, turn right on Rue Vincent Massey and drive 1.5km. From Dorval, Hwy 13 North, exit Hwy 440 East, Hwy 25 North...

COUNTRY HOME
CHALETS DES PINS

Carole Halbig and
Philippe Richomme
5749, Vincent Massey
Rawdon J0K 1S0
(450) 834-3401
fax (450) 834-1377
www.chaletsdespins.qc.ca
info@chaletsdespins.qc.ca

No. houses	4
No. rooms	1-4
No. people	1-10
WEEK-SUMMER	$700-1 005
WEEK-WINTER	$700-1 005
W/E-SUMMER	$260-620
W/E-WINTER	$260-620
DAY-SUMMER	$130-310
DAY-WINTER	$130-310

Taxes extra VS IT

Reduced rates: Jan. 14 to Feb. 11 and Mar. 17 to June 19
Open year round

Activities: 🚶 🏃 🚲 🛷 ⛷

FARM ACTIVITIES

Country-style Dining*:

7 BERGERIE DES NEIGES, St-Ambroise-de-Kildare 18

22 BERGERIE VOYNE, St-Jacques-de-Montcalm 18

Farm Excursion:

23 ARCHE DE NOÉ, Rawdon 30

* Registered trademark.

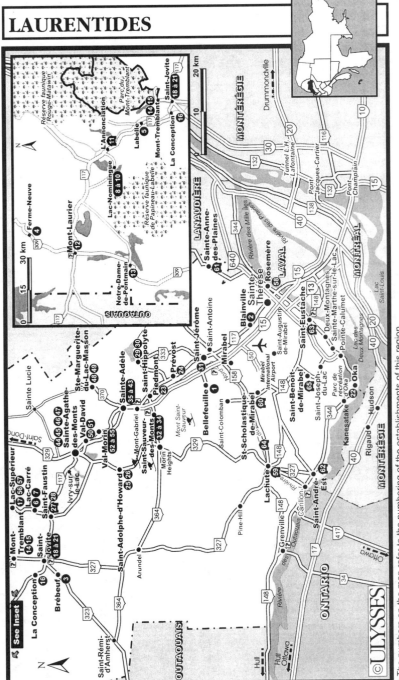

LAURENTIDES

* The numbers on the map refer to the numbering of the establishments of this region

© ULYSSES

1. BELLEFEUILLE

Panoramic mountain location, 20 min from Mirabel airport. Cross-country skiing at your doorstep, forest walks, private lake and healthy breakfasts. We are reserving a warm welcome, tranquillity, intimacy and comfort just for you... massage service available.

From Montréal or Mirabel, Hwy 15 North, Exit 43 West, Bellefeuille.Rue De Martigny becomes De la Montagne and Blvd. Lasalette. After the traffic lights and the church, right on Rue St-Camille, drive 4.8km.

B&B
GÎTE FLEURS DES BOIS

Monique F. Morin
and Rémi Gagnon
1331, rue St-Camille, R.R. #2
Bellefeuille J0R 1A0
(450) 438-7624

B&B	
single	$40-45
double	$55-60
triple	$85
child	$15

Taxes extra

Open: Jan. 5 to Dec.15

Number of rooms	5
rooms with private bath	2
shared wc	2
shared bathrooms	1

Activities:

2. BLAINVILLE

15 min from Mirabel, to fight the inconveniences of jet lag, we offer you the comfort and quietness of our home. At the foot of the Laurentides and 30 min from Montréal, it is a pleasant stop for cyclists. Biking, skiing and walking trails nearby.

From Mirabel, Hwy 15 South, Exit 31 twd St-Janvier. Right Rte 117, 3km. Right Rue Notre-Dame, left Rue J. Desrosiers. From Montréal, Hwy 15 North, Exit 25. Left Rte 117 for 3km, left 98th Ave.

B&B
LE GÎTE DU LYS

Francine Beauchemin
1237, Jacques-Desrosiers
Blainville J7C 3B2
(450) 437-4948
fax (450) 437-3658

B&B	
single	$35
double	$45-55
triple	$75
quad.	$90
child	$15

Open year round

Number of rooms	3
rooms in basement	3
shared bathrooms	1

Activities:

3. BRÉBEUF

Discover a charming inn situated just a stone's throw from Mont-Tremblant. Listen to the sound of the babbling river or gaze at a lingering sunset. In the morning, savour a breakfast prepared with seasonal ingredients. The hospitality and picturesque setting will make you want to come back year after year to «l'Été Indien».

From Montréal, Hwy 15, Rte 117 North. After St-Jovite, Exit 323 Brébeuf. Left at the lights 323 South. At Brébeuf, left before the bridge. From Ottawa, Rte 323 North for St-Jovite. At Brébeuf, turn right after the bridge.

B&B
AUBERGE L'ÉTÉ INDIEN

Johanne Pépin and
Luc Lemay
157 A, route 323
Brébeuf J0T 1B0
toll free 1-877-429-6622
(819) 429-6622
fax (819) 429-6922

B&B	
single	$60-70
double	$75-85
triple	$100
quad.	$115
child	$10

Taxes extra VS MC IT

Reduced rates: 3 nights and more
Open: Dec. 1 to Oct. 15

Number of rooms	4
rooms with private bath	1
shared bathrooms	2

Activities:

4. FERME-NEUVE

☀☀ F E ✖ P R8 TA

A quiet, cozy house with tremendous charm, artistic woodwork and full of windows. A picture-postcard landscape, 106 acres of fields, forest and a little river. Delicious, lavish cuisine. 20 minutes from the beaches of the Baskatong Reservoir, the devil's mountain and the Windigo Falls.

From Montréal, Hwy 15 North, then Rte 117. In Mont-Laurier, 309 North. In Ferme-Neuve, past the church, left at the ball park, left on Montée Gravel, 8km.

INN
AUBERGE AU BOIS
D'MON COEUR

Louison Morin
183, rang 4 Gravel
Ferme-Neuve J0W 1C0
(819) 587-3383
(819) 623-7143

	B&B	MAP
single	$45	$60-70
double	$60	$90-110
triple	$70	$115-145
quad.	$80	$140-180
child	$5	$15

Open year round

Number of rooms	4
shared bathrooms	2

Activities: 🏛 ⛵ 🚣 🎿 🚶

5. LABELLE

☀☀☀ F E 🏊 P 🚗 R5

20 min from Mont-Tremblant, close to the linear "Le P'tit Train du Nord" park, our house overlooks Lac Labelle, offering a magnificent view. Warm welcome, princely breakfasts, many activities: beach, canoe, hikes, cross-country skiing, snowshoeing, snowmobiling, packages for cyclists. Enjoy the four seasons...

From Montréal, Hwy 15 North, then 117 North up to Labelle. At the traffic lights, drive 4km. At the flashing lights, turn left on Ch. La Minerve, 1km. Turn left on Ch. Lac Labelle, 1km. Turn left on Ch. Saindon, 1km.

B&B
LA CLOCHE DE VERT

Thérèse and Normand Brunette
1080, chemin Saindon
Lac Labelle
Labelle J0T 1H0
(819) 686-5850
www.angelfire.com/
biz/cloche
clochedevert@bigfoot.com

B&B	
single	$40-50
double	$55-65
child	$10

Open year round

Number of rooms	3
rooms with sink	2
rooms with private bath	1
shared wc	1
shared bathrooms	1

Activities: 🎿 🚲 🚣 🏊 🏃

6. LAC-CARRÉ

☀☀☀ F E P 🚗 R.1 TA

"La Licorne", or The Unicorn, symbolizing freedom, invites you to share in its wonders and landscapes. After a day of cycling on the linear park 50 metres away, relax in our garden to the sound of waterfalls or go for a refreshing swim in the lake in front of the B&B. In winter, after skiing, relax in front of a fire. Mt Blanc 1km away, Tremblant 20km, good restaurants in St-Jovite 10km. At km 69.5 of the bike path.

From Montréal, Hwy 15 N. and Rte 117 N. After Ste-Agathe, 20km, Lac-Carré Exit, at the stop, right for 1km.

B&B
LA LICORNE

Patricia and Robin
1690, rue Principale
Lac-Carré J0T 1J1
(819) 688-3030
fax (819) 688-5020
www.boreale.net/licorne
lalicorne@sympatico.ca

B&B	
single	$40-50
double	$60-70
triple	$85
quad.	$90

VS

Open: Dec. 1 to Apr. 15,
May 1 to Oct. 31

Number of rooms	4
shared bathrooms	2

Activities: 🎿 🚶 🚲 🏊 🏃

7. LAC-CARRÉ

☀☀☀ | F | E | P | 🐕 | R.2 | TA

10km from St-Jovite and 18km from Mt-Tremblant, our septuagenarian house is a haven of peace for nature lovers. 50m from the linear park and 1km from Mont-Blanc, our B&B lets you relax on the beach of the lake, on the terrace or by the fire upon your arrival. Come morning, you will enjoy our now-famous hearty breakfast. Dinner and package-deals available.

From Montréal, Hwy 15 North and Rte 117 North. After Ste-Agathe drive 18km. Exit Lac-Carré. At 1st stop sign turn right, drive 1.5km, right on Rue de La Gare.

B&B
GÎTE DE LA GARE

Johanne Mathon and
Robert Freeman
362, de La Gare
St-Faustin, Lac-Carré
J0T 1J0
tel/fax (819) 688-6091
toll free 1-888-550-6091

B&B	
single	$50
double	$60

VS MC IT

Open year round

Number of rooms	4
shared bathrooms	2

Activities: 🚶 🚴 🏊 ⛷ 🏃

---

8. LAC-NOMININGUE

★★★ | F | E | 🐕 | ✕ | 🚗 | P | 🏊 | TA

By the cycling path, skidoo trail and the lake, our inn is the gateway to the Réserve Papineau-Labelle and its nature-related activities. We offer guests a delicious cocktail of gastronomy and relaxation: rooms with therapeutic baths, 5-course-dinner menu packages. Tourism Grand Prize 1999, hospitality and customer service. **See colour photos. Ad end of this region.**

From Montréal, Hwy 15 North and Rte 117. Pass L'Annonciation at the flashing light, Rte 321 South. After 8.8km, turn right on Ch. des Tilleuls (200 m.). By bike: atkm 141.5 of the P'tit Train du Nord bike path.

INN
AUBERGE-RESTAURANT
«CHEZ IGNACE»

Yolande Louis and
Ignace Denutte
1455, ch. des Tilleuls
Lac-Nomininingue J0W 1R0
(819) 278-0689
fax (819) 278-0751
www.laurentides.com

	B&B	MAP
single	$60-75	$75-95
double	$75-90	$118-138
triple	$110	$175
child	$10	$20

Taxes extra VS MC AM IT

Reduced rates: Mar. 15 to May 15 and Oct. 15 to Dec. 15, 3 nights and more 10% off
Open year round

Number of rooms	5
rooms with private bath	5

Activities: 🚶 🚴 🐎 ⛷ 🐎

---

9. LAC-NOMININGUE

★★★ | F | e | ♿ | 🐕 | ✕ | 🚗 | P | 🏊 | TA

Located on the shores of Lac Nomininingue and the Linear Park, Auberge Villa Bellerive is a renovated historic inn that is popular with cyclists and snowmobilists. Enjoy a coffee on the pier or in the dining room, which serves delectable six-course dinner. A terrace garden and a heated spa will delight you, even in winter, and the variety of our rooms will fulfill all of your desires. Discover our fine cuisine and cordial welcome. **See colour photos.**

Hwy 15 and 117 North. After L'Annonciation, at the flashing light, 321 South, 9km.km 142 Le P'tit Train du Nord bike path.

INN
AUBERGE VILLA BELLERIVE

Cécile L'Heureux and
Yvon Massé
1596, rue des Tilleuls
Lac Nomininingue J0W 1R0
toll free 1-800-786-3802
(819) 278-3802
fax (819) 278-0483
www.villabellerive.com
villabellerive@hotmail.com

	B&B	MAP
single	$60	$75-85
double	$75-125	$118-168
triple	$90-100	$165-195
quad.	$95-110	$200-240
child	$15	---

Taxes extra VS MC AM IT

Reduced rates: Mar. 15 to May 15, Oct. 15 to Dec.15
Open year round

Number of rooms	12
rooms with private bath	12

Activities: 🚤 🚶 🐎 🏃 🐎

10. LAC-NOMININGUE

☀☀☀☀ F E 🚭 P 🛏 🐕 ✕ R1 TA

Special Mention «Our beautiful Inns of Yesteryear» success 1999. Centenary manor on pristine ancestral site by the forest. Tourism 99 Grand Prize winner: "cycling/culture on the P'tit Train du Nord" package. We offer outdoor enthusiasts tasty food (garden-fresh home cooking in season), special atmosphere. Nominingue offers a full set of year-round activities. **See colour photos**

Rte 117, Rte 321. Chemin Tour du Lac to Rue Ignace, turn left. Turn right on Rue Sacré-Coeur.

**INN
LE PROVINCIALAT**

P. Seers and G. Petit
2292, Sacré-Coeur
Lac-Nominingue J0W 1R0
(819) 278-4928
toll free in Canada
1-877- 278-4928
fax (819) 278-3517
www.laurentides.
com/membres/002a.html

	B&B	MAP
single	$45-55	$63-73
double	$65-75	$100-110
triple	$75-90	$128-143
quad.	$110-140	$180-210
child	$15	$28

Taxes extra VS MC

Reduced rates: Oct. 31 to Dec. 15, Mar. 15 to May 15
Open year round

Number of rooms	5
rooms with private bath	2
rooms with sink	1
shared bathrooms	2

Activities: 🧍 🚲 🐎 🏃 🐴

---

11. L'ANNONCIATION

☀☀☀ F e P ✕ R5

We cleared this patch of mountainside land so that our small herd could graze and we could set up house comfortably. Former teachers, your hosts are genuine, unpretentious people who enjoy sharing the happiness of living with their guests according to old-fashioned values. A warm welcome awaits you. **Country-style Dining p 19 and Farm Stay p 39.**

From Montréal, Hwy 15 North and Rte 117 to L'Annonciation. Drive 4.3km past the hospital, and turn left on Chemin Laliberté. First house on the right.

**B&B
LA CLAIRIÈRE DE LA CÔTE**

Monique Lanthier and
Yves Bégin
16, chemin Laliberté
L'Annonciation J0T 1T0
(819) 275-2877
fax (819) 275-3363

	B&B
single	$35
double	$50

Open: Dec. 1 to Mar. 31 to May 1 to Oct. 31

Number of rooms	3
rooms in basement	3
shared wc	2
shared bathrooms	1

Activities: 🛷 🧍 🚲 🛶 🎿

---

12. MONT-LAURIER

☀☀☀ F e P R.1 TA

Memorable stay. Friendly welcome, considerations, cosy bed, lounge at your disposal: chats, reading, soft music, TV. Not to mention the breakfast!!! "As appetizing to the eyes as to the belly." Near the linear park. Welcome to our home with magnificent woodwork.

From Montréal, Hwy 15 N., Rte 117 to Mont-Laurier. We're on Boul A. Paquette, which is the extension of Rte 117. The inn is on your right.

**B&B
AUBERGE DE LA
MAISON GRENIER**

Joane and Gilbert Vincent
335, boul. A. Paquette
Mont-Laurier J9L 1K5
(819) 623-6306
fax (819) 623-5054
dominic.vincent@sympatico.ca

	B&B
single	$40
double	$55
triple	$70
child	$5

Taxes extra VS MC

Open year round

Number of rooms	5
rooms with sink	1
shared bathrooms	2

Activities: 🏛 🧍 🚲 🛶 🏃

13. MONT-LAURIER, NOTRE-DAME-DE-PONTMAIN ☀️☀️ F e ✕ 🚗 R6 TA

Set back from the road on a lakefront property, Gite de la Maison Canadienne has a completely wooden décor. The view of the river and the mountains will take your breath away. Activities: pool, hiking path, fishing and hunting. Rowboat, canoe and pedal-boat rentals. Evening meal with reservation. In April, maple syrup excursions. Other packages available.

From Montréal, Hwy 15 North and Rte 117. At Mont-Laurier, Rte 309 South, drive 30km, Rte 311 North, drive 1.6km. From Hull Hwy 50, Rte 309 North. After N-D-Pontmain, Rte 311 North, drive 1.6km.

B&B
GÎTE DE LA MAISON CANADIENNE

Françoise Morin and
Gaston Landreville
61 ch. Lac-du-Cerf
Notre-Dame-de-Pontmain
J0W 1S0
(819) 597-2460
fax (819) 597-4020
www.gite.qc.ca
info@gite.qc.ca

B&B	
single	$40
double	$55
child	$10-15

Open: Apr. 1 to Nov. 30

Number of rooms	3
shared bathrooms	2

Activities: 🏛 🚣 👣 🚴 🏇

14. MONT-TREMBLANT ★★★ F E 🚭 ♿ 🚗 P 🏊 R.1 TA

The warmth of a log house within your reach. Ten spacious rooms, each with its own rustic charm to welcome you. Newly built, it boasts a television, therapeutic bath, balcony and a view of magnificent Mont-Tremblant. Lounge with fireplace to warm you in winter, pool to refresh you in summer. Excellent breakfast. Prices higher in winter. **See colour photos.**

From Montréal, Hwy 15 North, Rte 117 North for 1.5km. After St-Jovite, turn right on Montée Ryan to Lac Tremblant, turn left twd the village. 1km on the left.

INN
AUBERGE LA PETITE CACHÉE

Manon Millette and
Normand Chalifour
2681, chemin Principal
C.P. 1009
Mont-Tremblant J0T 1Z0
(819) 425-2654
fax (819) 425-6892
www.petitecachee.com

B&B	
single	$70-100
double	$89-130
triple	$115-135
child	$15

Taxes extra VS MC AM IT

Reduced rates: May, June, Oct., Nov.
Open year round

Number of rooms	10
rooms with private bath	10

Activities: 🚣 👣 🚴 🎿 ⛷

15. MONT-TREMBLANT ★★★ F E ♿ P 🚗 🏊 🐕 R1 TA

«One of the nicest places to stay in the Tremblant area» *The Gazette '99*. Less than 1km from the ski resort of Tremblant. Cross-Country skiing and mountain bike trails at our doorstep. Close to the bike paths. Log house, spacious rooms, living room with fireplace. Prices higher in winter. Welcome! **See colour photos.**

From Montréal, Hwy 15 North, Rte 117 North. Pass St-Jovite at the traffic light, take Montée Ryan on your right until the end (stop). Turn left along the lake, at the stop (Rue Pinoteau) turn left. Le Lupin sign, up the hill.

INN
AUBERGE LE LUPIN

Sylvie Senécal and
Pierre Lachance
127, Pinoteau
Mont-Tremblant J0T 1Z0
(819) 425-5474
toll free 1-877-425-5474
fax (819) 425-6079
www.lelupin.com
lelupin@lelupin.com

B&B	
single	$69-85
double	$89-109
triple	$114-134
child	$15

Taxes extra VS MC AM ER IT

Reduced rates: May, June and Nov. (week days)
Open year round

Number of rooms	9
rooms with private bath	9
shared wc	1

Activities: 🚣 👣 🚴 🎿 ⛷

16. MONT-TREMBLANT, LA CONCEPTION ★★★ F E 🚭 🚤 P 🚗 R6 TA

Discover our inn, a peaceful place in the forest by Rivière Rouge, a few minutes from the "P'tit Train du Nord" bike path and the Tremblant ski resort. Cosy and comfortable rooms, lounge with fireplace. Canoes available. Johanne is an herbalist and Bob a Micmac with a passion for history and traditions. **See colour photos.**

From Montréal, Hwy 15 and 117 North. After St-Jovite at the lights, turn right on Montée Ryan, 5.1km. Turn left at the lights, Ch.Principal, 2.5km. Turn left on Lac Mercier twd Labelle, La Conception, 6km, right on des Tulipes, 1km.

INN
L'AUBERGE À LA
CROISÉE DES CHEMINS

Johanne Parent and
Bob Bourdon
4273, chemin des Tulipes
Mt-Tremblant, La Conception
JOT 1M0
(819) 686-5289
toll free 1-888-686-5289
fax (819) 686-9205
www.xchemins.com
xchemins@xchemins.com

B&B	
single	$60-90
double	$70-100
triple	$90-120
quad.	$110-140
child	$15

Taxes extra VS MC IT

Reduced rates: Nov. 1 to Dec. 17, May 15 to June 20
Open year round

Number of rooms	9
rooms with private bath	7
shared wc	2
shared bathrooms	1

Activities: 🚶 🏃 🚴 ⛷ 🏃

17. MONT-TREMBLANT, LAC-SUPÉRIEUR ☼☼☼ F E 🐕 🚤 P 🚗 R2.5 TA

At the entrance to the Mont-Tremblant park and on the north side of the mountain is a typical Canadian-style house embraced by nature. Linear park 2.5km away. Ski, bike and snowmobile package. Swimming pool, terrace, relax in front of the fireplace. Meals with reservations. Have your breakfast with the family and share the enthusiasm of your hosts. **Country Home p 185. See colour photos.**

From Montréal, Hwy 15 North, Rte 117 North, Exit St-Faustin/Lac-Carré. Right at the stop, 2.3km, follow signs to Parc Mont-Tremblant, drive 2.5km on Chemin Lac-Supérieur

B&B
GÎTE ET COUVERT
LA MARIE-CHAMPAGNE

Marie-France
and Denis Champagne
654, chemin Lac-Supérieur
Lac-Supérieur JOT 1J0
(819) 688-3780
fax (819) 688-3758
www.laurentides.com

B&B	
single	$40-50
double	$60-70
triple	$80
quad.	$100
child	$15

VS AM

Open: Dec. 1 to Oct. 31

Number of rooms	4
rooms with private bath	4

Activities: 🚤 🚶 🚴 🛷 ⛷

18. MONT-TREMBLANT, ST-JOVITE F e 🚭 P R2 TA

Come discover a unique Canadian log-wood *auberge* in the middle of our tranquil forests with a stunning view of Mont-Tremblant. Living room, cosy bedrooms and generous breakfasts. Your hosts, Cécile, Jean-Yves and Nathalie, will spoil you. Only 8min from the Tremblant ski slopes, golf courses and 2min from the bike path. Higher prices in winter.

From Montréal, Hwy 15 North, Rte 117. At the light after St-Jovite, turn right onto Montée Ryan. Drive 1km.

INN
AUBERGE DU BOIS JOLIT

Cécile and Jean-Yves Jolit
109, chemin de la Falaise
St-Jovite JOT 2H0
(819) 425-6886
toll free 1-877-425-6886
fax (819) 425-6883
www.mt-tremblant.com/bois-jolit/
bois-jolit@mt-tremblant.com

B&B	
single	$79-115
double	$79-115
triple	$99-139
quad.	$139-159
child	$12

Taxes extra VS MC

Reduced rates: May, June, Oct. and Nov. week days
Open year round

Number of rooms	8
rooms with private bath	8

Activities: 🚤 🚶 🚴 🛷 ⛷

19. MONT-TREMBLANT, ST-JOVITE

✹✹✹ F E 🚗 P R2 TA

Escape from the real world at our B&B and enjoy an old-world charm with modern-day conveniences. You will be pleasantly surprised when you taste our exquisite breakfasts garnished with generous helpings of fresh fruit. Great variety of activities within a short distance. Only 8km from Tremblant and Mt-Blanc, and 500 m from the Linear Park where you can go biking, snowmobiling or cross-country skiing. Our motto: to see you again.

From Montréal Hwy 15 and 117 North. Right at the first exit for St-Jovite, 100m. Right at the first intersection, Mtée Kavanagh, 1.8km.

B&B
GÎTE LA TREMBLANTE

France and Michel
1251, montée Kavanagh
Mont-Tremblant, St-Jovite
J0T 2H0
(819) 425-5959
toll free 1-877-425-5959
fax (819) 425-9404
www.st-jovite.com/tremblante
tremblante@st-jovite.com

B&B	
single	$45-60
double	$55-70
triple	$70-85

VS MC

Open year round

Number of rooms	3
rooms with private bath	3

Activities: 🧍 🚶 🚴 🏊 🏃

20. MONT-TREMBLANT, ST-JOVITE

✹✹✹ F E 🚫 P R.5

Situated 500m from the Linear Park Le P'tit Train du Nord and 10min from Mont-Tremblant, Le Second Souffle is a Canadian-style home in the hilly St-Jovite region. Sports, cultural and gastronomic activities are a stone's throw from the B&B. There are five rooms, each with their own private bath-room and unique décor. Unforgettable breakfasts served in a laid-back, friendly ambience.

From Montréal, Hwy 15 and Rte 117 North. At St-Jovite, Rue Ouimet and then immediately turn onto Kavanagh, drive 500 m.

B&B
LE SECOND SOUFFLE

Monique and
Jean-Marie Leduc
815, montée Kavanagh
St-Jovite
J0T 2H0
tel/fax (819) 429-6166

B&B	
single	$65
double	$75
triple	$95
child	$5

Taxes extra VS IT

Open year round

Number of rooms	5
rooms with private bath	5

Activities: 🧍 🚶 🚴 🏊 🏃

21. MONT-TREMBLANT, ST-JOVITE

✹✹✹✹ F E 🏊 P 🐕 R3 TA

Secluded in the Laurentian mountains and less than 10 minutes from Mont-Tremblant, Wilde's Heath is a magnificient Victorian mansion. Entirely furnished with late-19th-century antiques. Wilde's Heath confirms that castle living is alive and well in St-Jovite. Discover breathtaking panoramas and say goodbye to all your worries. Antique shop on premise. **See colour photos.**

From Montréal, Hwy 15 North and Rte 117. After St-Jovite, at the viaduct on your left twd Brébeuf, take Rte 323 for 1.6km, look for the sign "Wilde's Heath B&B".

B&B
WILDE'S HEATH B&B

«Lord» Daniel H.Wilde
268, Route 323
St-Jovite J0T 2H0
(819) 425-6859
fax (819) 425-7636

B&B	
single	$105-175
double	$125-195

VS MC AM IT

Open year round

Number of rooms	4
rooms with private bath	4

Activities: 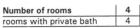 🏍 🧍 🚴 ⛷

22. OKA

☀☀☀ | F | e | ⊗ | 🏊 | P | R.5 | TA

A complete change of scenery 40 min from Mirabel, 45 min from Montréal. Enchanting site on a lake and around a pool. Bicycle path. Parc Oka nearby. In summer, water sports and golf available. In winter, cross-country skiing, ice-fishing, and snowmobilling.

From Mirabel, Hwy 15 South, exit onto Hwy 640 West to the end. Right on Rte 344 West to Oka, left on Rue Olier. Right on St-Sulpice, 8.5km from the end of Rte 640 West.

B&B
LA MAISON DUMOULIN

Pierrette Dumoulin-Roy
53, rue St-Sulpice
Oka J0N 1E0
(450) 479-6753

B&B	
single	$40-45-50
double	$50-55-60
child	$10

Open year round

Number of rooms	4
shared bathrooms	2

Activities: 🚣 🚶 🎿 🚴 ⛸

23. PIEDMONT

☀☀☀ | F | E | ⊗ | 🚗 | P | R3 | TA

La Chrysalide is a majestic cocoon in the mountains offering tranquillity and relaxation. Situated near St-Sauveur, it's in the heart of vibrant cultural and sporting events. Our rooms have a scenic view, jacuzzis, fireplaces and terraces. You will be impressed by our gourmet breakfasts. Come to La Chrysalide. A great time guaranteed!

From Montréal Hwy 15 North, turn right at Exit 58, Rte 117 North. Right at first light onto Ch. de la Gare. After the bridge, keep right on Ch. de la Rivière. Turn left at the 2nd stop sign onto Ch. des Grands Ducs. We are at the end of the private road.

B&B
LA CHRYSALIDE

Ginette Paré and Lauréan Martin
237, chemin des Grands Ducs
Piedmont J0R 1K0
(450) 227-0944
fax (450) 277-6930
www.laurentides.
com/membres/003a.html
laurean.martin@sympatico.ca

B&B	
single	$55-90
double	$65-100
triple	$80-115
child	$10

Reduced rates: 10% 2 nights and more and Apr., May, Nov.
Open year round

Number of rooms	5
rooms with private bath	3
shared wc	1
shared bathrooms	1

Activities: 🏛 ⚫ 🎿 🚴 🚤

24. PRÉVOST

☀☀☀ | F | E | ⊗ | ♿ | P | R1 | M1

5min from St-Sauveur, relaxing home for non-smoking adults (fireplaces in living and in dining room, panoramic view, Jacuzzi in the solarium, healthy breakfasts). 1km from Linear Park (200km) for biking. Transportation available. 5min from lake, flea market, antiques. Partialy weelchair accessible. Air conditioned, TV.

Hwy 15 North, Exit 55. You're on Rue Louis-Morin. Right on rue Morin, cross the bridge. Left on Rue De La Station. 1km past the traffic lights on Rte 117, left on Montée-Sauvage, right on Du Sommet, right on De La Voie Lactée.

B&B
À LA MONTAGNE
CHEZ MADELEINE ET PIERRE

Madeleine Sévigny
and Pierre Lavigne
1460, Voie Lactée, C.P. 92
Prévost J0R 1T0
(450) 224-4628
fax -daytime- (450) 224-4628
www.bbcanada.com/2074.html
chez_madeleine_et_pierre
@hotmail.com

B&B	
single	$40-70
double	$50-70

Reduced rates: 10% from the 3rd night
Open: June 1 to Oct. 15

Number of rooms	3
rooms with private bath	1
shared wc	1
shared bathrooms	1

Activities: 🏛 ⚫ 🚣 🚴 🏇

25. ST-ADOLPHE-D'HOWARD ☀☀☀ F E 🚭 P 🚗 R4 TA

Enter through a magnificient stone tower with a scent of cedar. Welcome to our peaceful home nestled in the mountains right on the lake. Relax in front of a fireplace. Spacious and lovingly decorated rooms await you for a special treat. As for breakfast...Wow! At L'Aube Douce, forget about your daily stress.

From Montréal, Hwy 15 N., Exit 60, Rte 364 W., up to Rte 329 N. Drive 10km, then left at Montée Lac Louise for 1.5km. turn right on Gais Lurons Rd. At the stop sign, turn left.

B&B
AUBE DOUCE

Michèle Ménard and
Gilles Meilleur
22, chemin de la Québécoise
St-Adolphe-d'Howard JOT 2B0
(819) 327-5048
fax (819) 327-5254
www.bbcanada.com/
2767.html

B&B	
single	$50-60
double	$60-80
triple	$80-105
child	$0-10

Open year round

Number of rooms	4
rooms with private bath	4

Activities: 🐟 🛶 🚴 🎿 🏃

---

26. ST-ADOLPHE-D'HOWARD ☀☀☀☀ F E 🚭 P 〰 R2

Located 8km from Sainte-Agathe facing Lac Saint-Joseph, come experience some of the greatest pleasures in life. Meticulously decorated rooms, private bathrooms, living room with balcony and view of the lake. Sumptuous breakfast served in the spacious dinning-room. A great place to rejuvenate yourself and practice aquatic or winter sports. Welcome to our friendly home.

From Montréal, Hwy 15, Exit 60 Rte 364 to Morin-Heights, Rte 329 to Saint-Adolphe, 3km after the town.

B&B
CHEZ BÉCASSINE

Nicole Sénécal
2875, chemin du Village
Saint-Adolphe d'Howard
JOT 2B0
(819) 327-5029
toll free 1-888-822-5029
fax (819) 327-3513
www.angelfire.com/mt/
chezbecassine/index.html
chezbecassine@hotmail.com

B&B	
single	$45-60
double	$70-95
child	$10-20

Taxes extra VS IT

Reduced rates: Nov. 1 to Dec. 15, Apr. 1 to May 15
Open year round

Number of rooms	4
rooms with private bath	4
shared wc	1

Activities: 🛶 ⛷ 🛷 🎿 🏃

---

27. ST-FAUSTIN ☀☀ F E 🚭 〰 P 🚗 ✕ R8

Discover shepparding traditions, simplicity, nature, culture and the time to relax. Large property to explore as much as contemplate. Lovely rooms connected to the sheepfold. Meals in season served in a family-style atmosphere in our intimate, round loghouse. An enchanting place! **Farm Stay p 39.**

From Montréal, Hwy 15 North. In St-Faustin, 2km after Mt-Blanc, left on Chemin la Sauvagine for 7km. From St-Jovite, Rte 327 South twd Arundel for 2km. Left on Chemin Paquette for 6km.

B&B
FERME DE LA
BUTTE MAGIQUE

Diane, Maud and children
1724, chemin de la Sauvagine
St-Faustin JOT 1J2
tel/fax (819) 425-5688
www.citeweb.net/bmagique
fermedelabuttemagique
@hotmail.com

	B&B	MAP
single	$47-57	$67-77
double	$67	$107
triple	$92	$152
child	$20	$28

Reduced rates: 10% 2 nights and more (B&B), except from Dec. 23 to Jan. 2 and Apr. 21 to 24
Open year round

Number of rooms	3
shared wc	1
shared bathrooms	1

Activities: 🚤 🚶 🚴 🎿 🏃

28. ST-FAUSTIN

F E P TA

Special Mention «Our beautiful Inns of yesteryear» success 1999. A former general store, our ancestral house has a welcoming spirit as do its hosts. 1km from the lake and the P'tit Train du Nord Linear Park. 15 min from Tremblant. Facing Mont Blanc. Reduced rates for skiing. We have a reputation for our good cuisine: summertime on the terrace and around the fire in winter. Group packages.

From Montréal or Mirabel Airport, Hwy 15 N. to St-Jérome. Continue to Ste-Agathe, Rte 117, 16km. Take the St-Faustin/Lac-Carré exit and follow the blue signs.

INN
LA BONNE ADRESSE

Odette Bélanger and
Jean-Marie Noël
1196, rue de la Pisciculture
St-Faustin J0T 2G0
(819) 688-6422
toll free 1-877-688-6422
fax (819) 688-5052
www.laurentides.com

	B&B	MAP
single	$50-75	$70-95
double	$65-100	$104-139
triple	$85-125	$143-184
quad.	$105-150	$183-228
child	$15	$25

Taxes extra VS MC

Open: Dec. 15 to Nov. 1

Number of rooms	7
rooms with private bath	3
shared bathrooms	2

Activities:

29. ST-HIPPOLYTE

★★ F E P R4 TA

Facing the lake, in the mountains rife with lush flora. Imagine the scene at dusk when the sun paints its canvas! Dining room with terrace, unparalleled view. Innovative, lavish fine cuisine. Discover edible flowers. Charming, comfortable rooms. Private beach, free watercraft, grade-A water. No motorboats allowed. Rest assured. 1st prize «Villages Fleuris». A true paradise! **See colour photos.**

Hwy 15 N., Exit 45 twd St-Hippolyte, left at 1st light for 16km to Rte 333 N. Turn left at the church, drive 4km, keep to the right, inn is 300 m further.

INN
AUBERGE LAC DU PIN ROUGE

Nicole Bouffard and
Yvan Trottier
81, chemin Lac-du-Pin-Rouge
St-Hippolyte J8A 3J3
(450) 563-2790
1-800-427-0840
www.laurentides.com

	B&B	MAP
single	$51-75	$84-108
double	$65-90	$129-151
triple	$88-119	$175-208
child	$20	à la carte

Taxes extra VS MC

Reduced rates: 40$ off for the second night (MAP), 4 nights and more 10% to 20%
Open: May 15 to Oct. 15

Number of rooms	6
rooms with private bath	4
rooms with sink	2
shared wc	3
shared bathrooms	2

Activities:

30. ST-HIPPOLYTE

F e P R2 TA

Peace and quiet is only 45 min from Montréal. L'Éveil sur le Lac has a terrace with a panoramic view, a water garden with a fountain and a living room with a fireplace. Access to a kitchenette. We offer bath therapy, massages, seaweed body wraps and other treatments. Swimming in the lake and free use of pedal-boats. Cycling and skiing in the Linear Park Le P'tit Train du Nord 6km away.

Hwy 15 Exit 45. Turn left at first light onto Rte 333, drive 9.3km. Turn left on Chemin du Lac Echo, drive 50 m. Right on Rue Desjardins, drive 1km then turn right on 88th Avenue, left at the stop sign.

B&B
L'ÉVEIL SUR LE LAC

Hugette Péloquin and
René St-Vincent
214, 92e avenue
St-Hippolyte J8A 1V1
tel/fax (514) 865-9485
toll free 1-888-224-9716
www.eveilsurlelac.cjb.net
eveil@aei.ca

	B&B
single	$38-45
double	$55-60
child	$10

VS MC

Reduced rates: 15% 3 nights and more
Open year round

Number of rooms	3
shared bathrooms	2

Activities:

31. ST-JÉRÔME

☀☀☀ F E 🚗 🐕 R.3 TA

Ten min from Mirabel airport and 30 min from Dorval, generous and considerate hospitality *à la québécoise*. Nice ambience, gourmet breakfast. Gérard, a history professor, is proud to tell you about his Québec! Located at 100 metres from the bicycle path "Le P'tit train du Nord".

Hwy 15 North, Exit 43 East twd downtown. After the bridge, right on Rue Labelle. At the lights, left on Rue du Palais (cathedral), left on Melançon street, 2nd light. B&B is 1 block away on the left.

B&B
L'ÉTAPE CHEZ MARIE-THÉRÈSE ET GÉRARD LEMAY

Marie-Thérèse and Gérard Lemay
430, rue Melançon
St-Jérôme J7Z 4K4
(450) 438-1043

B&B	
single	$40
double	$55
triple	$75
child	$15

Reduced rates: Nov.1 to Mar. 31
Open year round

Number of rooms	3
shared wc	1
shared bathrooms	2

Activities: 🏛 🦆 👤 🚶 🚴

---

32. ST-SAUVEUR-DES-MONTS

★ ★ F E 🏊 P 🚗 R2

Winner of the *Grand Prix du Tourisme Laurentides*: welcome and customer service 1997. Facing ski hills, 2km from town. Enchanting decor, tranquillity, attention and discretion. Heated pool, central air conditioning, flowered terrace, 2 rms with fireplaces, including one semi-basement suite. Many recreational/tourist activities nearby. But above all, relaxation, comfort and a warm welcome. Gourmet breakfast.

From Montréal, Hwy 15 N. left at Exit 60, at Rte 364 W. turn right, 3rd set of lights, left on Rue Principale, 2km.

INN
AUBERGE SOUS L'ÉDREDON

Carmelle Huppé and Andrée Cloutier
777, Principale
St-Sauveur-des-Monts
J0R 1R2
(450) 227-3131

B&B	
single	$55-80
double	$70-95
triple	$100-110
child	$10-15

Taxes extra VS MC

Reduced rates: Apr., May, Nov.,
and 10% 3 nights and more
Open year round

Number of rooms	7
rooms with private bath	5
rooms in semi-basement	1
shared bathrooms	1

Activities: 🦆 🚣 👤 🚴 ⛷

---

33. ST-SAUVEUR-DES-MONTS

☀☀☀ F E 🚭 P 🚗 🏊 ✖ TA

Lovely charming house. Cosy air conditioned non-smoking haven, peaceful setting in a very picturesque Laurentian Village. Fireplace, view of ski hills. Beautiful gardens and outdoor pool. Private bathrooms. Luxury suite with double whirlpool. Packages available: ski, dogsled, snowmobile, golf, biking, water slides, etc. Very warm ambiance, well travelled host speaking various language. Candlelit gourmet breakfast.

From Montréal Hwy 15 N., left at Exit 60. Right onto Rte 364 W. At 2nd light, right on Rue de la Gare. Left on Rue Principale 0.4km.

B&B
«AUX PETITS OISEAUX...»

Mireille and Benny
342, rue Principale
St-Sauveur-des-Monts J0R 1R0
(450) 227-6116
toll free 1-877-227-6116
fax (450) 227-6171
www.laurentides.com
auxpetitsoiseaux@
sympatico.ca

B&B	
single	$60-90
double	$65-115
triple	$90-140
quad.	$150-200
child	$10-20

Taxes extra VS MC AM

Reduced rates: Week days Apr.,
May , Oct., Nov., 3 nights and
more except summer and holidays
Open year round

Number of rooms	4
rooms with private bath	4
rooms in basement	1

Activities: 🦆 🚣 👤 🚴 ⛷

34. ST-SAUVEUR-DES-MONTS ☀☀☀☀ F e 🚫 🚗 P R.1

A charming B&B in the heart of Laurentian Mountains. Our ancestral home welcomes you with romantic bedrooms (two with fireplaces) and gourmet breakfasts. Stone fireplace in the common room. Minutes from boutiques, fine restaurants, ski and golf resorts. Smokefree. "A peaceful haven where your dreams have a good chance of coming true." *Le Bel Âge*

From Montréal, Hwy 15 North, turn left at Exit 60, turn right at Rte 364, turn right at the 3rd light onto Rue Principale.

B&B
LE BONNET D'OR B&B

Michelle McMillan and
Glen Bonney
405, rue Principale
St-Sauveur-des-Monts J0R 1R0
(450) 227-9669
toll free 1-877-277-9669
www.bbcanada.com/bonnetdor
bonnetdor@qc.aibn.com

B&B	
single	$75-105
double	$85-115
triple	$130

Taxes extra VS MC

Open year round

Number of rooms	5
rooms with private bath	5

Activities: 🍷 🎿 🚴 ⛷ 🏃

35. STE-ADÈLE ☀☀☀ F E 🚫 🏊 P 🚗 🐕 R.3 TA

Lovely Canadian house in the woodlands offers central air conditioning, comfort and relaxation. Very large family-size room that can accommodate up to 5 people. Incomparable breakfasts. Pool, hiking, cross-country skiing on site. 25 minutes from Mirabel, 50 from Dorval and 45 from Mont-Tremblant. 10% discount for 3 nights or more.

From Montréal or Mirabel Airport, Hwy 15 North, Exit 69, Rte 370 East, for 0.8km. Facing the "Clef des Champs" restaurant.

B&B
À LA BELLE IDÉE

Suzanne and Jean-François
894, de l'Arbre Sec
Ste-Adèle J8B 1X6
(450) 229-6173
Canada and USA only:
toll free 1-888-221-1313
fax (450) 229-5423
www.bbcanada.com/870.html
la.belle.idee@sympatico.ca

B&B	
single	$40-60
double	$55-75
triple	$75-90
quad.	$105
child	$0-10

Reduced rates: Apr.1 to June 14
Oct.15 to Dec. 14
Open year round

Number of rooms	4
rooms with private bath	2
shared bathrooms	1

Activities: 🍷 🎿 🚴 🛷 ⛷

36. STE-ADÈLE ☀☀☀ F E 🐕 🏊 P R4 TA

Large Canadian-style home, rustic ambiance, professionally appointed. 7-acre landscaped domain on which a river flows offering a magnificent panoramic view of the wilderness. Choice property for relaxation, canoeing, walking, swimming, cross-country skiing and snowshoeing. Sublime breakfasts, warm hosts. You will be enchanted with your stay.

From Montréal, Hwy 15 N., Exit 67. 7km on Rte 117 N. At Lac Millette, left on Chemin du Moulin for 2km. At the green barn, right on Des Engoulevents. Private road, keep left.

B&B
À L'ORÉE DU BOIS

Louise Durivage and
Robert Parizeau
4400, rue des Engoulevents
Ste-Adèle J8B 3J8
(450) 229-5455
www.bbcanada.
com/aloreedubois
aloreedubois@sympatico.ca

B&B	
single	$60-100
double	$80-100
triple	$100-120
child	$20

Taxes extra MC

Reduced rates: 10% 5 nights and more
Open year round

Number of rooms	4
rooms with sink	4
shared wc	2
shared showers	2

Activities: 🎿 🚴 🛷 ⛷ 🐕

37. STE-ADÈLE ★★ F E ♿ P 🚗 ✕ R.3 TA

Charming inn with country-style decor in the heart of the village! Fireplace, dining room. Many activities nearby. Packages: jaunt, health, lovers, snowmobiling, skiing, dogsledding, theatre, golf, cruise. Shuttle service. Some luxury rooms with double therapeutic bath, fireplace, TV, queen-size bed. Hearty breakfast to brighten up your mornings.

From Montréal, Hwy 15 North, Exit 67; at 4th lights, turn right onto Chemin Pierre-Péladeau. From Ste-Agathe, Hwy 15 South, Exit 69, left at first stop sign, right at next stop sign onto Chemin Pierre-Péladeau.

INN
AUBERGE AU NID DOUILLET

Martin Leduc
430, chemin Pierre-Péladeau
Ste-Adèle J8B 1Z4
(450) 229-6939
toll free 1-800-529-6939
fax (450) 229-6651
www.bbacanada.
com/1760.html

	B&B	MAP
single	$55-85	$69-99
double	$65-125	$99-159
triple	$85-135	$129-179
quad.	$95-145	$159-209
child	$0-15	$0-30

Taxes extra VS MC AM ER IT

Reduced rates: Apr., May, and Oct. week days, 15% 2 nights and more
Open year round

Number of rooms	16
rooms in basement	2
rooms with private bath	16

Activities: 👤 🚴 ⛷ 🐕

38. STE-ADÈLE ★★ F E 🚭 🏊 P R.5 TA

Our little love nest is tucked away between Montréal and Tremblant, amidst all the cultural and outdoor activities. Total relaxation is guaranteed. Friendly hosts, a night by the fire. In the morning, a big breakfast awaits in the solarium, where you can admire the birds, flowered garden, stream and heated pool. Enjoyable days and nights await. Spoil yourself.

From Montréal, Hwy 15 N., Exit 67, Rte 117, Boul Ste-Adèle for 2km. 25 min from Mirabel airport.

INN
AUBERGE BONNE NUIT BONJOUR

Gillian Lee and Timothy Eccles
1980, boul. Ste-Adèle
Ste-Adèle J8B 2N5
tel/fax (450) 229-7500
toll free 1-888-229-7500
www.bbcanada.com/
1607.html

B&B	
single	$55-65
double	$75-110
triple	$105
quad.	$125
child	$20

Taxes extra VS MC IT

Reduced rates: Apr. 1 to June 1, Nov. 1 to Dec. 1
Open year round

Number of rooms	6
rooms with private bath	4
shared bathrooms	1

Activities: 🍲 👤 ⛷ 🏃

39. STE-ADÈLE ☼☼☼ F e 🚭 🚗 P R.4 TA

Located near the bike and cross-country skiing path, Auberge de la Gare is a Victorian-style house from the *belle époque*. This rustic property is furnished with antiques, which complement the meticulous décor. We offer two different breakfasts, living room with fireplace, billiard table, reading room and more. Numerous sports activities, hydroplane, new concert theatre, cinema, art gallery, waterfall. Shuttle buses to the airports and excellent restaurants in the area. Terrace and Belgian specialities. **See colour photos. Ad end of this region.**

From Montréal, Hwy 15 North, Exit 69, 370 East 4km.

B&B
AUBERGE DE LA GARE

Geneviève Ostrowski and
Michel Gossiaux
1694, ch. Pierre-Péladeau
C.P. 2587
Ste-Adèle J8B 1Z5
(450) 228-3140
toll free 1-888-825-4273
fax (450) 228-1089
www.laurentides.
com/membres/006a.html

B&B	
single	$52-57
double	$60-65

Taxes extra VS MC IT

Open year round

Number of rooms	5
rooms with sink	5
shared wc	2
shared bathrooms	2

Activities: 🍲 👤 🚴 ⛷ 🐕

40. STE-ADÈLE

☀☀☀ F E 🐕 🏊 P 🚗 R6 TA

A home away from home! Our domain built on the mountainside is an oasis of peace and tranquillity! Warmth, relaxation and comfort blend together to offer you an unforgettable stay. Dream breakfasts that will fulfil you! Swimming pool on the premises. Parks, hikes, bikes path, ski resorts a stone's throw away. Golf, theatre and massage packages available.

From Montréal, Hwy 15 North, Exit 67. Right at the traffic lights Rue St-Joseph. At the stop sign, turn left on Rue Rolland, drive 3km.

B&B
AUBERGE DES SORBIERS B&B

Lise Fournier and Alain Parpal
4120, rue Rolland
Ste-Adèle J8B 1C7
(450) 229-3929
fax (450) 229-7510
www3.sympatico.ca/auberge.
des.sorbiers
/auberge.des.sorbiers
auberge.des.sorbiers
@sympatico.ca

B&B	
single	$55-65
double	$65-75
triple	$95
child	$20

Taxes extra VS

Reduced rates: 3 nights and more in Mar., Apr. and from Nov. 1 to Dec. 15
Open year round

Number of rooms	4
rooms with sink	2
rooms with private bath	2
shared bathrooms	1

Activities: 🍷 🎿 🚴 🏊 🏃

41. STE-ADÈLE

F E 🚫 🏊 P 🚗 R.5 TA

Located on an enchanted river with natural whirlpools, enjoy our old stone sauna, outdoor spa, massages, relaxation pavillion, walking paths and rest areas. A delicious breafast and tastefully decorated rooms await your visit. Adventure, romance, relaxation packages available. Come dream with us!

From Montréal, Hwy 15 North Exit 67, Rte 117, Boul Ste-Adèle, drive 3.6km. Stone house with blue roof, on left. 25 minutes from Mirabel Airport.

INN
AUBERGE ET SPA BEAUX RÊVES

Hannes Lamothe
2310, boul. Ste-Adèle rte 117
Ste-Adèle J8B 2N5
(450) 229-9226
toll free 1-800-279-7679
fax (450) 229-2999
www.beauxreves.com
bienvenue@beauxreves.com

B&B	
single	$60-75
double	$80-95
triple	$95-115
quad.	$95-135
child	$0-20

Taxes extra VS MC

Open year round

Number of rooms	7
rooms with private bath	7

Activities: 🎿 🚴 🛶 🎿 🐕

42. STE-ADÈLE

✒ F E 🚫 🚗 P R.3 TA

High above the valley! On mountainside, quiet area, near the lake and the city beach, ski Chanteclerc and many restaurants. Central air-conditioned inn, European charm, private balconies, V.I.P. suites. Splendid views! Stone fireplace, guests' living room, large indoor sauna and spa, outdoor snowbath! Learn German at breakfast!

From Montréal, Hwy 15 N. Exit 67, Rte 117, Blvd Ste-Adèle, left at the 4th light at Rue Morin, 0.3km, then turn left onto Rue Ouimet, drive 0.2km. 4th house on your left at the end of the street.

B&B
AUBERGE LA GIROUETTE
DES B&B

Helga Büchel Bélanger
941, rue Ouimet
Ste-Adèle J8B 2R3
tel/fax (450) 229-6433
toll free 1-800-301-6433
www.bbcanada.com/1536.html
la.girouette@securenet.net

B&B	
single	$55-90
double	$65-110
triple	$105-135
quad.	$120-160
child	$0-15

Taxes extra VS MC IT

Reduced rates: Apr., May and Nov.
Open year round

Number of rooms	5
rooms with pivate bath	5

Activities: 🛶 🎿 🚴 🏊 🏃

43. STE-ADÈLE

We'll welcome you like special company to our private property 5 min from all the activities in the Laurentians. Fireplace, piano, pinball, air conditioning, outdoor spa... everything to help you relax. Copious breakfast. Other meals by reservation

From Montréal or Mirabel, Hwy 15 N., Exit 69 twd Ste-Marguerite, Rte 370. Drive 6km, or 1.8km from linear park (bike path), on your right.

INN
AUX PINS DORÉS

Carmen Champagne and René Tremblay
2251, chemin Pierre-Péladeau
Ste-Adèle J8B 1Z7
(450) 228-4556
toll free 1-877-228-4556
fax (450) 228-1881
members.tripod.com/~pins

B&B	
single	$45-60
double	$55-75
triple	$85
quad.	$95
child	$0-10

Reduced rates: 2 nights or more during weeks except summertime and school holidays.

Open year round

Number of rooms	4
rooms with private bath	1
shared bathrooms	2

Activities:

---

44. STE-AGATHE-DES-MONTS

On the shore of Lac des Sables, our Inn has 5 luxurious thematic rooms, which include whirlpools for two, chimneys, balconies, sound systems, air conditioned, private bathrooms and breakfast served in the privacy of your own room. Massages available on the premises. Free use of our canoes, pedal-boats and bikes. Snowmobiling and other winter sports are nearby. 1 hour from Mtl and 35 min from Tremblant. **Ad end of guide.**

From Montréal, Hwy 15 N., Exit 86. Rte 117 N., 3rd light, left on Rue Principale, left on Ste-Lucie and left on Larocque.

INN
AUBERGE AUX NUITS DE RÊVE

Carol McCann and Christian Simon
14, Larocque Ouest
St-Agathe-des-Monts J8C 1A2
tel/fax (819) 326-5042
toll free 1-888-326-5042
www.polyinter.com/auberge-de-reve
auberge@polyinter.com

B&B	
single	$110-145
double	$110-145

Taxes extra VS MC

Reduced rates: Apr., May, Nov.
Open year round

Number of rooms	5
rooms with private bath	5

Activities:

---

45. STE-AGATHE-DES-MONTS

Special Mention «Our beautiful Inns of yesteryear» success 1999. Imagine a beautiful 100-year-old house where comfort is a living tradition. A fire burning in the hearth, Swedish massages. The colours of the changing seasons. The peaceful contentment of gathering twilight. 1 hour from Montréal, 35 min from Tremblant: 12 rms, including 8 with fireplace and whirlpool bath. **Ad end of guide.**

From Montréal, Hwy 15 N. Exit 86. Rte 117 N., at 5th lights turn left on Rue Préfontaine, right on Chemin Tour-du-Lac.

INN
AUBERGE DE LA TOUR DU LAC

Jean-Léo Legault
173, Tour-du-Lac
Ste-Agathe-des-Monts J8C 1B7
toll free 1-800-622-1735
(819) 326-4202
fax (819) 326-0341
www.delatour.qc.ca

B&B	
single	$73-103
double	$88-118
child	$15

Taxes extra VS MC AM ER IT

Reduced rates: Apr. and Nov.
Open year round

Number of rooms	12
rooms with private bath	12

Activities:

46. STE-AGATHE-DES-MONTS

F E 🚫 🐕 🛶 P R2 TA

Situated in the heart of a picturesque, quaint little village, Au Nid D'Hirondelles was built pieces on pieces. The Canadian-style decor with two fireplaces creates the atmosphere of a bygone era. In harmony with Mother Nature, we celebrate her changing seasons. After a night of restful sleep, you will be served a copious breakfast. Located between Mont-Tremblant and St-Sauveur, it's the ideal spot for sports enthusiasts and nature lovers.

From Montréal, Hwy 15 North to the end, drive 1km. Turn right on Chemin Mt-Castor, 1.5km.

B&B
AU NID D'HIRONDELLES

Suzanne and Michel Grêve
1235, des Hirondelles
Mont-Castor
Ste-Agathe-des-Monts J8C 2Z8
(819) 326-5413
toll free 1-888-826-5413
fax (819) 326-3839
www.nidhirondelles.qc.ca
gite@nidhirondelles.qc.ca

B&B	
single	$55
double	$70

Taxes extra VS IT

Open year round

Number of rooms	4
rooms with private bath	4

Activities: 🎿 ⛷ 🏃 🐎

---

47. STE-AGATHE-NORD

F E 🐕 🚗 P R5 TA

Relive the turn of the century in our manor. Built for Count d'Ivry in 1902, its original woodwork and stone fireplaces have been preserved. Nature and many outdoor activities are just outside your doorstep. There's swimming in Lac Manitou, as well as biking and snowmobiling on the P'tit Train du Nord path (1km). Discount for Mont-Blanc ski resort. A breakfast made with seasonal products is served up by your friendly hosts.

From Montréal, Hwy 15 North. When the highway ends and links up with Rte 117, first street on your left, Chemin Renaud.

INN
MANOIR D'IVRY B&B

Isabelle Taverna, Daniel Potvin,
Isabelle Giroux, Pascal Potvin
3800, chemin Renaud
Ste-Agathe-Nord J8C 2Z8
(819) 321-0858
www.manoirdivry.com
manoirdivry@ste-agathe.net

B&B	
single	$45-50
double	$55-60
triple	$75
quad.	$80
child	$5-10

Taxes extra VS

Reduced rates: Price for group, 5$ off/night, 3 nights and more
Open year round

Number of rooms	9
shared wc	1
shared bathrooms	3

Activities: 🚤 🛶 🎿 ⛷

---

48. STE-MARGUERITE-DU-LAC-MASSON

F e ✕ P R5 TA

A rustic ambience, a spacious home, the relaxing countryside, all this is waiting for you at Auberge au Phil de L'eau. But there's more: a terrace by the lake, a private beach, a fireplace, golfing, canoeing, swimming, summer theatre, ice skating, the list goes on. All this less than one hour from Montréal.

Hwy 15 North, Exit 69, 8km Rte 370 East. At "Les 2 Roses" residence, left on Chemin Guénette 4.5km.

B&B
AUBERGE AU PHIL DE L'EAU

Murielle Godin and
Philippe Gauzelin
150, ch. Guénette
Ste-Marguerite-du-Lac-Masson
JOT 1L0
(450) 228-1882
fax (450) 228-8271
www.laurentides.com

	B&B	MAP
single	$45-60	$60-85
double	$50-65	$80-115
triple	$80	$125-155
quad.	$95	$155-195

Taxes extra

Open year round

Number of rooms	5
shared wc	1
shared bathrooms	2

Activities: 🚤 ⛷ 🏃 🚴 🐎

49. STE-MARGUERITE-DU-LAC-MASSON

"The tranquillity of the forest, the beautiful setting, the sun-lit house, the warmth of two hearths, such warm-hearted people, an extra-special breakfast. The place had it all." Here you will find the contentment of a pleasant, informal home. Near St-Sauveur and Ste-Adèle, between Montréal and Mont Tremblant. 2km from the "Bistrot Champlain".

From Montréal, Hwy 15 North, Exit 69. Rte 370, 10.5km. After the cemetery and Sommet Vert, left on Lupin. Left on Rue Des Rapides, to the end of the street.

B&B
GÎTE DU LIÈVRE

Chantal Belisle and
Patrice Richard
34, Place du Lièvre
Ste-Marguerite-du-Lac-Masson
JOT 1L0
tel/fax (450) 228-4131
toll free Mtl (514) 823-4582
pages.citenet.net/
users/ctmx0131
gite_du_lievre@citenet.net

B&B	
single	$60
double	$65
triple	$80
quad.	$95

Open year round

Number of rooms	3
rooms with private bath	1
shared bathroomss	1

Activities:

---

50. VAL-DAVID

Warm house with charm of yesteryear, main floor made of unhewntimber, fireplace, veranda, garden. Family atmosphere; spacious, well-ventilated rooms; comfortable king-size bed. And what can we say about our breakfasts? Succumb to new flavours! Across from the linear park for cycling, cross-country skiing...

From Montréal, Hwy 15 North, Exit 76, Rte 117 North. In Val-David: right at 2nd lights onto Rue de l'Eglise, right on Rue de la Sapinière, 2nd block on the left.

B&B
LA CHAUMIÈRE AUX
MARGUERITES

Fabienne and Marc Girard
and their daughter Jéromine
1267, rue de la Sapinière
Val-David JOT 2N0
(819) 322-2043

B&B	
single	$60
double	$60
child	$0-10

VS

Reduced rates: 2 nights and more
Open year round

Number of rooms	2
shared bathrooms	1

Activities:

---

51. VAL-DAVID

Old-station-style inn on the summer bike path/winter ski trail ("*P'tit train du nord*"). Terrace on the Rivière du Nord. Ideal for lovers. Rooms on the river or trail. Transport to anywhere on the path (15-passenger minibus). Treks organized: cross-country ski, snowmobile, dogsled, bike, canoe, visits around Québec. At our restaurant: Québec beers and traditional food.

1 hr from Montréal, Hwy 15 N. or Rte 117 N., Exit 76 Val David, then take the 1st street on the left for 600 m.

INN
LE RELAIS DE LA PISTE

Anne-Marie and
Thierry Chaumont
1430, de l'Académie
Val-David JOT 2N0
(819) 322-2280
fax (819) 322-6658
lerelais@polyinter.com

	B&B	MAP
single	$68	$86
double	$75	$110
triple	$90	$145
quad.	$105	$180
child	$15	$30

Taxes extra VS AM IT

Reduced rates: Oct. 10 to
Oct. 31, Mar. 1 to Mar. 31
Open year round

Number of rooms	6
rooms with private bath	6

Activities:

52. VAL-MORIN ☀☀☀ F E P 🚗 R.5 TA

Laurentides Excellence Prize 1997-98. A cosy nest where you can relax in private. Lounge around the fire in the living room with its great view. Refine and gourmet breakfast. Easy access to the bike path (1km), cross-country and downhill skiing. Close to Val-David, Ste-Adèle, St-Sauveur and Mt-Tremblant (30 min). We can meet you at the airport, 40km to Mirabel, 75km to Dorval.

From Montréal or Mirabel, Hwy 15 North, Exit 76, Val-Morin. Rte 117, for 0.5km, turn right on Curé-Corbeil, to the end 1.5km, turn right on Rue Morin, 0.5km, corner of 8ᵉ rue.

B&B
LA «CHANT'OISEAU»

Martine and Marc Sabourin
5760, rue Morin
Val-Morin J0T 2R0
(819) 322-6660
fax (819) 323-3737
www.bbcanada.
com/3572.html

B&B	
single	$45
double	$60
triple	$80
child	$10-15

Reduced rates: From the second night, Oct. 15 to Dec. 15 and Jan. 15 to May 15
Open year round: except Nov.

Number of rooms	3
shared bathrooms	1

Activities: 🚤 🧍 🚴 🏊 🏃

53. VAL-MORIN ☀☀☀ F E ♿ 🚭 🏊 🚗 ✕ P TA

Near the P'tit Train du Nord linear trail for biking or skiing excursions. We also organize canoe trips throughout Québec. Large salon with foyer to have a coffee or read. Guests love our copious breakfasts and suppers. Les Florettes is located in a pleasant landscaped spot near a lake without a dock for motorboats.

From Montréal, Hwy 15 North, Exit 76, Rte 117 North, right on Curé-Corbeil, at the stop sign, right on Rue Morin, left on 7e Avenue until the end, then left on De La Gare.

B&B
LES FLORETTES

Micheline Boutin and
Jacques Allard
1803, de la Gare
Val-Morin J0T 2R0
(819) 322-7614
fax (819) 322-3029
escapade@polyinter.com

B&B	
single	$45
double	$65-70
child	$16

Taxes extra VS MC

Reduced rates: 10% 2 nights and more
Open year round

Number of rooms	5
rooms with private bath	1
shared bathrooms	2

Activities: 🚤 🧍 🚴 🏊 🏃

54. VAL-MORIN ★★ F E 🚭 P 🚗 🐕 R2 🏊 TA

Laurentides Excellence Prize 1999. Discover a piece of Laurentian heritage in this former general store and post office. The 2-acre property lies alongside "Parc Linéaire" and Lake Raymond. Bikes, canoes and pedalboats free. Relax on one of the porches in front of the lake, an ideal retreat to pass the time. Come enjoy our 5-course breakfast and exquisite hospitality. Gift certificate. **See colour photos.**

From Mtl, Hwy 15 N., Exit 76. Drive 0.5km on Rte 117 N., then right on Curé-Corbeil to the end. Right on Rue Morin, 0.5km, left at first stop, to the end of the street.

INN
LES JARDINS DE LA GARE B&B

Françoise and Alain
1790, 7ᵉ Avenue
Val-Morin J0T 2R0
tel/fax (819) 322-5559
toll free 1-888-322-4273
http://pages.infinit.net/
racetr/jardin.html

B&B	
single	$60-85
double	$80-110

Taxes extra VS IT

Reduced rates: Oct. 15 to Dec. 15, Apr. 1 to May 15
Open year round

Number of rooms	8
rooms with private bath	2
rooms with sink	2
shared wc	1
shared bathrooms	2

Activities: 🏛 🚤 🧍 🚴 🏃

55. VAL-MORIN

In the Laurentians, discover Lise & Camil's eden on a quiet lake surrounded by hills. In summer, take a deep breath while canoeing on the lake with loons and beavers. In winter, relax by an impressive fireplace after a day of skiing. Special packages: honeymoon, get together, Old Montréal. **See colour photos**

Hwy 15 North, Exit 76, Rte 117 North. First light, turn right on Morin. Follow signs to Far Hills. At stop sign after ski center, straight, 1.7km. Keep right on Ch. Lac Lasalle twd cul-de-sac.

B&B
NID D'AMOUR

Lise and Camil Bourque
6455, chemin du Lac Lasalle
Val-Morin J0T 2R0
tel/fax (819) 322-6379
toll free 1-888- 4321-NID
www.nidamour.qc.ca
nidamour@hotmail.com

B&B	
single	$70-90-100-120
double	$70-90-100-120

Taxes extra VS MC

Reduced rates: 2 nights and more (except 70$ rooms)
Open year round
(except during the Christmas Holidays)

Number of rooms	4
rooms with private bath	4

Activities:

56. MONT-TREMBLANT, LAC-SUPÉRIEUR

F | e | 🚗 | P | 🏊 | R2.5 | TA

In our cottage, you will live the life of Riley. After a fun-filled day, come home to a pool, terrace and fireplace in a tranquil environment. Explore the mountain, Parc du Mont-Tremblant and the beautiful Mont-Blanc 5km away. Seasonal tourist attractions. Unique setting in the Laurentian Mountains. **B&B p 171.**

From Montréal, Hwy 15 and Rte 117 North, St-Faustin/Lac-Carrée exit. Turn right at the stop sign, drive 2.3km following the signs for Parc du Montr-Tremblant, drive 2.5km on Ch. du Lac Supérieur.

COUNTRY HOME
LA PETITE CHAMPAGNE

Marie-France Champagne
654, ch. du Lac Supérieur
Lac-Supérieur
J0T 1J0
tel/fax (819) 688-3780
www.laurentides.com

No. houses	1
No. rooms	2
No. people	4
WEEK-SUMMER	$550
WEEK-WINTER	$550
W/E-SUMMER	$280
W/E-WINTER	$280
DAY-SUMMER	$140
DAY-WINTER	$140

VS AM

Open year round

Activities: 🚣 🎿 🚶 🚴 ⛷️

---

57. LAC-SUPÉRIEUR, MONT-TREMBLANT

F | E | ♿ | P | R1 | M.4 | TA

Hypnotized by the wind in the trees and an unforgetable view of the mountains. This carefully decorated home (1930) offers relaxation by the fireplace or access to nature; beach, lake, river. 7 min. from aera's two largest sites: the station and Parc du Mont-Tremblant. A few steps away: hiking trail, biking, cross-country skiing and three beautiful studios wich will also charm you.

Hwy 15 North, Rte 117 North, St-Faustin Exit. Right at stop sign, 2.3km, follow Mont-Tremblant Park and ski resort signs, continue for 9.5km.

COUNTRY HOME
LE VENT DU NORD

Géraldine and Jean Christie
1954, ch. du Lac Supérieur
Lac-Supérieur J0T 1P0
(819) 688-6140
fax (819) 688-3196

No. houses	4
No. rooms	1-4
No. people	1-14
WEEK-SUMMER	$350-950
WEEK-WINTER	$455-2450
W/E-SUMMER	$150-550
W/E-WINTER	$160-700

Taxes extra VS MC IT

Reduced rates: Nov.12 to Dec.18, Jan. 22 to Feb. 10, Mar. 26 to Apr. 20
Open year round

Activities: 🚣 🚶 🎿 ⛷️ 🏃

---

58. ROSEMÈRE

F | E | 🐕 | 🚗 | P | 🏊 | R.01 | M.03 | TA

Century house of the French-Canadian sculptor Louis-Philippe Hébert. This magnificient home has all the modern comforts. For business meetings or family get-togethers, it can accommodate 8 people. Reflecting of our recent past, it invites you to its peaceful surroundings on the banks of the 1000 Islands River. 20 min from Montréal, 5 min from Laval. **See colour photos.**

Hwy 15 North, Exit 19. Right at stop sign, left at first light, 1.5km on Grande-Côte. Right on Blvd Labelle, 0.5km. Right, reception at 125 Blvd Labelle (Hôtel Le Rivage).

COUNTRY HOME
LA MAISON DE L'ENCLOS

Christianne and Pierre Verville
463, Île Bélair Ouest
Rosemère
J7A 2G9
(450) 437-2171
toll free 1-888-437-2171
fax (450) 437-3005

No. houses	2
No. rooms	1-4
No. people	2-8
WEEK-SUMMER	$1 043-2 450
WEEK-WINTER	$1 043-2 450
W/E-SUMMER	$300-700
W/E-WINTER	$300-700
DAY-SUMMER	$150-350
DAY-WINTER	$150-350

Taxes extra VS MC AM ER IT

Open year round

Activities: 🏛️ 🦆 🚣 🛶 🚶

FARM ACTIVITIES

Farm Stays:

11 LA CLAIRIÈRE DE LA CÔTE, L'Annonciation 39

27 FERME DE LA BUTTE MAGIQUE, St-Faustin 39

Country-style Dining*:

59 AU PIED DE LA CHUTE, Lachute 19

60 AUX DOUCEURS DE LA RUCHE, Mirabel, St-Scholastique 20

11 LA CLAIRIÈRE DE LA CÔTE, L'Annonciation 19

61 LA CONCLUSION, Ste-Anne-des-Plaines 22

62 LA FERME CATHERINE, St-André Est 21

63 LE RÉGALIN, St-Eustache 21

64 LES RONDINS, Mirabel, Lachute 20

Farm Excursion:

65 INTERMIEL, St-Benoît, Mirabel 31

* Registered Trademark.

LAVAL

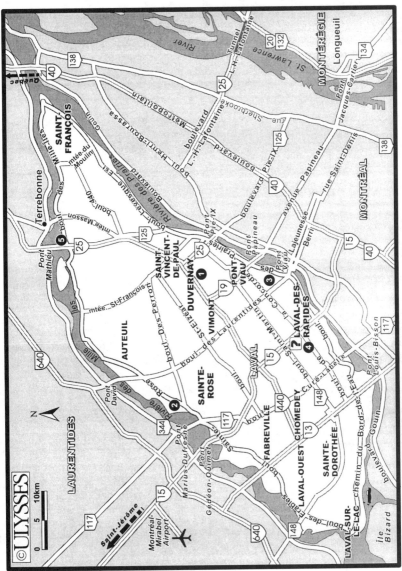

* The numbers on the map refer to the numbering of the establishments of this region

1. DUVERNAY EST

✹✹✹ | F | e | 🚭 | P | 🛶 | R.1

It is with great pride and joy that I invite you into my home in the countryside—and with a typically warm Gaspesian welcome. You will sleep peacefully in our cosy bedrooms. Located near conveniences and large centres. Sumptuous breakfast waits for you! "The flavour of Gaspé at the gateway to the metropolis."

Hwy 440, Exit 16 to Boulevard Lévesque East to Des Sapins, 1st street on your right, Des Cèdres.

B&B
LE GÎTE LA GASPÉSIENNE

Yvette Anglehart Grenier
85, rue des Cèdres
Duvernay est, Laval
H7A 2V7
(450) 665-8475

B&B	
single	$45
double	$55
child	$10

Open year round

Number of rooms	3
shared wc	1
rooms in basement	2
shared bathrooms	1

Activities: 𝅘 ⚶ 🚲 🛶 ⛷

2. LAVAL

✹✹✹ | F | E | 🚭 | 🚗 | P | 🛶 | R1 | TA

Welcome to the village of Vieux Ste-Rose in Laval, 30 minutes from Montréal and the Laurentides. We have had guests from 27 countries stay with us. Even businesspeople will feel like they are on vacation here, chatting away over breakfast before the Mille-Îles wildlife sanctuary. See you soon!

Hwy 15 (North or South), Exit 16, right on Boul. Ste-Rose, 2.5km to Rue des Patriotes (Vieux Ste-Rose restaurant on the corner). Turn left, continue for 0.9km.

B&B
GÎTE DU BORD DE L'EAU

Louise Trudeau
495, rue des Patriotes
Laval H7L 2L9
(450) 625-3785
fax (450) 625-8235
www.info-internet.
net./~trudeau
gite_d_eau@hotmail.com

B&B	
single	$47
double	$62
triple	$82
quad.	$102
child	$5-10-15

Open year round

Number of rooms	1
rooms with private bath	1

Activities: 🏛 🛶 🚤 𝅘 ⛷

3. LAVAL

✹✹✹ | F | E | 🚭 | 🐕 | P | R.25 | TA

Tourists and business people enjoy our cosy rooms including a magnificent suite with private bathroom and jacuzzi. Enjoy our breakfasts indoors or outdoors in the secluded garden, which has a fountain. Facing a park, just a 15min walk from metro Henri Bourassa, as well as cultural and recreational activities.

Hwy 15 North, Exit 7, Boulevard Cartier, left at first light. To the end, turn left onto St-Hubert, then right onto Lévesque.

B&B
GÎTE DU MARIGOT

Chantal Lachapelle
128, boulevard Lévesque Est
Laval H7G 1C2
(450) 668-0311
www3.sympatico.ca/
gitedumarigot/index.htm
gitedumarigot@sympatico.ca

B&B	
single	$45-60
double	$60-70
triple	$75-85
child	$5-10

Taxes extra

Open year round

Number of rooms	3
rooms with private bath	1
rooms with sink	3
shared bathrooms	1

Activities: 🏛 🍂 𝅘 ⚶ 🚲

4. LAVAL

✹✹✹ | F | e | ⊘ | P | 🛥 | 🐕 | R.75 | TA

Comfortable house located 3km from Montreal, near the Henri-Bourassa metro station. Shuttle service for those taking public transportation. Warm welcome, hearty breakfast to your liking and at your convenience. Children welcome. Living room, patio, BBQ, refrigerator, pantry, swimming pool, flowery terrace, large garden, swing.

From Montréal, Hwy 15 North, Exit 7, Boul. des Prairies East. From Mirabel, Hwy 15 South, Exit 7, eastbound Boul. des Prairies. After 13 blocks, left on Boul. Bon-Pasteur.

B&B
L'ABRI DU TEMPS

Marguerite and Raoul St-Jean
2, boul. Bon Pasteur
Laval-des-Rapides
H7N 3P9
tel/fax (450) 663-5094

B&B	
single	$47
double	$57-60
child	$15

Reduced rates: 15% after 7 consecutive nights
Open year round

Number of rooms	3
shared bathrooms	2

Activities: 🏛 🏄 🏌 🚶 🚲

---

5. LAVAL

✎ | F | e | ⊘ | 🛥 | P | R2

Facing Île-des-Moulins, Notre Maison sur la Rivière is sheltered by ash trees and watched over by herons. The babbling river, arts and culinary pleasures nearby will entice you to come visit our stone house, which has a fireplace and relaxing atmosphere. Our breakfasts are full of pleasant surprises. You will want to make this your first visit of many.

From Montréal, Boulevard Pie IX, Rte 25, Exit 20, turn right onto Boulevard des Milles-Îles, 1st stop sign, turn left on Rue Guglia, Dessureaux 1st street turn right.

B&B
NOTRE MAISON SUR LA RIVIÈRE

Viviane Charbonneau and
Serge Gaudreau
6125, Dessureaux
St-François, Laval
H7B 1B1
(450) 666-4095
fax (450) 666-6383
viviane.serge@sympatico.ca

B&B	
single	55-60 $
double	65-75 $

Taxes extra

Open year round: From June 1st, 2000

Number of rooms	2
rooms with sink	2
shared wc	1
shared bathrooms	1

Activities: 🏛 🍷 🛶 🚶 🐎

MAURICIE

La Tuque

Carignan

Lac Wawagamac

155

Rivière-aux-Rats

Réserve faunique du Saint-Maurice

Grande-Anse
②

Lac Mékinac

155

Rivière-Matawin

Saint-Joseph-de-Mékinac

Notre-Dame-des-Anges

Rivière

Saint-Roch-de-Mékinac

Sainte-Thècle

QUÉBEC CITY REGION

363

Saint-Ubalde

354

Mauricie National Park

Saint-Maurice

155

159

153

Saint-Tite
⑬

Saint-Adelphe

Réserve faunique Mastigouche

Grandes-Piles
④ à ⑥

Hérouxville
⑦ ⑧ ㉗

159

138

Lotbinière

Saint-Mathieu
⑫

Grand-Mère
③

Saint-Stanislas

Sainte-Anne-de-la-Pérade
⑭ ⑮

132

Shawinigan

Ste-Geneviève-de-Batiscan

Deschaillons

226

155

Shawinigan-Sud
⑯ ⑰

359

Batiscan
①

Saint-Pierre-les-Becquets

351

55

157

Saint-Maurice

40

Champlain

Sainte-Françoise

218

265

Saint-Paulin

153

Saint-Louis-de-France

St. Lawrence River

132

Manseau

20

Saint-Sévère

350

Trois-Rivières
⑱ à ㉓

Bécancour

Sainte-Marie-de-Blandford

263

Pointe-du-Lac
㉔ ㉕ ㉖

155

261

Saint-Louis-de-Blandford

Louiseville
⑨ ⑩ ⑪ ㉘

40

Lac Saint-Pierre

Nicolet

55

132

CENTRE-DU-QUÉBEC

Saint-Louis-de-Blandford

138

Baie-du-Febvre

Saint-Wenceslas

161

Sainte-Eulalie

Princeville

162

LANAUDIÈRE

Berthierville

Pierreville

226

Sainte-Perpétue

155

20

Victoriaville

116

Sorel

Saint-Elphège

255

259

161

Tracy

132

122

0   10   20km

N

© ULYSSES

* The numbers on the map refer to the numbering of the establishments of this region

1. BATISCAN

☀☀☀☀☀ F E 🚫 🚗 P 🏊 ✕ R2 TA

An enchanting B&B by the St. Lawrence River, on the Chemin du Roy, awaits you. Decor of a bygone era, a stone's throw from a superb, unknown beach, near Parc de la Batiscan, less than 40 minutes from Parc de la Mauricie, Village du Bûcheron, Cité de l'énergie, Forges du Saint-Maurice. Winter activities: snowshoeing, dogsledding, snowmobiling, snow scooter, ice fishing, sugar Shack. Mauricie Excellence Prize 1995-96. **See colour photos.**

Between Montréal and Québec City, Hwy 40, Batiscan Exit, twd Rte 361 South, Rte 138 West. 4km from the highway.

B&B
LE ST-ÉLIAS

Monique Bernier
951, Principale rte 138
Batiscan G0X 1A0
(418) 362-2712
fax (418) 362-2081
www.quebecweb.com/elias
monique.bernier@cgocable.ca

B&B	
single	$45-55
double	$60-70
child	$15

VS MC

Reduced rates: 3 nights and more
Open: Jan. 15 to Oct. 31

Number of rooms	4
shared wc	1
shared bathrooms	2

Activities: 🏛 🦪 🛶 🎿 🚲

---

2. GRANDE-ANSE

F E ✕ 🚗 P 🏊 R17 TA

Mrs. Anne "the queen of Mauricie" Stillman-McCormick's haven of peace since 1918, this estate offers an ideal setting in which to relive this great lady's past. Located on the shores of the St-Maurice, with wide expanses inviting you to relax, have fun and get a good dose of fresh air, then share adventures and anecdotes. Family-size suites.

From Montréal or Québec City, Hwy 40. At Trois-Rivières, Hwy 55 North and 155 twd La Tuque. On Rte 155, atkm 70.

B&B
MAISON GOYETTE

Domaine McCormick
5171, Route 155 Nord
Grande-Anse G0X 2C0
(819) 676-3388
fax (819) 676-3297

	B&B	MAP
single	$40	$50
double	$55	$80
child	$10	$15

Taxes extra

Reduced rates: 6 people or more
Open year round

Number of rooms	2
shared bathrooms	2

Activities: 🛶 🎿 🚣 ⛷ 🐕

---

3. GRAND-MÈRE

☀☀☀☀ F E 🎿 🐕 P R.1

Come as you are and relive a page of history with us, in large and comfortable rooms. Our lovely Victorian house, wich has painstakingly preserved its attractive features, stands proudly and majestically 20 min from Cité de l'Énergie and from the National Park, 5 min from the Grand-Mère golf course.

From Québec City, Hwy 40 West, Exit 220 twd Grand-Mère, 0.5km from the bridge. From Montréal, Hwy 40 East, Hwy 55 North, Exit 223, go all the way down 5e Ave. Circle the park and turn on to 3e Ave.

B&B
GÎTE LA BELLE AU
BOIS DORMANT

Valérie, Lucie,
Pierre and Pierrot Dumont
20, 3ᵉ Avenue
Grand-Mère G9T 2T3
(819) 538-6489
(819) 533-2572
www.knightsoft.ca/belle
minivalou@hotmail.com

B&B	
single	$60-80
double	$65-85

Open year round

Number of rooms	3
shared bathrooms	1
shared wc	1
rooms with private bath	1

Activities: 🎿 🚣 🚲 🏊 ⛷

4. GRANDES-PILES

★★★ F e TA

"Le Bôme, some Mauricie balm to bask in". Snug inside an ancestral home, you will discover a friendly inn with cozy, comfortable rooms during your stay. The French-Italian-flavoured cuisine is a must. The singular landscape of mountains scored by the St-Maurice river will draw you to its national park. This 3-star inn boasts a spa, sauna and tennis court.

Halfway between Montréal and Québec City. Hwy 40 to Trois-Rivières, Hwy 55 North and Rte 155 twd La Tuque. Lac St-Jean, 10km past Grand-Mère, follow roadsigns to the inn.

INN

AUBERGE-LE-BÔME

Matilde Mossa and
Jean-Claude Coydon
720, 2e Avenue
Grandes-Piles G0X 1H0
toll free 1-800- 538-2805
(819) 538-2805
fax (819) 538-5879
www.auberge-le-bome.qc.ca
auberge-le-bome@
infoteck.qc.ca

	B&B	MAP
single	$80-115	$115-150
double	$85-120	$150-170
triple	$95-130	$205-245
child	$10	$25

Taxes extra VS MC IT

Open year round

Number of rooms	**10**
rooms with private bath	10

Activities:

5. GRANDES-PILES

F E TA

The crew of Franc-Nord welcomes you. Breathtaking view of the St-Maurice River. You will enjoy our rooms and elegant terrace. Packages available: lumberjack town, energy town, black-bear watching, golfing and much more. Take one of the most beautiful cruises in Québec. A stone's throw from Mauricie's national park. ¡Hablamos español! **Advertisement on front inside cover.**

Halfway between Québec City and Montréal Hwy 40 to Hwy 55 North, Rte 155 North to La Tuque/Lac St-Jean. In the village, turn left at Garage Crevier.

B&B

CAPITAINERIE D'AUTREFOIS

Anie Desaulniers and
Mario Therrien
740, 3e Avenue
Grandes-Piles G0X 1H0
(819) 533-1234
toll free 1-877-213-1234
fax (819) 538-2966
http://site.voila.fr/gite
croisieres.des.piles@qc.aira.com

B&B	
single	$55-80
double	$55-80
triple	$85
quad.	$90
child	$10

VS

Reduced rates: Oct.15 to May 31

Open year round

Number of rooms	**3**
shared bathrooms	2

Activities:

6. GRANDES-PILES

★★ F e R.1 TA

Perched between the Rivière St-Maurice and the mountains, Château Crête, the jewel of the Mauricie, is ideal for those who love wild open spaces. What awaits: Mauricie National Park and its many activities; lumberjack village; Village d'Émilie; Cité de l'Énergie; all that and more... Visit our internet site. See you soon! **See colour photos.**

Halfway between Montréal and Québec City by Hwy 40, then 55 N., 155 twd la Tuque and Lac St-Jean. 60km from Trois-Rivières.

INN

LE CHÂTEAU CRÊTE

Micheline Bardor
740, 4e Avenue
Grandes-Piles G0X 1H0
(819) 538-8389
toll free 1-888-538-8389
fax (819) 538-7323
www3.sympatico.ca/
chateau_crete
chateau_crete@sympatico.ca

B&B	
single	$45-65
double	$60-80
triple	$75
quad.	$90

Taxes extra

Open year round

Number of rooms	**7**
rooms with private bath	2
rooms with sink	3
rooms in basement	3
shared wc	3
shared bathrooms	1

Activities:

7. HÉROUXVILLE

F ♿ ✕ P 🚗 ⛵ R2 TA

Share in the simplicity and joy of living on our family farm, in a B&B suited for young and old alike. In a country setting, enjoy communing with the animals, rediscover human warmth and enjoy a well-deserved rest. Interesting tourist attractions. B&B next to the main house. Air-conditioned. **Farm Stay p 40.**

From Montréal or Québec City, Hwy 40. At Trois-Rivières, Hwy 55 North to the end, Exit Rte 153 North. In Hérouxville, cross the train tracks and continue for 2km.

B&B
ACCUEIL LES SEMAILLES

Christine Naud and Lise Richer
1460, rang Saint-Pierre
Hérouxville G0X 1J0
(418) 365-5190
mapageweb.net/semailles.com

	B&B	MAP
single	$35	$43
double	$50	$66
child	$12	$15

Open year round

Number of rooms	5
shared bathrooms	2

Activities: 🏛 🐎 🐇 🦆 🏃

---

8. HÉROUXVILLE

F E 🚗 🐕 P R5 TA

A warm B&B located near Parc de la Mauricie between Montréal and Lac St-Jean. Come relax by the fire and sample grilled marshmallows. Family ambiance where it is pleasant to share our traditions with you. Prix Excellence Mauricie 1994-95. Recommended by the French guide 98. Snowshoe, skate and ski rentals. **Country Home p 200.**

Halfway between Québec City and Montréal by Hwy 20 or 40, take Hwy 55 N. via Trois-Rivières. At the end of Hwy 55, Exit Rte 153 N. At Hérouxville, at the flashing light, street beside the church.

B&B
MAISON TRUDEL

Nicole Jubinville
and Yves Trudel
543, Goulet
Hérouxville G0X 1J0
(418) 365-7624
fax (418) 365-7041
www.bbcanada.com/408.html
maison-trudel-quebec
@concepta.com

	B&B
single	$40
double	$50
triple	$75
child	$10

VS

Open year round

Number of rooms	4
shared bathrooms	3

Activities: 🍷 🛷 🎿 🐎 🎿

---

9. LOUISEVILLE

F E 🚫 ♿ 🚗 P 🐕 TA

The Carrefour is not only a prestigious B&B but also one of the most cultural in Québec. Our Queen-Anne house is the only official historic one in the village. Sumptuously furnished and decorated, it offers the utmost in comfort. Each of its four rooms is more opulent than the next. Discover its garden, as well.

From Montréal or Québec, Hwy 40, Exit 166 or 174 to Rte 138 twd downtown Louiseville. Corner Rte 349 and 138.

B&B
GÎTE DU CARREFOUR

Réal-Maurice Beauregard
11, av. St-Laurent Ouest
Louiseville J5V 1J3
tel/fax (819) 228-4932
www.giteducarrefour.qbc.net

	B&B
single	$45
double	$55

Open year round

Number of rooms	4
shared wc	1
shared bathrooms	3

Activities: 🏛 🛷 🎿 🚲 🐎

10. LOUISEVILLE

☀☀☀ F e 🚗 P R1

Built in 1858, the Victorian-era La Maison de l'Ancêtre has retained its architectural charms of yesteryear. Conveniently located 1km from the town centre, it offers guests a tasteful decor with quality furnishings in a peaceful oasis. Lavish breakfast complemented by homemade goods. Your hosts' warm, heart-felt welcome awaits.

From Montréal, Hwy 40, Exit 166. Rte 138 East, 3.5km. Rte 349, Rue Notre-Dame North, 1km. From Québec City, Hwy 40, Exit 174. Rte 138 West, 4.9km, Rte 349, Rue Notre-Dame North, 1km.

B&B
LA MAISON DE L'ANCÊTRE

Julienne Leblanc
491, Notre-Dame Nord
Louiseville J5V 1X9
(819) 228-8195

B&B	
single	$45-55
double	$50-60
triple	$65-75
child	$10

Open year round

Number of rooms	3
shared bathrooms	2

Activities: 🚶 🎿 🚴 ⛷ 🐎

---

11. LOUISEVILLE

F e 🚗 ✕ P R1 TA

Comfortable, peaceful Victorian farmhouse (1880). A romantic trip back in time. Quality and harmony, it has been called "a corner of paradise..." 10km from Ste-Ursule waterfalls, Lac St-Pierre. Dine on the farm (5 courses) with reservations. **Farm Stay p 40, Country-style Dining p 23, Country Home p 200 and Farm Excursion p 32. Ad end of guide.**

From Montréal or Québec City, Hwy 40, Exit 166. Rte 138 East, drive 2.4km to Rte 348 West. Left twd St-Ursule, drive 1.5km, 1st road on the right.

B&B
LE GÎTE DE LA SEIGNEURIE

Michel Gilbert
480, chemin du Golf
Louiseville J5V 2L4
tel/fax (819) 228-8224
m.gilbert@infoteck.qc.ca

	B&B	MAP
single	$45-70	$65-90
double	$60-90	$100-130
triple	$85	$145
quad.	$100	$180
child	$20	$30

Taxes extra

Open year round

Number of rooms	5
rooms with sink	2
rooms with private bath	1
shared bathrooms	2

Activities: 🏛 ⛷ 🚶 🚴

---

12. ST-MATHIEU-DU-PARC

F E P 🐕 R5 TA

Welcome to our haven of peace and harmony. 7km from Parc de la Mauricie. You're invited to l'Herbarium, a picturesque residence, enchanting and grandiose decor, amidst lakes, mountains, flower gardens. Friendly welcome, relaxing atmosphere, delicious breakfast. Picnics and hiking on site.

From Montréal, Hwy 40 East, Hwy 55 North, Exit 217. Rte 351 North, 12km. Right on Ch. St-François, 4km. Left on Ch. Principal, 1km. Right on Ch. St-Paul, 0.5km.

B&B
L'HERBARIUM

Anne-Marie Groleau
1950, chemin St-Paul
St-Mathieu-du-Parc G0X 1N0
(819) 532-2461

B&B	
single	$40-50
double	$55-65
triple	$75
child	$10

Open year round

Number of rooms	3
shared wc	1
shared bathrooms	1

Activities: 🚶 🚣 ⛷ 🚴 ⛸

13. ST-TITE

☀☀☀ F e 🚫 🐾 🚗 P 🛶 R.03 TA

Mauricie Excellence Prize 1999. In the Western-style town of St-Tite, discover our ancestral (1907) house renowned for its warm welcome, cozy decor and lavish breakfasts. Near Parc de la Mauricie, Village du Bûcheron, Cité de l'Energie, dogsledding, snowscooter. Restaurant dinner package by reservation. **See colour photos.**

From Québec City or Montréal, Hwy 40. At Trois-Rivières, Hwy 55 North, Exit Rte 153 North. In St-Tite, 500 m from the caisse populaire, on the left.

B&B
MAISON EMERY JACOB

Lucie Verret and Réal Trépanier
211, Notre-Dame
St-Tite G0X 3H0
(418) 365-5532
fax (418) 365-3957
www.maisonemeryjacob.qc.ca
emeryjac@globetrotter.net

B&B	
single	$40
double	$50
child	$10

VS AM

Reduced rates: Nov.1 to Mar. 30
Open year round

Number of rooms	4
shared wc	1
shared bathrooms	2

Activities: 🛶 🚲 🛷 🎿 🐎

14. STE-ANNE-DE-LA-PÉRADE

☀☀☀☀ F E ✕ P TA

On the Chemin du Roy, between "smelt" river and the forgotten *"marigotte"*, the timeless old Manoir Dauth offers a world of delightful packages: fishing, snowmobiling, dogsledding, sightseeing, croquet, cycling, mouthwatering cuisine and sweet dreams in a canopy bed.

Between Montréal (2 hours) and Québec City (1 hour) on Chemin du Roy (Rte 138), 100 m from the church. Via Hwy 40, Exit 236, right at 1st stop, left at 2nd stop, then 200 m.

INN
AUBERGE DU
MANOIR DAUTH

Lise Garceau and
Yvan Turgeon
21, boul. de Lanaudière
C.P. 111
Ste-Anne-de-la-Pérade
G0X 2J0
tel/fax (418) 325-3432
www.bbcanada.com/3193.html
manoir.dauth@tr.cgocable.ca

	B&B	PAM
single	$40-60	$53-73
double	$52-72	$78-98
triple	$64-84	$103-123
quad.	$76-96	$128-148
child	$10	$17

Taxes extra VS MC ER IT AM

Reduced rates: 20% 3 nights and more
Open year round

Number of rooms	5
rooms with private bath	1
shared wc	2
shared bathrooms	2

Activities: 🏛 🚲 🛷 🎿 🐎

15. STE-ANNE-DE-LA-PÉRADE

☀☀☀ F e 🐾 ✕ 🚗 P TA

Ancestral house where time has stopped. Stay in a historic monument; documents and furniture (1702). Part of the Heritage Tour. Magnificent French garden. Tommy-cod fishing is one way to enhance your stay. Step back in time in our museum-house.

On the Chemin du Roy, Rte 138, 2 hours from Montréal, 1 hour from Québec City, via Hwy 40, Exit 236, 2km east of the church.

INN
L'ARRÊT DU TEMPS

Serge Gervais
965, boul. de Lanaudière
Chemin du Roy
Ste-Anne-de-la-Pérade
G0X 2J0
(418) 325-3590

	B&B	MAP
single	$40-45	$55-60
double	$50-55	$80-85
triple	$65-70	$110-115
child	$15	on request

Taxes extra VS MC AM ER IT

Open year round

Number of rooms	3
shared wc	1
shared bathrooms	1

Activities: 🏛 🧍 🚶 🚲 🛶

16. SHAWINIGAN-SUD

☀☀☀ | F | E | 🐕 | 🚗 | P | 🛥 | R.5 | TA

Pamper yourselves at two artists' cozy place of refuge. Retire to your suite, born out of a dream. Behold the Cité de l'Énergie, enjoy the National Park. Private living room with fireplace, bathrooms with shower or whirlpool bath, garden with pool, breakfast on terrace, the only thing missing... is you.

From Trois-Rivières, Hwy 55 North, Exit 211, twd Cité de l'Énergie. Follow the signs H for hospital. After the hospital, turn left at the first stop on Rue Lacoursière, right at the 2nd stop on Adrienne-Choquette and right on Albert-Dufresne.

B&B
LES P'TITS POMMIERS

Michelle Fortin and
Jean-Louis Gagnon
2295, Albert-Dufresne
Shawinigan- Sud G9P 4Y6
(819) 537-0158
toll free 1-877-537-0158
fax (819) 537-4839
www.bbcanada.com/3460.html
pommiers@yahoo.com

B&B	
single	$45
double	$55
child	$10

VS

Open year round

Number of rooms	3
rooms in semi-basement	3
shared bathrooms	2

Activities: 🏊 ⚲ 🚶 🚴 🏃

17. SHAWINIGAN-SUD

☀☀☀ | F | e | 🚗 | P | R4 | TA

At the gate of the Cité de l'Énergie, the country in the city. Four rooms overlooking the St-Maurice: calm nights, tantalizing breakfast. Writer Adrienne Choquette once lived here; her words echo through Time. Pleasant old-fashioned decor; always pleasant and warm.

From Montréal or Québec City, Hwy 40. At Trois-Rivières, Hwy 55 N. Exit 211 twd Cité de l'Énergie, Rte 157. After bridges, right at the overpass Boul. du Capitaine. At the end, before the hill, go left on Ch. St-Laurent.

B&B
LE TEMPS DES VILLAGES

Reynald Roberge
155, chemin Saint-Laurent
Shawinigan-Sud G9P 1B6
tel/fax (819) 536-3487

B&B	
single	$50-60
double	$60-70
child	$10

Open year round

Number of rooms	4
shared wc	1
shared bathrooms	1

Activities: 🏛 ⚲ 🚶 🎿 🏃

18. TROIS-RIVIÈRES

F | E | 🚭 | 🍽 | P | TA

Our beautiful Victorian inn is nestled in the centre of town, on the way into historic Trois-Rivières, on a secluded, shady street. Rich oak woodwork, bevelled doors, gilding and lovely moulding, handed down from the old aristocracy. The elegant dining room, with its lustrous chandelier, lacework and old lamps is open to the public. Parking and air conditioning.

Hwy 40 Exit Trois-Rivières downtown. To Notre-Dame. Left on Rue Radisson (on your left). You'll see two big black awnings.

INN
AUBERGE DU BOURG

Monic and Jean-Marc Beaudoin
172, Radisson
Trois-Rivières G9A 2C3
(819) 373-2265
(819) 379-9198

	B&B	MAP
single	$50-70	$65-85
double	$60-80	$90-110

Taxes extra VS MC AM IT

Open year round

Number of rooms	4
rooms with sink	2
rooms with private bath	2
shared wc	2
shared bathrooms	1

Activities: 🛶 ⚲ 🚶 🚴 🛥

19. TROIS-RIVIÈRES

F e P R.3 TA

Family property! Grandpa Beau would be proud, his house welcomes so many people! Spacious, attractively decorated home whose attic rooms bring back wonderful childhood memories. You'll enjoy a generous breakfast complemented with garden-fresh vegetables. Near all tourist attractions and the university.

From Québec City, Hwy 40 West, Exit 199 to the town centre, right on Ste-Marguerite for 2km. From Montréal, Hwy 40, Exit 199. At 2nd light, left on Ste-Marguerite for 2km.

B&B
CHEZ GRAND'PAPA BEAU

Carmen and Yvon Beaudry
3305, rue Ste-Marguerite
Trois-Rivières G8Z 1X1
(819) 693-0385
www3.sympatico.ca/voir/gite/
grandpapa_beau@altavista.net

B&B	
single	$40
double	$50
triple	$60
quad.	$70
child	$10

VS

Open year round

Number of rooms	4
shared bathrooms	2

Activities:

20. TROIS-RIVIÈRES

F E P R.1 TA

Located in the heart of the town centre and just steps from old Trois-Rivières, a lovely centenary home housed in a former convent concealed by huge poplars. Original, clever decor. Furniture bequeathed by the community provides a warm and intimate atmosphere. Buffet breakfast in the refectory. Piano, TV and reading in the lounge. Parking. **See colour photos**

From Montréal, Hwy 40, Downtown Trois-Rivières Exit. Turn right at 1st lights, left at 2nd lights, right on Rue Bonaventure.

B&B
GÎTE DU PETIT COUVENT

Maryse Bergeron and
Martin Gagnon
466, Bonaventure
Trois-Rivières G9A 2B4
(819) 374-8052
toll free 1-800-582-4384
fax (819) 371-2430

B&B	
single	$45
double	$55-60
triple	$70
quad.	$85
child	$5-15

Open year round

Number of rooms	3
rooms with sink	3
shared wc	1
shared bathrooms	1

Activities:

21. TROIS-RIVIÈRES

F E P R.3 TA

Hundred-year-old house in the heart of the old, historic part of the city, facing the majestic St. Lawrence River. Abundance of campanulas on the property. Outdoor hot tub. Children welcome. Sweet treats await you. Gargantuan breakfast and friendly welcome. A galaxy of activities nearby.

From Montréal, Hwy 40, Exit downtown. Take Rue St-Rock, turn left at the end on Notre-Dame. Right on Rue des Casernes and left on des Ursulines.

B&B
GÎTE LA CAMPANULE

Kostas Grusudis and
Bertrand Dubé
634, Des Ursulines
Trois-Rivières G9A 5B4
(819) 373-1133
kg@infoteck.qc.ca

B&B	
single	$45
double	$55
child	$10

VS

Open year round

Number of rooms	3
shared bathrooms	1

Activities:

22. TROIS-RIVIÈRES

F E P R.1 TA

A must on the shores of the St-Laurent. Comfort, safety in an upscale decor. Gardens, pool and air conditioning. Renowned for its welcome and gastronomic breakfast. Good place for family get-togethers or with friends. One French guide commented: "In short, an excellent place for the price".

From Hwy 55, Exit Notre-Dame, to Rte 138 East, drive about 1km. At McDonald's, turn right on Rue Garceau. Right on Rue Notre-Dame, 5th house on the left.

B&B

GÎTE SAINT-LAURENT

Yolande and René Bronsard
4551, Notre-Dame
Trois-Rivières Ouest G9A 4Z4
tel/fax (819) 378-3533
rene.bronsard@sympatico.ca

B&B	
single	$50
double	$65

Taxes extra VS

Open year round

Number of rooms	**4**
rooms with sink	4
shared wc	2
shared bathrooms	1

Activities:

23. TROIS-RIVIÈRES

F E P R.7

Warm, English-style house located in Old Trois-Rivières. Parking, air conditioning, terrace, fireplace. A stone's throw from town centre, harbour park, restaurants, museum. Near Mauricie National Park, Cité de l'Énergie, Forges St-Maurice, saphouse. Children welcome.

Hwy 40, Exit 201, Boul. des Chenaux south, right, 1.6km. Right on Rte 138 West or St-Maurice, drive 0.8km. At the 4th traffic lights, at the church left on Rue St-Francois-Xavier, drive 0.7km.

B&B

MAISON WICKENDEN

Yolande Ferland
467, St-François-Xavier
Trois-Rivières G9A 1R1
tel/fax (819) 375-6219

B&B	
single	$45
double	$55
triple	$70
quad.	$80
child	$10

VS

Reduced rates: Nov. 1 to May 1
Open year round

Number of rooms	**3**
shared wc	1
shared bathrooms	1

Activities:

24. TROIS-RIVIÈRE, POINTE-DU-LAC

F e P R1.6 TA

Savour peace and quiet and the joy of living by the St. Lawrence River, halfway between Quebec City and Montreal. In an inn full of old memories, enjoy lavish breakfasts and gourmet cooking. Baie-Jolie also provides guests with an equipped conference room, free Internet access and laundry facilities.

From Montréal, Hwy 40 East, Exit 187, Rte 138 East, 7km. From Québec City, Hwy 40 West and 55 South, Notre-Dame Exit, Rte 138 West, 5km.

INN

AUBERGE BAIE-JOLIE

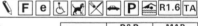

Barbara and Jacques Piccinelli
709 Notre-Dame, rte 138
Pointe-du-Lac G0X 1Z0
(819) 377-2226
(819) 377-3056
fax (819) 377-4221
www.baie-jolie.com
info@baie-jolie.com

	B&B	MAP
single	$40	$55
double	$60-65	$90-95
triple	$75-80	$120-125
quad.	$90-95	$150-155
child	$10	$20

Taxes extra VS MC AM ER IT

Reduced rates: 3 nights and more
Open year round

Number of rooms	**11**
rooms with private bath	11

Activities:

25. TROIS-RIVIÈRES, POINTE-DU-LAC

☀☀☀ | F | E | 🚗 | P | 🏊 | 🐕 | R1.6 | TA

10km from old Trois-Rivières and its harbour park, enchanting site right on the shores of the St. Larence River and Lac St-Pierre. Large garden, in-ground pool, picnic tables, B.B.Q. Calm and restful, close to all the sites you'll want to discover. Generous breakfast. Discount: 3 days or more. English, German, Italian, Spanish spoken. Flight packages available.

From Montréal, 130km, Hwy 40 E., Exit 187. Rte 138 E., 7km. From Mirabel, Hwy 15 S., 640 E., 40 E. From Québec City, 130km Hwy 40 W. and 55 S., Exit Notre-Dame, Rte 138 W., 5km.

B&B
GÎTE BAIE-JOLIE

Barbara and Jacques Piccinelli
711, Notre Dame route 138
Pointe-du-Lac G0X 1Z0
tel/fax (819) 377-3056
www.baie-jolie.com
jacques.piccinelli@
baie-jolie.com

B&B	
single	$35-40
double	$55-60
triple	$75-80
quad.	$95
child	$10

VS

Reduced rates: Oct.15 to May 31
Open: Dec. 1 to Oct. 31

Number of rooms	3
rooms with private bath	3

Activities: 🚣 🛷 🧍 🏃 🐎

26. TROIS-RIVIÈRES, POINTE-DU-LAC

☀☀☀ | F | e | 🚫 | 🏊 | 🚗 | P | R2

Excellence Prize Mauricie 1997-98. Are you seeking rest and tranquillity? At our lovely Canadian-style house we guarantee a relaxing time in a cosy atmosphere! Treat yourself to a generous, varied, fine quality breakfast. Go for a refreshing swim any time of the year in the indoor pool and enjoy a therapeutic bath. Air conditioning.

Montréal, Hwy 40 E., Exit 187, then Rte 138 E., 7km. Turn left on Rue des Saules to the end. From Québec City, Hwy 40 W., then Hwy 55 S., Notre-Dame Exit, Rte 138 W. for 5km, turn right on Rue des Saules to the end.

B&B
SOLEIL LEVANT

Léonie Lavoie and
Yves Pilon
300, av. des Saules
Pointe-du-Lac G0X 1Z0
tel/fax (819) 377-1571
toll free 1-877-8-SOLEIL
gitesoleillevant@qc.aira.com

B&B	
single	$40-45
double	$60-65
triple	$85
child	$15

Reduced rates: Nov. 1 to Mar. 31
Open year round

Number of rooms	3
shared bathrooms	2

Activities: 🏛 ☕ 🚣 🧍 🛷

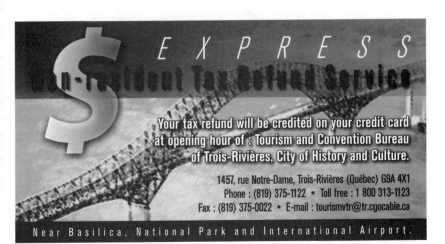

27. HÉROUXVILLE

F E P 🐕 🚗 R5 M1 TA

Heart of the Mauricie. From 1883, the house has kept its old-fashioned cachet, rooms have period decor. Located in the heart of the village, our place is ideal for relaxation and story-telling with family or friends. Close to Mauricie National Park, wild fishing, horseback riding, cycling, all winter sports. Backwoods cabin also available in the Upper Mauricie. **B&B p 193.**

Hwy 20 or 40, and Hwy 55 N. via Trois-Rivières. Exit Rte 153 N. At Hérouxville, at the flashing light, street beside the church.

COUNTRY HOME
MAISON TRUDEL

Nicole Jubinville and
Yves Trudel
543, Goulet
Hérouxville GOX 1J0
(418) 365-7624
fax (418) 365-7041
www.bbcanada.com/408.html
maison-trudel-quebec
@concepta.com

No. houses	1
No. rooms	6
No. people	14
WEEK-SUMMER	$600
WEEK-WINTER	$600
W/E-SUMMER	$300
W/E-WINTER	$300
DAY-SUMMER	$150
DAY-WINTER	$150

VS

Open year round

Activities: 🦪 ⛵ 🚲 🛶 🐎

28. LOUISEVILLE

F e 🚗 R1 M1.5 TA

Heritage home located on a farm surrounded by thousands of flowers. Take advantage of the gardens and tend your own! Ideal place to get into gardening or learn more. Gardening library. All-season guided excursions: hiking, canoeing, fishing, biking, snowshoeing, dogsledding... Ste-Ursule waterfalls, Lac St-Pierre. **Farm Stay p 40, B&B p 194, Country-style Dining p 23 and Farm Excursion p 32. Ad end of guide.**

From Montréal or from Québec City, Hwy 40, Exit 166. Rte 138 E., 2.4km to Rte 348 W. Left twd Ste-Ursule 1.5km. 1st road on the

COUNTRY HOME
LA MAISON DU JARDINIER

Michel Gilbert
480, chemin du Golf
Louiseville J5V 2L4
tel/fax (819) 228-8224
m.gilbert@infoteck.qc.ca

No. houses	1
No. rooms	3
No. people	4
WEEK-SUMMER	$400
WEEK-WINTER	$400
DAY-WINTER	$100

Taxes extra

Open year round

Activities: 🏛 🔧 🎿 🚲 🤸

🏚 FARM ACTIVITIES

Farm Stays:

7 ACCUEIL LES SEMAILLES, Hérouxville 40

11 FERME DE LA SEIGNEURIE, Louiseville 40

Country-style Dining *:

11 LA TABLE DE LA SEIGNEURIE, Louiseville 23

Farm Excursions:

11 LES JARDINS DE LA SEIGNEURIE, Louiseville 32

* Registered trademark.

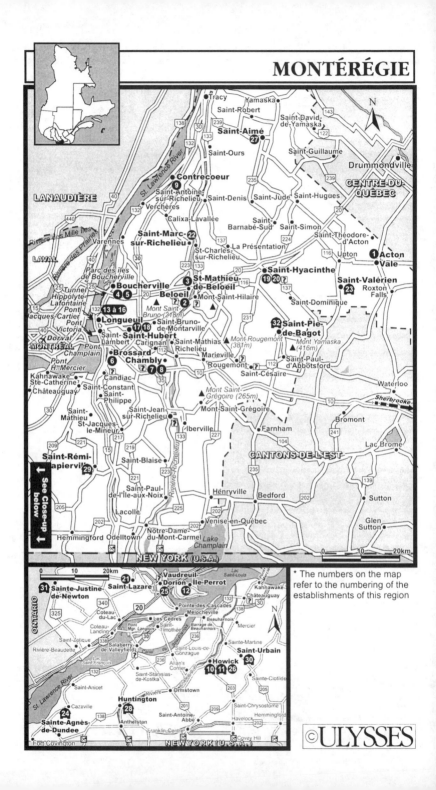

MONTÉRÉGIE

©ULYSSES

1. ACTON VALE

Between Montréal and Québec City, in cycling country, 2km from "La Campagnarde" path, 8km from La Dame de Cœur theatre, across from a golf course, what more could you ask for! Breakfast on the veranda. Take advantage of golf and cycling packages. It's about the simple pleasure in welcoming people from far and wide.

Hwy 20, Exit 147, right on Rte 116 for 17km. Or, Hwy 55, Rtes 139 and 116. Across from the golf course.

B&B
AUBERGE AUX P'TITS OIGNONS

Denise Morin and
Jacques McCaughan
1011, Route 116 Ouest
Acton Vale J0H 1A0
(450) 549-5116
fax (450) 549-6116
www.bbcanada.com/
1086.html
auberge@ntic.qc.ca

B&B	
single	$35-45
double	$50-60
triple	$65-75
quad.	$80
child	$10

VS MC

Open year round

Number of rooms	4
rooms with private bath	1
rooms in basement	3
shared wc	1
shared bathrooms	2

Activities:

2. BELOEIL

The Richelieu valley will win you over... 20 minutes from Montréal, stop and enjoy the peace and cozy charm of our ancestral home (1846) on the banks of the Rivière Richelieu, in the heart of Vieux Beloeil. Admire the beauty of Mont St-Hilaire. Copious breakfast; lace, china and silver.

Hwy 20, Exit 112, Rte 223 South, for 2.3km. House next to presbytery and church. From Rte 116, Rte 223 North, 0.8km.

B&B
BEAUX BRUNELLES

Fernande Vézina and
Raymond Chrétien
1030, rue Richelieu
Beloeil J3G 4R2
(450) 467-4700
fax (450) 467-4668
www.bbcanada.
com/beauxbrunelles
beauxbrunelles@convitech.ca

B&B	
single	$45-50
double	$60-65
triple	$75-80
quad.	$80-90
child	$0-10

Open year round

Number of rooms	5
shared bathrooms	2

Activities:

3. BELOEIL, ST-MATHIEU

20 min from Montreal. Snowshoe hiking on Mt-St-Hilaire, ski Mont St-Bruno; a stone's throw from summer theatres. In the country, 6km from Vieux Beloeil. With spacious rooms, our air conditoned ancestral house (1905) beneath the trees awaits you. Different breakfasts served in the warmth of our kitchen graced with a wood-burning stove.

From Montréal or Québec City, Hwy 20, Exit 109. On Rue St-Jean-Baptiste go north twd St-Mathieu-de-Beloeil, drive for 1km. Right on first street Ruisseau Sud for 3.8km.

B&B
LA MAISON DU GAZEBO

Monique and
Georges Blanchard
2054, Ruisseau Sud
St-Mathieu-de-Beloeil J3G 2C9
(450) 464-2430
fax (450) 464-4541
www.bbcanada.com/
maisondugazebo
gazebo@tourisme.cc

B&B	
single	$40-65
double	$55-65
triple	$70-80
child	$10

Reduced rates: 7th night free
Open year round

Number of rooms	3
shared wc	1
shared bathrooms	1

Activities:

4. BOUCHERVILLE

☀☀☀ F E 🚭 🐕 🚗 P 🏊 R1 TA

Located near the old village on the St. Lawrence, Highways 132, 20 and 30, restaurants and shops, this air-conditioned B&B offers spacious rooms, a huge kitchen, view on equipped terrace and in-ground pool. Free for children 10 and under. Hearty breakfast, Bilingual.

From Montréal, L.-H. Lafontaine tunnel, Hwy 20, Exit 92, left on Boul. Montagne (or right from Québec City). Drive 3km, cross Boul. Montarville, drive 1km, left on Étienne-Brûlé, right on Duluth.

B&B
CHEZ FLEUR DO

Doris Hupé
919, rue Duluth
Boucherville J4B 6Y5
(450) 449-5659

B&B	
single	$50
double	$65
triple	$80
child	$0-10

Open year round

Number of rooms	2
shared wc	1
shared bathrooms	2

Activities: 🛶 👤 🚶 🚴 ⛷

---

5. BOUCHERVILLE

☀☀☀ F E 🚭 P R.5 TA

Just 15 min from the sights of Montréal. Friendly atmosphere, we like to chat with people. Bicycles and tandems available for free; bike paths; bus to the Métro. Generous breakfasts, air conditioning and a small souvenir for everyone.

From Montréal by Louis-H. Lafontaine tunnel or from Québec City, Hwy 20, Exit 90 twd Varennes. Rte 132 East Exit 18, Montarville. Turn left to Boul. Fort St-Louis, turn left and drive 1.2km.

B&B
LE RELAIS DES ÎLES PERCÉES

Colette and Raymond LeBlanc
85, des Îles Percées
Boucherville J4B 2P1
tel/fax (450) 655-3342
www.total.net/
~lerelais/bb_en_ligne.htm
lerelais@total.net

B&B	
single	$40
double	$55
triple	$70
child	$10

VS

Open year round

Number of rooms	3
rooms in basement	2
shared bathrooms	2

Activities: 🏛 🍷 👤 🚴 🎿

---

6. BROSSARD

☀☀☀ F E 🏄 🐕 P R.5

Montérégie Excellence Prize 1999. Business or pleasure, for a single night or more, partake of our classic breakfast to the sound of music. Terrace and garden brightened by birdsong, flowery pool. Spacious room (1 to 5 people). Period furniture; 15 min from downtown, casino, Old Montreal. Corporate rates (Nov. to Apr.). Speciality: Alexandre Legrand's crepes.

From Montréal, Mirabel, Dorval, Hwy 15 S., Champlain bridge, Exit 8 West Taschereau-La Prairie, left on Rome, right on Niagara. From Québec City, Hwy 20, Exit 90 La Prairie-USA, Exit 53, Boul. Rome to Niagara, go right.

B&B
AU JARDIN D'ALEXANDRE

Diane and Jean-Marie Caissie
8135, Niagara
Brossard J4Y 2G2
(450) 445-2200
fax (450) 445-1244
www.bbcanada.com/
2462.html
b.bjardinsalex@videotron.ca

B&B	
single	$37
double	$50-55
triple	$65
quad.	$80
child	$10

Reduced rates: Nov. 1 to Apr. 30, 4 nights for the price of 3
Open year round

Number of rooms	1
shared bathrooms	1

Activities: 🛶 👤 🚶 🚴 ⛷

7. CHAMBLY

☼☼☼☼☼ 〔F〕〔e〕〔P〕〔🚗〕〔R.2〕〔TA〕

Provincial Excellence Prize 1999.
20 min from Montréal, Victorian house from 1914 with magnificent woodwork, period mouldings, fireplace and French doors. Breakfast on the veranda with a view of the mountains rising out of the water. Boat dock. Close to all the city's services and activities. Dinner by reservation. Air conditionned. **See colour photos.**

From Montréal, Hwy 10, Exit 22, Boul Fréchette to the end. Follow directions. Beside St-Joseph church.

B&B
AUBERGE L'AIR DU TEMPS

Lucie Chrétien and
Daniel Desgagné
124, Martel, Chambly J3L 1V3
(450) 658-1642
toll free 1-888-658-1642
fax (450) 658-2830
www.bbcanada.
com/3034.html

B&B	
single	$55
double	$69-79
triple	$99
quad.	$119

Taxes extra VS AM

Open year round: except Nov.

Number of rooms	5
rooms with private bath	5

Activities: 🛶 ⛴ 🎣 🚴 🐎

8. CHAMBLY

☼☼☼☼☼ 〔F〕〔E〕〔🏊〕〔P〕〔🚗〕〔R.2〕〔TA〕

This old Fort Chambly officer's residence, transformed into a luxurious manor, offers a panoramic view, a superb ambiance and exceptional comfort. Make it a base to visit Montréal (20 min) and the Valley of Forts, and let yourself be serenaded by the songs of the rapids or the flames of the 3 fireplaces. Spacious rooms with TV and modem access. Gastronomic breakfast. Free access to our outdoor tennis club. Rated 3 diamonds by the AAA (CAA). **See colour photos.**

Hwy 10 (Exit 22), Rte 112 or Rte 223, then follow the signs for Fort Chambly. The Maison Ducharme is next to the guardhouse.

B&B
LA MAISON DUCHARME

Danielle Deland and
Edouard Bonaldo
10, de Richelieu
Chambly J3L 2B9
(450) 447-1220
toll free 1-888-387-1220
fax (450) 447-1018
www.mlink.net/~ducharme
maison.ducharme@mlink.net

B&B	
single	$90-105
double	$105-120
triple	$125-140
child	$20

Taxes extra VS MC

Reduced rates: Oct. 15 to May 12
Open year round

Number of rooms	4
rooms with private bath	4

Activities: 🛶 🎣 🚴 🏊 ⛷

9. CONTRECOEUR

☼☼☼☼ 〔F〕〔e〕〔🚫〕〔🚗〕〔P〕〔🏠〕〔R.1〕

Are you looking for an escape from the hectic pace of life today? Do you want to have a great time and be pampered? Then succumb to the allure of our charming B&B, which offers a friendly and cosy ambiance, and a kitchen full of exciting flavours. Imagine listening to music by candlelight, lounging in a hammock, relaxing in a pool, reading in a garden, going on a pedalboat trip to some islands, or cycling on a country road. Let all your worries trickle off you like water off a duck's back.

From Montréal, Hwy 20 and 30 East, Exit 158, Rte 132 East, 1.6km.

B&B
LES MALARDS

Hélène Delisle
4741, Marie-Victorin
Contrecoeur J0L 1C0
(450) 587-5581

B&B	
single	$50
double	$65

Taxes extra

Reduced rates: 20% 3 nights and more
Open year round

Number of rooms	3
rooms with sink	2
shared bathrooms	2

Activities: 🛶 ⛴ 🎣 🚴 ⛷

10. HOWICK

Welcome to our century-old house situated in the country-side. Feed the animals, swim, cycle, canoe, fish and finally relax around an evening campfire by the river. Visit our antique shop where we also recycle wood, doors and windows into reproductions on antique furniture. **Farm stay p 40 and Country Home p 212.**

30km from Montréal. From Mercier bridge, Rte 138 West, then Rte 203 to Riverfield (about 9km). At the church, turn right on Rang des Écossais and cross the bridge; we are on the left.

B&B
AUBERGE LA CHAUMIÈRE

Patricia Rae and
Suzanne Chéné
1071, rang Des Écossais
Howick, Riverfield J0S 1G0
(450) 825-0702
info@lachaumiere.qc.ca

	B&B	MAP
single	$35	$53
double	$50	$86
child	$10	$25

VS

Reduced rates: Nov. 1 to Apr. 30
Open year round

Number of rooms	4
shared bathrooms	2

Activities:

11. HOWICK

Welcome to our 150-acre 5th-generation dairy farm. Enjoy feeding small animals, campfire, take a hay ride, cycle or relax by our inground pool. Non-smokers please. A delicious home-baked breakfast is served! We have been receiving guests for more than 12 years. Smoke free B&B. **Farm Stay p 41.**

From Montréal, Hwy 20 West, Mercier bridge, Rte 138 West. Rte 203 to Howick (about 40km). Cross the bridge, turn left on Rue Lambton. Take English River Road and drive 2km.

B&B
HAZELBRAE FARM

Gloria and John Peddie
1650, English River Road
Howick J0S 1G0
(450) 825-2390

B&B	
single	$30
double	$50
child	$5-9

Open year round

Number of rooms	3
rooms with private bath	1
shared wc	1
shared bathrooms	2

Activities:

12. ÎLE PERROT

Situated on Lac Deux-Montagnes in the middle of the wilderness, our B&B offers a beautiful view facing the north: Oka, the L'Îsle aux Tourtes bridge and some small colourful islands. It also offers peace and tranquillity with a large landscaped property and some magnificent places to relax by the water's edge.

Hwy 20 West, right at the first light when you arrive on Île Perrot, after the train track, drive 1.6km. Turn right on Roy. Last house by the water.

B&B
GÎTE DE L'ÎLE

Nicole Frappier
10, rue Roy
Île Perrot J7V 8W3
tel/fax (514) 425-0965
(514) 592-2248

B&B	
single	$60
double	$75

Open year round

Number of rooms	2
shared bathrooms	2

Activities:

13. LONGUEUIL

☀☀☀ | F | e | 🚫 | 🚗 | P | R1 | TA

On the South Shore, 10 minutes from downtown Montreal, on a quiet street near the metro in the heart of Vieux Longueuil, a welcoming house invites you to come relax in a warm ambiance. Come as you are and enjoy its charming rooms and good breakfast.

From Montréal, Jacques-Cartier bridge, keep left, Rte 132. From Hwy 20, Exit 8, right on Rue St-Charles, right on Quinn at the Esso, 100 m. Ste-Élizabeth, on the left.

B&B
GÎTE LA BRUNANTE

Louise Bélisle
480, Ste-Elisabeth
Longueuil J4H 1K4
(450) 442-7691

B&B	
single	$40-50
double	$50-65
triple	$75
child	$10

Open year round

Number of rooms	2
rooms with sink	1
shared bathrooms	2

Activities: 🚣 👤 🚶 🚲 ⛷

14. LONGUEUIL

☀☀☀ | F | e | 🐕 | P | R1 | TA

La Maison de Madame Dufour is a friendly place in a peaceful area near downtown Montréal. Come stay in a cozy setting and soak up the tranquil atmosphere. Relax in our 2 suites or our two living rooms. Savour a delicious breakfast of crepes or eggs served on a bed of onions. An oasis of peace that will provide you with wonderful memories. See you soon! Your host, *Gaby*.

From Montréal or Québec City, Route 132, Exit Roland-Therrien. Drive about 4km to Rue Desormeaux; turn left and continue to Berthelet.

B&B
LA MAISON DE
MADAME DUFOUR

Gaby Dufour
1260, Berthelet
Longueuil J4M 1G3
(450) 448-6531

B&B	
single	$65-75
double	$65-85
triple	$90-110
quad.	$115-135
child	$15

MC

Reduced rates: -15% from Nov.1 to May 1
Open year round

Number of rooms	5
rooms in basement	2
shared bathrooms	3

Activities: 🏛 🍷 🚣 🚶 🚲

15. LONGUEUIL

☀☀☀ | F | e | ♿ | 🚗 | 🐕 | R.2 | TA

Come take advantage of a poetic ambience in a warm century-old house in the heart of Vieux Longueuil. Succulent breakfasts served on the terrace in the summer. Close to downtown Montréal by Métro or the ferry. Reductions for stays of 3 nights and more.

From Montréal, Jacques-Cartier Bridge, keep left, Exit Rte 132 or Hwy 20 immediately right, Exit Rue St-Charles. From Rte 132, Exit 8. Rue St-Charles and right on Rue St-Jean. Located behind Longueuil Town Hall.

B&B
LE REFUGE DU POÈTE

Louise Vézina
320, rue Longueuil
Longueuil J4H 1H4
(450) 442-3688

B&B	
single	$45-50
double	$50-60
triple	$60-70
child	$10

Reduced rates: -5$ night, 3 nights and more
Open year round

Number of rooms	2
rooms with sink	1
rooms with private bath	1
shared bathrooms	2

Activities: 🏛 🚣 👤 🚲 ⛷

16. LONGUEUIL
✎ F E 🚗 R.01 TA

Conveniently located near restaurants in the heart of Vieux-Longueuil (10min from Montréal). You will be charmed by our flower garden as you enjoy your breakfast listening to the sound of a waterfall. Our B&B offers two air-conditioned rooms with private bathrooms. We respect your privacy. See you soon!

From Montréal, Jacques-Cartier Bridge, keep left, Rte 132 exit or Hwy 20 and turn right immediately, St-Charles exit. Behind city hall, Rue Longueuil.

B&B
L'OASIS DU VIEUX-LONGUEUIL

Luc Desbiens
316, de Longueuil
Longueuil J4H 1H4
(450) 670-9839
fax (514) 598-2894

B&B	
single	$45-55
double	$50-60

Reduced rates: week days
Open year round

Number of rooms	2
rooms with private bath	2

Activities: 🏛 🚣 ⚲ 🚲 🏃

17. ST-HUBERT
☀☀☀ F e P 🚗 R.5 TA

Excellence Prize Montérégie 1997-98. 7km south of Montréal, easy access to major highways. Great place to get away. All the activities of Montréal on your doorstep. Biodôme, festivals, Gilles Villeneuve racetrack, etc. Wake up to our regional specialties and breads. Looking forward to your visit.

From Montréal, Hwy 20 East to Hwy 30 West or Hwy 10 East to Hwy 30 Exit 115. Rte 112 West (Boul. Cousineau) for 3.7km, left on Rue Prince Charles, right on Rue Primot, left on Rue Latour.

B&B
AUX DEUX LUCARNES

Ginette and
Jean-Marie Laplante
3310, Latour
St-Hubert J3Y 4V9
(450) 656-1224
fax (450) 656-0851
www.bbcanada.com/
2345.html
auxdeuxlucarnes@
sympatico.ca

B&B	
single	$40
double	$55-60

Reduced rates: Oct. 15 to Apr.15 for long stays
Open year round

Number of rooms	4
rooms with sink	3
rooms with private bath	1
shared bathrooms	2

Activities: 🦪 ⚲ 🏃 🚲 🏃

18. ST-HUBERT
☀☀☀ F e 🚫 P R.75

A base for all your activities in Montérégie: cycling, golfing, Parc Safari, cruise, summer theatre, festival, museum, etc. For a short or long stay, it will be our pleasure to welcome you to the quietness of the suburbs. Right near Montréal, a few kilometres from the highways. Simple & quiet ambiance.

From Montréal via the Champlain bridge, Boul. Milan to Brossard, change to Gaétan Boucher in St-Hubert, left on Normand, right on Harding. In Québec City, via Hwy 10, 20, 30.

B&B
CHEZ GRAND-MAMAN
JACQUELINE

Jacqueline Castonguay
4545, Harding
Saint-Hubert J3Y 2K5
(450) 676-8667

B&B	
single	$35
double	$45
triple	$55
quad.	$65
child	$0-5

Open year round

Number of rooms	1
rooms with private bath	1
rooms in basement	1
shared bathrooms	1

Activities: 🏛 🚣 🚲 🎿 🏃

19. ST-HYACINTHE

☀☀☀☀☀ F E 🚭 🏊 P 🚗 🐕 R.2 TA

Montérégie Excellence Prize 1996-97. An English garden hidden in the heart of the town. 1km from the convention centre and agriculture campus. In summertime the spa, the plant and water gardens offer complete relaxation. Antiques, paintings, paintings and books will warm you up in winter. Scrumptious home-made breakfasts on the menu. Come and share our house! Montérégie Excellence Prize 1996-97.

From Montréal or Québec City, Hwy 20, Exit 130. Boul Laframboise to the arch. Rue Bourdages turn right, Rue Bourassa turn right, Rue Raymond, turn left.

B&B
LE JARDIN CACHÉ

Carmen and Bernard Avard
2465, avenue Raymond
St-Hyacinthe J2S 5W4
(450) 773-2231
fax (450) 773-9099
www.bbcanada.
com/lejardincache
jardincache@sympatico.ca

B&B	
single	$40-50
double	$55-65

Taxes extra VS MC

Reduced rates: corporate rates and Oct. 1 to May 31
Open year round

Number of rooms	3
shared bathrooms	2

Activities: 🦪 🧍 🚶 🚴 🐎

20. ST-HYACINTHE

☀☀☀☀ F E 🚭 P 🚗 R.8 TA

Let yourselves be pampered in our warm and peaceful nest, located in a quiet neighbourhood. Romantic decor. Delicious breakfast in the solarium. Rest area filled with birdsong near the water garden and amidst flowers. Little considerations guaranteed. Golf, horseback riding, canoeing and pedal boating only a 5-minute drive away.

Hwy 20, Exit 123, twd St-Hyacinthe, drive 7km. Turn right at the 1st lights, Boul. Laurier. Left at the 2nd lights, Dieppe. 2nd street turn right.

B&B
LE NID FLEURI

Suzanne and Gilles Cournoyer
5985, Garnier
St-Hyacinthe J2S 2E8
(450) 773-0750
www3.sympatico.ca/nid.fleuri
nid.fleuri@sympatico.ca

B&B	
single	$40-50
double	$50-60

VS

Reduced rates: Sep. 15 to Dec. 15 and Apr. 1to May 31
Open: Apr. 1 to Dec 15

Number of rooms	3
shared wc	1
shared bathrooms	1

Activities: 🦪 🧍 🚶 🚴 🐎

21. ST-LAZARE-DE-VAUDREUIL

☀☀☀☀ F E 🚭 P 🚗 R1 🍴 TA

Located 20min from Dorval airport, at the gateway to Montreal, on the road to Ottawa and Niagara Falls. Enjoy a relaxing stay in a country setting, where Mother Nature's rivers, birds, flowery gardens and small woodlands, as well as quality, comfort and gastronomy, await. The only thing missing is you! Many packages. New: air conditioning.

Hwy 20 and/or Hwy 40, St-Lazare-bound Exit 22 to Chemin Ste-Angélique.

B&B
HALTE DE RESSOURCEMENT

Lise Bisson
2565, ch Ste-Angélique
St-Lazare-de-Vaudreuil
J7T 2K6
(514) 990-7825
fax (450) 455-1786
http://ressourcement.
citeglobe.com
ressourcement@citeglobe.com

	B&B	MAP
single	$50-70	$70-90
double	$65-85	$85-105
triple	$85-105	$105-125
quad.	$105-125	$125-145
child	$10-15	$20-25

MC AM

Reduced rates: 10% Oct. 30 to May 1, except Dec. 15 to Jan. 15
Open year round

Number of rooms	4
rooms with private bath	1
shared bathrooms	3
rooms with sink	2

Activities: 🦪 🚤 🧍 🚴 🤸

22. ST-MARC-SUR-RICHELIEU ☀☀☀☀ F E P R.25 TA

Less than 30 min from Montréal, the enchantment begins by following the Richelieu River and the small country roads, continues in the theatres, restaurants and art galleries, and ends in the warm ambiance of our house. We offer guests three spacious rooms with private bathrooms and a most delicious breakfast. You'll be back...

Take Exit 112 off Hwy 20 and follow the 223 North.

B&B
LE VIREVENT

Johanne Jeannotte
511, rue Richelieu
Saint-Marc-sur-Richelieu
JOL 2E0
(450) 584-3618
www.generation.net/
~neige/virevent/virevent.htm
neige@generation.net

B&B	
single	$40
double	$55
triple	$70
quad.	$85

Open year round

Number of rooms	3
rooms with private bath	3

Activities: 🏛 🦪 🚲 🐎 🛷

23. ST-VALÉRIEN ✎ F E ✗ P ≋

Your host, a veterinarian, will greet you with a warm welcome and will share his passion for animals, plants and nature with you. Located on the border of Montérégie and the Eastern Townships, La Rabouillère is a unique farm. You can dine at the farm (reservations required). Pool, jacuzzi, play area. Near summer theatre, bike path, zoo and downhill skiing. **Country-style Dining p 25, Farm Excursion p 33, Farm Stay p 41.**

From Montréal, Hwy 20, Exit E.141 for St-Valérien. Once in town, drive down Chemin Milton and turn right at 1st street, 2nd flashing light.

B&B
LA RABOUILLÈRE

Pierre Pilon
1073 rang Egypte
St-Valérien J0H 2B0
(450) 793-2329
(450) 793-4998
fax (450) 793-2529

B&B	
single	$50-60
double	$60-75
triple	$90
child	$15

Taxes extra VS

Open year round

Number of rooms	2
shared bathrooms	2

Activities: 🦪 🛶 🚶 🚲 🏃

24. STE-AGNÈS-DE-DUNDEE ☀☀ F e 🚗 🐕 ✗ P R10 TA

Peaceful country setting, flowering gardens, roomy house, columns and balconies reminiscent of Louisiana. 15km: Dundee border to New York, 5km: Lac St-François wildlife reserve and Droulers archeological site (prehistoric Iroquois village), borrow a bike, golf, lake, waterskiing, snowmobiling. Lunch and dinner specials by reservation. Looking forward to your visit! **Farm Stay p 41.**

Rte 132 from Valleyfield to Cazaville, left on Montée Cazaville to Ch. Ridge, turn right, 8th house on the left.

B&B
LE GÎTE CHEZ MIMI

Émilienne Marlier
5891, chemin Ridge
Ste-Agnès J0S 1L0
(450) 264-4115
toll free 1-877-264-4115

B&B	
single	$45
double	$55
triple	$65
quad.	$80
child	$10

Taxes extra VS MC

Open year round

Number of rooms	3
rooms with sink	2
shared bathrooms	1

Activities: 🛶 🚶 🚲 🐎 🛷

25. VAUDREUIL-DORION

☀☀☀ | F | e | 🐕 | 🏊 | P | R1 | TA

Our B&B offers a superb view of Lac des Deux-Montagnes and its sailboats. Nearby: shopping centre, restaurant and museum. Come lounge around our pool and patio or rest in the relaxation room of our veranda. A generous breakfast served with home-made goods will complete your stay. We look forward to welcoming you.

From Montréal, Hwy 40 West, Exit 35, at the traffic lights right on Rue St-Charles, 1km. At the convenience store turn right on Chemin de L'Anse, 0.4km. 3rd house on left.

B&B
GÎTE DE L'ANSE

Denise and Gilles Angell
154, chemin de l'Anse
Vaudreuil-Dorion J7V 8P3
(450) 424-0693

B&B	
single	$45
double	$55-65
child	$5-10

Open: May 1 to Oct. 31

Number of rooms	2
shared bathrooms	2

Activities: 🏛 🍴 🛶 🎿 🚴

To Ensure Your Satisfaction

Bed & Breakfast, Country Inn,
Country and City Homes, Farm Stay,
Country-Style Dining, Farm Excursion :

680 establishments fall into these
6 categories, and all are accredited and regularly
inspected according to a code of ethics and standards
of quality for hospitality, layout and decor, safety,
cleanliness, comfort and meals served.

The Fédération des Agricotours du Québec
25 years of hospitality
1975-2000

ACCRÉDITÉ PAR
AGRICOTOURS
QUALITÉ ✦ CONFORT

26. HOWICK

`F` `E` `🚗` `P` `🏊` `R.5` `M6` `TA`

Small chalet suitable for a pleasant family farm stay. Antique reproduction shop onsite, camfire by the river, canoeing, swimming, biking. **Farm Stay p 40 and B&B p 206.**

30km from Montréal. From Mercier bridge, Rte 138 West, then Rte 203 to Riverfield, about 9km. At the church, turn right on Rang des Écossais and cross the bridge; we are on the left.

COUNTRY HOME
AUBERGE LA CHAUMIÈRE

Patricia Rae and
Suzanne Chéné
1071, rang des Écossais
Howick, Riverfield J0S 1G0
(450) 825-0702
chaumiere@mailexcite.com

No. houses	1
No. rooms	4
No. people	6
WEEK-SUMMER	$450
W/E-SUMMER	$200
DAY-SUMMER	$100

VS

Open: June 1 to Sep. 30

Activities: 🎿 🚲 🐎 🏃 🐕

---

27. ST-AIMÉ

`F` `E` `♿` `P` `🏊` `R1` `M2` `TA`

One hour from Montréal. House in farming country. Comfort, fire in the hearth. By the Yamaska river. Canoe. 20 minutes from Odanak Indian reservation, Sorel Islands cruise, Gibelotte and Western festivals. Admire Canada geese and snow geese. Golfing, skidooing, Cyclo-Québec path at our door. **Ad end of the guide.**

From Montréal, Hwy 20 twd St-Hyacinthe, Exit 130 North, right at 3rd light onto the 235 North. Massueville left on Royale, 2km. From Sorel, 132 East, before Yamaska bridge right on Rang Bord de l'Eau, 8km.

COUNTRY HOME
MAISON BOIS-MENU

Nicole Larocque and
Gaétan Boismenu
387, rang Bord de l'Eau
St-Aimé, Massueville J0G 1K0
(450) 788-2466
www.chez.com/boismenu
boismenu@chez.com

No. houses	1
No. rooms	4
No. people	8
WEEK-SUMMER	$350
WEEK-WINTER	$350
W/E-SUMMER	$160
W/E-WINTER	$160
DAY-SUMMER	$100
DAY-WINTER	$100

Open year round

Activities: 🏛 🍂 🚤  🎿

FARM ACTIVITIES

*Registered trademark.

MONTRÉAL REGION

ISLAND OF MONTRÉAL

MONTRÉAL

© ULYSSES

* The numbers on the map refer to the numbering of the establishments of this region

1. ÎLE BIZARD  F E P R4

Situated on a peaceful, rustic island, Gîte Île Bizard is a modern and
comfortable B&B with two spacious
bedrooms. Vibrating bed in one
room, and whirlpool in the other.
Breakfasts on the terrace. Come
for a visit! It won't be your last!

From Montréal, Hwy 20 or Hwy 40
West, Exit Boul. St-Jean North. Left
on Boul. Pierrefonds, right on Jac-
ques Bizard (bridge). Left at 1st light
on Rue Cherrier, right on Rue de
L'Église, to the end of the street, at
"Le Bizard" stop. From Mirabel, Hwy
15 South and 40 West...

B&B
GÎTE ÎLE BIZARD

Osithe Paulin
1993 Bord du Lac
Île Bizard H9E 1P9
(514) 620-0766
fax (514) 620-2384
www.bbcanada.com/3069.html
osithepaulin@hotmail.com

B&B	
single	$50
double	$60
triple	$75
quad.	$90
child	$6-12

Reduced rates: Sep.1 to May 31
Open year round

Number of rooms	2
rooms with private bath	1
rooms in semi basement	1
shared bathrooms	1

Activities: 🏛 ⛴ 🧍 🚶 🚲

2. LACHINE  F e P R2 TA

Tourists or businesspeople, we
offer you tranquillity only 20 minutes from Montréal and 10 minutes
from the Dorval Airport. The cycling
path on our doorstep leads to Old
Montréal, running past many historic and tourist attractions. "Surprise" breakfast for stamina, pool
for fitness.

From Montréal, 20 W., Exit 58, left
on 55ᵉ Ave. Straight to Victoria.
Turn left then take 1st right, 53ᵉ Ave
to the river. Left to 50ᵉ Ave and left
at the 1st dead end.

B&B
LES LORRAINS

Viviane and Jean-Paul Mineur
21, 50ᵉ Avenue
Lachine H8T 2T4
(514) 634-0884
www.aei.ca/~lorrains
lorrains@aei.ca

B&B	
single	$40-50
double	$60
child	$10

Reduced rates: 10% from the 4th
night
Open year round

Number of rooms	2
shared bathroom	1

Activities: 🏛 ⛴ 🚶 🚲 ⛷

3. MONTRÉAL F e P R.1

Historic Victorian house with a private garden facing a cosy park. 3
min walk from Métro, 5 min drive
from downtown and Old Montréal.
Outdoor market and many antique
dealers in the area. Free private
parking and easy access from highway. Bicycles available. Charming
and friendly.

Atwater exit on Ville-Marie express-
way (720). Take St-Antoine (one
way) until you meet Rue Agnès, left.
From Champlain bridge, Exit Atwa-
ter. Straight on Atwater after the
tunnel, to St-Antoine...

B&B
À BONHEUR D'OCCASION

Francine Maurice
846, rue Agnès
Montréal H4C 2P8
tel/fax (514) 935-5898
www.bbcanada.com/526.html

B&B	
single	$50-55-75
double	$70-75-95
triple	$90
child	$10

Taxes extra

Reduced rates: Nov. 1 to
Dec. 15, Jan. 15 to Apr. 15
Open year round

Number of rooms	5
rooms with private bath	2
shared bathroom	1

Activities: 🏛 ⛴ 🚶 🚲

4. MONTRÉAL

✺✺✺ F E 🚫 P R.1 TA

Right downtown, a large sunny house with southern decor, period furniture, a garden and terraces. Suites with whirlpool bath and wood-burning fireplace. Rooms with phone, voice mail, modem hookup, TV, hair dryer, makeup mirror, bathrobes, goosedown duvet, etc. 50m from the metro. "A gem." says Michel Vastel of *Le Soleil*. **See photo back cover/inside flap.**

Ville-Marie Hwy (720 Est), Rue Guy Exit. At 1st lights, right on René-Lévesque; at 2nd lights, right on southbound Rue Guy, 1st street on the left after Hotel Days Inn. Lucien-L'Allier metro station.

B&B
À BON MATIN

1393, av. Argyle
Montréal H3G 1V5
(514) 931-9167
toll free 1-800-588-5280
fax (514) 931-1621
www.bonsmatins.com

B&B	
single	$85-145
double	$95-155
triple	$115-175
quad.	$135-195
child	$10

Taxes extra VS MC AM ER IT

Open year round

Number of rooms	5
rooms with private bath	5

Activities: 🏛 🍴 ⛴ 🚣 🚴

---

5. MONTRÉAL

✺✺✺ F e 🏊 P R.1 TA

Located in a residential neighbourhood, on a quiet street, we offer a warm welcome, family atmosphere and copious breakfast. Free parking, flowered terrace, pool and T.V. in room. Near services (0.1km), buses, Crémazie Métro, highways, bicycle path and olympic pool (0.8km).

Easy access from Dorval and Mirabel airports. From Dorval, rte 520 East twd Hwy 40 East, Exit 73, Ave. Christophe-Colomb north, 1km. Rue Legendre, right and drive 0.2km to Ave. André-Grasset, turn left. First street turn right. From Mirabel, Hwy 15 South twd 40 East...

B&B
À LA BELLE VIE

Lorraine and Camille Grondin
1408, Jacques Lemaistre
Montréal H2M 2C1
(514) 381-5778
fax (514) 381-3966
www.bbcanada.com/3399.html
alabellevie@hotmail.com

B&B	
single	$50
double	$60
child	$10

Open year round

Number of rooms	2
shared bathroom	1

Activities: 🏛 🚣 🎿 🚴 🏃

---

6. MONTRÉAL

✺✺✺ F E 🚫 🚗 R.2 TA

A park and a flowery garden surround a B&B offering an incomparable welcome. Easy parking. Here will you find everythings a B&B has to offer: comfort, discrete environment, varied breakfasts, information. Everything to make your stay a memorable one... when one has a lucky star!

From the Jacques-Cartier bridge, Boul. De Lorimier North right on Boul. St-Joseph. Left on 3rd street, Messier, left on Rue Laurier, right on Rue de Bordeaux. From the North, Rue Papineau South, left on Boul. St-Joseph, left on Rue Bordeaux at the traffic lights.

B&B
À LA BONNE ÉTOILE

Louise Lemire and
Christian Guéric
5193, rue de Bordeaux
Montréal H2H 2A6
(514) 525-1698
www.bbcanada.com/
1947.html

B&B	
single	$50-55
double	$60-65
triple	$85

Reduced rates: Nov. 1 to Apr. 30
Open year round

Number of rooms	2
shared bathroom	1

Activities: 🏛 🍴 ⛴ 🚣 🚴

7. MONTRÉAL ☀☀ F E 🐕 R.1

Simple comfort in a grand old house 2 minutes walking distance from the metro, restaurants, cultural and entertainment activities. Warm welcome, very good and lively breakfast, spacious rooms, 10% off for stays of 5 days or more. Parking available.

From the airports, take the shuttle to the Voyageur bus terminal. Métro Mont-Royal, go right until St-Hubert. By car, Rue Sherbrooke, East to St-Hubert, heading North.

B&B
À LA DORMANCE

Chantal Savoye
and Eddy Lessard
4425, St-Hubert
Montréal H2J 2X1
(514) 529-0179
fax (514) 529-1079
dormance@microtec.net

B&B	
single	$50
double	$70
triple	$85
child	$0-10

Reduced rates: 10% 5 nights and more
Open year round

Number of rooms	5
shared wc	1
shared bathroom	2

Activities: 🏛 ⛴ 🚣 🧍 🚴

8. MONTRÉAL F e 🚫 R.2

The next best thing to home. Steps from Berri-UQAM metro, bus terminal, old port, museums, restaurants. Ancestral home, roof-top terrace, huge rooms, living room, good breakfasts. Low-season: extended-stay rates. See you soon...

From the terminus, walk one street to the east. By Métro, Berri-UQAM, exit Place Dupuis. By car, Hwy Ville-Marie (720), Berri Exit, right on Ontario, right on St-André, right on de Maisonneuve, right on St-Christophe.

B&B
À L'ADRESSE DU CENTRE-VILLE

Nathalie Messier and
Robert Groleau
1673, St-Christophe
Montréal H2L 3W7
(514) 528-9516
fax (514) 528-2746
www.bbcanada.com/657.html
adresvil@dsuper.net

B&B	
single	$50-60
double	$60-75
triple	$85-100

Reduced rates: Nov. 1 to Mar. 31
Open year round

Number of rooms	4
shared bathroom	2

Activities: 🏛 🍴 ⛴ 🧍 🚴

9. MONTRÉAL ☀☀☀ F E 🚫 🐕 P R.1 TA

Montréal Excellence Prize 1999. The «people's favorite» Prize. Meet colourful Montrealer Denis and Sacha (gentle canine public-relations director). The front door is the city, the back yard is the country, inside it is homey. Across the street from the Olympic Park & the Pie-ix metro. Must try fresh fruit salad, French toast, croissant and jelly. Clean as a whistle. Regional finalist for the «Québec Grand Prize of Tourism 1999, hospitality and customer service».

From Dorval, 520 E., 40 E., Exit 76, Boul Pie-IX S., 4km. From Mirabel, 15 S., 40 E., Exit 76. From downtown, east on Sherbrooke, right on Boul. Pie-IX South.

B&B
AU GÎTE OLYMPIQUE

Denis Boulianne
2752, boul.Pie-IX
Montréal H1V 2E9
(514) 254-5423
toll free (CAN and USA)
1-888-254-5423
fax (514) 254-4753
www.dsuper.net/~olympic
olympic@dsuper.net

B&B	
single	$60-75
double	$75-95
triple	$90-115
child	$15

Taxes extra VS MC AM

Reduced rates: Nov. 1 to Dec. 23, Jan. 2 to Apr. 30
Open year round

Number of rooms	5
rooms with private bath	5
rooms in semi-basement	3

Activities: 🍴 🚣 🧍 🚴 🎿

10. MONTRÉAL

☀☀ F E ⊘ R.1 TA

Victorian house with age-old woodwork on a quiet street facing Square St-Louis. Ten minutes' walking distance from downtown and Old Montreal, in the heart of the Latin Quarter. Lavish breakfasts and warm welcome.

From Dorval, Hwy 20 and Rte 720 East, Boul. St-Laurent North Exit. After 1km, turn right on Ave. des Pins, right on Ave. Laval. Sherbrooke metro station, Rigaud St. exit.

B&B
AUX PORTES DE LA NUIT

Christiane and Philippe Boscher
3496, av. Laval
Montréal H2X 3C8
(514) 848-0833
www.bbcanada.com/767.html

B&B	
single	$60-80
double	$70-90
triple	$85-100
quad.	$110-135
child	$10

Open year round

Number of rooms	5
shared bathrooms	1
rooms with private bath	3

Activities: 🏛 🦪 ⛴ 🚶 🚲

11. MONTRÉAL

☀☀☀ F E ⊘ R.1 TA

If at night the cats are grey, the mornings won't be any less colourful... Gourmet breakfasts, different every morning. Cheerful atmosphere in a relaxing decor. Near Old Montreal, 2 steps away from Rue St-Denis and festival sites. 15min walk to downtown. Metro and bus close to this lovely Victorian house facing Parc Lafontaine. Free parking in area.

Near the Jacques-Cartier bridge on Sherbrooke East. Métro Sherbrooke or bus #24.

B&B
B&B CHAGRI

Eve Bettez
1268, Sherbrooke Est
Montréal H2L 1M1
tel/fax (514) 524-1691
www.colba.net/~
chagri/
chagri@colba.net

B&B	
single	$55-60
double	$70-80
triple	$75-90
quad.	$100-110
child	$10

Reduced rates: Nov. to Apr.
Open year round

Number of rooms	3
shared wc	1
shared bathroom	1

Activities: 🏛 🦪 ⛴ 🚲 ⛷

12. MONTRÉAL

F E P R.5 TA

Our old house facing Lafontaine park and surrounded by greenery has been entirely renovated; Botanical Gardens, Olympic Park and summer theatres are nearby. Copious breakfast, cosy and modern comfort, whirlpool bath. Refined atmosphere, original works of art. An oasis of peace and tranquillity. Private parking.

From Dorval, twd Montréal Hwy 40 E., Exit Papineau S., drive 5km. From Métro Papineau, bus #45 N., 2nd stop after Sherbrooke.

B&B
CHEZ FRANÇOIS

François Baillergeau
4031, Papineau
Montréal H2K 4K2
(514) 239-4638
fax (514) 596-2961
www.bbcanada.
com/2838.html

B&B	
single	$60-65
double	$75-95
triple	$90-120
child	$5-10

Taxes extra VS

Open year round

Number of rooms	5
rooms with private bath	3
rooms with sink	1
shared bathroom	1

Activities: 🏛 🦪 ⛴ 🚶 🚲

13. MONTRÉAL

F E 🚫 R.1 TA

An artist and sociologist, I'm touched by your trust in me when making your reservations, as well as your desire to enjoy your time here. Thank you! I serve unforgettable healthy, refined breakfasts to your liking and offer information about Montréal. Located in the quiet Centre-Sud district, 5 min walking distance from Berri metro and the bus terminal. **City Home p 225.**

Ville-Marie Hwy (720 Est), Downtown-bound Exit. Vieux-Port/Vieux-Mtl/St-Laurent/Berri Exit 6 twd Berri. Left on Rue Berri, right on Rue Ste-Catherine, left on Rue Wolfe.

B&B
GÎTE GRÉGOIRE

Christine Grégoire
1766, rue Wolfe
Montréal H2L 3J8
(514) 524-8086
www.gregoire.qc.ca
bb@gregoire.qc.ca

B&B	
single	$55-60
double	$75-80
triple	$100-110
child	$15

VS

Reduced rates: Nov. 1 to Apr. 30
5 nights and more
Open year round

Number of rooms	2
shared bathroom	1

Activities: 🏛 ⛵ 🚶 🚴 ⛷

14. MONTRÉAL

☀☀☀ F e R.1 TA

Soothed by the stately trees lining the quiet street, right by a lively avenue of shops and restaurants sure to delight strollers, near the metro to explore the city, our B&B offers an ambiance where time stands still, to fully enjoy a comfortable stay and savour the morning's lavish breakfasts.

From the Jacques-Cartier bridge, Rue de Lormier. Left on Sherbrooke Est. Right on Émile-Duployé. Left on Rachel Est. Right on Boyer. From Mont-Royal metro station, right to the exit. Right on Boyer.

B&B
GÎTE LA CINQUIÈME SAISON

Jean-Yves Goupil
4396, rue Boyer
Montréal H2J 3E1
(514) 522-6439
fax (514) 522-6192
www.bbcanada.com/1952.html
cinquieme.saison
@sympatico.ca

B&B	
single	$55
double	$65

Taxes extra VS MC IT

Reduced rates: Nov. 1 to Apr. 30
Open year round

Number of rooms	5
shared wc	1
shared bathroom	1
shared showers	1

Activities: 🏛 🍷 ⛵ 🎣 🚴

15. MONTRÉAL

F e R.5 TA

Right downtown! Parking. Near all services. Residential district, at the edge of the festivals. Room with cable-tv, radio, phone and ventilation. Visitors can use kitchen. A short walk to the Palais des Congrès, museums, hospitals, universities and shopping centre. Complete musical breakfast. "An excellent address" according to travellers. **City Home p 225.**

Métro Place-des-Arts, Jeanne-Mance exit, bus 80, 2nd stop, walk straight. By car: downtown, 4 streets west of Boul. St-Laurent and one street north of Sherbrooke, between Milton and Prince-Arthur.

B&B
GÎTE TOURISTIQUE
ET APPARTEMENTS
DU CENTRE-VILLE

Bruno Bernard
3523, Jeanne-Mance
Montréal H2X 2K2
(514) 845-0431
fax (514) 845-0262
www3.sympatico.ca/app
app@sympatico.ca

B&B	
single	$50-55
double	$65-75
triple	$85

Taxes extra VS MC AM

Open year round

Number of rooms	3
shared wc	1
shared bathroom	1

Activities: 🏛 ⛵ 🚶 🚴 ⛷

16. MONTRÉAL

☀☀☀ F E 🐕 P R.1 TA

In the heart of the city, the peacefulness of the country. Located at the foot of a tree-lined stairway, come admire the house's interior architecture, skylights, fireplace and antique furniture. Comfortable bedrooms. As for the garden, several terraces look out onto English gardens and the wooded and flowered alley. Private parking.

Métro Berri, Voyageur terminal. By car, Hwy Ville-Marie (720) Exit Berri. Turn left on Berri, right on Rue Ontario East, 2nd street on left. Or Jacques-Cartier bridge, to Sherbrooke, turn left at 1st traffic lights, Rue Ontario for 1km, turn right.

B&B
LA MAISON CACHÉE

Yvette Beigbeder
2121, St-Christophe
Montréal H2L 3X1
(514) 522-4451
fax (514) 522-1870
www.cam.org/
~mcachee/index.html
mcachee@cam.org

B&B	
single	$65-75
double	$70-80

VS MC

Open year round

Number of rooms	3
shared bathroom	1

Activities: 🏛 🦪 ⛴ 🚲 🏃

17. MONTRÉAL

F e R.1 TA

A few min from the Old Montréal market, St-Denis and Ste-Catherine, the yellow house right in the midst of Montréal's cultural, social and tourist activities. This ancestral house's unique character and tranquillity will add to your stay. Good advice on activities, restaurants, entertainment.

Hwy 20, Rte 132, Jacques-Cartier bridge twd Rue Sherbrooke, left on Ontario, drive 1.2km, right on St-Hubert.

B&B
LA MAISON JAUNE

Sylvain Binette and
François Legault
2017, St-Hubert
Montréal H2L 3Z6
(514) 524-8851
fax (514) 521-7352

B&B	
single	$55
double	$70-80
triple	$80-95
quad.	$95-125

Taxes extra

Reduced rates: Nov. 1 to Apr. 30
Open year round

Number of rooms	5
shared wc	2
shared bathroom	2

Activities: 🏛 🦪 ⛴ 🛶 🚲

18. MONTRÉAL

☀☀☀ F E 🚭 🏊 P R1 TA

Montréal 1996-97 Excellence Prize. Located by the St. Lawrence River, 25min from downtown, this 1900 house will charm you with its garden, flowers and in-ground swimming pool. Lavish breakfast on the terrace. The country right in the city. Private parking. Children welcome. **See colour photos.**

From Dorval, Rte 520 E, Hwy 40 E, Exit 87, Tricentenaire to Notre-Dame, turn right, 200 m. From Mirabel, Hwy 15 S, 40 E, Exit 87... From Hwy 20, Lafontaine tunnel, 1st Exit, twd East. Drive south: Notre-Dame, twd East.

B&B
LA VICTORIENNE

Aimée and Julien Roy
12560, rue Notre-Dame Est
Montréal H1B 2Z1
(514) 645-8328
fax (514) 255-3493

B&B	
single	$40
double	$50
triple	$65
child	$0-5

Open: May 1 to Oct. 15

Number of rooms	3
rooms with sink	1
shared bathroom	2

Activities: ⛴ 🛶 🚶 🏃 🚲

19. MONTRÉAL

☀☀☀ | F | E | ⊘ | 🛶 | R1 | TA

This is the place for comfort and a warm welcome at a low price. Close to the Olympic tower, L'Assomption metro and 10 min from the botanical garden. Breakfasts are made with fresh, quality ingredients and you can have as much as you like. Pool, bikes available, free laundry.

From Mirabel Hwy 40 East, Boul. Lacordaire South Exit. Drive down to Boul. Rosemont and turn right, continue to Rue Lemay (2nd street, turn right). From Dorval, Hwy 520 East to Hwy 40 East...

B&B
«LE 6400»
COUETTE ET CAFÉ
BED & BREAKFAST

Lise and Jean-Pierre Durand
6400, rue Lemay
Montréal H1T 2L5
(514) 259-6400
www.agricotours.qc.ca

B&B	
single	$35-45
double	$55-65

Reduced rates: Nov. 1 to Apr. 30
Open year round

Number of rooms	2
shared bathroom	1

Activities: 🛶 🏊 🧍 🚶 🚲

20. MONTRÉAL

☀☀☀ | F | E | ⊘ | P | R.2 | TA

Right near a vast park, our large and sunny room with private entrance and parking awaits you. It provides easy access to expressways and airports while offering you a guaranteed haven of peace with healthy breakfasts and private garden. Come enjoy the metropolis in a warm and intimate ambiance.

From Dorval, 520 East, Hwy 40 East, Exit 73 Ave. Papineau North. From Mirabel, Hwy 15 South, 440 East, 19 South, Ave. Papineau South. We are 0.6km east of Ave. Papineau, via Prieur (two blocks south of Gouin Blvd.).

B&B
LE CLOS DES ÉPINETTES

Diane Teolis and Léo Lavergne
10358, Parthenais, app. 1
Montréal H2B 2L7
(514) 382-0737
www.bbcanada.
com/3181.html
leclos@vl.videotron.ca

B&B	
single	$55
double	$65
triple	$85
quad.	$95
child	$5-10

Open year round

Number of rooms	1
rooms with private bath	1
rooms in semi-basement	1

Activities: 🏛 🧍 🚶 🚲 ⛷

21. MONTRÉAL

☀☀☀ | F | E | R1 | TA

Lovely Victorian house (marble fireplace) a stone's throw from festival sites, restaurants, museums, shops. Quiet and centrally located historic district. Relaxed ambiance with a soothing decor, home-made jams and rooms tempting one to take a nap. Friendly young hosts respectful of everyone's space. Make yourselves at home!

From Mirabel or Toronto, Hwy 40 East, St-Denis Exit, 6km. Right on Des Pins, right on Laval. From Québec City, Hwy 20, Rte 132, J.-Cartier bridge, left on Sherbrooke, right on St-Denis, left on Des Pins, right on Laval.

B&B
LE ZÈBRE

Jean-François Pépin and
Éric Fourlanty
3767, avenue Laval
Montréal H2W 2H8
(514) 844-9868
www.bbcanada.com/2729.html
lezebre@mlink.net

B&B	
single	$55
double	$70
triple	$90

Taxes extra

Reduced rates: 10% 5 nights and more
Open: May 1 to Oct. 31

Number of rooms	3
shared bathroom	2

Activities: 🏛 🍷 🛶 🚣 🚲

22. MONTRÉAL

☀☀ F E 🚫 R.1 TA

Square Saint-Louis is a peace of the countryside downtown. Everything is within walking distance: museums, exhibitions, restaurants, shopping, Old Montréal, etc. After a long day, relax in the park filled with birdsong. At breakfast, we eat, chat, laugh and start all over again! **See colour photos.**

From Dorval, Hwy 20 East, then Hwy 720 East, Boul. St-Laurent North Exit. Continue for 1km, then right on Ave. des Pins, right on Ave. Laval, left on St-Louis square. Or Sherbrooke metro station, Rigaud exit.

B&B
PIERRE ET DOMINIQUE

Dominique Bousquet
and Pierre Bilodeau
271, Carré St-Louis
Montréal H2X 1A3
(514) 286-0307
www.pierdom.qc.ca
info@pierdom.qc.ca

B&B	
single	$40-55
double	$70-85
triple	$100
quad.	$115
child	$15

Open year round

Number of rooms	3
rooms with sink	2
shared bathroom	1

Activities: 🏛 👤 🚶 🚲 ⛷

23. MONTRÉAL

☀☀ F E 🚫 🐕 P R.1

In the heart of the Latin Quarter (restaurants-nightclubs-theatres-boutiques). Easy parking. Garden, hammocks. Quiet, safe street. 2 min from Métro. Near the bike path, international events: Jazz Festival, Just For Laughs, World Film Festival. 6-person suite. Superb lovers' suite. Family or group rooms (2 to 6 people).

Airports: Voyageur bus terminus, Métro Mont-Royal. By Car: twd downtown. Berri is parallel to St-Denis (2 streets to the east). 4272 Berri is between Mont-Royal and Rachel.

B&B
SHÉZELLES

Lucie Dextras and
Lyne St-Amand
4272, Berri
Montréal H2J 2P8
(514) 849-8694
cell. (514) 943-2526
fax (514) 528-8290
www.bbcanada.com/2469.html
shez.masq@sympatico.ca

B&B	
single	$40-85
double	$60-100

Reduced rates: 10% 7 consecutives nights and more
Open year round

Number of rooms	4
rooms with private bath	1
shared bathroom	1

Activities: 🏛 🍷 🏊 🚣 🚲

24. MONTRÉAL-NORD

☀☀ F E 🚫 🐕 🦫 P 🏊 R.5 TA

Located in Montréal Nord, Hâvre Sportif 2000 is a peaceful spot outside the hustle and bustle of the metropolis and less than 30min from downtown. The facility has a pool, *pétanque* (a game of bowls), croquet, mini-golf and a weight room for sports enthusiasts. Kitchenette and laundromat. Enjoy breakfast in the brand-new solarium.

From Dorval, Hwy 40 East, Exit St-Michel to the north, right on Prieur. From Mirabel, Hwy 15 South, 40 East, Exit St-Michel...

B&B
HAVRE SPORTIF 2000

Guy Doré
3375, rue Prieur
Montréal-Nord H1H 2K8
(514) 852-4261
fax (514) 852-5187
pages.infinit.net/hsportif/
havresportif2000@videotron.ca

B&B	
single	$50
double	$50-60
triple	$60-70
child	$0-10

Taxes extra VS MC AM IT

Reduced rates: Sep. 1 to May 31
Open year round

Number of rooms	5
shared wc	3
shared bathrooms	2

Activities: 🚣 🚲

25. MONTRÉAL, NOTRE-DAME-DE-GRÂCE

☀☀☀☀ F E 🚫 🚗 P R1

Pretty Victorian House located in the heart of the Monkland village in N.D.G. Close to the restaurants and boutiques. 15min from Dorval airport via Hwy 20 or 40. Convenient access to downtown attractions by Metro (Villa Maria station). Our rooms are comfortable and well-furnished. Hingston House is filled with warmth.

From Dorval airport, Côte-de-Liesse East and Décarie South (Hwy 15), Exit Sherbrooke West turn right, right on Hingston.

B&B
MAISON HINGSTON 4335

Hélène Groulx
4335 Hingston
Montréal
H4A 2J8
(514) 484-3396

B&B	
single	$50-55
double	$60-65

Open year round

Number of rooms	2
shared bathrooms	1

Activities: 🏛 ⛴ 🏄 👣 🚲

26. MONTRÉAL, NOTRE-DAME-DE-GRÂCE

☀☀☀☀ F E 🚫 P R.25 TA

1999 Ulysses Grand Prize, hospitality and customer service. Picturesque Victorian manor offers luxurious rooms, total comfort, King and Queen size beds and the warmth of antique furnishings. Only steps away from the cafés and shops of Monkland Village, near Decarie Hwy leading to Dorval Airport and straight to the downtown core, near the Villa-Maria metro station with its easy access to the "underground city".

Decarie Hwy, Côte-St-Luc/Queen Mary Exit, head west on Côte-St-Luc to Somerled, left on Somerled to Havard, right on Harvard, we're located corner of Harvard and Somerled.

B&B
MANOIR HARVARD

Robert and Lyne Bertrand
4805, avenue Harvard
Notre-Dame-de-Grâce,
Montréal H3X 3P1
(514) 488-3570
fax (514) 369-5778
www.bbcanada.com/1963.html
alrc@sympatico.ca

B&B	
single	$145-155-165
double	$145-155-165

Taxes extra VS MC ER IT

Open year round

Number of rooms	4
rooms with private bath	4

Activities: 🏛 ⛴ 👣 🚲

27. PIERREFONDS

☀☀☀☀ F E 🚫 P 🚗 R.1 TA

Air-conditioned, renovated ranch house in west-end Montréal, close to Dorval airport, accessible from downtown via Rtes 40 or 20. Free off-the-street parking. Cozy bedrooms, spacious meeting rooms, piano, fireplaces, screened veranda, well-kept grounds. Healty & hearty breakfast. A restful place to return to.

Coming from Dorval Airport, Hwy 20 West, 7km, until Boul Saint-Jean, Exit 50 N., proceed on St-Jean for 7km, then left on Boul Pierrefonds, 1.4km, turn left again at Rue Paiement.

B&B
GÎTE MAISON JACQUES

Micheline and Fernand Jacques
4444, rue Paiement
Pierrefonds H9H 2S7
(514) 696-2450
fax (514) 696-2564
www.maisonjacques.qc.ca
gite.maison.jacques
@sympatico.ca

B&B	
single	$43-46
double	$59-63
triple	$84
quad.	$107
child	$6-12

MC AM VS

Reduced rates: 7% seniors and 4 nights and more
Open: Jan. 29 to Nov. 30

Number of rooms	3
rooms with private bath	3
rooms in basement	1

Activities: 🏛 👣 🚶 🐎

28. VERDUN

☀☀ F E ⊘ P R.7 TA

Sunny and peaceful with private entrance and parking just 10 min from downtown (museums, festivals, theatres). Close to beautiful park along St. Lawrence River banks (cycling, hiking, rafting in line skating). Quick access to airports and regional activities via Hwys. Discount on 4 nights and more.

From Dorval, Hwy 20 East, Hwy 15 South. From the south, Champlain bridge to Hwy 15 North, La Vérendrye Exit, turn left at 6th light onto Stéphens, left on Beurling and left on Rolland.

B&B
PACANE ET POTIRON
CAFÉ COUETTE

Nathalie Ménard and
Jean-Pierre Bernier
1430, Rolland
Verdun H4H 2G6
(514) 769-8315
www.bbcanada.com/3464.html
jpb_nm@hotmail.com

B&B	
single	$50-70
double	$70-95
child	$15

VS MC

Reduced rates: 10% Oct. 15 to Dec. 10 and Jan. 15 to Apr. 15
Open year round

Number of rooms	2
shared bathroom	1

Activities: 🚤 🚴 🏃 🎿 🏃

29. MONTRÉAL

F e R1 TA

Beautifully furnished apartments in a prime, central location! Fully equipped kitchen. Daily, weekly or monthly rentals. Balcony, television, radio, telephone, pool and air conditioning. Great view of the city. Near festivals, Palais des Congrès, shopping centre, universities and hospitals. Parking. Great value for your dollar. **B&B p 219.**

Metro Place-des-Arts, Jeanne-Mance exit, bus #80, get off at the 2nd bus stop, walk right. By car, situated downtown four streets west of Boul. St-Laurent and 1 street north of Sherbrooke between Milton and Prince-Arthur.

CITY HOME
APPARTEMENTS MEUBLÉS
MONTRÉAL CENTRE-VILLE

Bruno Bernard
3463, rue Ste-Famille
Office 008
Montréal H2X 2K7
(514) 845-0431
fax (514) 845-0262
www3.sympatico.ca/app
app@sympatico.ca

No. apt.	8
No. rooms	4
No. people	1-4
WEEK-SUMMER	$500-600
WEEK-WINTER	$475-575
W/E-SUMMER	$160-250
W/E-WINTER	$80-125
DAY-SUMMER	$80-125
DAY-WINTER	$75-120

Taxes extra VS MC AM

Reduced rates: Oct. 21 to June 1
Open year round

Activities: 🏛 🍴 ⛵ 🚶 🚴

30. MONTRÉAL

F E ⊘ P R.1 M.1 TA

Nice, big 4-room apartment in south-central Montreal, the media and arts district known as "the Village", where the population is the most diverse of any Canadian city. Private entrance, phone, whirlpool bath, stove, fridge, microwave oven, TV, patio door, terrace, garden. View of the city, trees and sky. Safe, quiet and comfortable. **B&B p 219.**

Ville-Marie Hwy (720) twd downtown, Exit Vieux-Port/Vieux-Mtl/St-Laurent/Berri twd Berri. Left on Rue Berri, right on Rue Ste-Catherine, left on Rue Wolfe.

CITY HOME
MAISON GRÉGOIRE

Christine Grégoire
1766, rue Wolfe
Montréal H2L 3J8
(514) 524-8086
www.gregoire.qc.ca
maison@gregoire.qc.ca

No. houses	1
No. rooms	2
No. people	4-5
WEEK-SUMMER	$875-1000
WEEK-WINTER	$650-850
W/E-SUMMER	$330-400
W/E-WINTER	$270-325
DAY-SUMMER	$165-200
DAY-WINTER	$135-170

VS ER

Reduced rates: Nov. 1 to Apr. 30
Open year round

Activities: 🏛 ⛴ 🚶 🚴 🏃

31. ST-LAURENT

F E ⊘ 🚗 P R.4 M.2 TA

Lovely 3 1/2 (living room, kitchen, bathroom). Very roomy, quiet, fully equipped, phone, cable TV, stereo. Residential district, near Marcel Laurin city park, Raymond Bourque arena, shopping centres, 5 min. from Côte-Vertu metro, 15 min. from downtown Montréal, 10 min. from Dorval airport. Access to garden, laundry. Parking. Personalized welcome.

Reach Hwy 40, Exit 67 (Marcel Laurin North), drive about 1.5km. Turn left on Place Thimens. At the stop sign, turn left on Alexis-Nihon, right on Hufford and left on Sigouin.

CITY HOME
STUDIO MARHABA

Assia and Ammar Sassi
2265, Sigouin
St-Laurent H4R 1L6
(514) 335-7931
(514) 744-9732
fax (514) 335-2177

No. houses	1
No. rooms	1
No. people	1-3
WEEK-SUMMER	$350-500
WEEK-WINTER	$250-350
W/E-SUMMER	$100-180
W/E-WINTER	$60-140
DAY-SUMMER	$60-100
DAY-WINTER	$40-80

MC IT

Reduced rates: Nov. 1 to Apr. 30
Open year round

Activities: 🏛 ⛴ ⛵ 🚴 🏃

FARM ACTIVITIES

Farm Excursions *:

32 FERME ÉCOLOGIQUE DU PARC-NATURE DU CAP-SAINT-JEAN, Pierrefonds 35

* Registered trademark.

25 years of hospitality
1975 - 2000

For 25 years, the host members of the
Fédération des Agricotours du Québec have been committed
to offering you genuine, high-quality choices
for accommodation and agricultural tourism.

This has made Agricotours the largest high-quality network
in Quebec, and your confidence has helped in its success.

For this reason, our network host members hope that they
may, with their traditional warm welcome, continue to help
you discover the best of Quebec for many more years to come.

*You'll always feel welcome
in the Agricotours network.*

OUTAOUAIS

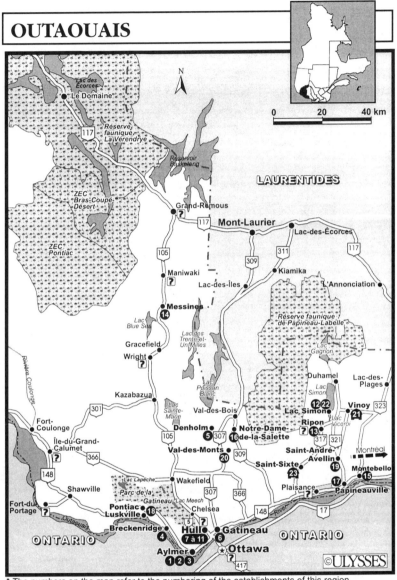

Lac des
Écorces
Le Domaine

N

0   20   40 km

117
Réserve
faunique
La Vérendrye

Réservoir
Baskatong

LAURENTIDES

ZEC
Bras-Coupé-
Désert

Grand-Remous
?

117   Mont-Laurier   Lac-des-Écorces

ZEC
Pontiac

105

311   117
309

Kiamika   L'Annonciation

Maniwaki
?

Lac-des-Îles

Messines
14

Lac
Blue Sea

Réserve faunique
de Papineau-Labelle

Gracefield

Lac des
Trente-et-
Un Milles

Lac
Gagnon

Wright
?

Rivière Coulonge

Kazabazua

301

Lac
Sainte-
Marie

Lac
Poisson
Blanc

Duhamel

Lac-des-
Plages

Lac
Simon

Fort-
Coulonge

Île-du-Grand-
Calumet
?

366

Val-des-Bois

Lac Simon
12 22

Vinoy
21

323

148

Denholm
5   307

Notre-Dame-
16 de-la-Salette

Ripon
?   13

Lac
Viceroi

317   321

105
Val-des-Monts
20

309

Saint-André-
Avellin
19

Montréal

Shawville

Lac Lapêche

Parc de la
Gatineau

Wakefield

307

366

Saint-Sixte

23

Montebello
17   15

Fort-du-
Portage
?

Pontiac
Luskville   18

Lac Meech

Chelsea

148

Plaisance
?

Papineauville

River

Breckenridge
4

5

Hull
7 à 11

Gatineau
6

17

ONTARIO

Aylmer
1 2 3

Ottawa

ONTARIO

©ULYSSES

417

* The numbers on the map refer to the numbering of the establishments of this region

1. AYLMER

☀☀☀ F E Ⓢ P R1

10 min from Ottawa/Hull. Artist home, 3 spacious rooms, 1 with balcony. Enjoy fine breakfast on terrace surrounded by trees and flowers by trees and flowers, or in a dining room aglowed with morning light. Peacefull environnement close to everything: ski, golf, parks, beaches, bike paths, museums. Air conditionning.

Via Ottawa, Hwy 417, exit 123: Island Park Dr. to Champlain Bridge, After bridge, left 2nd light on Aylmer Rd. (Rte 148). Pass 4th traffic lights, turn left on Lakeview (no 32).

B&B
GÎTE ENCHANTÉ

Rita Rodrigue
32, Lakeview
Aylmer J9H 2A1
(819) 682-0695

B&B	
single	$50-60-70
double	$55-65-75
triple	$65-75-85
child	$10

Reduced rates: Oct. 15 to Apr.30
Open year round

Number of rooms	3
shared wc	1
shared bathrooms	1
rooms in basement	1

Activities: 🏛 ⚓ 🚶 🚲 🏃

2. AYLMER

☀☀☀ F E Ⓢ 🐾 🚗 P 🏊 R.5

B&B surrounded by magnificent woodlands. Healthy breakfast served on a large terrace around the pool and relaxation packages. Near the Aylmer marina, Gatineau Park, cycling paths, footpaths, golf courses, Hull and Ottawa tourist attractions. Computerized office and shuttle service available. Bike shed, private parking lot.

Hwy 417 W., Exit 123, Island Park Drive (2 km) cross Champlain bridge, 2nd light left on Ch. Aylmer (6 km), right on Wilfrid Lavigne (1 km) cross Hwy McConnell Laramée, 2nd street on right (cul-de-sac).

B&B
L'ÉQUINESSENCE

Joanne Tessier and
Hélène Tremblay
120, avenue Des Ormes
Aylmer J9J 1S9
(819) 685-3555
toll free 1-888-909-1061
fax (819) 684-2424
equinessence@sprint.ca

B&B	
single	$45-55
double	$70-80

VS IT

Open year round

Number of rooms	2
rooms with private bath	1
rooms in basement	1
shared bathrooms	1

Activities: 🚶 🚶 🚲 🎿 🏃

3. AYLMER

☀☀☀ F E P Ⓢ R1

Provincial Excellence Prize 1996-97. A few minutes from Ottawa/Hull, this charming residence is referred to by many guests as "their home away from home". A warm welcome, comfortable rooms, attention to details and great breakfasts are a winning combination. Close to bike and ski trails, golfing, Gatineau Park. Air conditionning and private parking.

From Montréal, Hwy 417, in Ottawa Exit 123, follow Island Park, cross Champlain Bridge to 148 West sign, left, drive 2 km. From Hull, follow Boul. Taché W. wich change for Aylmer Rd. Drive 1 km past Chateau Cartier Hotel.

B&B
L'ESCAPADE B&B

Lise and Rhéal Charron
912, chemin d'Aylmer
Aylmer J9H 5T8
(819) 772-2388
toll free 1-877-882-7755
fax (819) 772-4354
www.bbcanada.com/279.html
escapade@mondenet.com

B&B	
single	$50-60
double	$65-75
triple	$80-90

VS

Open year round

Number of rooms	3
rooms with sink	2
shared wc	1
shared bathrooms	1

Activities: 🏛 🍷 🚶 🚲 🏃

4. AYLMER, BRECKENRIDGE

☀☀☀ | F | E | 🚭 | P | R1 | TA

Our split-level home offers you comfort, tranquillity and a warm welcome. Take the time to enjoy nature in the magnificent woods bordering the Outaouais River. 20 min to the Parliament and Ottawa's other tourist attractions. Bicycle storage available. Generous breakfast.

From Montréal, Hwy 417, in Ottawa Exit 123 (Island Park Drive) follow Island Park, cross Champlain Bridge to 148 West sign. From the Aylmer city hall, right on Eardley Street for 5 km. Left on Terry Fox twd the river, right on Cedarvale.

B&B
MAISON BON REPOS

Denyse and Guy Bergeron
37, Cedarvale, Breckenridge
Aylmer, Pontiac J0X 2G0
(819) 682-1498
tel/fax (819) 684-6821
www.bbcanada.com/3276.html
denise.bergeron2
@sympatico.ca

B&B	
single	$40-45
double	$50-60

Open year round

Number of rooms	3
rooms with private bath	2
shared bathrooms	1

Activities: 🛶 ⛷ 🚶 🚲 ⛷

5. DENHOLM

★ ★ | F | E | 🚭 | ✖ | P | TA

"What a peaceful haven! I loved absolutely everything...The most warm of welcomes and exquisite meals. Everything is wonderful here!" Enjoy the splendour of nature at La maison des merisiers. Located 45min from Ottawa-Hull, our Inn is a country home in the mountains. Cosy atmosphere: woodwork, fireplace, piano, antiques and gorgeous décor. Lunch meal plan available. **See colour photos.**

From Montréal, Rte 148 W. From Gatineau, Rte 307 N. to St-Pierre de Wakefield. From the metal bridge, drive 8.5 km left Ch. des Voyageurs, twd Denholm, at stop sign, left on Chemin Paugan to Low 5.2 km.

INN
AUBERGE LA MAISON DES
MERISIERS

Claire Poulin and Michel Régnière
991, chemin Paugan
Denholm J8N 9B6
(819) 457-1209
fax (819) 457-1115
www.aubergedesmerisiers.com
info@aubergedesmerisiers.com

	B&B	MAP
single	$61	$81
double	$70	$112
triple	$10	$20

Taxes extra VS

Open year round

Number of rooms	7
shared wc	1
Shared bathrooms	3

Activities: 🛶 ⛷ 🚶 ⛷ 🤸

6. GATINEAU

☀☀ | F | E | 🐕 | P | 🛶 | R1 | TA

Warm and peaceful B&B; breakfast in gazebo, inground swimming pool, resting areas. On a hill, view on Gatineau, Hull and Ottawa; 15min from parliament, casino, Musée des Civilisations, bike baths, Gatineau park and golf course. Tourist information available on site.

From Hwy 417, Exit St-Nicholas to Hull, Hwy 50 East, Exit Maloney, left on Main, left on Magnus, right on Craik. From Montréal, Rte 148, right on Main, etc. From Maniwaki, Hwy 5 S., Hwy 50 East...

B&B
LA MAISON SUR LA COLLINE

Josée and Jean-Pierre Allain
520 rue Craik
Gatineau J8P 5N7
(819) 663-3185
fax (819) 663-7108
www.bbcanada.com/1376.html
allain@magma.ca

B&B	
single	$50
double	$60
triple	$75

VS MC

Open year round

Number of rooms	2
rooms with private wc	1
shared bathrooms	2

Activities: 🏛 🍷 🛶 🚶 🚲

7. HULL

☀☀☀ F E 🚭 P 🚗 R1 TA

Come experience Outaouais hospitality at its best, in a peaceful area right near downtown Hull, Ottawa and Parc de la Gatineau. Unforgettable breakfasts served in a solarium looking out onto a rose garden... or a blanket of snow. A place for people of all different ages and all different cultures! Se habla español!

From the Queensway, Exit Nicholas, Hull to the Hwy 5 North, Mont-Bleu Exit. Turn right on Boul. Riel to Normandie. From Montréal, via the 148 West, take the 5 North and follow the directions above.

B&B
AU NORMANDIE

Colette and Guy Claveau
67, rue de la Normandie
Hull J8Z 1N6
tel/fax (819) 595-2191
www.bbcanada.com/
1024.html
claveau@admin.uottawa.ca

B&B	
single	$50-60
double	$60-70
child	$10

VS

Open year round

Number of rooms	3
rooms in basement	1
rooms with private bath	1
shared bathrooms	1

Activities: 🏛 🐸 🚶 🚴 🎿

8. HULL

☀☀☀ F P R1 TA

An invitation to relax in a calm spot, near Gatineau Park, bike paths and walking trails. Country charm in the city. Warm welcome. Comfortable rooms and delicious breakfasts. Living room with fireplace, piano and TV. A few min from Ottawa, the casino and museums. Make yourself at home.

From Queensway, Nicholas Exit twd Hull and Hwy 5 N.; Mt-Bleu Exit. Right on Boul. Mt-Bleu, on the hill go left. Take Rue des Bouleaux, turns into des Ormes. From Mtl, Rte 148, Hwy 5 N... as above.

B&B
AU PIGNON SUR LE PARC

Fernande Béchard-Brazeau
63, des Ormes
Hull J8Y 6K6
(819) 777-5559
fax (819) 777-0597
brazeau-a@sympatico.ca

B&B	
single	$50
double	$60
triple	$80
quad.	$100
child	$10-15

Open year round

Number of rooms	3
rooms in basement	1
shared bathrooms	2

Activities: 🏛 🐸 🚶 🚴 🏃

9. HULL

☀☀☀ F E 🚭 P 🚗 R2 TA

Comfort and tranquility just minutes from Ottawa (museums) and the casino; 2 min from Parc de la Gatineau, bike paths. Attentive service. Finely decorated, air-conditioned house with living room, fireplace. Breakfast on the terrace, by magnificent woodlands and a golf course. Bike shed. Welcome!

Hwy 417, Mann Exit, then King Edward twd Hull, Hwy 5 North, Hautes-Plaines Exit 8, left on Rue du Contrefort, right on Du Versant. From Montréal, Rte 148 West. In Hull, Hwy 5 North...

B&B
AU VERSANT
DE LA MONTAGNE

Ghyslaine Vézina
19, du Versant
Hull J8Z 2T8
(819) 776-3760
fax (819) 776-2453
www.bbcanada.com/3577.html
auversant@sympatico.ca

B&B	
single	$50
double	$60
triple	$85
quad.	$100
child	$10

VS

Open year round

Number of rooms	3
rooms in semi-basement	1
shared bathrooms	2

Activities: 🏛 ⛵ 🚶 🚴 🏃

10. HULL

🔆🔆🔆 F e 🚫 🐕 P R.5

Welcoming Victorian house, lovingly decorated. A few minute's walk to Ottawa, Parliament, museums, Rideau Canal, etc. Access to bicycles and to the nicest bike paths. Casino 5 min away by car. Private parking, copious breakfast. Recommended by La Presse, in Dec. '94 and August '97.

From Montréal, Rte 148 then 550. Exit Hull West, Exit Boul Maisonneuve, left on Verdun, left on Champlain. From Montréal, Hwy 417, Exit Mann (becomes King Edouard), Cartier McDonald bridge Exit Boul Maisonneuve.

B&B
COUETTE ET CROISSANT

Anne Picard Allard
330, rue Champlain
Hull J8X 3S2
(819) 771-2200

B&B	
single	$50-55
double	$60-65
triple	$85

VS

Open: Apr. 1 to Oct. 31

Number of rooms	3
rooms with private bath	1
rooms in basement	1
shared bathrooms	2

Activities: 🏛 🍷 ⛵ 🚲 🏃

11. HULL

F E 🚫 🐕 P R1 TA

By Gatineau Park, a few minutes from downtown Hull and Ottawa. Welcome to our home with modern-classical decor and family ambiance. You will enjoy comfort, quiet and hearty breakfasts while abandoning yourselves to tourist activities such as: museums, outdoors, etc. See you soon! Families welcome.

From Ottawa or Rte 148 via Montréal, take Hwy 5 North, St-Raymond Exit toward Rte 148 West, right on Ch. Pink, left on Des Peupliers, left on Atmosphère, right on Astrolabe.

B&B
MANOIR DES CÈDRES

Christiane and Yvon Charron
5, rue de l'Astrolabe # 1
Hull J9A 2W1
(819) 778-7276
fax (819) 778-6502

B&B	
single	$55
double	$65
triple	$80
quad.	$95
child	$10

Open year round

Number of rooms	2
shared wc	1
rooms in basement	2
shared bathrooms	1

Activities: 🏛 👫 🏃 🚲 🏃

12. LAC-SIMON, CHÉNÉVILLE

🔆🔆🔆 F E 🐕 ✖ P 〰 R1 TA

Are you looking for a getaway? Come rejuvenate yourself in the countryside in a picturesque setting offering a stunning panoramic view of the lakes and mountains year-round. Fine sand private beach. Our rooms, generous breakfasts, *table d'hôte* meal plan and the magnificent view will delight you. **Country home p 235.**

From Montréal, Rte 148 West or from Ottawa Rte 148 East to Papineauville and Rte 321 North. At Chénéville, Rte 315 West for 1.3 km. Turn right onto Chemin Tour-du-Lac and drive 1.5 km, then turn left onto Chemin Marcelais.

B&B
DOMAINE AUX CROCOLLINES

Thérèse Croteau and
Franz Collinge
642, chemin Marcelais
Lac-Simon, Chénéville
JOV 1EO
tel/fax (819) 428-9262

B&B	
single	$45
double	$60
triple	$75
child	$10

Reduced rates : Apr.1 to June 14, Nov.1 to Dec. 20, 10% 3 nights and more
Open year round

Number of rooms	2
rooms with sink	2
shared wc	1
shared bathrooms	1

Activities: 🦫 👫 ⛵ 🏃 🐎

13. LAC-VICEROI (CANTON DE RIPON)

F E 🚭 🛶 P 🛏 ✕ R5 TA

Stately residence with turrets, period furniture, grand piano and organ. Family or gourmet cooking. Family-size room for 4 people. All our activities are free: canoeing on the river in front, trout fishing, dogsledding, tennis. Packages for our summer theatre.

From Montréal, Rte 148 W. From Ottawa-Hull, Hwy 50 and Rte 148 E. At Papineauville, Rte 321 N, 27 km. At 4 lanes, left on Rte 317. After the bridge, right on Ch. des Guides, 1.6 km, right at the sign, 0.09 km.

B&B
CHÂTEAU ÉPI D'OR

Claire and Charles Dussault
15, chemin Périard
Canton de Ripon, Lac-Viceroi
J0V 1V0
(819) 428-7120

	B&B	MAP
single	$40	$47.50
double	$50	$65
child	$10	$15

Taxes extra VS MC

Open year round

Number of rooms	4
rooms with private bath	4
shared bathrooms	1

Activities: 🍸 🛥 🛷 🎿 🐎

---

14. MESSINES

☀☀☀ F E 🚭 ✕ 🚗 P 🛶 TA

Outaouais Excellence Prize 1999. Located in a peaceful, enchanting setting in Haute-Gatineau, our inn has a tranquil atmosphere that will envelop you in a pleasant sense of well-being. The fine cuisine served in our restaurant is among the best in the Outaouais. Golf, horseback riding, downhill and cross-country skiing, etc.

From Ottawa/Hull, take Hwy 5 North and Rte 105 twd Maniwaki. Turn left at the flashing light in Messines. From Montréal, Hwy 15 North, Rte 117 North in St-Jovite to Grand-Remous. Turn left on Rte 105 South, to Maniwaki...

INN
MAISON LA CRÉMAILLÈRE

Andrée and André Dompierre
24, chemin de la Montagne
Messines J0X 2J0
(819) 465-2202
toll free 1-877-465-2202
fax (819) 465-5368
www.lacremailliere.qc.ca
la.cremailliere@ireseau.com

B&B	
single	$50-70
double	$65-85
child	$10

Taxes extra VS MC IT

Open year round

Number of rooms	5
rooms with private bath	3
rooms with sink	1
shared wc	3
shared bathrooms	2

Activities: 🛥 🎣 🚴 🛷 🎿

---

15. MONTEBELLO

☀☀☀☀ F E 🚭 🛶 P R1 TA

Let yourself be seduced by the enchanting decor, warm reception and creature comforts of the spacious rooms. Prestigious house. 45-acre property 3km from Château Montebello. Foyer. In-ground pool, canoeing, pedal-boating. Health packages, fishing, sea kayaking, dogsledding... a dream vacation!

From Montréal, Ottawa-Hull-bound Hwy 40 West; Hawkesbury Exit, Rte 148 West, 2 km before Montebello. From Ottawa-Hull, Hwy 50 and Rte 148 East to Montebello; 2 km east of the village.

B&B
JARDINS DE RÊVES

Michelle Lachance
1190, Côte du Front
Montebello J0V 1L0
(819) 423-1188
fax (819) 423-2084
www.bbcanada.
com/2878.html
jardins.reves@orbit.qc.ca

B&B	
single	$65
double	$85
triple	$100
quad.	$115
child	$15

Taxes extra VS MC IT

Open year round

Number of rooms	5
rooms with private bath	5

Activities: 🚶 🚴 🐎 🛶 🎿

16. NOTRE-DAME-DE-LA-SALETTE

☼☼☼☼ | F | E | ☒ | P | ⛵ | R.5 | TA

Looking for peace and tranquillity? That is just what our B&B offers. Located by a river surrounded by mountains. Our farm animals graze on our 9-acre park. We rent snowmobiles and V.T.T. 10 min away, «Club Vacances Royal»awaits you with various outdoor activities.

2.5 hours from Montréal, take Hwy 40 West twd Ottawa-Hull; take the Hawksbury Exit to Cumberland. Take the ferry at traffic light then Rte 309 twd Buckingham. After Buckingham, drive 27 km and cross the bridge at left.

B&B
DOMAINE DE LA MAISON
BLANCHE

Doreen Desjardins and
Jean-Georges Burda
C.P. 185
Notre-Dame de la Salette
JOX 2L0
(819) 766-2529
fax (819) 766-2572
www.impactmrk.com/mb

B&B	
single	$55
double	$65
triple	$80

Taxes extra VS

Open : Jan.15 to Dec. 20

Number of rooms	4
shared wc	1
shared bathrooms	2

Activities: 🦌 ⛷ ⚲ 🚶 🛷

---

17. PAPINEAUVILLE, MONTEBELLO

F | E | ⛵ | P | R.5 | TA

Our 150-year-old house will charm you. Peaceful environement. Just 5 km from Chateau Montebello, 65 km from Hull/Ottawa. Home-made jams, outdoor pool. Nearby you will find: golf, horseback riding, rafting, cross-country skiing, ice- fishing. Golf packages available.

Halfway between Montréal and Hull-Ottawa by Rte 148. From Montréal to Papineauville, right on Rue Joseph Lucien Malo at the corner with the Ultramar garage.

B&B
À L'ORÉE DU MOULIN

Suzanne Lacasse
170, Joseph Lucien Malo
Papineauville, Montebello
JOV 1R0
tel/fax (819) 427-8534
www.destinationquebec.
com/ftpdocs/oree/oree.htm

B&B	
single	$45
double	$60
triple	$85
child	$15

VS

Open year round

Number of rooms	4
shared bathrooms	2

Activities: 🏛 ⚲ 🐎 🏃

---

18. PONTIAC, LUSKVILLE

☼☼☼ | F | E | ⊘ | 🐕 | P | R2 | TA

Outaouais Excellence Prize 1997-98. Large one-story log house, impressive stone fireplace. Pine grove, 25 kilometres from Ottawa, near Gatineau Park. On site: old forge; cycling, snowshoeing, canoeing; reflexology, Reiki. Paddle down Ottawa River in a canoe while singing to the rhythm of the oars.

From Hull, Ch de la Montagne N. After 17.5 km, right on Ch. Crégheur, 2nd house on the right. From Ottawa, cross a bridge, take the 148 W., 16.5 km after Aylmer, take Ch. Crégheur, 1.5 km.

B&B
AU CHARME
DE LA MONTAGNE

Thérèse André and
Armand Ducharme
368, chemin Crégheur
Pontiac, Luskville JOX 2G0
(819) 455-9158
fax (819) 455-2706

B&B	
single	$45-55
double	$55-65
triple	$75-85
child	$10

VS

Reduced rates : 10% 3 nights and more
Open year round

Number of rooms	3
shared bathrooms	2
rooms with sink	3

Activities: ⚲ 🚶 🐎 🏃

19. ST-ANDRÉ-AVELLIN ☼☼☼☼ F E P R.5 TA

Hundred-year-old house on the heritage tour in the historic heart of the village. Victorian period furniture. 4 cosy romantic rooms. Solarium. Restaurants, shops, attractions and services close by. The charm and simplicity of days gone by... Friendly welcome.

From Montréal, Rte 148 West or from Ottawa-Hull Hwy 50 and Rte 148 East to Papineauville. Rte 321 North, 12 km. In St-André-Avellin, turn left in front of the church, grey-stone house on the left.

B&B
L'ANCESTRALE

Ginette Louisseize
and Bertin Mailloux
19, rue St-André
St-André-Avellin J0V 1W0
(819) 983-3232
fax (819) 983-3466

B&B	
single	$45
double	$60

Taxes extra

Open year round

Number of rooms	5
rooms in basement	1
rooms with private bath	2
shared wc	2
shared bathrooms	1

Activities: 🦆 🏊 ♨ 🚴 🎿

---

20. VAL-DES-MONTS ☼☼☼ F e 🚫 P 🏊 R2

Country B&B near lakes, forests and wide expanses, 25 kilometres from Hull-Ottawa. Nearby: fish breeding, saphouse, skidoo trails (rentals available) and cross-country skiing, cycling paths, Laflèche cave. On site: bee-keeping, pool, recreation canoes.

From Montréal, Rte 148 W. or from Ottawa/Hull, Hwy 50 twd Montréal, Exit Boul. Lorrain, 10.5 km on Rte 366 N., left on Rue École (at the dépanneur), go for 1 km, right on Prud'homme.

B&B
AUX PETITS OISEAUX

Gaétane and Laurent Rousseau
6, Prud'homme
Val-des-Monts J8N 7C2
(819) 671-2513
www.cyberus.ca/
~rousseau/gite
rousseau@cyberus.ca

B&B	
single	$45
double	$55
child	$10

Open year round

Number of rooms	2
rooms with sink	1
shared bathrooms	2

Activities: ♨ 🎿 🚴 🛷 🎿

---

21. VINOY, CHÉNÉVILLE F E P 🚗 ❌ TA

In a stream-laced wooded valley, retreat where period decor revives old memories while creating new ones and time is measured by the passing of the seasons. A farmyard enchants children, cosy corners invite lovers' whispers, nature's bounty nurtures the camaraderie of old friends. Taste each season at its peak, from strawberry summers to wonderland winters. Outaouais Excellence Prize 1995-96. **Farm stay p 42. See colour photos.**

From Montréal, Rte 148 West. From Ottawa/Hull, Hwy 50, Rte 148 East to Papineauville. North on Rte 321. 12 km from St-André-Avellin, right on montée Vinoy, 5 km.

INN
LES JARDINS DE VINOY

Súzânne Benoît and
André Chagnon
497, Montée Vinoy Ouest
Vinoy, Chénéville J0V 1E0
(819) 428-3774
fax (819) 428-1877
www.jardinsdevinoy.qc.ca
a.chagnon@orbit.qc.ca

	B&B	MAP
single	$50-65	$69-84
double	$65-80	$103-118
triple	$80-95	$137-152
quad.	$95-110	$171-186
child	$15	$24.50

Taxes extra VS MC

Reduced rates: Sep. 6 to June 22
Open year round

Number of rooms	5
rooms with private bath	1
shared wc	1
shared bathrooms	2

Activities: 🏊 ♨ 🚴 🎿 🐕

22. LAC-SIMON, CHÉNÉVILLE

Are you looking for a getaway? Come rejuvenate yourself in the countryside in a picturesque setting offering a stunning panoramic view of the lakes and mountains year-round. Fine sand private beach. Charming and comfortable homes for a pleasant stay. If you wish, a *Table d'hôte* meal plan in our residence is available. **B&B p 231.**

From Montréal, Rte 148 West or from Ottawa Rte 148 East to Papineauville and Rte 321 North. At Chénéville, Rte 315 West for 1.3 km. Turn right onto Chemin Tour-du-Lac and drive 1.5 km, then turn left onto Chemin Marcelais.

COUNTRY HOME
DOMAINE AUX CROCOLLINES

Thérèse Croteau and
Franz Collinge
642, chemin Marcelais
Lac-Simon, Chénéville
J0V 1E0
tel/fax (819) 428-9262

No. houses	5
No. rooms	1-4
No. people	1-8
WEEK-SUMMER	$525-735
WEEK-WINTER	$475-665
W/E-SUMMER	$150-210
DAY-WINTER	$130-190 /2dys

Open year round

Activities:

FARM ACTIVITIES

Farm Stay:

21 LES JARDINS DE VINOY, Vinoy, Chénéville

Country-style Dining*:

23 FERME CAVALIER, St-Sixte

* Registered trademark.

QUÉBEC CITY REGION

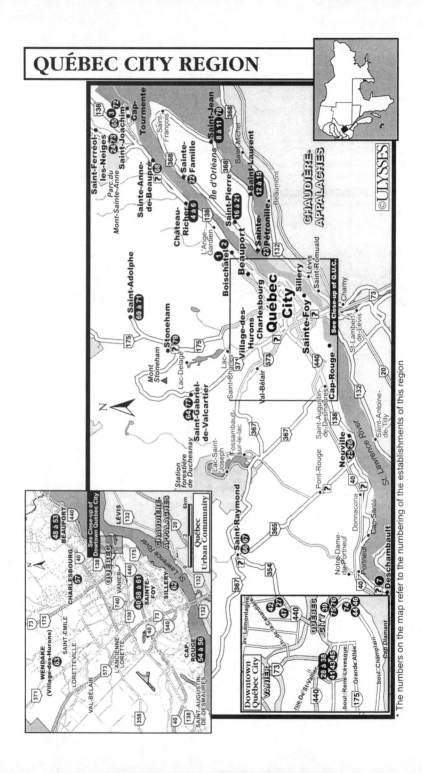

© ULYSSES

* The numbers on the map refer to the numbering of the establishments of this region

1. BOISCHATEL

☀☀☀ F e 🚫 P 🚗 R.2 TA

Large Canadian house in the heart of all the attractions in the Québec City area. 300 metres from the Montmorency falls, opposite Île d'Orléans. 10 minutes from Old Québec City. Fax and Internet service on site. Copious and varied breakfast. Whale excursion reservations. Free parking.

From Montréal, Hwy 20 E. or Hwy 40 E. twd Ste-Anne-de-Beaupré. Left at Côte-de-l'Église, Boischatel Exit, 1.6km after Chutes Montmorency (at 1st traffic lights). Head up the hill, left on Ave. Royale, 0.6km.

B&B
AU GÎTE DE LA CHUTE

Claire and Jean-Guy Bédard
5143, avenue Royale
Boischatel G0A 1H0
tel/fax (418) 822-3789
www.clic.net/~bedard
/5143gite
5143gite@clic.net

B&B	
single	$40-45
double	$55-65
child	$15

Reduced rates: 3 nights or more
Open year round

Number of rooms	5
rooms in basement	3
shared wc	1
shared bathrooms	2

Activities: 🐚 🏃 ⛴ 🚴 🎿

2. BOISCHATEL

☀☀ F e 🚗 P R2

Ten minutes from Quebec City, "Le Refuge du Voyageur" offers an exceptional view of the city, the St. Lawrence River, the Pont de l'Île bridge and Île d'Orléans. Rustic decor, spacious rooms with balcony and a family-size suite with kitchenette.

From Québec City, Hwy Dufferin-Montmorency East, Boischatel Exit. Côte de l'église, to Ave. Royale. One minute's drive, on your right.

B&B
LE REFUGE DU VOYAGEUR

Raynald Vézina
5516, avenue Royale
Boischatel G0A 1H0
(418) 822-2589

B&B	
single	$50
double	$60
triple	$75
quad.	$90
child	$0-10

Reduced rates: Nov. 1 to June 1
Open year round

Number of rooms	2
rooms with private bath	2

Activities: 🏛 🐚 🚴 🎿 🏃

3. CAP-TOURMENTE, MONT-STE-ANNE

☀☀☀ F E 🚫 🐕 P 🛶 R1 TA

In the heart of Cap-Tourmente, 12 min from Mont Ste-Anne (view of the slopes), house with 5 rooms with private bathrooms. Lodging also in the hosts' house (right next to the B&B) where breakfast is served. On site: outdoor pool, hiking or cross-country skiing to the falls and the sugar shack. **Country home p 261.**

From Québec City, Henri IV Hwy N., twd 40 E., Ste-Anne-de-Beaupré, Rte 138 E., twd St-Joachim, Cap-Tourmente.

B&B
GÎTE DE L'OIE DES NEIGES

Gisèle Perron
390, ch. du Cap Tourmente
St-Joachim G0A 3X0
(418) 827-5153
tel/fax (418) 827-2246
www.bbcanada.com/
2690.html
melifre@total.net

B&B	
single	$45
double	$75
triple	$100
quad.	$125
child	$15

VS

Open year round

Number of rooms	5
rooms with private bath	5

Activities: 🛶 🏃 🚶 🎿 🏃

4. CHÂTEAU-RICHER

The warm welcome of a small inn, an ancestral house restored to its original style, only 15 minutes from the centre of Québec City, facing Île d'Orléans, and 20 minutes from Mont-Ste-Anne. Hablamos español.

Rte 138 East Twd Ste-Anne-de-Beaupré, after the Île d'Orléans bridge, left on Rte du Petit-Pré, right on Ave. Royale, 9km after Chutes Montmorency.

INN
AUBERGE DU PETIT PRÉ

Ginette Dion and Yvon Boyer
7126, avenue Royale
Château-Richer G0A 1N0
(418) 824-3852
fax (418) 824-3098

B&B	
single	$50-60
double	$60-70
triple	$85
quad.	$100
child	$15

Taxes extra VS MC AM IT

Open year round

Number of rooms	4
shared wc	1
shared bathrooms	2

Activities: 🏛 ⚲ 🚴 ⛵ ⛷

---

5. CHÂTEAU-RICHER

★★★ F E 🚫 P ✖ TA

Between Mont Ste-Anne and Québec City, in the heart of the Beaupré region, treat yourself to an incomparable stay at our home, along with delicious meals from the Baker restaurant. You will find all the charm of a country home. Rooms in the Inn or the pavilion.

East of Québec City, Rte 138 East. To Ste-Anne-de-Beaupré. 18.5km from the Montmorency falls. Watch for "Baker" on the roof of the restaurant.

INN
BAKER

Gaston Cloutier
8790, avenue Royale
Château-Richer G0A 1N0
(418) 824-4478
(418) 824-4852
fax (418) 824-4412
www.auberge-baker.qc.ca
gcloutier@auberge-baker.qc.ca

	B&B	MAP
single	$59-85	$90-115
double	$65-89	$124-150
triple	$80-104	$170-195
quad.	$95-120	$215-245
child	$10	$32

Taxes extra VS MC AM ER IT

Reduced rates: Apr. 6 to June 23 and Oct. 11to Dec. 22
Open year round

Number of rooms	6
rooms with sink	4
rooms with private bath	2
shared bathrooms	2

Activities: 🚣 ⚲ 🏂 🏃

---

6. CHÂTEAU-RICHER

☀☀☀ F E P ✖ TA

Fifteen minutes from Old Québec City and 10 minutes from Mont-Ste-Anne, stay in a magnificent Victorian house (1868). Hearty home-made breakfast with exceptional view of the river and Île d'Orléans. Large lounge with fireplace. Exquisite, cosy, traditionally furnished rooms. Dinner by reservation. Delicious French cuisine. We speak German.

From Québec City, Rte 138 East. Drive 15km past the Île d'Orléans bridge. In Château-Richer, left at the traffic lights on Rue Dick, right on Ave. Royale, left on Côte Ste-Achillée, drive 100 feet, left on Rue Pichette.

INN
LE PETIT SÉJOUR

Pascal Steffan,
Christiane and Anne-Marie
394, Pichette
Château-Richer G0A 1N0
(418) 824-3654
fax (418) 824-9356
www.quebecweb.com
/petitsejour
petitsejour@globetrotter.net

	B&B	MAP
single	$50-70	$80-100
double	$60-85	$120-145
triple	$85-100	$175-190
quad.	$100-115	$220-235

Taxes extra VS MC

Reduced rates: 5% 3 nights and more
Open year round

Number of rooms	5
rooms with private bath	1
shared wc	1
shared bathrooms	2

Activities: 🏛 🚣 ⚲ 🏃 🏂

7. DESCHAMBAULT ★★ F E P 🛶 ⊠ R4 TA

With the St. Lawrence, the falls and Rivière Belisle at its feet, this large hundred-year-old Victorian, nicknamed "the little château", will transport you back in time with flowers, lace and a decor from days gone by. Evening meal of creative and meticulously prepared meals. Snowmobiling, sleigh rides, cross-country skiing, ice-fishing. **See colour photos.**

From Montréal or Québec City, Hwy 40, Exit 254, drive 1.6km to the river. Turn left onto Rte 138 (Chemin du Roy), drive 2km. Turn left at the Inn "Chemin du Roy" sign, Rue St-Laurent.

INN
AUBERGE CHEMIN DU ROY

Francine Bouthat and
Gilles Laberge
106, rue St-Laurent
Deschambault G0A 1S0
(418) 286-6958
toll free 1-800-933-7040

	B&B	MAP
single	$64-89	$89-114
double	$79-104	$129-154
triple	$94-119	$169-194
quad.	$129	$229
child	$10	$20-30

Taxes extra VS MC

Open year round

Number of rooms	8
rooms with private bath	8

Activities: 🏛 ⚓ 🧍 🚲 🎿

8. ÎLE D'ORLÉANS, ST-JEAN ☀☀☀ F e P R.1 TA

We are 25 minutes from Québec City, in an ancestral home very close to the river, and near museums, theatres, handicraft boutiques, art galleries, and restaurants. Friendly atmosphere and hearty breakfast. We will do everything we can to make your stay a pleasant one. Welcome to Île d'Orléans.

From Québec City, Rte 440 East twd Ste-Anne-de-Beaupré, Île d'Orléans Exit. At the traffic lights, go straight ahead for 20km. House on the right, corner of Chemin du Quai.

B&B
GÎTE DU QUAI

Rita and Grégoire Roux
1686, chemin Royal
Saint-Jean, Île d'Orléans
G0A 3W0
(418) 829-2278

B&B	
single	$40
double	$45-50
triple	$70
quad.	$90
child	$10-15

Reduced rates: May 1 to June 1, Oct.1 to Oct. 31
Open: May 1 to Oct. 31

Number of rooms	3
shared bathrooms	2

Activities: 🏛 🦆 ⚓ 🧍 🚲

9. ÎLE D'ORLÉANS, ST-JEAN ☀☀☀ F E ⊠ P R.5 TA

Ancestral home, where calm and tranquillity are the most important things. View of the river. Bedrooms with natural wood and sinks. Twenty minutes from Québec City. Close to first seigneury on Île d'Orléans. A gem of a find!

From Québec City, Rte 440 East twd Ste-Anne-de-Beaupré, Exit Île d'Orléans. At the traffic lights, straight on for 17.7km. Turn left on first street after the Manoir Mauvide de Genest, at the top of the hill, 1st green and white house.

B&B
LA MAISON SUR LA CÔTE

Hélène and Pierre Morissette
1477, chemin Royal
St-Jean, Île d'Orléans
G0A 3W0
(418) 829-2971
fax (418) 829-0991

B&B	
single	$50
double	$55
triple	$75

MC

Open: Apr. 1 to Oct. 31

Number of rooms	4
rooms with sink	4
shared bathrooms	2

Activities: 🏛 🦆 🛶 ⚓ 🚲

10. ÎLE D'ORLÉANS, ST-JEAN ☀☀☀☀☀ F E P 🚭 R8 TA

Located 25 min from old Quebec City, a new house 400 m from the road, near the river, offers quiet and comfort: rooms with queen-size bed and balcony with St. Lawrence River view (1 room with 2 single beds), 2 living rooms and a dining room. Full breakfasts made up of homemade goods. Looking forward to seeing you soon.

From Québec City, Hwy 40 or 440 East twd Ste-Anne-de-Beaupré, Île d'Orléans Exit. At traffic lights, straight ahead to St-Laurent and St-Jean. 2.4km past the St-Jean church.

B&B
LE GIRON DE L'ISLE

Lucie and Gérard Lambert
120, chemin des Lièges
St-Jean, Île d'Orléans
G0A 3W0
(418) 829-0985
toll free 1-888-280-6636
fax (418) 829-1059
giron@iname.com

B&B	
single	$59-69-85
double	$69-79-95
triple	$99-109-125
quad.	$119-129-145
child	$20

VS MC

Reduced rates: Oct. 15 to Dec. 15 and from Jan. 15 to Apr. 30
Open year round
with reservations Oct. 15 to Apr. 30

Number of rooms	3
shared bathrooms	3

Activities: 🏛 👤 🚲 ⛷ 🐎

---

11. ÎLE D'ORLÉANS, ST-JEAN ☀☀☀ F E P 🚭 🐕 R.5 TA

If you're looking for a peaceful and comfortable place, our 18th-century replica of an old farm house, situated on a cliff, is awaiting you. Your hosts: Yolande, Claude and Valentine the cat.

From Québec City, Rte 138 East twd Ste-Anne-de-Beaupré, Île d'Orléans Exit. After the bridge straight ahead for 17.5km. At the B&B sign, turn left, the house is on your right on the cliff.

B&B
LE MAS DE L'ISLE

Yolande and Claude Dumesnil
1155, chemin Royal
St-Jean, Île d'Orléans
G0A 3W0
tel/fax (418) 829-1213
www.bbcanada.com/382.html
sorciere@total.net

B&B	
single	$55
double	$60
triple	$90
quad.	$115
child	$20

VS

Reduced rates: $10 discount/room, Oct. 1 to Apr. 30
Open year round

Number of rooms	3
shared bathrooms	2

Activities: 🏛 🛥 🚤 👤 🚲

---

12. ÎLE D'ORLÉANS, ST-LAURENT ☀☀☀ F E P 🚭 R.5

By the shores of the St. Lawrence River on a vast property far from the road, surrounded by trees and flowers, a large, peaceful house invites rest. All rooms have a view of the river. Complete breakfast. Your hosts' desire: that you feel at home at "Aux Capucines" and that you experience the beauty of Île d'Orléans.

From Québec City, Hwy 40 East twd Ste-Anne-de-Beaupré, Exit Île d'Orléans. After the bridge at the traffic lights, straight for 12km. House on river side.

B&B
AUX CAPUCINES
SUR LE BORD DE L'EAU

Mariette and
Jean-Marc Bouffard
625, chemin Royal
St-Laurent de l'Île d'Orléans
G0A 3Z0
(418) 829-3017
www.bbcanada.com/2689.html
jmmb@globetrotter.net

B&B	
single	$55-60
double	$60-65

Open year round

Number of rooms	3
shared bathrooms	1

Activities: 🦆 🛥 👤 🚶 🚲

13. ÎLE D'ORLÉANS, ST-LAURENT

☀☀☀ F e ⊘ P R.5 TA

The St. Lawrence at your feet! Between the rhythm of the waves breaking on the beach and the silent force of the rising tide, we offer an interlude of peace and rest. Air conditioned. Appetizing breakfast, welcome worthy of our most honoured traditions... Off-season rates for 2 nights or more.

From Québec City, Hwy 440 East twd Ste-Anne-de-Beaupré, Île d'Orléans Exit. After the bridge, at the traffic lights, go straight for 11km. House on the right.

B&B
GÎTE «EAU VIVE»

Micheline and Michel Turgeon
909, chemin Royal
St-Laurent de l'Île d'Orléans
G0A 3Z0
(418) 829-3270
michelineturgeon@hotmail.com

B&B	
single	$55-65
double	$55-65
triple	$85
child	$15

Reduced rates: 2 nights or more Nov. 1 to Apr. 30
Open: Jan. 1 to Nov. 30

Number of rooms	3
rooms with private bath	1
shared bathrooms	1

Activities: 🦆 ⛴ 🚶 🚲 🐎

14. ÎLE D'ORLÉANS, ST-LAURENT

☀☀☀☀ F e P 🚗 〰 R.1 TA

Come drop anchor at our hundred-year-old house, right in the heart of town, on the river a few steps away from the marina. The horizon is constantly changing and the landscape transforms with the rhythm of the tide. Library with 2,500 books, reading room, heated pool. Excusions on the St.Lawrence River. Equiped for seafood cooking.

From Québec City, Hwy 40 E. or 440 E. twd Ste-Anne-de-Beaupré, Exit 325 Île d'Orléans. After the bridge, at the lights, go straight for 8km. About 0.2km after the church, house on the riverside.

B&B
LA CHAUMIÈRE DU NOTAIRE

June and Jacques Bouffard
1449, chemin Royal
St-Laurent, Île d'Orléans
G0A 3Z0
(418) 828-2180
fax (418) 653-1023

B&B	
single	$80-90
double	$80-90
child	$10

Open: May 1 to Oct. 31

Number of rooms	2
rooms with private bath	2

Activities: ⛴ 🏄 🚶 🎿 🏃

15. ÎLE D'ORLÉANS, ST-LAURENT

✎ F E ⊘ 🚗 P 〰 R2 TA

Our lovely Victorian home, which has exquisite air-conditioned bedrooms, will delight you. Come and enjoy a royal breakfast while admiring the majestic St. Lawrence River. The beauty of our landscaped property is only equalled by the melody of the birds. You will be surprised how good it feels to let yourself be pampered. At L'Oasis de Rêves, your dreams come true.

From Québec City, Hwy 40 East to Ste-Anne-de-Beaupré, Île d'Orléans exit. At the traffic light, continue straight ahead. Drive 5km past St-Laurent church.

B&B
L'OASIS DE RÊVES

Lyette Chedore and Jean Tardif
179, chemin Royal
St-Laurent de l'île d'Orléans
G0A 3Z0
(418) 829-3473
(418) 570-0634
fax (418) 829-0053

B&B	
single	$80
double	$90
triple	$105
child	$15

Open: May 1 to Oct. 31

Number of rooms	2
rooms with private bath	2
shared bathrooms	1

Activities: 🏛 🦆 ⛴ 🚶 🚲

16. ÎLE D'ORLÉANS, ST-PIERRE

★★ F E P ⊠ R2 TA

Situated next door to the oldest church in Québec, Auberge Le Vieux Presbytère is a beautiful, large ancestral home. Speciality restaurant: game and seafood. The 150,000-ft property has American buffalo, wapitis (large deer) and ostriches. Breathtaking view. Only 15min from Québec City. Bike rental on site.

From Québec City, Hwy Dufferin-Montmorency, Île d'Orléans exit. Left at the light. At the town centre of Saint-Pierre, left between the two churches.

INN
AUBERGE LE VIEUX PRESBYTÈRE

Louise Lapointe and
Hughes L'Heureux
1247, Mgr. D'Esgly
Saint-Pierre, Île d'Orléans
G0A 4E0
(418) 828-9723
toll free 1-888-828-9723
fax (418) 828-2189
www.presbytere.com

	B&B	MAP
single	$50-90	$70-105
double	$60-100	$110-145
triple	$80-115	$159-190
quad.	$95-130	$204-235
child	$10-15	---

Taxes extra VS MC AM ER IT

Open year round

Number of rooms	8
rooms with private bath	6
shared wc	2
shared bathrooms	1

Activities:

17. ÎLE D'ORLÉANS, ST-PIERRE

☀☀☀ F e P R1 TA

Located near the Pont de l'Île, our B&B is only 10 min east of Québec City, 5 min from the Chutes Montmorency, and 20 min from Ste-Anne-de-Beaupré. With us, comfort, spotlessness, intimacy and generous breakfasts are guaranteed! Bike and motorcycle storage. One room with private entrance. "Crépuscule" is also the explosion of brilliant fall colours. Welcome.

From Québec City, Hwy 40 East or 440 East, twd Ste-Anne-de-Beaupré, Exit 325 Île d'Orléans. At the traffic lights at top of the hill, straight for about 1km. B&B on left.

B&B
CRÉPUSCULE

Louise Hamel
863, rue Prévost
St-Pierre-de-l'Île, Île d'Orléans
G0A 4E0
(418) 828-9425
louise.hamel3@sympatico.ca

B&B	
single	$50
double	$60
triple	$75
quad.	$90
child	$10

Open year round

Number of rooms	3
rooms with private bath	3

Activities:

18. ÎLE D'ORLÉANS, ST-PIERRE

☀☀☀☀ F e ⊘ 🐕 P R1

Only 5min from the island's bridge and 15min from Vieux-Québec, Domaine Steinbach, a 300-year-old heritage house, offers two old-style rooms with exposed beams and stone walls. You will be able to visit our interpretation centre and have some free samples. Incredible view of the St. Lawrence River, the Beaupré coast, as well as the orchards and small farm animals. What great memories are made of!

Drive about 5km after crossing the island's bridge.

B&B
DOMAINE STEINBACH

Claire and Philippe Steinbach
2205 Chemin Royal
Saint-Pierre de l'Île d'Orléans
G0A 4E0
(418) 828-0000
fax (418) 828-0777
domstein@total.net

B&B	
single	$60
double	$65-75
triple	$90-100
child	$25

Taxes extra VS MC IT

Open: May 1 to Oct. 31

Number of rooms	2
shared bathrooms	1

Activities:

19. ÎLE D'ORLÉANS, ST-PIERRE

☀☀☀☀ F e ⊘ P R1 TA

Welcome to the B&B "Bel Horizon", the gateway to Île d'Orléans, only 15 min from Québec City. Comfort, intimacy, complete breakfast. View of the river, facing Chutes Mont-morency. 5 rooms (12 people): 2 on ground-floor, 3 on first floor, family suite, private bathroom. Ideal for family and groups. Shared bathrooms for couples (if not in a group). Reserve now!

At entrance to Québec City, Rte 440 or Hwy 40 East twd Ste-Anne-de-Beaupré. Drive about 35km, Exit 325 Île d'Orléans. At the top of the hill, at the lights, turn right, 1km.

B&B
GÎTE «BEL HORIZON»

Yvette and Paul-Émile Vézina
402, chemin Royal
St-Pierre, Île d'Orléans
G0A 4E0
(418) 828-9207
fax (418) 828-2618
quebecweb.com
/gpq/belhorizon

B&B	
single	$50-60
double	$55-70
triple	$80
quad.	$90-110
child	$15

Reduced rates: Feb. 1 to May 31
10% 4 nights and more
5% 4 rooms
Open: Feb. 1 to Nov. 1

Number of rooms	5
rooms with private bath	3
shared bathrooms	1

Activities: 🏛 🛶 ⚓ 🎿 🚴

20. ÎLE D'ORLÉANS, ST-PIERRE

☀☀☀☀ F E 🐕 🚗 P R.5

Seated on one of most beautiful sites on Île d'Orléans, nestled in a vineyard, our ancestral home will greet you with history. A visit of the vineyard and free sampling of our products are offered. Three renovated rooms combining com-fort and intimacy. The breakfasts are memorable!

Located at the entrance to Île d'Orléans, 2km from the traffic light to the left, just before the village of Saint-Pierre.

B&B
LA MAISON DU VIGNOBLE

Lise Roy
1071, chemin Royal
St-Pierre-de-l'Île d'Orléans
G0A 4E0
(418) 828-9562

B&B	
single	$45-60
double	$60-80
triple	$75-95
quad.	$110
child	$15

VS MC

Open year round

Number of rooms	3
rooms with private bath	1
shared bathrooms	2

Activities: 🛶 🎿 🚴 🎿 🐎

21. ÎLE D'ORLÉANS, ST-PIERRE

☀☀☀ F E P ✕ TA

A house with over 200 years of history... is cosy comfort where antique furniture and dried flowers encourage calm and relaxation. Come share authentic and refined country cooking in the intimacy of the dining room. Relax by the fire in the living room or in the garden near the farmyard.

From Québec City, Hwy 40 or 440 East twd Ste-Anne-de-Beaupré, Île d'Orléans Exit. Left at the traffic light. Drive 3km.

INN
L'AUBERGE SUR LES PENDANTS

Chantale Vigneault and
Jean-Christophe L'Allier
1463, chemin Royal
St-Pierre, Île d'Orléans
G0A 4E0
(418) 828-1139

	B&B	MAP
single	$52	$76
double	$62	$110
triple	$77	$149
quad.	$92	$188
child	$10	$18

Taxes extra VS MC IT AM

Open year round

Number of rooms	5
shared bathroom	2

Activities: 🛶 🎿 🚴 ⚓ 🎿

22. ÎLE D'ORLÉANS, STE-FAMILLE

☀☀☀☀ F E 🚗 P 🐕 R.03 TA

The wind has carried us to all the continents and we've brought back the scents, great life experiences, a different way of doing things and the desire to share. Hundred-year-old house, adjoining shop, view of the river and the Laurentians, walking path, cycling, X-country skiing, snowshoeing, picnic baskets. We speak Japanese, French and English.

From Québec City, Rte 440 E. twd Ste-Anne-de-Beaupré, Île d'Orléans Exit. Left at the lights, straight for 13km.

B&B
AU TOIT BLEU

Loulou and Iris Germain
3879, chemin Royal
Ste-Famille, Île d'Orléans
G0A 3P0
(418) 829-1078
fax (418) 829-3052
toitbleu@total.net

B&B	
single	$40-60
double	$55-65
triple	$80
quad.	$95
child	$10

VS AM

Reduced rates: 10% 3 nights and more, Nov. 1 to May 1, except Christmas Holiday
Open year round

Number of rooms	3
shared bathroom	2

Activities: 🚴 🛶 ⛷ 🎿 🐎

23. ÎLE D'ORLÉANS, STE-PÉTRONILLE

☀☀☀ F E P ♿ R.5

Enchanting setting on magical Île d'Orléans. Come discover the art of living in harmony with the past in our home, amidst a century and a half of history. The magnificent view of the majestic St. Lawrence and a visit to the Chutes Montmorency will leave you with unforgettable memories. To top it all off, we offer generous breakfasts and hospitality worthy of the finest establishments; a wonderful stay awaits you.

From Québec City, Rte 138 and Hwy 40 or 440 twd St-Anne-de-Beaupré, Île d'Orléans Exit. Right at the lights after the bridge, 3.5km.

B&B
LE 91 DU BOUT DE L'ÎLE

Jeanne Trottier
91, chemin Royal,
ch. du Bout de l'Île
Ste-Pétronille, Île d'Orléans
G0A 4C0
(418) 828-2678

B&B	
single	$45-50
double	$55-60
triple	$75-80

Reduced rates: Nov. 1 to Apr. 1
Open year round

Number of rooms	4
rooms with sink	2
shared bathrooms	2

Activities: 🏛 ⚲ 🍴 🎿 ⛷

24. MONT-STE-ANNE, ST-FERRÉOL

☀☀☀ F E 🚭 P 🚗 R1 TA

5 min from Mt Ste-Anne, 30 min from Québec City, discover the calm and comfort of soundproof rooms, twin or queen-size beds, sinks, suites, living room with fireplace. Magnificent scenic view. Nearby: Sept Chutes (falls), Grand Canyon, Cap Tourmente, skiing, cycling, golf, walking trails, snowmobiling, horseback riding, dogsledding. Ski packages.

From Québec City, Rte 138 East., 40km. At Beaupré, to Mont-Ste-Anne, Rte 360, 10km. From Baie-St-Paul, Rte 138 W., 30km, Rte 360 to St-Ferréol. After the 7 Chutes, drive 3km.

B&B
LES AROLLES

Claire Boutet and Gilles Dumas
3489, av. Royale, route 360
St-Ferréol-les-Neiges
G0A 3R0
tel/fax (418) 826-2136
quebecweb.com/gpq/arolles
javert@megaquebec.com

B&B	
single	$50-60
double	$65-80
child	$0-15

VS MC

Open year round

Number of rooms	5
rooms with sink	3
rooms with private bath	1
shared bathrooms	2

Activities: 🏃 🚶 🚴 🎿 ⛷

25. NEUVILLE

F e P R2 TA

All the charm of the country 15 minutes from Québec City. View of the St .Lawrence, the perfect spot. Large property, woods, terrace with inground pool. Generous breakfast served on the terrace or in the dining room. Living room with TV, pool room. Bikes available. Large parking lot.

From Montréal, Hwy 40 East, Exit 281 Neuville, Rte 138 East, for 6km. From Québec City, Hwy 40 West, Exit 298, Rte 138 West, 10.4km.

B&B
LE GÎTE DE NEUVILLE

Louise Côté and
Ernest Germain
173, Route 138
Neuville G0A 2R0
(418) 876-3779
(418) 876-3060
fax (418) 876-3780
legitedeneuville@hotmail.com

B&B	
single	$40
double	$55
child	$15

VS IT

Open year round

Number of rooms	3
shared wc	2
shared bathrooms	1

Activities: 🐚 ⛵ 🎿 🚲 🛥

26. NEUVILLE

☀☀☀ F E P R1 TA

15 min from Québec City, in one of the prettiest villages in Québec, discover many ancestral houses. Stunning view of the St. Lawrence. Relax on the terrace, in the sunroom or near the fireplace. Air conditioned. Nearby: marina, antiques, theatre and dogsledding. Guides tours of the village and church. Bikes available.

From Montréal or Québec City, Hwy 40, Exit 285, to Neuville (Route 138), drive 3km.

B&B
MAISON DUBUC

Madeleine and Antoine Dubuc
421, rue des Érables
Neuville G0A 2R0
tel/fax (418) 876-2573
www.bbcanada.
com/2687.html

B&B	
single	$40
double	$55
child	$10

Open: Dec. 1 to Mar. 31,
May 1 to Oct. 31

Number of rooms	2
shared bathroom	1

Activities: 🏛 🛥 🎿 🚲 🛥

27. QUÉBEC

F E 🚭 ♿ 🏊 P R.1 TA

Located 3min from Vieux-Québec and the convention centre, Abat-Jour B&B will fill your stay with unforgettable pleasant memories. Travel back in time and revel in the culture and history of Québec. Go for a bike ride on the Corridor de Cheminots, explore Domaine Maizeret, Parc Montmorency and much more. Cordial reception and personalized service. Delicious breakfasts. See you soon!

Hwy 20, Pierre-Laporte bridge or Hwy 40 to Ste-Anne-de-Beaupré, Exit 316. At the 1st stop sign, take Rue Chamfleury straight to the 8th stop sign, left De Fondville drive 700 m.

B&B
ABAT-JOUR B&B

Nadia El-Ghandouri
2064, De Fondville
Québec G1J 1X6
(418) 666-6654
(418) 265-4853
fax (418) 666-8400
quebecweb.com/abatjour

B&B	
single	$50
double	$60
triple	$75
quad.	$90
suite	$110-140
child	$10

Open year round

Number of rooms	3
suite with private bath	1
rooms with sink	3
shared wc	1
shared bathrooms	1

Activities: 🏛 🛥 🎿 🚲 🎿

28. QUÉBEC

※※※ F E 🚳 🐕 R.1 TA

Vacation at L'Heure Douce in old Québec City, close to the convention centre and all services. Ancestral house with comfortable rooms. Dining room reserved for guests. Panoramic view and balcony where you'll relax with a drink and watch the sun go down. Québécois, continental and vegetarian breakfast. We'll give you some good suggestions.

Hwy 20, Pierre-Laporte bridge, Boul. Laurier Exit, Rue Cartier, left, right on Chemin Ste-Foy, left on St-Augustin to Richelieu. Hwy 40, Boul. Charest, twd dowtown. Right on Dorchester, drive up côte d'Abraham, right on Richelieu.

B&B
ACCUEIL B&B L'HEURE DOUCE

Diane Dumont
704, Richelieu
Québec G1R 1K7
tel/fax (418) 649-1935
www.bbcanada.
com/2695.html
jacques.gagne1@sympatico.ca

B&B	
single	$50-55
double	$65-70
triple	$75-85
quad.	$100-110
child	$15

Taxes extra VS

Open year round

Number of rooms	3
shared bathroom	2

Activities: 🏛 ⚓ 🚴 🎿 🐎

29. QUÉBEC

※※※ F e P 🚳 R.8

Cosy house built in 1930, near the Musée du Québec; you'll admire the river and greenery of the Plains of Abraham as you walk towards the old city. Exquisite breakfast, served in the flowery garden or the dining room. We'll chat about art and the history of our beautiful city. Free parking.

Hwy 20, Pierre-Laporte bridge, Boul. Laurier to downtown. 7.9km from the bridge, turn on Avenue Murray. From Hwy 40, Avenue St-Sacrement South, left on Chemin St-Louis, drive 1.3km..

B&B
À LA CAMPAGNE EN VILLE

Marie Archambault
1160, avenue Murray
Québec G1S 3B6
(418) 683-6638

B&B	
single	$55
double	$65
child	$15

Reduced rates: 4 nights or more
Open year round

Number of rooms	2
shared wc	1
shared bathrooms	1

Activities: 🏛 ⚓ 🚶 🚴 🏃

30. QUÉBEC

※※※ F E 🚳 P R.5

Discover enchantment in this beautiful, turn-of-the-century Tudor-style home, near national parks and Vieux-Québec. Top-quality lodging under a gabled roof. Private parking, sheltered in winter months. Office and internet computer facilities upon request. Discrete, personal attention to travellers' needs.

From Montréal, Hwy 20 East to Québec City. After the Pierre-Laporte bridge, follow Boul. Laurier to old Québec. Turn left onto Ave. Moncton at the Plains of Abraham.

B&B
À LA MAISON TUDOR

J. Cecil Kilfoil
1037, avenue Moncton
Québec (QC) G1S 2Y9
(418) 686-1033
fax (418) 686-6066
www.clic.net/~ckilfoil
ckilfoil@clic.net

B&B	
single	$65-85
double	$75-85
triple	$95-105
child	$15

Taxes extra VS MC ER

Reduced rates: Oct. 15 to Dec18
and Jan. 5 to June 22
Open year round

Number of rooms	2
shared wc	1
shared bathrooms	1

Activities: 🏛 🚶 🚴 🎿 🏃

31. QUÉBEC

✹✹✹✹ F E 🚫 R.5

Nearly 100-years old, solarium overflowing with plants and a panoramic view of the Laurentians. Situated in a safe residential area of town, it's the ideal place for a peaceful stay. A short stroll away from the heart of Vieux-Québec, the convention centre, the Musée du Québec, the Plains of Abraham and Cartier, Gand-Allée and Saint-Jean streets. Breakfast served in the dining room.

Hwy 20 P. Laporte bridge, exit Blvd Laurier, 9km, left on Cartier, right on Ste Foy-St-Jean, right on Turnbull, right on Lockweel at the stop sign.

B&B
À L'ÉTOILE DE ROSIE

Marie-Denise Saint-Gelais
66, rue Lockwell
Québec G1R 1V7
(418) 648-1044
fax (418) 648-0184
www.bbcanada.com/2165.html
etoilerosie@sympatico.ca

B&B	
single	$75-80
double	$75-80
child	$15

Reduced rates: Nov.1 to Dec.15, Feb.15 to Mar.30
Open year round

Number of rooms	3
shared bathrooms	1

Activities: 🏛 🚴 🛶 🎿 🐎

32. QUÉBEC

✹✹✹ F E 🚫 R1 TA

Situated in Vieux-Québec, a stone's throw from the Plains of Abraham, le Musée du Québec, fine dining and terrace-cafés, Au 2e Balcon is an English-style B&B dating from 1926. Spacious and comfortable rooms await, as do hearty breakfasts. Parking available. **Country Home p 263, no 78.**

From Hwy 20, Pierre-Laporte bridge, Blvd Laurier exit, left on Rue Cartier, left again on the 2nd street. Or Hwy 40, Avenue St-Sacrement South, left on Chemin St-Louis, left on Rue Cartier and left on the 2nd street.

B&B
AU 2ᵉ BALCON

Anik Roy and Chantal Javaux
204, Aberdeen
Québec G1R 2C8
(418) 649-0141
fax (418) 529-6227
www.troisbalcons.qc.ca
chantaljavaux@sympatico.ca

B&B	
single	$55-60
double	$70
triple	$90-100
quad.	$120
child	$15

Taxes extra VS MC

Open year round

Number of rooms	2
shared bathrooms	1

Activities: 🏛 🎿 🚴 🎿 🏃

33. QUÉBEC

✹✹✹ F E 🐕 R.5 TA

At the Croissant de Lune in old Québec, you will be enchanted by our 19th-century home with two cosy bedrooms, varied and delicious breakfasts, warm hospitality and all the tourist information you may need. Reservations and informations via e-mail all year long, and by phone from July 1st 2000.

Hwy 20, pont Pierre-Laporte (bridge), Boul. Laurier, left Rue Cartier, right on Chemin Ste-Foy, right on Rue des Zouaves, right on St-Gabriel.

B&B
AU CROISSANT DE LUNE

Louise St-Laurent and
René Gilbert
594, rue St-Gabriel
Québec G1R 1W3
(418) 522-6366
www.bbcanada.com/2396.html
aucroissantdelune@hotmail.com

B&B	
single	$60
double	$70

VS

Open year round

Number of rooms	2
shared bathrooms	1

Activities: 🏛 🦪 🛶 🚴 🎿

34. QUÉBEC

✎ F 🐕 🚗 P R.25

In the heart of the marvellous Montcalm district, near the Plains of Abraham, a stone's throw from Rue Cartier, with restaurants, cafés and shops, "Au Maric" offers you a warm welcome. Quiet and comfortable rooms. Lavish breakfast with music.

Hwy 20, Pierre-Laporte bridge, Boul. Laurier twd downtown. Turn left on Ave. Des érables, after crossing Chemin Ste-Foy or Hwy 40, right on l'Aqueduc.

B&B
AU MARIC

Micheline Rioux
470, des Franciscains
Québec G1S 2R1
(418) 688-9341

B&B	
single	$55
double	$65
triple	$80

Open: May 1 to Oct. 31

Number of rooms	2
shared bathrooms	1

Activities: 🏛 🏊 🏄 🕯 🚲

35. QUÉBEC

☀☀☀☀ F E P 🚗 🚭 🐕 R1 TA

In downtown Québec City, a neighbourhood with European charm, restaurants, cafés and boutiques. Located just 2 min from the Plains of Abraham and the Museum of Québec. Old Québec City is a 10-min walk away. Gourmet breakfast. **Country Home p 263, no 78. See colour photos.**

Hwy 20, Pierre-Laporte bridge, Boul. Laurier to downtown (Grande-Allée). 8.7km after the bridge, turn on Cartier, then left on Saunders. Or Hwy 40, Boul. Charest East, right on St-Sacrement South, left on Chemin Ste-Foy, right on Rue Cartier, right on Saunders.

B&B
AUX TROIS BALCONS

Chantal Javaux and
Paul Simard
130, Saunders
Québec G1R 2E3
(418) 525-5611
fax (418) 529-6227
www.troisbalcons.qc.ca
chantaljavaux@sympatico.ca

B&B	
single	$55-65
double	$70-90
triple	$85-100
quad.	$110
child	$10

Taxes extra VS MC

Reduced rates: 7 consecutives nights for the price of 6
Open year round

Number of rooms	4
rooms with private bath	3
shared bathrooms	1

Activities: 🏛 🏊 🚲 🎿 🏃

36. QUÉBEC

☀☀☀ F E 🚭 P 🚗 R.1 TA

Stone house dating from 1830, 200 m from the walls of the old city and the convention centre (Centre des Congrès). Lively family atmosphere full of surprises. Garden in summer, a crackling fire in winter, old-fashioned character, cosy, indoor greenery, excellent music and copious breakfasts complete with a serving of helpful tourist advice. Parking.

Hwy 40, Charest E., twd downtown, right on Dorchester, drive-up côte d'Abraham, right on Richelieu. Or Hwy 20, pont Pierre-Laporte, Boul. Laurier, left on Cartier, right on Ste-Foy, left on St-Augustin, left on Richelieu

B&B
B&B À L'AUGUSTINE

Caroline Collet and
Kamal Elhaji
775, Richelieu
Québec G1R 1K8
tel/fax (418) 648-1072
www.oricom.ca/augustine/
bb.html
carocol@oricom.ca

B&B	
single	$50
double	$65
triple	$85
child	$15

Reduced rates: Nov. 1 to Jan. 31 and Feb. 20 to Apr. 30
Open year round

Number of rooms	3
shared bathroom	2

Activities: 🏛 🏊 🚲 🛷 🎿

37. QUÉBEC

✎ F E R.1 TA

Magnificent Victorian home just steps from old Québec City in the heart of the Faubourg St-Jean-Baptiste: historic, artistic and early settlement district. I am a professional artist. Large, comfortable rooms. 2 rooms with private bathroom, two double beds and fridge. One room with private but separate bathroom, good ventilation. Copious breakfast.

Boul. Laurier to Québec City. After the parliament, Hwy Dufferin to the left, right on Rue St-Jean. Left at the first traffic lights, Rue d'Aiguillon. Cross Dufferin again to Côte St-Geneviève.

B&B
B&B CHEZ PIERRE

Pierre Côté
636, rue d'Aiguillon
Québec G1R 1M5
(418) 522-2173
welcome.to/chezpierre

B&B	
single	$60-85
double	$70-95
triple	$100-120
quad.	$125-145

Taxes extra VS MC

Reduced rates: Feb. 1 to May 31
Open: Dec. 1 to Oct. 31

Number of rooms	7
rooms with private bath	5
rooms with sink	1
shared bathrooms	1

Activities: 🏛 ⛴ 🚣 🚴 🏃

38. QUÉBEC

✎ F e 🚫 🐕 🚗 P R.5 TA

Located on a peaceful street in the heart of a lively area a short distance from the Plains of Abraham, Grande-Allée, Grand-Théâtre, and a 10 min walk from Vieux-Québec and the convention centre. A few rooms with queen-size beds and living rooms available. Hearty breakfasts. Discount for stays of three nights or longer. Free parking.

From Montréal, Hwy 20, P.-Laporte bridge, Boul. Laurier to downtown. Left on Ave. de la Tour 8.8km from the bridge. Or, Hwy 40, right on Rue St-Sacrement Sud. Left on Chemin St-Louis, drive 2.6km.

B&B
B&B DE LA TOUR

Hugette Rodrigue and
André Blanchet
1080, avenue de la Tour
Québec G1R 2W7
(418) 525-8775

B&B	
single	$55-60
double	$70-75
triple	$90
child	$15

Reduced rates: 3 nights and more
Open: Dec. 1 to Oct. 20

Number of rooms	3
rooms with sink	2
shared bathrooms	2

Activities: 🏛 ⛴ 🎿 🚴 🏃

39. QUÉBEC

☀☀☀ F e 🐕 R.3 TA

On a quiet street in the heart of the Old City, a stone's throw from Château Frontenac and the river. Fully renovated hundred-year-old house. Clean and comfortable rooms. Breakfast in the Victorian dining room served by your young Quebec hosts mindful of your well-being.

Hwy 20, Laporte bridge, Boul. Laurier Exit, twd Vieux-Québec. After the Porte St-Louis, turn right at 1st light on d'Auteuil, left on Ste-Geneviève and left on des Grisons.

B&B
B&B DES GRISONS

Claudine Desbois and
Jocelyn Santerre
1, rue des Grisons
Québec G1R 4M6
(418) 694-1461
fax (418) 694-9204
bbcanada.com/2608.html
jsanterr@videotron.ca

B&B	
single	$60
double	$65-75
triple	$95

MC

Reduced rates: Nov. 1 to Feb. 1
and Mar. 15 to May 15
Open year round

Number of rooms	3
shared bathroom	2

Activities: 🏛 🍷 ⛴ 🚴 🎿

40. QUÉBEC

☀☀☀ | F | E | 🚭 | 🐕 | 🚗 | P | R1 | TA

Warm house located on a quiet street near services, restaurants, university, hospitals, shopping centres, 5 minutes from the Old City. Family ambiance, opportunities for great conversations! Facilities for children. Healthy breakfast served in our dining room. Storage for skis and bikes.

Hwy 20, Pierre-Laporte bridge, downtown Québec City twd Boul. Laurier. Past Université Laval, turn left on Ave. Des Gouverneurs, left on Boul. René Lévesque, left on Madeleine-de-Verchères.

B&B
B&B LA BEDONDAINE

Sylvie and Gaétan Tessier
912, Madeleine-de-Verchères
Québec G1S 4K7
(418) 681-0783
www.bbcanada.com
/2851.html

B&B	
single	$40-45
double	$50-60
child	$10

Reduced rates: Sep. 1 to May 31
Open year round

Number of rooms	3
rooms with private bath	1
rooms in semi-basement	2
shared bathroom	1

Activities: 🏛 🏃 🚲 🎿 ⛷

41. QUÉBEC

☀☀☀☀ | F | e | 🚭 | 🚗 | P | R1

Near the Plains of Abraham, old Quebec City, museums and major places of interest, a lovely old house, prestigious inland Montcalm district, spacious rooms with distinctive styles, large living room with fireplace, central air conditioning, private parking lot. **See colour photos.**

Hwy 20, Pierre-Laporte bridge, Boul. Laurier twd downtown, Chemin St-Louis to Ave. des Laurentides, 6km. Or, Hwy 40, right on St-Sacrement, 1.5km, left on Chemin St-Louis to Ave. des Laurentides, 1.2km.

B&B
B&B MAISON LESAGE

Jean-Luc Lesage and
Yves Ruel
760, chemin St-Louis
Québec G1S 1C3
(418) 682-9959
www.bbcanada.com/
3282.html
bbmaisonlesageyr@videotron.ca

B&B	
single	$70-75
double	$85-90

Taxes extra VS

Open year round

Number of rooms	4
rooms with private bath	4

Activities: 🏛 🏃 🚲 🎿 ⛷

42. QUÉBEC

☀☀☀☀ | F | E | ✕ | P | 🚗 | 🐕 | R.1 | TA

Québec Excellence Prize 1999. Regional winner of Québec Tourism Grand Prizes for hospitality and customer service (1995); Classification Hébergement Québec «4 suns». Located at 5 min (1.5km or 1mile) from «fortified Old Québec». Central air conditioning, pool table, bikes, parking, table d'hôte.

Hwy 20 P. Laporte bridge, or Hwy 40 E., twd Ste-Anne-de-Beaupré, Exit 316, staight ahead untill Chemin de la Canardière. Turn right to 1720.

B&B
CHEZ MONSIEUR GILLES[2]

Gilles Clavet
1720, chemin de la Canardière
Québec G1J 2E3
(418) 821-8778
fax (418) 821-8776
www3.sympatico.ca/mgilles
mgilles@sympatico.ca

B&B	
single	$65-100
double	$75-110
triple	$90-125
quad.	$105-140
child	$15

Taxes extra VS ER

Open year round

Number of rooms	5
rooms with sink	2
rooms with private bath	3
shared wc	2
shared bathrooms	3

Activities: 🏛 ⛴ 🏃 🚲 🎿

43. QUÉBEC

☀☀☀ | F | e | 🚭 | P | R.01 | TA

Gîte du Parc is a century-old home bathed in the tranquillity of the Montcalm area, 2 min from the Plains of Abraham, le Musée du Québec and a stone's throw from Vieux-Québec. You will be delighted by our friendly welcome, helpful tourist information on Québec City, spacious, attractively decorated rooms, copious breakfasts and free parking.

From Montréal, Hwy 20, Pierre-Laporte bridge, exit Boul. Laurier. Left on Des Érables, then left on Fraser.

B&B
GÎTE DU PARC

Henriette Hamel and
René Thivierge
345, rue Fraser
Québec G1S 1R2
(418) 683-8603
fax (418) 683-8431
giteduparc@moncourrier.com

B&B	
single	$60-70
double	$70-85
triple	$85-100

Open year round

Number of rooms	2
shared bathrooms	1

Activities: 🏛 🦪 ⛷ 🚶 🎿

44. QUÉBEC

☀☀☀☀ | F | E | 🚭 | 🚗 | R1 | TA

Grand ancestral Irish house from 1832 (UNESCO World Heritage Site), below Prom. des Gouverneurs, the Citadelle, 10 min walk from Petit Champlain. Quiet street with free parking; elegant, restful rooms; lux. bathrooms; authentic style and decor. Unique breakfasts. Next to Cap-Blanc apts.; priv. bathrooms; ideal for families, friends, honeymooners...**City Home p 261 no 74. See colour photos.**

From Hwy 20, 40 or 73, Pierre-Laporte bridge, Boul. Champlain Exit 132, follow the river for 10km, left at 6th lights, Rue Champlain, 1km from the ferry.

B&B
HAYDEN'S WEXFORD HOUSE

Jean and Louise
450, rue Champlain
Québec G1K 4J3
(418) 524-0524
fax (418) 648-8995
www.bbcanada.com/
haydenwexfordhouse
haydenwexfordhouse@
videotron.net

B&B	
single	$75
double	$85

Taxes extra VS MC

Open year round

Number of rooms	4
shared wc	3
shared bathrooms	2

Activities: 🏛 ⛴ 🛶 🚲 🏊

45. QUÉBEC

F | e | 🚭 | 🐕 | 🚗 | P | R4 | TA

French artist's home located in "Upper Town" and in the cultural heart of Québec City. Personalised welcome, cosiness, relaxation, tranquillity and security. Special meals (for diabetics). Two cats. Near most tourist attractions, shops, boutiques, restaurants.

Chemin Ste-Foy to "Vieux Québec". Turn left on Rue Désy street. La Coule Douce is on Dolbeau street, 2nd street on your left.

B&B
LA COULE DOUCE

Michel Champagne
473, rue Dolbeau
Québec G1S 2R6
(418) 527-2940
fax (418) 527-0288
pages.infinit.net/hotel/
quebec.html
ntherio@videotron.ca

B&B	
single	$55
double	$65
triple	$100
quad.	$125

Open year round

Number of rooms	2
shared bathrooms	1

Activities: 🏛 🦪 ⛷ 🚲 🏊

46. QUÉBEC

⁕⁕⁕⁕ F e 🐾 P R.5 TA

Charming house with view of the river located in a historic district, near the Plains of Abraham, Place Royale, renowned places of interest and restaurants. Opposite a park, public pool, cycling path. Very lovely and comfortable rooms, canopy beds, balcony, free parking, flowery courtyard and lavish breakfasts indoors or outdoors.

Hwy 20, Pierre-Laporte bridge, Exit 132, Boul. Champlain, left at 6th traffic light onto Rue Champlain, at the foot of the Cap-Blanc stairway. 1km, then left of the Québec City-Lévis ferry (opposite the park).

B&B
L'ANSE DES MÈRES

Linda Pelchat
553, rue Champlain
Québec G1K 4J4
tel/fax (418) 649-8553
www.anse-des-meres.qc.ca
Info@anse-des-meres.qc.ca

B&B	
single	$50-85
double	$75-100
triple	$100-115
quad.	$130
5-6 people	$145-160

VS AM

Reduced rates: Nov.15 to Jan.30
Open year round

Number of rooms	3
shared wc	1
shared bathrooms	1

Activities: 🏛 🥾 🛳 🏌 🚲

---

47. QUÉBEC

⁕⁕⁕⁕ F E 🚭 🚗 R1 TA

Downtown, 2 min from old Québec City, a former schoolhouse (historic monument, 1849) serves as a setting for a comfortable stay in the old capital. Lovely garden, warm fireplace and good local-style breakfast. In our studio, learn about etching and silk-screen printing. Near businesses, cultural events, transport. Come discover our «secret garden».

After the Parliament, left on Honoré-Mercier, then eastbound Hwy Dufferin, Exit 22. At 1st lights, turn left and continue to the end, left to 3e Rue, on the left.

B&B
LE JARDIN SECRET

André Lemieux
and Yves Dumaresq
699 and 701, 3ᵉ Rue
Québec G1J 2V5
(418) 640-7321
tel/fax (418) 529-5587

B&B	
single	$45-55
double	$60-70

VS

Open: Mar. 1 to Nov. 30

Number of rooms	3
rooms with private bath	1
shared bathrooms	1

Activities: 🏛 🧗 🛳 🚲 🎿

---

48. QUÉBEC, BEAUPORT

⁕⁕ F e P R.5 TA

Panoramic view: St. Lawrence River, Île d'Orléans, Parc Montmorency. All you have to do is cross the street to discover the charms of Parc de la Chute Montmorency with its picnic sites, trails and manor, etc... 10km from old Québec City and 4km from Île d'Orléans. Between Mont-Ste-Anne and Stoneham.

From Montréal, twd Ste-Anne-de-Beaupré, Exit 322, turn left, drive 2.3km. Corner Royale and Avenue Larue. From the Côte-Nord, twd Montréal, exit 322, etc... (facing Manoir Montmorency).

B&B
EN HAUT DE LA CHUTE
MONTMORENCY

Gisèle and Bertrand Tremblay
2515, avenue Royale
Beauport G1C 1S2
tel/fax (418) 666-4755
gisele@oricom.ca

B&B	
single	$40
double	$55-65
triple	$70-80
child	$10

Open year round

Number of rooms	3
rooms with private bath	1
rooms with sink	2
rooms in basement	2
shared wc	2
shared bathrooms	1

Activities: 🏛 🥾 🧗 🚶 🚲

49. QUÉBEC, BEAUPORT

☀☀☀ F E P ⬛ 🚫 R.5 TA

Our B&B is located on the oldest road in Québec City, 10 min from old Québec City, 1km from the Montmorency falls, 30 min from Mont-St-Anne. Come relax in the outdoor pool and the large garden. Bike/ski shed. And what a delicious breakfast! Québec Region Excellence Prize 1997-98. **See colour photos.**

From Montréal, Hwy 40 East; from the Cote-Nord, Hwy 40 West, Exit 322. From Québec City, Hwy 440, Exit 29, Exit 322, left on Boul. des Chutes, left at Esso station, right on Ave. Royale, 0.5km.

B&B
MAISON ANCESTRALE
THOMASSIN

Madeleine Guay
2161, avenue Royale
Beauport G1C 1N9
(418) 663-6067
fax (418) 660-8616

B&B	
single	$40
double	$52
triple	$70
quad.	$87

Taxes extra

Open year round

Number of rooms	4
shared bathrooms	2

Activities: 🍴 🛶 🕴 🚲 ⛷

50. QUÉBEC, BEAUPORT

☀☀☀ F e 🚫 ✕ P R.3 TA

Ancestral house in Old Beauport. Near the Montmorency Falls, Île d'Orléans, the Old City (5 minutes) and Mont-Sainte-Anne (30 minutes). The master chef invites you to partake of a hearty breakfast, table d'hôte delicacies in an art-gallery-like decor.

Hwy 40 twd Ste-Anne-de-Beaupré. Seigneuriale South Exit, right on Ave. Royale. From Old Québec: Hwy Dufferin, Exit François-de-Laval, right on Ave. Royale.

B&B
LA MAISON DUFRESNE

France Collin and Michel Nigen
505, avenue Royale
Beauport G1E 1Y3
(418) 666-4004
toll free 1-877-747-4004
fax (418) 663-0119
www.mlink.net/~dufresne
dufresne@mlink.net

	B&B	MAP
single	$50	$70
double	$65	$105
triple	$80	$140
child	$10	$20

Taxes extra VS MC

Reduced rates: Nov.1 to Apr. 30
Open year round

Number of rooms	3
rooms with sink	3
shared wc	1
shared bathrooms	1

Activities: 🏛 🍴 🍷 ⛷ 🎿

51. QUÉBEC, BEAUPORT

☀☀☀ F E 🚫 🐕 🛏 P ⬛ R.3 TA

Le Gîte du Vieux-Bourg is a welcoming 100-year-old home situated in the historic area of Beauport. Biking and hiking paths nearby. Only 5 min from Vieux-Québec, Montmorency falls, half way between Mont Ste-Anne and Stoneham. Large family-size bedrooms can accommodate four to five people. Pool. Tasty home-made breakfasts served on the terrace or in the solarium.

Hwy 40 East, Exit 320, right on Rue Seigneuriale and right on Royale. From Vieux-Québec, Hwy 440 East, François de Laval exit, right on Royale.

B&B
LE GÎTE DU VIEUX-BOURG

Marielle Viel and
Benoit Couturier
492, avenue Royale
Beauport G1E 1Y1
tel/fax (418) 661-0116
www3.sympatico.ca
/vieux-bourg
vieux-bourg@sympatico.ca

B&B	
single	$50-70
double	$60-85
triple	$75-100
quad.	$115
child	$10

VS

Reduced rates: Nov.1 to Apr. 30
Open year round

Number of rooms	4
rooms with private bath	1
rooms with sink	1
shared wc	1
shared bathrooms	2

Activities: 🍴 🛶 🕴 🚲 ⛷

52. QUÉBEC, BEAUPORT

✹✹✹✹✹ F E ♿ 🚫 ⛴ P 🏊 R.2

Built in 1875, Manoir Vallée will make your relive the warmth and ambiance of yesteryear. Located 5min from Vieux-Québec and the Montmorency Falls. Relax in our spacious rooms with stone walls and a romantic decor. You will appreciate our old-fashioned breakfasts. Relaxation room, suite with kitchen.

From Montreal, Hwy 40 East, or from Côte-Nord, Hwy 40 West, Exit Rue Labelle, go down until Royale, right, 10th house facing "Ultramar".

B&B
LE MANOIR VALLÉE

Francine Huot, Kevin Strassburg, Carlos and Rosalee
907, avenue Royale
Beauport G1E 1Z9
(418) 660-3855
(418) 666-5421
fax (418) 660-8792
kevenstr@total.net

B&B	
single	$65-85
double	$65-95
triple	$75-105
quad.	$85-115
child	$5

VS MC IT

Reduced rates: Nov.1 to Apr. 30
Open year round

Number of rooms	4
rooms with rpivate bath	4

Activities: ⛴ 🚣 🚴 ⛷

53. QUÉBEC, BEAUPORT

✹✹✹ F E P 🏊 R.5

Le Petit Manoir is located on the historic site of Chute Montmorency, with the St. Lawrence River and Île d'Orléans in the backdrop. Representing living history, this 19th-century bourgeois residence have kept its original allure and character. Bordered by two peaceful streams, the property will seduce you with comfort and make you succumb to its charms. Vieux-Québec and Mont Ste-Anne nearby.

Hwy 40 to Ste-Anne-de-Beaupré, Exit 322, left on Boulevard des Chutes, right on Côte du Moulin.

B&B
LE PETIT MANOIR DU
SAULT MONTMORENCY

Nycole Giroux and
Jean-Pierre Morneau
63, côte du Moulin
Beauport G1C 2L7
(418) 663-6510
fax (418) 663-8996
petitmanoir@hotmail.com

B&B	
single	$60
double	$75

VS MC AM

Reduced rates: Nov.1 to Apr. 30
Open year round

Number of rooms	2
shared bathrooms	1

Activities: 🍷 🚴 ⛷ 🏃

54. QUÉBEC, CAP-ROUGE

✹✹✹✹✹ F E P 🚫 🚗 R1 TA

15 min from Old Québec, close to the bridges, English-style cottage (1991) B&B. Peaceful and welcoming, with parking, terrace and flower gardens. Nearby: marina, paths along the rivers, art galleries, restaurants, shopping centres. Generous breakfast served by your hosts.

Hwy 20, after the bridges, Exit 133, right on Ch. St-Louis, to the end (3km), Louis-Francœur is to the right. Or, Hwy 40 Duplessis Hwy Exit Ch. Ste-Foy. Go right, to Louis-Francœur, 2.5km.

B&B
GÎTE LA JOLIE ROCHELLE

Huguette Couture and
Martin Larochelle
1450, Louis-Francœur
Cap-Rouge, Pointe-Ste-Foy
G1Y 1N6
(418) 653-4326
fax (418) 653-6061
www.bbcanada.com/3211.html

B&B	
single	$50
double	$60
child	$10-15

Open year round

Number of rooms	3
shared wc	1
shared bathrooms	1

Activities: 🏛 ⛴ 🚶 🚴

55. QUÉBEC, CAP-ROUGE

✹✹✹ F E P 🚫 R.5 TA

The Feeney house is 200 years old, close to the river and the village. Enjoy the friendly ambiance around the fireplace. Old village, extraordinary history, water park and long beaches along the St. Lawrence allow for pleasant and relaxing walks. Meet some of the local "Carougeois", visit the studios of artists, potters, sculptors.

From Montréal, Hwy 20 East, Pierre-Laporte bridge Exit Hwy Duplessis, Exit Chemin Ste-Foy twd Cap-Rouge. Go down the hill, follow the river, Rue St-Félix is after the stop sign.

B&B
LA MAISON FEENEY

Louise Fortier and
André Létourneau
4352, St-Félix
Cap-Rouge G1Y 3A5
(418) 651-3970
www.bbcanada.com/2755.html
maisonfeeney@sympatico.ca

B&B	
single	$50
double	$60
triple	$75
quad.	$90
child	$12

Open year round

Number of rooms	3
rooms with sink	2
shared wc	1
shared bathrooms	1

Activities: 🏛 🍴 ⛴ 🎿 🚶

56. QUÉBEC, CAP-ROUGE

✹✹✹ F e P 🚫 R.5 TA

Large house (comfort, quiet, rest) 15km from old Quebec City. Varied, all-you-can-eat homemade breakfast. Private living room. Free parking. Flower garden, whirlpool bath. Nearby: golf course, footpath, St. Lawrence River, marina, art gallery, big shopping centre. Family suite (kitchenette, private bathroom).

From Montréal: Hwy 20 East, Pierre-Laporte bridge, Chemin St-Louis West Exit to Louis Francoeur. Left on Chemin Ste-Foy, Rue St-Félix, right on Rue du Golf. Or, Rte 138 to Cap-Rouge.

B&B
L'HYDRANGÉE BLEUE

Yvan Denis
1451, du Golf
Cap-Rouge G1Y 2T6
(418) 657-5609
fax (418) 657-7918

B&B	
single	$40-50
double	$50-60
triple	$65-75
quad.	$80-90
child	$10

Open year round

Number of rooms	2
rooms with private bath	1
shared bathrooms	1
rooms in basement	1

Activities: 🏛 🍴 ⛴ 🎿 🚶

57. QUÉBEC, CHARLESBOURG

✹✹✹ F E 🚫 P R.25 TA

"Health Speciality B&B" 10min from old Quebec City and tourist activities. 22km bike path/cross-country-skiing trail from the city to the wildlife reserves. Bike rentals. Good, warm ambiance. Singular breakfast, natural/organic food. Body-care packages: seaweed wraps with musicotherapy. Rates on request. Complimentary drinks and health snacks.

Pierre-Laporte bridge twd Chicoutimi, Hwy 40 East, Exit 313, Hwy 73 North, Exit 151, Boul. Jean Talon. Turn right at 1st lights and continue to Boul. H.-Bourassa, turn right, 0.25km.

B&B
LE GÎTE DU NATUROPATHE

France Villeneuve and
François Létourneau
9385, boul. Henri-Bourassa
Charlesbourg, G1G 4E5
(418) 624-2328
fax (418) 624-9836
www.bbcanada.com/gitenaturo
gitenaturo@sympatico.ca

B&B	
single	$45
double	$60
child	$15

Taxes extra VS

Reduced rates: 10% 4 nights or more
Open year round

Number of rooms	2
shared bathrooms	1

Activities: 🏛 🎿 🚶 ⛷ 🛷

58. QUÉBEC, STE-FOY

✹✹✹ F E 🚳 🚗 P R1 TA

Only a few minutes from downtown and not far from the airport, Le Gîte du Centenaire is a spectacular century-old home with a magnificent location in a rural area. Country-style breakfast. Large property with fruit trees, vegetable garden and flowers. Great variety of activities such as hiking, snowmobiling, horseback riding, golfing and summer theatre.

Hwy 40, Exit Rte 138 East, Exit Boulevard Hamel, 298 East, left on Rue Labelle for 1km. Hwy 20 Pierre-Laporte bridge, Duplessis Exit. Exit left on Boulevard Hamel, right on Rue Labelle for 1km.

B&B
B&B DU CENTENAIRE

Claire Harvey
1204, Labelle
Ste-Foy G2E 3L9
tel/fax (418) 872-4818
pages.infinit.net/lauclair/gite

B&B	
single	$40
double	$60
child	$10

Reduced rates: 20% Oct. 30 to Apr. 30
Open year round

Number of rooms	2
shared wc	1
shared bathrooms	1

Activities: 🏛 🍴 ⛴ 🏌 🚲

59. QUÉBEC, STE-FOY

✹✹✹ F E 🚳 P 🚗 R.5 TA

Ten minutes from Old Québec City, quiet residential district, access to highways. Warm ambiance, comfortable rooms with sink, generous breakfast. Walking distance from Université Laval, big shopping centres, public transport, cinema, restaurants. Free and easy parking.

From Montréal, Hwy 20, take Pierre Laporte bridge, Boul. Laurier, right at 5th light onto Rue Jean Dequen to Rue Lapointe. Hwy 40, take Hwy Duplessis South, Boul. Laurier, right at 5th light...

B&B
LA MAISON LECLERC

Nicole Chabot
and Conrad Leclerc
2613, rue Lapointe
Ste-Foy G1W 3K3
(418) 653-8936
fax (418) 653-5266
www.bbcanada.
com/2693.html
lamaisonleclerc@videotron.ca

B&B	
single	$40
double	$55
child	$0-15

VS MC

Reduced rates: 3 nights and more, and Nov. 1 to May 31
Open year round

Number of rooms	5
rooms with sink	2
rooms in basement	2
shared bathrooms	2

Activities: 🏛 ⛴ 🏃 🚲 🎿

60. QUÉBEC, STE-FOY

✹✹ F 🚳 P R.5 TA

House located in the heart of the town of Ste-Foy, 1km from the Pierre-Laporte bridge. Very close to the largest shopping centres in Québec City, the bus terminal, the post office, banks, hospitals. Chilean-style breakfast available. We speak Spanish very well.

After the Pierre-Laporte bridge towards downtown Québec City, Boul. Laurier Exit. At the 2nd traffic lights, turn left. Right on Rue Légaré, and right again on the next street.

B&B
MAISON DINA

Dina Saéz-Velozo
2850, rue Fontaine
Ste-Foy G1V 2H8
(418) 652-1013

B&B	
single	$40
double	$50
child	$12

Open: June 1 to Oct. 30

Number of rooms	3
rooms in basement	2
shared bathrooms	2

Activities: 🏛 🍴 ⛴ 🏌 🚲

61. QUÉBEC, STE-FOY

☀☀☀ F e P 🚗 R.1 TA

Canadian-style house located in a calm residential neighborhood, near services, shopping centre, public transport and expressways. 5 min from the airport and Université Laval. 10 min from old Québec City. Warm atmosphere, comfortable rooms, living room, copious breakfast, central air conditioning system. Welcome. Québec City Region Excellence Prize 94-95.

From Montréal, Hwy 20 East to Québec City, Pierre-Laporte bridge, Boul. Laurier Exit. At the 1st traffic lights, turn right on Rue Lavigerie, at the 3rd street, right on Rue de la Seine.

B&B
MONIQUE ET ANDRÉ
SAINT-AUBIN

Monique and André
Saint-Aubin
3045, rue de la Seine
Ste-Foy G1W 1H8
(418) 658-0685
fax (418) 658-8466
www.qbc.clic.net/~staubin
staubin@qbc.clic.net

B&B	
single	$45
double	$60
triple	$80
child	$10

Reduced rates: Nov.1 to Apr. 30
Open year round

Number of rooms	3
shared bathrooms	3

Activities: 🏛 🍴 ⛴ 🎿 🏃

62. QUÉBEC, SILLERY

☀☀☀ F E P 🚳 R.2 TA

White, English-style house dating back to the 1930s surrounded by hundred-year-old trees. Exceptional neighbourhood. Fireplace, terrace, large rooms, king and queen-size beds. Varied, home-made breakfast. Nearby: Université de Laval, Plains of Abraham, old Québec City and just steps from Cataraqui. Welcome.

Hwy 20, Pierre-Laporte Bridge, Boul Laurier to Québec City. 3.9km from bridge right on Rue Maguire. Right on Ch. St-Louis. Hwy 40, Boul. Duplessis South Exit to Boul. Laurier...

B&B
B&B LES CORNICHES

Francine C. DuSault
2052, chemin St-Louis
Sillery, Québec G1T 1P4
(418) 681-9318
fax (418) 681-4028

B&B	
single	$55
double	$65-75
triple	$90
child	$15

VS

Open year round

Number of rooms	3
rooms with private bath	1
shared bathrooms	2

Activities: 🏛 ⛴ 🧍 🚲 🏃

63. QUÉBEC, WENDAKE

☀☀☀ F E P 🚗 R.25 TA

Century-old house where the past mingles with the present. Friendly atmosphere, in which Native art transports guests back in time. Breakfast with a Huron flavour. The Bear, Wolf and Turtle Rooms await you. Located in the heart of the old village of Huron-Wendat, which you can explore, and 15 min from Québec City and area ski resorts. Guided tours of historic sites.

From Québec City, Hwy 73 and Hwy 369 to Loretteville. The B&B is located on a street parallel to Boul. Bastien, drive up Rue Gabriel Vincent and you're there.

B&B
LA MAISON AORHENCHE

Line Gros-Louis
90, François Gros-Louis,
C.P. 110
Wendake G0A 4V0
(418) 847-0646
fax (418) 847-4527
aorenche@sympatico.ca

B&B	
single	$55-65
double	$65-75
triple	$95
quad.	$115
child	$15

Open year round

Number of rooms	3
rooms with private bath	1
shared bathrooms	1

Activities: 🏛 🧍 🏃 🚲 🐎 🛶

64. ST-GABRIEL-DE-VALCARTIER

 F E P R8 TA

Large country house with vast English-style garden with thousands of flowers. Indoor pool and tennis court. Near Parc de la Jacques-Cartier, Village Vacances Valcartier, Stoneham ski resort, etc. All-you-can-eat breakfast and panoramic view. 200 acres of back country 30 min from Quebec City! **Farm Stay p 42, Country Home p 262.**

From Québec City, Hwy Henri IV, Rte 573 twd Rte 369, take "Entrée Base Militaire", "Rte de Transit, Valcartier Village" at exit, Rte 371 N, right at 1st light. From east of Québec City, Rte 175 twd Chicoutimi, Exit 167, Rte 371 S...

B&B
LE GÎTE DES EQUERRES

Annette Légaré
171, 5ᵉ Avenue Rte 371
St-Gabriel-de-Valcartier
G0A 4S0
(418) 844-2424
toll free 1-877-844-2424
fax (418) 844-1607
www.auxancienscanadiens.
qc.ca/gite.html
gite@auxanciens
canadiens.qc.ca

B&B	
single	$55-65
double	$70-80
triple	$85-95
quad.	$100
child	$10

Taxes extra VS MC

Reduced rates: 50% 4th night
Open year round

Number of rooms	3
rooms with private bath	3

Activities:

65. ST-JOACHIM

 F E P R10

À L'Abri de la Tourmente is a 175-year-old Québécois home, which has a refined decor, a pastoral setting, a 723-acre property, magnificent private waterfalls, as well as an apple orchard called "Produit du Terroir." A restful stay is assured. The property has a cider factory, home-made jams and jellies, maple syrup and fresh eggs. Choice of several different breakfasts. Visit Cap-Tourmente and Mont Ste-Anne. We will soon be offering evening meals.

Rte 138 East to Beaupré. Follow signs to St-Joachim, Cap-Tourmente.

B&B
À L'ABRI DE LA TOURMENTE

Marie-Christine Perreault and
Jean-Nil Bouchard
200, chemin Cap Tourmente
St-Joachim G0A 3X0
(418) 827-3025
toll free 1-888-530-3025
fax (418)827-3694
www.carpediem.
qc.ca/abri_de_la_tourmente
abritou@mlink.net

B&B	
single	$70-80
double	$95-125
triple	$145

Taxes extra VS MC

Reduced rates: 10% 5 nights and more
Open year round

Number of rooms	5
rooms with private bath	5

Activities:

66. ST-RAYMOND

 F E P R.2 TA

Lovely, turn-of-the-century brick house surrounded by equally charming neighbours. A short bike ride away from the cycling path, three strides from nature (canoeing, hiking, skidooing, skiing, gliding...). Colours, local flavours and exotic aromas mingle here. Prices include taxes and services.

Hwy 40, Rte 365 North, at 1st light in the village turn right, a little past the church. By Bike: St-Raymond Exit on the path, follow road toward downtown. By snowmobile: via trail 365.

INN
LA VOISINE

Odile Pelletier and
Denis Baribault
443, Saint-Joseph
Saint-Raymond G3L 1K1
(418) 337-4139
fax (418) 337-3109
voisine@globetrotter.net

	B&B	MAP
single	$45-55	$60-70
double	$60-70	$90-100
triple	$75-85	$120-130
child	$15	$25

VS MC IT

Open year round

Number of rooms	5
rooms with sink	5
rooms with private bath	1
shared wc	1
shared bathrooms	2

Activities:

67. ST-RAYMOND ☀☀ F E 🚫 P R3 TA

See, smell and taste the difference in the quietness of the countryside; access to cycling path, skidoo trail and the river. Get back in touch with your inner self by getting some fresh air, taking part in merry encounters and sharing a breakfast of fresh home-made products. Welcome to our home.

From Montréal or Québec City, Hwy 40, twd Pont-Rouge/St-Raymond Exit 281, Rte 365 for about 25km. After Côte Joyeuse, Rue St-Pierre, 1st street on left, straight toward Chute Panet, 4km.

B&B
SENS SAINT-RAYMOND NID

Christine Robert and
Louis Vallée
570, rte de Chute Panet
St-Raymond G3L 4P2
(418) 337-1430

B&B	
single	$30-50
double	$45-75
child	$0-15

Open year round

Number of rooms	3
rooms with sink	1
shared wc	2
shared bathrooms	1

Activities: 🎿 🚲 ⛷ 🏃

68. STE-ANNE-DE-BEAUPRÉ ☀☀☀ F e P 🚫 R1 TA

Pretty country house (1909) located 10 min from Mont Ste-Anne and 20 min from Québec City. Nearby: Cap Tourmente, Grand Canyon, Sept-Chutes. Generous breakfast served in the sun-room with view of the river. Cosy bedrooms decorated with care. Fireplace in living room. Ski and mountain-bike packages at Mont Ste-Anne and Le Massif. Small farm: goats, rabbits...

From Québec City, Rte 138 East to Ste-Anne-de-Beaupré. 6km from Château-Richer, after the Écomusée du Miel, turn left on Rue Paré. At the end, Ave. Royale, turn right.

B&B
LA MAISON D'ULYSSE

Carole Trottier and
Raymond Allard
9140, av. Royale
Ste-Anne-de-Beaupré G0A 3C0
(418) 827-8224

B&B	
single	$45
double	$60-65
triple	$75
child	$0-15

Taxes extra VS MC

Open year round

Number of rooms	4
rooms with sink	2
rooms with private bath	1
shared bathrooms	2

Activities: 🏛 🎿 ⛷ 🏃 🐎

69. STONEHAM, ST-ADOLPHE ☀☀☀ F e ♿ P 🚫 R5 TA

Country style house, 20 minutes from Québec City, in the mountains, relive the charming era of little inns when travellers spent the evening telling tales in front of a stone fireplace. Enjoy a night in one of our romantic rooms until it's time for breakfast. Closest B&B to Parc de la Jacques-Cartier.

From Québec City, Hwy 73 N. twd Chicoutimi. At the intersection with 175 N. (after Exit 167 - Stoneham) drive 7km to the sign for St-Adolphe. Right on St-Edmond, drive 1.7km.

B&B
AUBERGE LA SAUVAGINE

Francine Beauregard and
Pierre Desautels
544, rue St-Edmond
Stoneham G0A 4P0
(418) 848-6128
fax (418) 848-7866
www.clic.net/~sauvagin/
sauvagin@clic.net

B&B	
single	$50-80
double	$60-80
triple	$75-100
quad.	$120
child	$10-20

Open year round

Number of rooms	3
rooms with private bath	1
rooms with sink	1
shared wc	1
shared bathrooms	1

Activities: 🎿 🏃 ⛷ 🏃 🐎

70. STONEHAM, ST-ADOLPHE

Near Jacques-Cartier Park, our farm offers you: walking trails, river, lake with wriggling trout, bountiful greenery and rock gardens, small-scale maple grove and many small animals. Lunch with home-made and farm products awaits you at this B&B separated from our house.

From Québec City, Hwy 73 N., twd Chicoutimi. At the intersection with 175 N. (After Exit 167 - Stoneham) drive 7km to the sign for St-Adolphe. Right on rue St-Edmond and drive 3km.

B&B
AUBERGE DE LA FERME
ST-ADOLPHE

Jocelyne Couillard and
George Legendre
1035, rue St-Edmond
Stoneham, St-Adolphe
G0A 4P0
(418) 848-2879
fax (418) 848-6949
www.qbc.clic.net/
~geleg/auberge/
geleg@qbc.clic.net

B&B	
single	$45
double	$55
child	$10-15

Taxes extra

Open year round

Number of rooms	3
shared bathrooms	2

Activities:

71. STONEHAM, ST-ADOLPHE

Overlooking the valley at 1,700 ft. in altitude, our B&B offers a grand view of the Jacques-Cartier mountains. Enjoy Stoneham ski resort, cross-country skiing (Camp Mercier), J.-Cartier Park, rafting, hikes, fall colours. Fine country B&B before Parc des Laurentides. Dinner package Dec. 1 to Mar. 31: 2 nights, 2 dinners, 2 breakfasts for $155/couple.

From Québec City, Hwy 73 twd Chicoutimi. Hwy 73 Nord. Do not get off at Exit 167 (Stoneham), but 7km farther at St-Adolphe sign. Turn right on Rue St-Edmond and continue for 5km. Left on Rue Lepire.

B&B
AU SOMMET DES RÊVES

Christine Venditto
and Gilles Benoit
25, rue Lepire
Stoneham G0A 4P0
(418) 848-6154
fax (418) 848-8686
www.bbcanada.com/
2042.html

B&B	
single	$45
double	$60
triple	$80
quad.	$100
child	$12

VS MC

Reduced rates: 10$/room (dbl +), Apr. to June and Sep. to Nov.
Open year round

Number of rooms	3
shared bathrooms	1

Activities:

72. CAP-TOURMENTE, MONT-STE-ANNE

F E P 🏠 R1 M7 TA

In the heart of Cap-Tourmente, 12 min from Mont Ste-Anne (view of the slopes). House with five guestrooms with private baths, kitchen with dishwasher, family room, small sitting room with cable TV, washer and dryer, pool table in the basement. Covered pool in the warm weather, hiking, cross-country skiing and mountain biking (visit the falls and the sugar shack). Also: skiing, golf, horseback riding, etc. **B&B p 237.**

From Québec City, Hwy. Henri IV North, to 40 East Ste-Anne-de-Beaupré, Rte 138 East, twd St-Joachim, Cap-Tourmente.

COUNTRY HOME
L'OIE DES NEIGES

Gisèle Perron
390, ch. du Cap Tourmente
St-Joachim G0A 3X0
(418) 827-5153
tel/fax (418) 827-2246
www.bbcanada.com/
2690.html
melifre@total.net

No. houses	1
No. rooms	5
No. people	4-16
WEEK-SUMMER	$795-1200
WEEK-WINTER	$795-1200
W/E-SUMMER	$550-650
W/E-WINTER	$550-650
DAY-SUMMER	$350-450
DAY-WINTER	$350-450

VS

Open year round

Activities: 🚶 🎿 🚴 🛷 🎿

73. MONT-STE -ANNE, ST-FERRÉOL

F E P R.5 M.5 TA

Savour the tranquillity of our lovely country homes, ancestral or recent, 30 min from downtown Québec City, at the edge of Charlevoix. Dreamy, legendary spot, in a small typical Québécois town. Houses are well equipped and can comfortably accommodate 4 to 30 people, and even up to 50! We are nestled at the foot of Mt Ste-Anne, a year-round internationally renown resort. **See colour photos.**

1km after Mt Ste-Anne, as you enter the small town of St-Ferréol-les-Neiges.

COUNTRY HOME
CHALETS-VILLAGE
MONT-SAINTE-ANNE

Marie Flynn and Gilles Éthier
C.P. 275
Ste-Anne-de-Beaupré G0A 3C0
tel/fax (418) 650-2030
toll free 1-800-461-2030
Visit us on the Internet:
www.chalets-village.qc.ca

No. house	8
No. rooms	2-8
No. people	4-30
WEEK-SUMMER	$525-2500
WEEK-WINTER	$500-6000
W/E-SUMMER	$150-1300
W/E-WINTER	$180-2000

Taxes extra VS MC

Reduced rates: spring and fall
Open year round

Activities: 🚶 🎿 🛷 🎿 ⛸

74. QUÉBEC

F E 🚭 🚗 M1 R1 TA

Next to Hayden's Wexford House B&B, exec. suites in 1847 building. Elegantly furnished and decorated, with charm of yesteryear, stone/brick walls, wood floors. queen-size beds, new bathrooms, living-room nook, daily upkeep, phone, computer hookup. Breakfast avail. Ideal for business or pleasure. 2-night-stay minimum. Reduced rates from 4 weeks. **B&B p 251, no 44. See colour photos.**

From Hwy 20, 40 or 73, Pierre-La-porte bridge, Boul. Champlain Exit 132, follow the river for 10km; at 6th light, left on Rue Champlain, 1km from the ferry.

CITY HOME
LES SUITES-APPARTEMENTS
DU CAP-BLANC

Jean and Louise
444, rue Champlain
Québec G1K 4J3
(418) 524-6137
fax (418) 648-8995
www.bbcanada.com/
haydenwexfordhouse
haydenwexfordhouse
@videotron.net

No. apartments	4
No. rooms	1
No. people	1-4
DAY-SUMMER	$125-170
DAY-WINTER	$125-170

Taxes extra VS MC

Open year round

Activities: 🏛 🛶 🎣 🚴 ⛸

75. QUÉBEC

| F | e | P | R.01 | M.01 |

For business or pleasure, the Maison Calou, in the shadow of Château Frontenac, invites you to the cosy comfort of its fully equipped, 3 or 4-room suites with parking. Explore the history so close at hand (typical streets, museums, churches) and the present (restaurants, shows, shops, street performers). Monthly rental available. **Country Home p 263, no 79.**

Hwy 20, Laporte bridge, Boul. Laurier Exit twd Old Québec City. After the St-Louis gate, 4th street, go left. Parking at the back.

CITY HOME
MAISON CHALOU

Mariette Poirier and
Jean Dreyer
40, des Jardins
Québec G1R 4L7
(418) 628-9913
(418) 655-6364
www.quebecweb.com/chalou
jdreyer@sutton.com

No. apartments	1
No. rooms	1
No. people	4
WEEK-SUMMER	$500
WEEK-WINTER	$500
W/E-SUMMER	$160
W/E-WINTER	$160
DAY-SUMMER	$85
DAY-WINTER	$85

Open year round

Activities: 🏛 🍂 ⚔ 🚶 🎿

76. QUÉBEC

| F | E | 🚭 | 🐕 | P | R.01 | M.2 | TA |

A comfortable English-style house with 3 balconies, 2 bathrooms, equipped kitchen and a piano all in the heart of lovely Québec City. Right near the Old City, the Plains of Abraham, Musée du Québec, bustling Rue Cartier and the Grand-Théâtre. Near roads leading to Île d'Orléans, Mont-Ste-Anne. **Country Home in Bas-St-Laurent, p 64, no 39.**

On Rue St-Jean near the intersection of Rue Turnbull at the beginning of the St-Jean-Baptiste district. 3 blocks west of Rue Cartier and 7 blocks east of Porte St-Jean, 3 blocks north of Boul. René-Lévesque.

CITY HOME
RÉSIDENCE THIBAUDEAU

Chantal Brisson and
Serge Thibaudeau
230, rue St-Jean
Québec G1R 1P1
(418) 640-9255
fax (418) 640-0795
www.craph.org/mti
sthibau@globetrotter.net

No. houses	1
No. rooms	3
No. people	6
WEEK-SUMMER	$800
WEEK-WINTER	$800
W/E-SUMMER	$400
W/E-WINTER	$400

Open year round

Activities: 🏛 🍂 🚶 🚴

77. ST-GABRIEL-DE-VALCARTIER

| F | E | P | 🏊 | M8 | R8 | TA |

This 100-year-old farmhouse has a completely rustic and authentic style. Fully equipped kitchen, three bedrooms, laundry room, bedding, television, and veranda with a B.B.Q. Four-sun facility next door with interior pool, tennis. Only 30min from Québec City. **Farm Stay p 42 and B&B p 258.**

From Québec City, Hwy Henri IV, Rte 573 to Rte 369, take "Entrée base militaire," follow "route de Transit Valcartier Village." At the exit, turn right on Rte 371 North at 1st light. From eastern Québec, to Chicoutimi Rte 175, Exit 167, Rte 371 South.

COUNTRY HOME
LE GÎTE DES ÉQUERRES
«MAISON LE MAS»

Annette Légaré
171, 5ᵉ avenue rte 371
St-Gabriel-de-Valcartier G0A 4S0
(418) 844-2424
toll free 1-877-844-2424
fax (418) 844-1607
www.auxancienscanadiens.
qc.ca/gite.html
gite@auxancienscanadiens.qc.ca

No. houses	1
No. rooms	3
No. people	10
WEEK-SUMMER	$800
WEEK-WINTER	$800
W/E-SUMMER	$300
W/E-WINTER	$300

Taxes extra VS MC

open year round

Activities: 🚶 ⛷ 🎣 🎿 🐎

78. ST-JEAN, ÎLE D'ORLÉANS

| F | E | 🚫 | P | R2 | M1 | TA |

La Petite Cuisine d'Été is a small house on agricultural land where strawberries are grown. There are farm birds, as well as bike and walking paths that pass through the fields and woods. The town has beautiful old-fashioned homes, and a beach is only 2km away. 25 min from Québec City. **B&B p 247, no 32 and p 248, no 35.**

From Québec City, Hwy 440, Île d'Orléans exit, at the light after the bridge, drive straight to the intersection, turn left and head east from the St-Jean bridge for 20km.

COUNTRY HOME
LA PETITE CUISINE D'ÉTÉ

Chantal and Basile Javaux
995, chemin Royal
St-Jean, Île d'Orléans G0A 3W0
(418) 829-2241
fax (418) 529-6227
www.troisbalcons.qc.ca
chantaljavaux@sympatico.ca

No. houses	1
No. rooms	1
No. people	2-4
WEEK-SUMMER	$375
WEEK-WINTER	$300
W/E-SUMMER	$150
W/E-WINTER	$150

Taxes extra VS MC

Reduced rates: Nov.1 to May 31
Open year round

Activities: 🏛 🖼 ⛵ 🚶 🚴

79. STONEHAM

| F | e | P | 🏊 | R.25 | M4 |

On the mountainside, in the heart of the Stoneham ski resort, we invite you to the comfort of a magnificent, fully equipped house. Take the time to live. Ski or snowboard down the slopes; once the snow has melted, enjoy a host of activities on site or in the neighbourhood. Explore the past and present in Old Québec, only 20 minutes away. **City Home p 262, no 75.**

Hwy 75 North, Exit 167 (Stoneham). Follow "Station Touristique" signs. At the resort, before the chalet, turn right, turn right at the end, go under the bridge to Chemin Des Skieurs.

COUNTRY HOME
LE TEMPS DE VIVRE

Mariette Poirier and
Jean Dreyer
14, chemin Des Skieurs
Stoneham G0A 4P0
(418) 628-9913
(418) 655-6364
www.quebecweb.com/temps
jdreyer@sutton.com

No. houses	1
No. rooms	3
No. people	10
WEEK-SUMMER	$1000
WEEK-WINTER	$1500-1800
W/E-SUMMER	$400
W/E-WINTER	$600
DAY-SUMMER	$225
DAY-WINTER	$350

Reduced rates: Sep. 15 to Dec. 1 and Apr. 15 to June 15
Open year round

Activities: ⛵ 🚶 🚶 🐎 🎿

FARM ACTIVITIES

Farm stay:

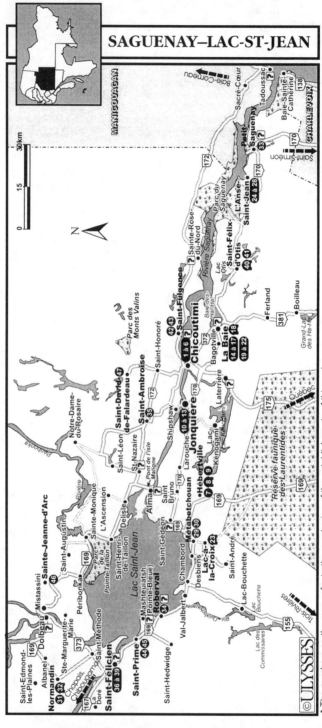

SAGUENAY–LAC-ST-JEAN

* The numbers on the map refer to the numbering of the establishments of this region

© ULYSSES

1. CHICOUTIMI

Very cozy. Near downtown Chicoutimi. On the banks of the Rivière Saguenay. Steps away from the old port, the Pulperie, Marjolaine cruises, bike path, the Promenade and the famous white house that survived the flood. Winter: Carnaval, skiing, snowmobiling and ice fishing. Breakfast served in a splendid dining room with a view of the fjord.

From Québec City, Rte 175 to Chicoutimi. Boul Talbot to the end, left on Rue Jacques-Cartier. At the 2nd lights (by the hospital), turn right again and head down to Blvd Saguenay E., turn right to 782.

B&B
À LA PROMENADE

Lisette Blackburn and
Jacques Grenon
782, boul. Saguenay Est
Chicoutimi G7H 1L3
tel/fax (418) 543-9997
www.bbcanada.
com/1936.html

B&B	
single	$40
double	$60
triple	$90
child	$15

Open year round

Number of rooms	3
rooms with sink	3
shared wc	1
shared bathrooms	1

Activities:

---

2. CHICOUTIMI

We are known for our hospitality. Located behind the Montagnais hotel, near restaurants, the university, shopping centres; 10min from the airport. A peaceful place with magnificent terrace with swimming pool, Saguenay-style breakfasts. Reduced rates and laundry service (2 days or more). Packages: show, saphouse, snowmobiling, dogsledding.

From Québec City, Rte 175 N., Boul. Talbot; after shopping mall, corner «Burger King», left on Boul. Université, left 1st lights onto Rue Thérèse-Casgrain, right 1st stop. From Tadoussac, Rte 172 S., Boul. Talbot...

B&B
AU FIL DES SAISONS

Murielle Boulé
524, Marguerite-Tellier
Chicoutimi G7H 6C1
(418) 543-1839
(418) 698-5193 poste 2269
fax (418) 693-0163
aufildessaisons@hotmail.com

B&B	
single	$50
double	$60
triple	$80
quad.	$100
child	$10-20

VS MC

Reduced rates: May 1 to June 15 and from Sep. 15 to Oct. 30
Open year round

Number of rooms	4
shared bathrooms	2
rooms in basement	2

Activities:

---

3. CHICOUTIMI

If you enjoy the simple things in life, welcome to our home! You are invited to my house surrounded by flowers with an exceptional view of the Saguenay. Delight in a visit to the greenhouses. Cosy comfort, air conditioned rooms and a delicious breakfast will whet your appetite after a good night's rest. Intimacy, calm and pleasures of long ago. A deserved break.

From Québec City, Rte 175 to Chicoutimi. Boul Talbot, left on Boul Université, to the end. Right on Boul St-Paul, at the 2nd traffic lights, left on Rue Price. Next traffic lights, left on Boul Saguenay, 1km.

B&B
GÎTE AUX MILLE FLEURS

Ghislaine Morin
976, boul. Saguenay Ouest
Chicoutimi G7J 1A5
(418) 545-9256

B&B	
single	$40
double	$55
child	$15

Reduced rates: Oct. 1 to Oct. 15
Open: May 15 to Oct. 15

Number of rooms	3
shared bathrooms	1

Activities:

4. CHICOUTIMI

☀☀☀ F e 🚫 P 🐕 R7

Overlooking a majestic fjord, this very quiet B&B is centrally located, close to town, with all its attractions and services. The rooms are cosy and the copious and varied breakfast are served in a spacious dining room with a panoramic view of the river. Welcome all.

From Québec City, Rte 175 North to Chicoutimi. Right on Boul. Université Est (near the shopping centre), left on Boul. Saguenay and take the first right (after the golf course), Rang St-Martin, drive 6.8km.

B&B
GÎTE DE LA BERNACHE

Denise Ouellet
3647, rang St-Martin
Chicoutimi G7H 5A7
(418) 549-4960
fax (418) 549-9814

B&B	
single	$40
double	$55-60
triple	$75
child	$10-15

Open year round

Number of rooms	4
rooms with sink	3
rooms in basement	1
shared wc	1
shared bathrooms	2

Activities: 🦆 ⛵ 🚶 🚲 🛶

5. CHICOUTIMI

☀☀☀ F E 🚫 🐕 🚗 P R.1

Come relax on the veranda of our house in the shade of our magnificent linden tree. Located on an historic street near the cathedral and close to the Saguenay, restaurants and attractions, our home, which was built in 1915, is a haven of peace. The old-fashioned-style rooms are spacious and cosy. Rest, quiet and hearty breakfasts await.

From Québec City, Hwy 175 to Chicoutimi. Boulevard Talbot to the end, turn left on Jacques-Cartier, then right on Du Séminaire, 2nd street.

B&B
LA MAISON DU SÉMINAIRE

Gaëtane Harvey
285, rue de Séminaire
Chicoutimi G7H 4J4
(418) 543-4724
fax (418) 545-2195
http://pages.infinit.net/gitesemi
giteseminaire@videotron.ca

B&B	
single	$50
double	$65
triple	$80
child	$15

MC

Open year round

Number of rooms	2
shared wc	1
shared bathrooms	1

Activities: 🏛 ⛵ 🚶 🚲 🛶

6. CHICOUTIMI

☀☀☀ F ♿ P R2 TA

Just east of Chicoutimi on a vast property with a commanding view of the city and the Rivière Saguenay, Le Chardonneret is a comfortable home away from home. Copious breakfasts. Various services 0.6km away: bank, pharmacy, convenience store, gas station. Welcome to my home.

From Québec City, Rte 175 North to Chicoutimi. Right on Boul. Université East (near the shopping centre), left on Boul. Saguenay. After the Hôtel Parasol, right on Boul. Renaud. 2nd house on the left.

B&B
LE CHARDONNERET

Claire Tremblay
1253, boul. Renaud
Chicoutimi G7H 3N7
(418) 543-9336
lechardonneret@videotron.ca

B&B	
single	$40
double	$55-60
triple	$75
child	$15

Reduced rates: 10% Oct.1 to Feb. 15
Open: May 1 to Feb. 15

Number of rooms	3
rooms with sink	1
shared bathrooms	2

Activities: 🏛 🦆 ⛵ 🚶 🚲

7. HÉBERTVILLE

★ ★ F e P 🚗 🏊 ✕ TA

Presbytery built in 1917. Historical character and period furniture. Warm reception, intimate dining room, refined cuisine, spacious comfortable and warm rooms with full bathrooms. Conference room, peaceful, calm, inspires creativity. In the heart of the Saguenay-Lac-St-Jean region with its activities. Looking forward to your visit. **See colour photos.**

From Rte 169, (don't go to the town of Hébertville), head twd Mont Lac Vert, 3km. Across from the municipal campground.

AUBERGE
AUBERGE PRESBYTÈRE
MONT LAC VERT

The Tremblay family
335, rang Lac-Vert
Hébertville G8N 1M1
(418) 344-1548
toll free 1-800-818-1548
fax (418) 344-1013

	B&B	MAP
single	$50	$70
double	$65	$130
triple	$90	$180
quad.	$105	$225
child	$10	$20

Taxes extra VS MC IT

Reduced rates: Oct. 1 to Nov. 30
Apr. 1 to June 1
Open year round

Number of rooms	6
rooms with private bath	6

Activities: 🚣 🚶 🚲 🛶 🎿

8. HÉBERTVILLE

☀☀☀ F 🏊 P 🚗 ✕ R1 TA

B&B on the farm, charming welcome. Perfect location for visiting the entire region. Come share in our family life and visit our dairy farm in the shade of Parc des Laurentides. Children welcome. Pool, beach, mountain biking, skating and roller-blading track, fishing, playing field. Downhill and cross-country skiing, ice-fishing, inner-tubes sliding. **Farm Stay p 42.**

From Parc des Laurentides, Rte 169. 1st village, Rue St-Isidore.

B&B
FERME CAROLE and
JACQUES MARTEL

Carole and Jacques Martel
474, St-Isidore
Hébertville G8N 1L7
(418) 344-1323

	B&B
single	$35
double	$45
triple	$65
quad.	$85
child	$10

Open year round

Number of rooms	3
shared bathrooms	2

Activities: 🚣 🚲 🚶 🛶 🎿

9. HÉBERTVILLE

☀☀ F e 🚗 P 🐕 R4 TA

Visit an area where nature still offers adventure. Ancestral house in French-speaking land welcomes you year round. Activities; fishing cruises on Lac St-Jean available. Our B&B is located between Tadoussac (70 min), for whale-watching, and the St-Félicien zoo (45 min). We look forward to sharing pleasant family moments with you. Dinner on request.

From Parc des Laurentides, Rte 169 North, 6km, twd Robertval.

B&B
GÎTE BELLE-RIVIÈRE

Marie-Alice Bouchard
872, rang Caron, rte 169
Hébertville G8N 1B6
(418) 344-4345
fax (418) 344-1933
bouchard@digicom.qc.ca

	B&B
single	$30
double	$45
triple	$65
quad.	$85
child	$10

Open year round

Number of rooms	4
rooms with sink	1
shared bathrooms	2

Activities: 🛶 🚶 🚲 🛶 🎿

10. JONQUIÈRE

☀☀☀ F 🚫 🏊 P 🚗 R1

Saguenay-Lac-St-Jean Excellence Prize 1995-96 and finalist in 1997-98. 5 min walk from downtown. Soundproof rooms with sinks and TVs. Breakfast in the sunroom with a view of the river. One-of-a-kind aluminum footbridge, private beach, rowboat, pedal boat, fishing, bike path nearby. Rest and tranquillity guaranteed.

From Québec City, Rte 175 and Rte 170, left to Jonquière, drive 11.2km. Take Boul. Harvey, drive 2.8km, left on Rue St-Jean-Baptiste, (St-Raphaël parish) drive 1.1km. Left on Rue des Saules.

B&B
GÎTE DE LA RIVIÈRE
AUX SABLES

Marie and Jean Eudes Girard
4076, des Saules
Jonquière
G8A 2G7
(418) 547-5101
fax (418) 547-6939

B&B	
single	$40
double	$50-55
triple	$70
quad.	$85
child	$10

Open year round

Number of rooms	4
rooms with sink	4
rooms in basement	4
shared bathrooms	2

Activities: 🦆 🚤 ⛷ 🎣 🚲

11. JONQUIÈRE

☀☀☀ F e 🚗 P 🏊 R.5

Conveniently located in the heart of Saguenay close to various festivals, our B&B has a garden overflowing with fruits and vegetables, which accompany every breakfast. This peaceful retreat has a homey atmosphere. Little ones will be delighted by its pool. Older folks enjoy walking on the paths that run along Rivière-aux-Sables and Mont-Jacob. Our B&B warmly welcomes you and takes care of your every need.

From Québec City, Rtes 175 and 170, left to Jonquière, drive 11.2km. Boulevard Harvey, drive 2.8km, left on Rue St-Jean-Baptiste, drive 0.5km right on Rue Du Pont, left on Rue Ste-Gertrude.

B&B
GÎTE TOURISTIQUE DU
MONT-JACOB

Ghislaine and Laurien Tremblay
2313, rue Sainte-Gertrude
Jonquière G8A 1Y1
(418) 547-8934
fax (418) 547-0864

B&B	
single	$40
double	$50
triple	$70
child	$0-10

Open year round

Number of rooms	3
rooms in basement	1
shared bathrooms	1

Activities: 🏛 🦆 🚲 🚤 🤸

12. JONQUIÈRE

☀☀☀ F E 🚫 P 🚗 🏊 R1 TA

Winner of the Saguenay-Lac-St-Jean Excellence Prize 1998, finalist in 1999. It is a great pleasure to welcome you to our very warm home: large solarium; TV in every room, decorated with particular care. Spectacular garden and in-ground pool encourage relaxation. Near bar-restaurants, the sports centre and the CEGEP.

In Jonquière's town centre, at St-Dominique and Boul. Harvey, head south to the Irving gas station, left on Rue des Hirondelles, left on 1st street (Des Merles).

B&B
LE MERLEAU

Andrée Côté and Léo April
2456, des Merles
Jonquière G7X 8B3
(418) 542-1093
fax (418) 542-1031

B&B	
single	$40
double	$50-55
triple	$70
quad.	$85
child	$10

Reduced rates: Sep. 1 to May 31 20% 3 nights and more
Open year round

Number of rooms	5
rooms in basement	2
shared bathrooms	3

Activities: 🚤 ⛷ 🎣 🚲 🏇

13. JONQUIÈRE

☀☀☀ | F | e | 🚫 | 🐕 | 🚗 | P | R.5 | TA

Warm welcome in a charming, perfectly comfortable 1900s house. Picturesque, historic Arvida district near Alcan plant, the Manoir, the aluminum bridge and tourist, cultural and sports activities. Near the Québecissime show, with the bike path at our doorstep. Snowmobiling and dogsledding packages available. Original, hearty breakfast.

From Quebec City, Rte 175 North; in Chicoutimi, Jonquière-bound Rte 170 for 8km, right on Rue Mellon for 3km to roundabout, Boul. Saguenay to Jonquière, about 80 m, on the right.

B&B
LE MITAN

Denise F. Blackburn
2840, boul. Saguenay
Jonquière G7S 2H3
(418) 548-7388
fax (418) 548-3415
www.multimania.com/lemitan/
denisefblackburn@hotmail.com

B&B	
single	$40
double	$60
child	$15

Open year round

Number of rooms	3
rooms with sink	3
shared bathrooms	2
rooms in basement	1

Activities: 🐟 ⛴ 🎣 🚲 ⛷

14. LA BAIE

☀☀☀ | F | a | 🚫 | 🚗 | P | R.5

Conveniently located in the heart of all the tourist attractions, our cosy B&B has soundproof rooms with air-conditioning and televisions. The dining room has a panoramic view and for breakfast, secret pancakes, and shrimp at his best—just one way to thank you for staying with us.

Rte 175 North and 170 East or Rte 138 East and 170 West to Boulevard de la Grande Baie South. After the bridge, drive 0.9km, turn right on Avenue Lavoie, and then left on the 2nd street. Right at the corner.

B&B
À BAIE DES HA! HA!

Régis Sergerie
1131, 2ᵉ rue
La Baie
G7B 2G5
(418) 544-2508
toll free 1-877-244-2508

B&B	
single	50-55 $
double	55-60 $

Reduced rates: Sep.1 to June 15
Open year round

Number of rooms	3
rooms with sink	2
shared wc	2
shared bathrooms	1

Activities: 🐟 ⛴ 🎣 🚶 🚲

15. LA BAIE

☀☀☀ | F | e | 🚗 | P | 🏊 | 🚫 | 🐕 | R3

Located by the water, every room has its own private entrance and balcony, offering a superb view. Walk along the shoreline, watch the tides, discover the artist-host's granite sculptures. Evening beach campfires, for those who so desire. If nature enchants you, one day is not enough. Winter rate: $45 for 2. Ice-fishing and dog-sledding packages.

From the Parc des Laurentides, Rtes 175 North and 170 East to Boul de la Grande-Baie Sud. After the Musée du Fjord drive approx. 5km. From St-Siméon, Rte 170 North. On the water side, a huge granite block marks the entrance.

B&B
À FLEUR DE PIERRE

Colette Létourneau and
Carrol Tremblay
6788, boul. Grande-Baie Sud
La Baie G7B 3P6
(418) 544-3260

B&B	
single	$45-50
double	$55-60
triple	$70-75
quad.	$85
child	$10

Reduced rates: Oct. 1 to May 31
Open year round

Number of rooms	3
rooms with private bath	1
shared bathrooms	1

Activities: 🐟 🏛 ⛴ 🚤 🚶

16. LA BAIE

☀☀☀ F E 🚗 P 🛶 🐕 R.1 TA

Located at the heart of La Baie, on the shore of the Saguenay fjord, a few metres from the Parc Mars promenade. Spacious house offers tranquillity and comfort. Rooms for one, two or four people available. Hearty breakfast. Restaurants nearby. Large garage for up to 8 motorbikes or skidoos.

20km from Chicoutimi. From Québec City, Rtes 175 North and 170 East or Rtes 138 East and 170 West. At the Ville de La Baie, Rue Victoria is parallel to Parc Mars alongside the water.

B&B
À LA MAISON
DU DOCTEUR TANGUAY

Janine Minier and Pierre Lemay
547, rue Victoria
La Baie G7B 3M5
(418) 544-3515
toll free 1-877-544-3515

B&B	
single	$40-45
double	$50-60
triple	$70
quad.	$85
child	$10

Reduced rates: Jan.1 to May 1
Open year round

Number of rooms	5
rooms in basement	3
shared bathrooms	2

Activities: 🚶 🛶 🚣 🚴 🛶

17. LA BAIE

☀☀☀ F E 🚫 P 🛶 R1 TA

15,000 square metres of land right at the edge of the water (*au bord de l'eau*), in town, an outstanding location with a spectacular view, spacious rooms. Here, the "bay" (*baie*) is the sea; it is a vast stretch of salt water, and its 7-metre tides transform the landscape. Five min from the theatre and various activities, but in a world of its own. Hearty breakfasts, homey atmosphere.

From Parc des Laurentides, Rte 175 North, then 170 East to Boul Grande-Baie South. Drive 1.5km past the Musée du Fjord. Make sure not to drive right past the house; you can't see it from the road!

B&B
AU BORD DE L'EAU
La Baie G7B 3P6

Lyne Fortin and Réjean Ouellet
5208, boul. Grande-Baie Sud
La Baie G7B 3P6
(418) 544-0892
toll free 1-888-811-0892
fax (418) 544-5432
rejean.ouellet@sympatico.ca

B&B	
single	$45-70
double	$60-85
triple	$75-100
quad.	$90-115
child	$10

VS MC

Reduced rates: Sep.1 to May 31
Open year round

Number of rooms	4
rooms with private bath	2
shared bathrooms	1

Activities: 🛶 🚣 🚴 🛶 🎿

18. LA BAIE

☀☀☀ F e 🐕 🛶 P R2

Come live an incredible experience with the Gagné family at the "Chez Grand-Maman" B&B where you will find tranquillity in picturesque surroundings. You'll experience extraordinary things on our farm by the Baie des HA! HA! We will make you feel at home. **Farm Stay p 43.**

From Parc des Laurentides, Rtes 175 North and 170 East towards "Ville de la Baie", Rue Bagot. Left on Rue Victoria for about 2km. Straight ahead, 1st farm, "Alain Gagné".

B&B
CHEZ GRAND-MAMAN

Jacinthe Bouchard and
Alain Gagné
1254, chemin St-Joseph
La Baie G7B 3N9
(418) 544-7396
(418) 697-0517
fax (418) 544-0392

B&B	
single	$35
double	$45
triple	$65
child	$10-12

Open year round

Number of rooms	3
shared bathrooms	2

Activities: 🛶 🚣 🎣 🚴 🎿

19. LA BAIE

☀☀☀ F E P 🚗 ⛴ R.1 TA

Saguenay-Lac-St-Jean Excellence Prize 1996-97. Simple, warm exchanges will soon make us fast friends. Located by the water, all rooms have private entrance, patio door and view of the bay. 3 have private bathrooms. Short walk from various activities: cruises, park, restaurants, bike/footpaths. Breakfast in solarium. Ice-fishing packages. Welcome.

From Québec City, Rtes 175 North and 170 East to La Baie. From Rue Bagot, straight ahead to Rue Victoria, left to Damase-Potvin, left on Rue Simard.

B&B
GÎTE BELLE-VUE

Monique and Régent Goyette
1442, Simard
La Baie G7B 2X9
(418) 544-4598
fax (418) 544-5861
www.royaume.com/
gite-bellevue
bellevue@royaume.com

B&B	
single	$50-60
double	$55-70
triple	$70-85
quad.	$100
child	$15

Reduced rates: 20% Oct.1 to May 31
Open year round

Number of rooms	5
rooms with private bath	3
shared bathrooms	1

Activities: 🐚 🚣 ⛷ 🛶 🏃

20. LA BAIE

☀☀☀ F 🚗 P R2 TA

To rediscover the charm of the countryside of long ago, drop anchor off l'Anse-à-Benjamin. Near all services: theatre, walking trails, marina, skating rink. Pleasant rooms. Enjoy our B&B winter or summer. Outfitter of fishing cabins. Packages available upon request.

From Parc des Laurentides, Rtes 175 North and 170 East to Ville de la Baie, Rue Bagot. Left on Rue Victoria, keep right for 2km.

B&B
GÎTE DE LA PÊCHE BLANCHE

Laurence Blanchette and
Jean-Claude Simard
1352, route de
l'Anse-à-Benjamin
La Baie G7B 3N9
tel/fax (418) 544-4176

B&B	
single	$40
double	$45-55
triple	$55
child	$10

Open year round

Number of rooms	4
rooms in basement	3
shared bathrooms	2

Activities: 🐚 🛶 ⛷ 🏃 🛷

21. LA BAIE

☀☀☀ F e 🚗 P R1

Located on the heights of Ville de La Baie, in the heart of most activities, our warm and comfortable B&B has acquired an enviable reputation with tourists over the last 10 years. A magnificent landscaped garden offers our guests a quiet haven. Lavish breakfast; motorcycle garage, bicycles at guests' disposal.

From Parc des Laurentides, Rtes 175 North and 170 East to La Baie. Rue Bagot to intersection, left on Rue des Pins.

B&B
GÎTE DES PINS

Doris Bolduc and
Freddy Pouliot
1273, rue des Pins
La Baie G7B 3H7
(418) 544-5178

B&B	
single	$40
double	$50
triple	$60
quad.	$70
child	$10

Reduced rates: May 1 to June 15 and Sep. 1 to Oct. 31
Open: May 1 to Oct. 31

Number of rooms	3
rooms in basement	2
shared bathrooms	1

Activities: 🏛 🛶 ⛷ 🏃 🚲

22. LA BAIE

⚹⚹⚹ F | e | ♿ | P | 🚗 | R2 | TA

2km west of Ville de La Baie and 12km east of Chicoutimi. You are welcome in our ancestral home. You will enjoy staying with us. We will serve you breakfast with fresh farm products. We will be happy to meet you. Near the "Fabuleuse Histoire du Royaume".

From Parc des Laurentides, Rtes 175 North, and 170 East to Ville de La Baie. At the 2nd traffic lights, straight to Rue Victoria, turn left. Drive 2km on Victoria which becomes St-Joseph. 2nd house on right after flashing light.

B&B
LA MAISON DES ANCÊTRES

Judith and Germain Simard
1722, chemin St-Joseph
La Baie G7B 3N9
(418) 544-2925
fax (418) 544-0241

B&B	
single	$35
double	$45
triple	$60
child	$10

Open: May 1 to Oct. 31

Number of rooms	4
shared bathrooms	2

Activities: 🏛 🦆 🚣 🚶 🚴

23. LAC-À-LA-CROIX

⚹⚹⚹ F | e | 🚗 | P | R8 | TA

Century-old farmhouse where we like to keep up traditions: a toast to friends, home-made meals, cows in their pyjamas in the fall. Well-located for touring the region. Traditional recipes to be shared. Cross-country skiing on the farm and near the mountain. **Farm Stay p 43.**

From Parc des Laurentides, Rte 169, 1e Rang on the left before the village of Hébertville. Drive 11km.

B&B

Céline and Georges Martin
1311, Rang 3
Lac-à-la-Croix G0W 1W0
tel/fax (418) 349-2583

B&B	
single	$28
double	$42
child	$12

Open year round

Number of rooms	3
shared wc	2
shared bathrooms	1

Activities: 🚣 🚴 ⛷ 🏃 🐎

24. L'ANSE-ST-JEAN

★ ★ F | E | P | ✕ | TA

A kingdom in the heart of Parc Saguenay. Facing the covered bridge, with a large veranda off the rooms. Big living room with fireplace. Recommended for its game, fish and seafood dishes; 15% off for inn guests. Direct access to snowmobile trails. Skiing, fjord and ice fishing nearby. **Ad end of this region**

Rte 170 twd L'Anse-St-Jean. Take Rue St-Jean-Baptiste twd the dock. The inn is 0.2km from the church, facing the covered bridge.

INN
AUBERGE DES CÉVENNES

Enid Bertrand and
Louis Mario Dufour
294, rue St-Jean-Baptiste
L'Anse-St-Jean G0V 1J0
(418) 272-3180
toll free 1-877-272-3180
fax (418) 272-1131
auberge-des-cevennes.qc.ca
auberge-des-cevennes
@royaume.com

	B&B	MAP
single	$57-62	$79-84
double	$64-69	$108-113
triple	$91	$157
quad.	$98	$186

Taxes extra VS MC ER IT

Reduced rates: Sep. 4 to Dec. 22 and Jan. 6 to June 23
Open year round

Number of rooms	8
rooms with private bath	8

Activities: 🚣 🏃 🏇 🛷 🎿

25. L'ANSE-ST-JEAN

F e P R.3

Ancestral home caressed by the majestic Saguenay Fjord. Your eyes can't open wide enough to take in all that nature has to offer. The cozy, comfortable rooms bring you back to the turn of the century. Walking trails are at our doorstep. Horseback riding, mini-cruises up the fjord, sea kayaks, mountain bikes, salmon fishing, ski and ice-fishing available.

From Québec City, Rte 175, Parc des Laurentides to Chicoutimi. Or Rte 138 to St-Siméon, Rte 170 to Anse-St-Jean. Rue St-Jean-Baptiste, 8km to Saguenay Fjord.

B&B
AU NID DE L'ANSE

Suzanne and Ronald Bilodeau
376, St-Jean-Baptiste
L'Anse-St-Jean G0V 1J0
(418) 272-2273
(418) 549-1807
fax (418) 549-9284

B&B	
single	$50-55
double	$55-60
triple	$80-85

Open: Mar. 1 to Oct. 30

Number of rooms	3
shared wc	1
shared bathrooms	1

Activities:

26. L'ANSE-ST-JEAN

F e P R1.5 TA

Cosy Québec-style house echoing the colours of the fjord. Breakfast in the sunroom with river and mountain view. Rest in comfortable rooms, relax and daydream to the sound of the river. Nearby: walking trails, horseback riding, sea kayaking, fjord cruises, mountain biking, salmon fishing. Françoise (the homebody) and François (the sportsman) offer simple hospitality.

From Québec City, via St-Siméon, Rtes 138 E. and 170 to Anse-St-Jean. Via Chicoutimi, Rtes 175, then 170, Rue Principale de l'Anse for 3.5km.

B&B
LA PANTOUFLARDE

Françoise Potvin and
François Asselin
129, St-Jean-Baptiste
L'Anse-St-Jean G0V 1J0
(418) 272-2182
(418) 545-1099
fax (418) 545-1914

B&B	
single	$40
double	$55
triple	$70
quad.	$85

Open: June 1 to Oct. 31

Number of rooms	3
shared bathrooms	2
rooms with sink	2

Activities:

27. L'ANSE-ST-JEAN

F E P R3 TA

Located near Parc du Saguenay and Rivière St-Jean, Gîte Du Barrage de L'Anse has comfortable rooms, a cosy fireplace and scrumptious breakfasts. Views of L'Homme Qui Sommeille Mountain and other natural wonders. Near hiking trails, horseback riding, sea kayaking, ferryboats on the fjord, biking and fishing for trout, salmon and smelt. In winter: downhill and cross-country skiing and ice fishing.

Via St-Siméon or Ville la Baie, Rte 170 to the km 71 marker, Rue Côté facing our sign.

B&B
LE GÎTE DU BARRAGE DE L'ANSE

Elisabeth Ross and
Egide Lessard
3, rue Côté
L'Anse-St-Jean
G0V 1J0
(418) 272-3387
fax (418) 272-1388
egide@royaume.com

B&B	
single	$40-45
double	$50-55-60
triple	$65-75
child	$10-15

Open year round

Number of rooms	3
rooms in basement	1
shared bathrooms	2

Activities:

28. L'ANSE-ST-JEAN

☀︎☀︎☀︎ F E ♿ 🏊 P R1.5 TA

"...A beautiful terrace and river behind the B&B is ideal for enjoying a good book, and offers a splendid view of the mountains. Your host offers a friendly welcome into his sunny and spacious home; beautiful rooms will help put your worried behind you. Budget-conscious travellers in search of the utmost in comfort will find it here." A French tourist.

From Québec City via St-Siméon, Rtes 138 East and 170 to Anse St-Jean; via Chicoutimi, Rtes 175 and 170. Take the main street of Anse St-Jean and drive 3.5km.

B&B
LE GLOBE-TROTTER

Anne Lambert and
André Bouchard
131, St-Jean-Baptiste
L'Anse-St-Jean G0V 1J0
tel/fax (418) 272-2353
bur: (418) 272-2124
www.bbcanada.com/322.html
andreb7@hotmail.com

B&B	
single	$45
double	$55
child	$15

Open: Mar. 1 to Oct. 31

Number of rooms	3
rooms with private bath	1
shared bathrooms	1

Activities: 🚣 🐟 🧍 🚴 🐎

---

29. MÉTABETCHOUAN

☀︎☀︎☀︎ F 🚗 P 🏖 R.5 TA

At Berthe and Jean-Charles's, in a quiet and intimate spot right near the lake. Let yourselves be charmed by the flowers and birds. Five-kilometre-long beach with services and landscaped promenade. Concert at music camp, summer theatre, golf course, horseback riding, cycling path, special breakfasts.

From Parc des Laurentides, Rte 169 twd Roberval. In Métabetchouan: 1st exit, keep turning right.

B&B
AU SOLEIL COUCHANT

Berthe and Jean-Charles Fortin
31-2, rue Foyer du Lac
Métabetchouan G0W 2A0
(418) 349-2138
fax (418) 349-2203
www.mediom.qc.ca/~gil/soleil

B&B	
single	$40
double	$50
child	$0-10

Open year round

Number of rooms	3
shared wc	1
shared bathrooms	1

Activities: 🚣 🐟 🏇 🏃

---

30. MÉTABETCHOUAN

F e P R.4 TA

Majestic turn-of-the-century Victorian house crowned by stately maples. Where uniformity stops to make way for the pleasures of refinement. Large dining room inspired by the charms of the past. Cozy rooms, delicious brunch, music, flowers and little considerations. 3 rooms with antique bath. Nearby: beach and cycling path. **See colour photos.**

From Québec City, Rte 169 North twd Roberval. From La Tuque: Rte 155 to Chambord, turn right heading toward Alma. In Métabetchouan: enter on Rue Principale, near the church opposite the post office.

INN
AUBERGE LA MAISON LAMY

Lise Girard and Normand Doré
56, rue St-André
Métabetchouan G0W 2A0
(418) 349-3686
toll free 1-888-565-3686
www.bbcanada.com/
2733.html

B&B		
single	$50-60	
double	$60-75	
triple	$75	
quad.	$90	
child	$10	

Taxes extra VS MC IT

Reduced rates: Oct. 15 to Dec.15 and Jan. 5 to June 1
Open year round

Number of rooms	6
rooms with bath and sink	3
rooms with sink	3
shared bathrooms	3

Activities: 🐟 🧍 🚴 🚣 🎿

31. NORMANDIN

☼☼☼ F e 🚭 🐕 P R8 TA

"What a joy to find this haven of peace and harmony after a day of travelling." Everything to "recharge your batteries": peace and quiet, wide expanses and beautiful grounds. Personalized breakfasts. Singular decor. You will be greeted like the special guest that you are! Motorcycle and bicycle garage. Seven minutes from the Grands Jardins.

From Parc des Laurentides, Rte 169 toward Roberval then St-Félicien, St-Méthode and Normandin. At traffic light, toward St-Thomas Didyme 8km.

B&B
LE GÎTE DU PASSERIN

Gaétane Savard and
Philippe Laliberté
2292, St-Cyrille
Normandin G8M 4K5
(418) 274-2170

B&B	
single	$40
double	$55-65
triple	$70
child	$15

Reduced rates: Sep. 30 to May 31
Open year round

Number of rooms	3
shared bathrooms	2

Activities: 🚣 🧍 🚲 🛶 🏃

32. NORMANDIN

☼☼☼ F e 🚭 P 🏊 R4 TA

Saguenay-Lac-St-Jean Excellence Prize 1999. Follow your heart, stomach or desire for freedom to our spacious country house, a former general store. Facilities include: living-room solarium, pool, fireplace, swing, small farm. 3km from bike path, 4km from Grands Jardins. Finally, treat yourself to our Makadan breakfast. Motorcycle/bicycle garage. **Farm Stay p 43.**

From Parc des Laurentides, Rte 169 twd Robertval and St-Félicien, St-Méthode, Normandin. At the lights, twd St-Thomas Didyme, 3km.

B&B
LES GÎTES MAKADAN

Micheline Villeneuve and
Daniel Bergeron
1728, St-Cyrille
Normandin G8M 4K5
(418) 274-2867
toll free 1-877-625-2326
www.destinationquebec.
com/ftpdocs/makadan/
makadan.htm
makadan@destination.ca

B&B	
single	$40-55
double	$55-75
triple	$70-85
quad.	$95
child	$15

VS

Reduced rates: Sep. 30 to
May 31
Open year round

Number of rooms	5
rooms with private bath	1
shared bathrooms	2

Activties: 🚣 🧍 🚲 🏃 🛶

33. PETIT-SAGUENAY

★ ★ F e 🚗 P ❌ R1 TA

In an old rural inn, we have recreated the warm and intimate ambiance of a large country house. Located on the mountainside, facing the salmon river, at the entrance of Parc Saguenay. Cruise tickets: Fjord and whales. Snowbiling. The warmth of the hearth, a meal worthy of our hospitality, receiving you will be a pleasure.

From St-Siméon in the Charlevoix region, take Rte 170 towards Chicoutimi for about 50km. The inn is located 100 m from the tourist booth, an hour from Tadoussac and Chicoutimi.

INN
AUBERGE LES 2 PIGNONS

Régine Morin
117, route 170
Petit-Saguenay G0V 1N0
(418) 272-3091
fax (418) 272-1125
www.royaume.com/
auberge-2-pignons
auberge-2-pignons
@royaume.com

	B&B	MAP
single	$47-57	$67-77
double	$54-74	$97-114
triple	$79-89	$139-149
quad.	$94-104	$174-184
child	$12	$27

Taxes extra VS MC ER IT
Reduced rates: Sep. 15 to Dec 15
and Mar. to June 15
Open year round

Number of rooms	8
rooms with sink	1
rooms with private bath	6
shared wc	2
shared bathrooms	2

Activities: 🛶 🏇 🧍 🛶 ⛷

34. ROBERVAL

☀☀☀ F 🚗 P 🏊 R6 TA

Come relax by splendid Lac St-Jean, a veritable inland sea. Take advantage of a well-deserved quiet moment and stretch out on our private beach near the house. It gives us great pleasure to have you as our guests.

From Parc des Laurentides, Rte 169. We are 3.5km from the Val-Jalbert bridge. From La Tuque, Rte 155 to Chambord. Turn left to Roberval, Rte 169, drive 10km B&B on your left.

B&B
LA MAISON AU TOIT ROUGE

Yolande Lalancette and
Raynald Girard
1345, boul. de l'Anse,
route 169
Roberval G8H 2N1
(418) 275-3290

B&B	
single	$35
double	$45
child	$10

Open: May 15 to Sep. 30

Number of rooms	3
shared bathrooms	2

Activities: 🏛 ⛴ 🚣 🎣 🚴

---

35. ST-AMBROISE-DE-CHICOUTIMI

☀☀☀ F e 🚭 🐕 🚗 P 🍴 R.5 TA

In the heart of Saguenay-Lac-St-Jean, a country farmhouse with a garden, flowers, farmyard, lake, and trout stream. Cozy beds, choice breakfasts and, by reservation, delicious Saguenay meals. Also, 3- to 6-day "all-inclusive" packages. In summer: fishing, blueberry picking. In winter: snowmobiling, dogsledding, skiing, ice fishing.

Rte 172 between Chicoutimi and Alma. Near St-Ambroise, take Rte Bégin and drive 3km along paved road. Turn right on Rang 9, drive 500 m along gravel road.

B&B
AUX PIGNONS VERTS

Ghislaine Ouellet and
Jean-Claude Villeneuve
925, Rang 9
St-Ambroise-de-Chicoutimi
G7P 2A4
(418) 672-2172
fax (418) 672-6622
www.saglac.qc.ca/~
ambroise/pignon/pignon.htm
pignonsverts@sympatico.ca

B&B	
single	$45
double	$55-65
child	$25

VS

Open year round

Number of rooms	3
shared bathrooms	2

Activities: 🎣 🎿 ⛷ 🛷 🐕

---

36. ST-FÉLICIEN

🖊 F e 🚭 🚗 P R.1

Ten metres from the Ashuapmushuan River, and boasting a large terrace. What a joy to meet people from all over the world. Tourist attractions: zoo (6km), falls (5km), Val-Jalbert (20km). Located near the town centre. Come meet us for a pleasant time. Special little considerations await you.

From Parc des Laurentides, Rte 169 twd Roberal to St-Félicien; located opposite "Mets Chinois". From Dolbeau, at 2nd light, left on Sacré-Coeur; located opposite "Mets Chinois".

B&B
À FLEUR D'EAU

Claudette Nadeau and
Paul Hébert
1016, Sacré-Coeur
St-Félicien G8K 1R5
(418) 679-0784

B&B	
single	$35
double	$45-50
triple	$55-60
quad.	$65
child	$10

Reduced rates: Oct. 1 to June 1
Open year round

Number of rooms	5
rooms with private bath	2
shared wc	1
shared bathrooms	3

Activities: 🏛 ⛴ 🚣 🎣 🚴

37. ST-FÉLICIEN

☀☀☀ F e P 🚗 R2

If you like the charm of the country, you'll be enchanted by our surroundings. A warm welcome in a calming and restful atmosphere. A sitting room is at your disposal. Evenings outdoors around the campfire lead to good conversation. Healthy, generous breakfast. 3km to town, 6km to the zoo. Reduced rates: September to June.

From Parc des Laurentides, Rte 169 towards Roberval to St-Félicien. At the 1st traffic lights, turn left on Rue Notre-Dame, drive 2.6km. Right on Rang Double, drive 0.7km.

B&B
À LA FERME HÉBERT

Céline Giroux and
J-Jacques Hébert
1070, rang Double
St-Félicien G8K 2N8
(418) 679-0574

B&B	
single	$40
double	$45
triple	$60
child	$10

Taxes extra

Reduced rates: 2 nights and more, Sep. 1 to June 15
Open year round

Number of rooms	4
rooms with sink	1
rooms in basement	2
shared bathrooms	2

Activities: 🦪 🌰 🚲 🛶 🐎

38. ST-FÉLICIEN

☀☀☀ F P R2 TA

With my easy smile and the simplicity of the people of the Lac St-Jean region, I've got a warm welcome ready for you. Bedrooms with fans, generous breakfast, relaxing spot, country calm and sitting room with wood-burning stove. We will be happy to have you. Nearby: zoo, water-slides, autodrome, kayaking, horseback riding centre.

From Parc des Laurentides, Rte 169 twd Roberval to St-Félicien. At the 1st traffic lights, Rue Notre-Dame left, drive 2.4km and turn left on Rang Double. Drive 0.8km.

B&B
AU DOMAINE TREMBLAY

Lucienne and Robert
677, rang Double
St-Félicien G8K 2N8
(418) 679-0169

B&B	
single	$30
double	$45
child	$5-15

Reduced rates: Oct.1 to May 15
Open year round

Number of rooms	4
shared bathrooms	2

Activities: 🦪 🚲 👤 🐎 🛶

39. ST-FÉLICIEN

☀☀☀ F e P R4 TA

"Chez Denise" you'll discover the hospitality of the people of Lac-St-Jean. Large house located at the heart of tourist activities: zoo, race-car track, car museum (2km away), drive-in, golf, etc. Fishing possible. It is our pleasure to welcome you.

From Parc des Laurentides, Rte 169 to Roberval. From La Tuque, Rte 155 to Chambord, turn left to Roberval to St-Félicien. At the 2nd traffic lights turn left, 5km. From Dolbeau at the 2nd traffic lights, drive 5km.

B&B
GÎTE CHEZ DENISE

Denise and Louis-Marie Gagnon
1430, rang Double
St-Félicien G8K 2N8
tel/fax (418) 679-1498

B&B	
single	$35
double	$45-50
child	$7-15

Open year round

Number of rooms	4
shared bathrooms	2

Activities: 🛶 🌰 👤 🎿 🤸

40. ST-FÉLIX-D'OTIS

Country farm between La Baie and Rivière-Eternité with animals running free, flowers, decorative garden. A relaxing, rejuvenating haven where life flows with the seasons. Outdoor pool, air-conditioned house. Healthy breakfast, oven-fresh bread, wild berries. Near: Parc Saguenay, Site de la Nouvelle France and «La Fabuleuse Histoire d'un Royaume». Guided beaver-watching tour. **Farm Stay p 43.**

From Parc des Laurentides, Rtes 175 North and 170 East. From St-Siméon, Rte 170 North twd Chicoutimi.

B&B
GÎTE DE LA BASSE-COUR

Huguette Morin and
Régis Girard
271, rue Principale, route 170
St-Félix-d'Otis G0V 1M0
(418) 544-8766

B&B	
single	$40
double	$50
triple	$70
quad.	$80
child	$5-15

Open year round

Number of rooms	3
shared bathrooms	2

Activities:

---

41. ST-FÉLIX-D'OTIS

The fjord route invites you: Lac Otis, beach, canoeing fishing, kayaking. Backdrop for the film Black Robe, the traditions and customs of the Amerindians and the first colonists in an Iroquois village. 15km from Rivière Éternité; cruises, cliffs, hiking trails, beavers and town of La Baie (Fabuleuse and Jos Maquillon). Copious breakfasts, blueberry crepes; tv, tourist info. Come and chat with us.

From Parc des Laurentides, Rtes 175 North and 170 East. Or from St-Siméon, Rte 170 North towards Chicoutimi.

B&B
MAISON JONCAS

Dorina Joncas
291, rue Principale
Route 170 Est, C.P. 51
St-Félix-d'Otis G0V 1M0
(418) 544-5953

B&B	
single	$30
double	$40-45
triple	$60
quad.	$65
child	$5-8

Open: May 1 to Nov. 1

Number of rooms	2
shared wc	1
shared bathrooms	1

Activities:

---

42. ST-FULGENCE

Fairy tales are often set in enchanted forests like this. La Futaie is a wooded, 160-ha property between the Saguenay Fjord and Mont Valin. Do a bit of fishing in our wild lake. We serve *ouananiche*, fresh-water salmon (Montagnais called them "the little lost ones"), you can even catch your own! In winter: snowmobile base with excursion services.

Between St-Fulgence and St-Rose-du-Nord, Rte 172. 21km from Dubuc bridge in Chicoutimi and 115km from Tadoussac.

INN
AUBERGE LA FUTAIE

Jocelyne and Benoît Girard
1061, boul. Tadoussac
St-Fulgence G0V 1S0
tel/fax (418) 674-2581
grap@saglac.qc.ca

B&B	
single	$50-65
double	$60-75
triple	$75-90
quad.	$90-105
child	$10-15

Taxes extra VS MC IT

Open year round

Number of rooms	6
rooms with private bath	1
shared wc	1
shared bathrooms	2

Activities:

43. ST-FULGENCE

☀☀☀☀ F E 🐕 P ✕ 🏊 R8 TA

La Maraîchère du Saguenay, our ancestral home, our old barn and our latest addition, a tiny house similar to our old home. Warm, stunning, cosy rooms with antique furnishings. A grandiose fjord and magnificent parks nearby, Mont-Valin, Saguenay and Cap-Jaseux. Kayaking, canoeing, hiking, dogsleding, snowmobiling plus all the activities we can organise for you. Dinner available, must reserve ahead of time. See you soon.

From Chicoutimi, 8km past Dubuc bridge, Rte 172 towards Tadoussac. Turn left 400 m after Esso station.

B&B
LA MARAÎCHÈRE
DU SAGUENAY

Adèle Copeman and
Rodrigue Langevin
97, boul. Tadoussac
St-Fulgence GOV 1S0
(418) 674-9384
(418) 674-2247
fax (418) 674-1055
www.maraichere.langevin.net
maraichere@langevin.net

B&B	
single	$55-65
double	$65-75
triple	$80-100
quad.	$95-125
child	$0-30

Taxes extra VS MC

Open year round

Number of rooms	4
rooms with private bath	2
shared bathrooms	1

Activities: 🚶 🚲 🛶 🎿 🐎

44. ST-PRIME

☀☀☀ F 🐕 P R4 TA

Come pay us a visit. Discover the dairy farm's animals and natural surroundings. Make a date for some relaxation and tranquillity. Warm welcome. Savour an original, generous breakfast. Your trip will make for wonderful memories. Close: Zoo St-Félicien, Cheddar museum, native village, pioneer mill, ghost village, etc.

From Parc des Laurentides, Rte 169 twd Roberval. At St-Prime, across from the church, left on 15e Avenue for 3.3km, right for 4.1km.

B&B
GÎTE FERME DU PATURIN

Francine Villeneuve and
Yvan Grenier
1028, Rang 3
St-Prime G8J 1X5
tel/fax (418) 251-2837

B&B	
single	$35-40
double	$50-55
child	$5-12

Open year round

Number of rooms	4
rooms with private bath	1
shared bathrooms	2

Activities: 🏛 🛶 🎿 🚲 🛶

45. ST-PRIME

☀☀☀☀ F P 🐕 🏊 R4 TA

Century-old house on a dairy farm, on one of the prettiest farm roads, surrounded by lovely gardens, waterfalls, pool. If you like the space and tranquillity of the country, you'll feel at home at our house. It will be our pleasure to share special moments with you. Visit the farm. Located amidst all the main tourist attractions of Lac-St-Jean: St-Félicien zoo, Indian and ghost town, cheddar museum, pioneer mills, hydraulic-plane tours, etc.

From Parc des Laurentides, Rte 169 to Roberval. In St-Prime, facing the church, turn left on 15e Ave. Drive 3.3km, turn right, drive 2km.

B&B
LA MAISON CAMPAGNARDE

Brigitte Boivin and
Roger Taillon
850, Rang 3
St-Prime G8J 1X3
tel/fax (418) 251-3235
briro@destination.ca

B&B	
single	$40
double	$50-55
child	$5-12

Open year round

Number of rooms	4
shared wc	1
shared bathrooms	1

Activities: 🏛 🦆 🛶 🚲

46. STE-JEANNE-D'ARC

☀☀☀ F P R7 TA

Peaceful forestry farm, 2km from Route 169. Old house with antique furniture, fans in the rooms. Home-made breakfasts, fishing with your host. Near Louis Hémon museum, old mill, covered bridge, Parc de la Pointe Taillon, blueberry field, bike/skidoo trails. All-terrain vehicle and snowmobile rentals.

From Parc des Laurentides, Rte 169 twd Robertval, Ste-Jeanne-d'Arc. Bypass the village, continue on Rte 169, 7.5km. Left twd St-Augustin, 0.9km. At 1st curve, straight on Rte Harvey, 1.5km. Right on Ch. Lapointe.

B&B
FERME HARVEY

Denise Bouchard and
Bertrand Harvey
230, chemin Lapointe
Ste-Jeanne-d'Arc G0W 1E0
(418) 276-2810

B&B	
single	$30-35
double	$45-50
triple	$65-70
child	$5-12

Reduced rates: 10% 3 nights and more
Open year round

Number of rooms	3
shared bathrooms	2

Activities: 🏖 🚲 🚶 🛷 🐎

25 years of hospitality
1975 - 2000

For 25 years, the host members of the
Fédération des Agricotours du Québec have been committed
to offering you genuine, high-quality choices
for accommodation and agricultural tourism.

This has made Agricotours the largest high-quality network
in Quebec, and your confidence has helped in its success.

For this reason, our network host members hope that they
may, with their traditional warm welcome, continue to help
you discover the best of Quebec for many more years to come.

You'll always feel welcome
in the Agricotours network.

47. ST-DAVID-DE-FALARDEAU

F E ☒ P ⊟ ☒ ☒ R3 M3 TA

Come and discover our little paradise on an enchanting and charming site, next to the forest. A magnificent log chalet, fully equipped, facing a little lake and our pack of huskies. Discover our original table d'hôte menu and our winter activities. Sleigh rides, snowmobiling, ice-fishing. Close by: rafting, archery, fishing and swimming. We look forward to welcoming you.

From Québec City, Rte 175 N. In Chicoutimi, take the Dubuc bridge, Rte 172 W. to the "FALARDEAU" sign. In Falardeau, right at the church, right after the corner store, right on the 3rd street, 1.7km.

COUNTRY HOME
LES CHIENS and GÎTE
DU GRAND NORD

Valérie Dorgebray
Lot 18, Lac Durand #2
St-David-de-Falardeau
GOV 1C0
(418) 673-7717
fax (418)673-4072
www.chiens-gite.qc.ca
chiensgite@hotmail.com

No. houses	1
No. rooms	1
No. people	7
WEEK-SUMMER	$347.^{75}
WEEK-WINTER	$304.^{28}
W/E-SUMMER	$217.^{35}
W/E-WINTER	$217.^{35}
DAY-SUMMER	$17.^{38}
DAY-WINTER	$17.^{38}

Taxes extra

Open year round

Activities:

FARM ACTIVITIES

Farm Stays:

* Registered trademark

-B-

-H-

ACCOMMODATION

Your opinion is important for the continued EXCELLENCE of our guide.

In order to continue to improve the network and the quality of the services it offers, please send your comments and suggestions to: Fédération des Agricotours, C.P. 1000 succ., M, Montréal, Québec, H1V 3R2.

Win a free stay !

Each year, Agricotours awards a prize of EXCELLENCE to several of its members. The selection is based on clients' commentary cards, therefore we invite you to fill out the following card to show your appreciation and win the chance of staying at one of our members' establishments for free!

What was your overall experience?

RECEPTION
Friendliness and availability of hosts, special details

_____
_____
_____
_____

YOUR ROOM
Comfort of beds, overall comfort of room, cleanliness, quality of bedding

_____
_____
_____
_____

MEALS
Quality of food, quality of presentation, flexibility of serving times

_____
_____
_____
_____

HOUSE
Comfort, cleanliness, decor, general impression of the site

_____
_____
_____
_____

BATHROOM
Appropriate installation, cleanliness

_____
_____
_____
_____

Comments and suggestions

_____
_____
_____
_____
_____
_____
_____
_____
_____

YOUR OVERALL APPRECIATION

Excellent ☐   Good ☐

Very good ☐   Poor ☐

For our statistics

Was this your first experience with the Agricotours network?

☐ Yes
☐ No   How many times_____

Profession _____

Age

☐ 8-19   ☐ 20-29   ☐ 30-39   ☐ 40-49
☐ 50-59   ☐ 60-69   ☐ 70 and
                          more

YOUR NAME	
YOUR ADDRESS	STREET
	CITY
	COUNTRY POSTAL CODE
NAME OF THE ESTABLISHMENT VISITED	
DATE OF VISIT	
MUNICIPALITY OR REGION	

ACCOMMODATION

Your opinion is important for the continued EXCELLENCE of our guide.

In order to continue to improve the network and the quality of the services it offers, please send your comments and suggestions to: Fédération des Agricotours, C.P. 1000 succ., M, Montréal, Québec, H1V 3R2.

Win a free stay !

Each year, Agricotours awards a prize of EXCELLENCE to several of its members. The selection is based on clients' commentary cards, therefore we invite you to fill out the following card to show your appreciation and win the chance of staying at one of our members' establishments for free!

What was your overall experience?

RECEPTION
Friendliness and availability of hosts, special details

_____

_____

_____

_____

YOUR ROOM
Comfort of beds, overall comfort of room, cleanliness, quality of bedding

_____

_____

_____

_____

MEALS
Quality of food, quality of presentation, flexibility of serving times

_____

_____

_____

_____

HOUSE
Comfort, cleanliness, decor, general impression of the site

_____

_____

_____

_____

BATHROOM
Appropriate installation, cleanliness

_____

_____

_____

_____

Comments and suggestions

_____
_____
_____
_____
_____
_____
_____
_____
_____

YOUR OVERALL APPRECIATION

Excellent ☐   Good ☐

Very good ☐   Poor ☐

For our statistics

Was this your first experience with the Agricotours network?

☐ Yes

☐ No   How many times_____

Profession _____

Age

☐ 8-19   ☐ 20-29   ☐ 30-39   ☐ 40-49

☐ 50-59   ☐ 60-69   ☐ 70 and more

YOUR NAME	
YOUR ADDRESS	STREET
	CITY
	COUNTRY POSTAL CODE
NAME OF THE ESTABLISHMENT VISITED	
DATE OF VISIT	
MUNICIPALITY OR REGION	

ACCOMMODATION

Your opinion is important for the continued EXCELLENCE of our guide.

In order to continue to improve the network and the quality of the services it offers, please send your comments and suggestions to: Fédération des Agricotours, C.P. 1000 succ., M, Montréal, Québec, H1V 3R2.

Win a free stay !

Each year, Agricotours awards a prize of EXCELLENCE to several of its members. The selection is based on clients' commentary cards, therefore we invite you to fill out the following card to show your appreciation and win the chance of staying at one of our members' establishments for free!

What was your overall experience?

RECEPTION
Friendliness and availability of hosts, special details

_____

_____

_____

_____

YOUR ROOM
Comfort of beds, overall comfort of room, cleanliness, quality of bedding

_____

_____

_____

_____

MEALS
Quality of food, quality of presentation, flexibility of serving times

_____

_____

_____

_____

HOUSE
Comfort, cleanliness, decor, general impression of the site

_____

_____

_____

_____

BATHROOM
Appropriate installation, cleanliness

_____

_____

_____

_____

Comments and suggestions

_____
_____
_____
_____
_____
_____
_____
_____
_____

YOUR OVERALL APPRECIATION

Excellent ☐   Good ☐

Very good ☐   Poor ☐

For our statistics

Was this your first experience with the Agricotours network?

☐ Yes
☐ No   How many times_____

Profession _____

Age

☐ 8-19   ☐ 20-29   ☐ 30-39   ☐ 40-49
☐ 50-59   ☐ 60-69   ☐ 70 and
                                        more

YOUR NAME		
YOUR ADDRESS	STREET	
	CITY	
	COUNTRY	POSTAL CODE
NAME OF THE ESTABLISHMENT VISITED		
DATE OF VISIT		
MUNICIPALITY OR REGION		

COUNTRY DINING

Your opinion is important for the continued EXCELLENCE of our guide.

In order to continue to improve the network and the quality of the services it offers, please send your comments and suggestions to: Fédération des Agricotours, C.P. 1000 succ., M, Montréal, Québec, H1V 3R2.

Win a free stay !

Each year, Agricotours awards a prize of EXCELLENCE to several of its members. The selection is based on clients' commentary cards, therefore we invite you to fill out the following card to show your appreciation and win the chance of staying at one of our members' establishments for free!

What was your overall experience?

	Excellent	Very good	Good	Poor
ACCESSIBILITY, EASY TO FIND				
WELCOME				
-friendliness of hosts	□	□	□	□
-availability of hosts	□	□	□	□
THE MEAL				
-quality of the food	□	□	□	□
-freshness of ingredients	□	□	□	□
-quality of presentation	□	□	□	□
-quantity of food served	□	□	□	□
THE DINING ROOM				
-comfort	□	□	□	□
-cleanliness	□	□	□	□
ROOMS IN GENERAL				
-comfort	□	□	□	□
-cleanliness	□	□	□	□
OVERALL IMPRESSION				
-exterior of the house	□	□	□	□
-out-buildings	□	□	□	□
-fields	□	□	□	□
-cattle	□	□	□	□
-garden (in season)	□	□	□	□
Tour of the area suggested by hosts	□	□	□	□
Quality-price ratio	□	□	□	□

Comments and suggestions

_____
_____
_____
_____
_____
_____
_____
_____

YOUR OVERALL APPRECIATION

Excellent ☐   Good ☐

Very good ☐   Poor ☐

For our statistics

Was this your first experience with the Agricotours network?

☐ Yes

☐ No   How many times_____

Profession _____

Age

☐ 8-19   ☐ 20-29   ☐ 30-39   ☐ 40-49

☐ 50-59   ☐ 60-69   ☐ 70 and more

YOUR NAME		
YOUR ADDRESS	STREET	
	CITY	
	COUNTRY	POSTAL CODE
NAME OF THE ESTABLISHMENT VISITED		
DATE OF VISIT		
MUNICIPALITY OR REGION		

Order Form

ULYSSES TRAVEL GUIDES

☐ Atlantic Canada .... $24.95 CAN $17.95 US	☐ Martinique .... $24.95 CAN $17.95 US
☐ Bahamas .... $24.95 CAN $17.95 US	☐ Miami .... $9.95 CAN $12.95 US
☐ Beaches of Maine .... $12.95 CAN $9.95 US	☐ Montréal .... $19.95 CAN $14.95 US
☐ Bed & Breakfasts .... $13.95 CAN in Québec $10.95 US	☐ New Orleans .... $17.95 CAN $12.95 US
☐ Belize .... $16.95 CAN $12.95 US	☐ New York City .... $19.95 CAN $14.95 US
☐ Calgary .... $17.95 CAN $12.95 US	☐ Nicaragua .... $24.95 CAN $17.95 US
☐ Canada .... $29.95 CAN $21.95 US	☐ Ontario .... $27.95 CAN $19.95US
☐ Chicago .... $19.95 CAN $14.95 US	☐ Ottawa .... $17.95 CAN $12.95 US
☐ Chile .... $27.95 CAN $17.95 US	☐ Panamá .... $24.95 CAN $17.95 US
☐ Colombia .... $29.95 CAN $21.95 US	☐ Peru .... $27.95 CAN $19.95 US
☐ Costa Rica .... $27.95 CAN $19.95 US	☐ Portugal .... $24.95 CAN $16.95 US
☐ Cuba .... $24.95 CAN $17.95 US	☐ Puerto Rico .... $24.95 CAN $17.95 US
☐ Dominican .... $24.95 CAN Republic $17.95 US	☐ Provence - .... $29.95 CAN Côte d'Azur $21.95US
☐ Ecuador and .... $24.95 CAN Galapagos Islands $17.95 US	☐ Québec .... $29.95 CAN $21.95 US
☐ El Salvador .... $22.95 CAN $14.95 US	☐ Québec and Ontario .... $9.95 CAN with Via $7.95 US
☐ Guadeloupe .... $24.95 CAN $17.95 US	☐ Seattle .... $17.95 CAN $12.95 US
☐ Guatemala .... $24.95 CAN $17.95 US	☐ Toronto .... $18.95 CAN $13.95 US
☐ Honduras .... $24.95 CAN $17.95 US	☐ Vancouver .... $17.95 CAN $12.95 US
☐ Jamaica .... $24.95 CAN $17.95 US	☐ Washington D.C. .... $18.95 CAN $13.95 US
☐ Lisbon .... $18.95 CAN $13.95 US	☐ Western Canada .... $29.95 CAN $21.95 US
☐ Louisiana .... $29.95 CAN $21.95 US	

ULYSSES DUE SOUTH

☐ Acapulco .... $14.95 CAN $9.95 US	☐ Huatulco - Oaxaca .... $17.95 CAN Puerto Escondido $12.95 US
☐ Los Cabos .... $14.95 CAN and La Paz $10.95 US	☐ Cartagena .... $12.95 CAN (Colombia) $9.95 US
☐ Cancún & .... $19.95 CAN Riviera Maya $14.95 US	☐ Belize .... $16.95 CAN $12.95 US
☐ Cancun Cozumel .... $17.95 CAN $12.95 US	☐ St. Martin and .... $16.95 CAN St. Barts $12.95 US
☐ Puerto Vallarta .... $14.95 CAN $9.95 US	☐ Guadalajara .... $17.95 CAN $12.95 US

ULYSSES GREEN ESCAPES

☐ Cycling in France .... $22.95 CAN
                                       $16.95 US
☐ Cycling in Ontario .... $22.95 CAN
                                       $16.95 US
☐ Biking Montréal .... $3.95 CAN

☐ Hiking in the .... $19.95 CAN
   Northeastern U.S. $13.95 US
☐ Hiking in Québec .... $19.95 CAN
                                       $13.95 US

ULYSSES CONVERSATION GUIDES

☐ French for Better Travel .... $9.95 CAN
                                       $6.95 US

☐ Spanish for Better Travel .... $9.95 CAN
                                       $6.95 US

ULYSSES TRAVEL JOURNAL

☐ Ulysses Travel Journal .... $9.95 CAN
   (Colours) $7.95 US

☐ Ulysses Travel Journal .... $14.95 CAN
   80 Days $9.95 US

TITLE	QUANTITY	PRICE	TOTAL

Name	Sub-total	
Address	Postage & Handling	$4.00
....		
....	Sub-total	
Telephone		
Fax	G.S.T. in Canada 7%	
E-mail		
Payment : ☐ Money Order ☐ Visa ☐ MasterCard	TOTAL	
Card Number		
Expiry date		
Signature		

ULYSSES TRAVEL GUIDES
4176 St-Denis
Montréal, Québec, H2W 2M5
tel (514) 843-9447 fax (514) 843-9448
Toll free: 1-877-542-7247
www.ulyssesguides.com
info@ulysses.ca

See more...
Québec & Ontario
...suivez la carte!

Québec

Ontario

OTTAWA

MONTRÉAL

QUÉBEC

New York

ALBANY

Votre passeport transport!

Your Transport Passport!

Venez voir toute la beauté et l'histoire du **Québec** et de l'**Ontario**.

Hiver comme été...Rout•Pass vous fera découvrir des festivals à n'en plus finir, des grandes villes accueillantes et des paysages grandioses. À vous de fixer l'itinéraire et le rythme...car nos 35 transporteurs vous offrent des horaires **super-flexibles!**

Prenez **deux semaines** et voyagez à votre gré.
Le prix?... Moins de 17 $ par jour.

You're invited to come discover the beauty and history of **Québec** and **Ontario**.

Winter or summer, choose Rout•Pass and discover the most surprising festivals and events, livable big cities and countryside that will take your breath away. Our intercity bus network covers the map and the 35 participating carriers offer **very flexible** departure schedules... so you'll determine your own itinerary and rhythm.

Take **two weeks** and travel at your leisure!
Less than $17. per day.

Info/contact:

Veuillez consulter le catalogue de votre grossiste préféré ou communiquer avec nous :
Please consult your tour wholesaler's catalogue or contact us directly:

Rout•Pass Service Marketing Department:
505, est boul. de Maisonneuve Blvd E.
Montréal, Qc, Canada H2L 4R6
Fax: 1-877-849-2601 (sans frais / toll free)
Internet : http://www.omca.com

BUS AGENTS D'AUTOCAR – Telephone Information téléphonique :

Toronto	(416) 393-7911
Québec	(418) 525-3000
Montréal	(514) 842-2281
Ottawa	(613) 238-5900

Save up* to 20%

GET AN EYEFUL

Take advantage of our **GET AN EYEFUL** package to visit four of Montréal's major tourist attractions !

BIODÔME
Experience a unique feast for the senses as you explore four ecosystems from the Americas.

MONTRÉAL TOWER AT THE OLYMPIC PARK
Enjoy a breathtaking view of Montréal from the world's tallest inclined tower.

Tickets available at the ticket office of each tourist attraction and "Au Gîte Olympique" Bed & Breakfast.

Open all year round.

Complimentary shuttle service between all four tourist attractions and the Viau metro station.

INSECTARIUM
Discover the fascinating world of insects at this unique museum.

BOTANICAL GARDEN
Celebrate nature's diversity at one of the world's largest attractions of its kind.

Informations:

Botanical Garden-Insectarium	872-1400
Biodôme	868-3000
Montréal Tower	252-8687

* On the individual regular admission fee of each tourist attraction.

PARC OLYMPIQUE MONTRÉAL

Ville de Montréal

MÉTRO Viau

THE BACKROADS OF SOUTHERN QUÉBEC
IN MONTÉRÉGIE
Country flavours and historical roots

Ask for the Montérégie
tourist guide
Phone: (450) 469-0069
Fax: (450) 469-1139
info@tourisme-monteregie.qc.ca
www.tourisme-monteregie.qc.ca

MORE THAN ATTRACTIONS
...PEOPLE!

TOURISME
MONTÉRÉGIE

THE UNION DES PRODUCTEURS AGRICOLES AND ITS 45,000 MEMBERS INVITE YOU TO VISIT RURAL QUEBEC

L'UNION
DES PRODUCTEURS
AGRICOLES

UPA

Le Gîte
de la
Seigneurie

In the real Quebec's country side, in the same site, you will find our five agrotourism services: B & B, nice country-style meal, country house rental, guided tour of the old romantic gardens and the farm shop.

(See Mauricie Region)

Agrotourism destination by excellence!

Six years in operation, six awards of excellence!

180, chemin du Golf, Louiseville J5V 2L4 / mgilbert@infoteck.qc.ca / Tel. & Fax: 819-228-8224

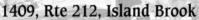
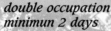

Hochelaga-Maisonneuve *It's Montréal at heart!*

Only 15 minutes from Downtown by metro or car, **Hochelaga-Maisonneuve** is a unique section of the city.

Home to the **Tower of Montréal**, the tallest inclined tower in the world, it also boasts the **Olympic Stadium**, the **Botanical Gardens**, the **Insectarium**, the **Biodôme**, and, we must not forget **Maurice "Rocket" Richard's Universe**, a museum devoted to one of the greatest players for the Montréal Canadiens hockey team.

Hochelaga-Maisonneuve is also...

HERITAGE A unique and faithful reflection of the life of an industrial city of the early 20th century, with impressive heritage buildings such as the **Très-Saint-Nom-de-Jésus** Church which has a famous **Casavant organ**, one of the most powerful in North America, the **Château Dufresne** with its sumptuous decoration and numerous **Beaux-Arts style buildings** such as the **Morgan Baths** or the **Maisonneuve Market**.

VOYAGE IN TIME Thanks to our **animated tour** (theatre and music) called **"In the steps of La Bolduc"** which offers an original way to discover the major attractions of the neighbourhood and to learn all about the life and work of one of Québec's most celebrated singers of the Pre-War period.

AGREEABLE STROLL Along **typical Montréal streets** either in the company of one of our guides or by yourself, with stops in our café-restaurants from time to time.

DISCOVERY A cultural life which is both intense and varied. On the **Market Place** in the summer months, shows, concerts, Sunday brunches and activities for the whole family are on the program.

PLEASURE The atmosphere of a traditional market at the **Maisonneuve Public Market** and shopping on **Promenade Ontario**.

Tourisme Hochelaga-Maisonneuve *welcomes you!*

Information **(514) 256-4636**
Web Site **www.tourismemaisonneuve.qc.ca**

LOCATION Pelletier

AUTOS • CAMIONS • MINIBUS

www.locationpelletier.com

SHORT-TERM RENTAL

We offer A GREAT VARIETY
of **new vehicles** to answer
ALL YOUR NEEDS.

QUEBEC	LAVAL	MONTREAL
Quebec Airport	Mirabel Airport	Dorval Airport
Tel.: **(418) 681-0678**	Tel.: **(450) 669-1474**	Tel.: **(514) 728-3622**
Fax: (418) 681-3963	Fax: (450) 669-3471	Fax: (514) 728-7388

Our competitive prices will please you !